POLAND

BUSINESS AND INVESTMENT OPPORTUNITIES YEARBOOK

International Business Publications, USA
Washington DC, USA - Poland

POLAND

BUSINESS AND INVESTMENT OPPORTUNITIES YEARBOOK

APDATED ANNUALLY

We express our sincere appreciation to all government agencies and international organizations which provided information and other materials for this yearbook

Cover Design: International Business Publications, USA

2007 6th Edition Updated Reprint International Business Publications, USA
ISBN 0-7397-7717-3

For customer service and information, please contact:

in the USA: **International Business Publications, USA**
P.O.Box 15343, Washington, DC 20003
Phone: (202) 546-2103, Fax: (202) 546-3275.
E-mail: rusric@erols.com

Printed in the USA

POLAND

BUSINESS AND INVESTMENT OPPORTUNITIES YEARBOOK

TABLE OF CONTENTS

STRATEGIC AND DEVELOPMENT PROFILES

BUSINESS AND DEVELOPMENT PROFILES

Capital (largest city)	Warsaw [3]) 52°13′N 21°02′E
Official language	Polish[2]
Government	Parliamentary republic
- President	Lech Kaczyński
- Prime minister	Jarosław Kaczyński
Formation	
- Christianisation[4]	966
- Redeclared	November 11, 1918
Accession to EU	May 1, 2004
Area	
- Total	312,685[3] km² (68th) 120,728 sq mi
- Water (%)	2.65
Population	
- 2006 estimate	38,128,000 (32nd)
- 2002 census	38,230,080
- Density	121.9/km² (83rd) 319.9/sq mi
GDP (PPP)	2006 estimate
- Total	$546.543 billion (23rd)
- Per capita	$14,400 (48th)
HDI (2004)	0.862 (high) (37th)
Currency	Złoty (PLN)
Time zone	CET (UTC+1)
- Summer (DST)	CEST (UTC+2)
Internet TLD	.pl[5]
Calling code	+48

Poland (Polish: *Polska*), officially the **Republic of Poland** (Polish: *Rzeczpospolita Polska*), is a country in Central Europe. It is bordered by Germany to the west, the Czech Republic and Slovakia to the south, Ukraine and Belarus to the east, and the Baltic Sea, Lithuania, and Russia (in the form of the Kaliningrad Oblast exclave) to the north. It also shares a maritime border with Denmark and Sweden.

The first Polish state was born in 966. Poland became a kingdom in 1025, and in 1569 it cemented a long association with the Grand Duchy of Lithuania by uniting to form the Polish-Lithuanian Commonwealth. The Commonwealth collapsed in 1795, and the Poles were without a state for 123 years. Poland regained its independence in 1918 but lost it again in World War II, emerging several years later as a satellite of the Soviet Union. In 1989 it threw off the communist yoke and became what is informally known as the **Third Polish Republic**. Poland is member of the European Union, NATO, the United Nations, and the World Trade Organization.

GEOGRAPHY

Location: Central Europe, east of Germany
Geographic coordinates: 52 00 N, 20 00 E
Map references: Europe
Area:
total: 312,683 sq km
land: 304,510 sq km
water: 8,173 sq km
Area - comparative: slightly smaller than New Mexico

Land boundaries:
total: 2,888 km
border countries: Belarus 605 km, Czech Republic 658 km, Germany 456 km, Lithuania 91 km, Russia (Kaliningrad Oblast) 206 km, Slovakia 444 km, Ukraine 428 km

Coastline: 491 km
Maritime claims:
exclusive economic zone : defined by international treaties
territorial sea: 12 nm
Climate: temperate with cold, cloudy, moderately severe winters with frequent precipitation; mild summers with frequent showers and thundershowers
Terrain: mostly flat plain; mountains along southern border

Elevation extremes:
lowest point: Raczki Elblaskie -2 m
highest point: Rysy 2,499 m

Natural resources: coal, sulfur, copper, natural gas, silver, lead, salt

Land use:
arable land: 47%
permanent crops : 1%
permanent pastures: 13%
forests and woodland: 29%
other: 10%

Irrigated land: 1,000 sq km
Natural hazards: NA

Environment - current issues: situation has improved since 1989 due to decline in heavy industry and increased environmental concern by postcommunist governments; air pollution nonetheless remains serious because of sulfur dioxide emissions from coal-fired power plants, and the resulting acid rain has caused forest damage; water pollution from industrial and municipal sources is also a problem, as is disposal of hazardous wastes

Environment - international agreements:
party to: Air Pollution, Antarctic-Environmental Protocol, Antarctic Treaty, Biodiversity, Climate Change, Endangered Species, Environmental Modification, Hazardous Wastes, Marine Dumping, Nuclear Test Ban, Ozone Layer Protection, Ship Pollution, Wetlands, Whaling
signed, but not ratified: Air Pollution-Nitrogen Oxides, Air Pollution-Sulphur 94, Law of the Sea

Base 802627AI (R00812) 9-00

Geography - note: historically, an area of conflict because of flat terrain and the lack of natural barriers on the North European Plain

PEOPLE

Population: 38,615,239

Age structure:
0-14 years: 21% (male 4,235,659; female 4,038,016)
15-64 years : 67% (male 12,842,909; female 13,020,736)
65 years and over: 12% (male 1,698,505; female 2,779,414) (July 2004 est.)

Population growth rate: 0%
Birth rate: 10.18 births/1,000 population
Death rate: 9.82 deaths/1,000 population
Net migration rate: -0.4 migrant(s)/1,000 population

Sex ratio:
at birth : 1.06 male(s)/female
under 15 years: 1.05 male(s)/female
15-64 years: 0.99 male(s)/female
65 years and over: 0.61 male(s)/female
total population: 0.95 male(s)/female

Infant mortality rate: 13.6 deaths/1,000 live births

Life expectancy at birth:
total population: 72.47 years
male : 68.27 years
female: 76.91 years

Total fertility rate: 1.43 children born/woman

Nationality:
noun: Pole(s)
adjective: Polish

Ethnic groups: Polish 97.6%, German 1.3%, Ukrainian 0.6%, Byelorussian 0.5% (1990 est.)
Religions: Roman Catholic 95% (about 75% practicing), Eastern Orthodox, Protestant, and other 5%
Languages: Polish

Literacy:
definition: age 15 and over can read and write
total population: 99%
male: 99%
female: 98% (1978 est.)

GOVERNMENT

Country name:
conventional long form : Republic of Poland
conventional short form: Poland
local long form: Rzeczpospolita Polska
local short form: Polska

Data code: PL
Government type: democratic state
National capital: Warsaw

Administrative divisions: 49 provinces (wojewodztwa, singular - wojewodztwo); Biala Podlaska, Bialystok, Bielsko Biala, Bydgoszcz, Chelm, Ciechanow, Czestochowa, Elblag, Gdansk, Gorzow, Jelenia Gora, Kalisz, Katowice, Kielce, Konin, Koszalin, Krakow, Krosno, Legnica, Leszno, Lodz, Lomza, Lublin, Nowy Sacz, Olsztyn, Opole, Ostroleka, Pila, Piotrkow, Plock, Poznan, Przemysl, Radom, Rzeszow, Siedlce, Sieradz, Skierniewice, Slupsk, Suwalki, Szczecin, Tarnobrzeg, Tarnow, Torun, Walbrzych, Warszawa, Wloclawek, Wroclaw, Zamosc, Zielona Gora

Independence: 11 November 1918 (independent republic proclaimed)
National holiday: Constitution Day, 3 May (1791)
Constitution: interim "small constitution" came into effect in December 1992 supplementing the heavily amended constitution of 22 July 1952; referendum for a new constitution to be held 25 May 2004

Legal system: mixture of Continental (Napoleonic) civil law and holdover communist legal theory; changes being gradually introduced as part of broader democratization process; limited judicial review of legislative acts; has not accepted compulsory ICJ jurisdiction

Suffrage: 18 years of age; universal

Executive branch: Poland

chief of state: President Lech KACZYNSKI (since 23 December 2005)
head of government: Prime Minister Jaroslaw KACZYNSKI (since 10 July 2006); Deputy Prime Ministers Ludwik DORN (since 23 November 2005), Roman GIERTYCH (since 5 May 2006), Zyta GILOWSKA (since 22 September 2006), Andrzej LEPPER (since 16 October 2006)
cabinet: Council of Ministers responsible to the prime minister and the Sejm; the prime minister proposes, the president appoints, and the Sejm approves the Council of Ministers
elections: president elected by popular vote for a five-year term (eligible for a second term); election last held 9 and 23 October 2005 (next to be held October 2010); prime minister and deputy prime ministers appointed by the president and confirmed by the Sejm
election results: Lech KACZYNSKI elected president; percent of popular vote - Lech KACZYNSKI 54%, Donald Tusk 46%

Legislative branch: bicameral legislature consisting of an upper house, the Senate or Senat (100 seats; members are elected by a majority vote on a provincial basis to serve four-year terms), and a lower house, the Sejm (460 seats; members are elected under a complex system of proportional representation to serve four-year terms); the designation of National Assembly or Zgromadzenie Narodowe is only used on those rare occasions when the two houses meet jointly
elections: Senate - last held 25 September 2005 (next to be held by September 2009); Sejm elections last held 25 September 2005 (next to be held by September 2009)
election results: Senate - percent of vote by party - NA%; seats by party - PiS 49, PO 34, LPR 7, SO 3, PSL 2, independents 5; Sejm - percent of vote by party - PiS 27%, PO 24.1%, SO 11.4%,

SLD 11.3%, LPR 8%, PSL 7%, other 11.2%; seats by party - PiS 155, PO 133, SO 56, SLD 55, LPR 34, PSL 25, German minorities 2
note: two seats are assigned to ethnic minority parties in the Sejm only **Judicial branch:** Supreme Court, judges are appointed by the president on the recommendation of the National Council of Judiciary

Political parties and leaders:
post-Communist: Democratic Left Alliance or SLD (Social Democracy of Poland) Jozef OLEKSY; Polish Peasant Party or PSL Waldemar PAWLAK
post-Solidarity parties: Freedom Union or UW (Democratic Union and Liberal Democratic Congress merged to form Freedom Union) Leszek BALCEROWICZ; Christian-National Union or ZCHN Marian PILKA; Center Alliance Party or PC Jaroslaw KACZYNSKI; Peasant Alliance or PL Gabriel JANOWSKI; Solidarity Electoral Action or AWS Marian KRZAKLEWSKI; Union of Labor or UP Ryszard BUGAJ; Conservative Party or PK Aleksander HALL; Nonparty Reform Bloc or BBWR Jacek LIPINSKI; Nonparty Reform Block United for Elections or BBWR-SW Jerzy GWIZDZ
non-Communist, non-Solidarity : Movement for the Reconstruction of Poland or ROP Jan OLSZEWSKI; Confederation for an Independent Poland or KPN Leszek MOCZULSKI; German Minority or MN Gerhardt BARTODZIEJ; Union of Real Politics or UPR Janusz KORWIN-MIKKE

Political pressure groups and leaders: powerful Roman Catholic Church; Solidarity (trade union); All Poland Trade Union Alliance or OPZZ (trade union)

International organization participation: Australia Group, BIS, BSEC (observer), CBSS, CCC, CE, CEI, CERN, EBRD, ECE, EU (applicant), FAO, IAEA, IBRD, ICAO, ICFTU, ICRM, IDA, IFC, IFRCS, IHO, ILO, IMF, IMO, Inmarsat, Intelsat, Interpol, IOC, IOM, ISO, ITU, MINURSO, NACC, NAM (guest), NSG, OAS (observer), OECD, OSCE, PCA, PFP, UN, UN Security Council (temporary), UNAVEM III, UNCTAD, UNDOF, UNESCO, UNIDO, UNIFIL, UNIKOM, UNMIBH, UNMOP, UNMOT, UNOMIG, UNPREDEP, UNTAES, UPU, WCL, WEU (associate partner), WFTU, WHO, WIPO, WMO, WToO, WTrO, ZC

Diplomatic representation in the US:
chief of mission : Ambassador Jerzy KOZMINSKI
chancery: 2640 16th Street NW, Washington, DC 20009
telephone: 1 (202) 234-3800 through 3802
FAX: 1 (202) 328-6271
consulate(s) general : Chicago, Los Angeles, and New York

Diplomatic representation from the US:
chief of mission: Ambassador Nicholas Andrew REY
embassy: Aleje Ujazdowskie 29/31, Warsaw
mailing address: American Embassy Warsaw, US Department of State, Washington, DC 20521-5010
telephone: 48 (2) 628-30-41
FAX: 48 (2) 628-82-98
consulate(s) general: Krakow

Flag description: two equal horizontal bands of white (top) and red; similar to the flags of Indonesia and Monaco which are red (top) and white

ECONOMY

Economy - overview: In 1996, Poland continued to make good progress in the difficult transition to a market economy. The transition began on 1 January 1990, when the new democratic government instituted shock therapy by decontrolling prices, slashing subsidies, and drastically reducing import barriers. Although real GDP fell sharply in 1990 and 1991, in 1992 Poland became the first country in the region to resume economic growth with a 2.6% increase.

Growth advanced to 3.8% in 1993, 5.2% in 1994, 6.5% in 1995, and 6.0% in 1996. Most of the growth since 1991 has come from the booming private sector, which now accounts for more than 60% of GDP, attributable mostly to the creation of new private firms. Large-scale industry still remains largely in state hands. The trade and current account balances officially are in deficit but in fact both have comfortable surpluses because of large, unrecorded sales to cross-border visitors. The government has promised to extend privatization and social welfare reform and to maintain fiscal and monetary discipline. As for external debt, the burden was sharply reduced by reschedulings and write-offs of both private and official debt during 1991-95.

GDP: purchasing power parity - $246.3 billion
GDP - real growth rate: 6%
GDP - per capita: purchasing power parity - $6,400
GDP - composition by sector:
agriculture : 6%
industry: 40%
services: 54%
Inflation rate - consumer price index: 18.8%
Labor force:
total: 17.662 million
by occupation: industry and construction 32.0%, agriculture 27.6%, trade, transport, and communications 14.7%, government and other 25.7% (1992)
Unemployment rate: 13.3% (yearend 1996)
Budget:
revenues: $37.1 billion
expenditures: $40.6 billion, including capital expenditures of $NA
Industries: machine building, iron and steel, coal mining, chemicals, shipbuilding, food processing, glass, beverages, textiles
Industrial production growth rate: 8.5%
Electricity - capacity: 29.64 million kW
Electricity - production: 127.42 billion kWh
Electricity - consumption per capita: 3,124 kWh
Agriculture - products: potatoes, milk, fruits, vegetables, wheat; poultry and eggs; pork, beef
Exports:
total value: $30.9 billion (f.o.b)
commodities: intermediate goods 38%, machinery and transport equipment 23%, consumer goods 21%, foodstuffs 10%, fuels 7%
partners : Germany 35.7%, Netherlands 5.9%, Russia 5.4%, Italy 4.9%
Imports:
total value: $34.6 billion (f.o.b)
commodities: machinery and transport equipment 32%, intermediate goods 20%, chemicals 15%, consumer goods 9%, food 9%, fuels 8%
partners: Germany 27.5%, Italy 8.4%, Russia 6.8%, UK 5.3%
Debt - external: $45.8 billion
Economic aid:
recipient: Western governments and institutions pledged $22 billion in grants and loans during 1990-94, but much of the money has not been disbursed
Currency: 1 zloty (Zl) = 100 groszy

Exchange rates: zlotych per US dollar - 3.2355 (2005), 3.6576 (2004), 3.8891 (2003), 4.08 (2002), 4.0939 (2001)
note: zlotych is the plural form of zloty
Fiscal year: calendar year

COMMUNICATIONS

Telephones - main lines in use:	11.803 million
Telephones - mobile cellular:	29,166,400
Telephone system:	*general assessment:* modernization of the telecommunications network has accelerated with market based competition finalized in 2003; fixed-line service, dominated by the former state-owned company, is dwarfed by the growth in wireless telephony *domestic:* wireless service, available since 1993 (GSM service available since 1996) and provided by three nation-wide networks, has grown rapidly in response to the weak fixed-line coverage; third generation UMTS service available in urban areas; cellular coverage is generally good with more gaps in the east; fixed-line service is growing slowly and still lags in rural areas *international:* country code - 48; international direct dialing with automated exchanges; satellite earth station - 1 (Intelsat, Eutelsat, Inmarsat, and Intersputnik)
Radio broadcast stations:	AM 14, FM 777, shortwave 1
Television broadcast stations:	40
Internet country code:	.pl
Internet hosts:	358,476
Internet users:	10.6 million

TRANSPORTATION

Railways:
total: 24,313 km
broad gauge : 652 km 1.520-m gauge
standard gauge: 22,243 km 1.435-m gauge (11,648 km electrified; 8,978 km double track)
narrow gauge: 1,418 km various gauges including 1.000-m, 0.785-m, 0.750-m, and 0.600-m

Highways:
total: 372,479 km
paved : 243,229 km (including 257 km of expressways)
unpaved: 129,250 km
Waterways: 3,997 km navigable rivers and canals (1991)
Pipelines: crude oil 1,986 km; petroleum products 360 km; natural gas 4,600 km (1992)
Ports and harbors: Gdansk, Gdynia, Gliwice, Kolobrzeg, Szczecin, Swinoujscie, Ustka, Warsaw, Wrocaw

Merchant marine:
total: 125 ships (1,000 GRT or over) totaling 1,952,937 GRT/2,933,887 DWT
ships by type: bulk 72, cargo 30, chemical tanker 4, container 7, passenger 1, refrigerated cargo 2, roll-on/roll-off cargo 4, short-sea passenger 5
note: Poland owns an additional 16 ships (1,000 GRT or over) totaling 233,906 DWT operating under the registries of The Bahamas, Cyprus, Liberia, Saint Vincent and the Grenadines, and Vanuatu
Airports: 134
Airports - with paved runways:
total: 69
over 3,047 m: 2
2,438 to 3,047 m: 30
1,524 to 2,437 m: 27
914 to 1,523 m : 3
under 914 m: 7
Airports - with unpaved runways:
total: 65
2,438 to 3,047 m: 5
1,524 to 2,437 m: 10
914 to 1,523 m : 32
under 914 m: 18

MILITARY

Military branches: Army, Navy, Air and Air Defense Force
Military manpower - military age: 19 years of age
Military manpower - availability:
males age 15-49: 10,321,399
Military manpower - fit for military service:
males: 8,030,056
Military manpower - reaching military age annually:
males: 327,862
Military expenditures - dollar figure: $3.46 billion
Military expenditures - percent of GDP: 2.3%

TRANSNATIONAL ISSUES

Disputes - international: none

Illicit drugs: major illicit producer of amphetamines for the international market; transshipment point for Asian and Latin American illicit drugs to Western Europe

IMPORTANT INFORMATION FOR UNDERSTANDING POLAND[1]

Official Name: Republic of Poland

PROFILE

GEOGRAPHY

[1] This section based in part on the US State Department materials

Area: 312,683 sq. km. (120,725 sq. mi.); about the size of New Mexico.
Cities : *Capital*--Warsaw (pop. 1,626,100). *Other cities*--Lodz (825,600), Krakow (746,000), Wroclaw (641,000), Poznan (582,800), Gdansk (463,000).
Terrain: Flat plain, except mountains along southern border.
Climate: Temperate continental.

PEOPLE

Nationality: *Noun*--Pole(s). *Adjective*--Polish.
Population: 39 million.
Annual growth rate: Negligible.
Ethnic groups: Polish 98%, German, Ukrainian, Belorussian, Lithuanian.
Religions: Roman Catholic 90%, Eastern Orthodox, Uniate, Protestant, Judaism.
Language: Polish.
Literacy: 98%.
Health : *Infant mortality rate*--15/1,000. *Life expectancy*--males 66 yrs., females 75 yrs.
Work force: 18.0 million. *Industry and construction*--30.4%; *agriculture*--27%; *trade and business*--25.1%; *government and other*--17.6%.

Poland today is ethnically almost homogeneous (98% Polish), in contrast with the preÐWorld War II period, when there were significant ethnic minoritiesÐÐ4.5 million Ukrainians, 3 million Jews, 1 million Belorussians, and 800,000 Germans. The majority of the Jews were murdered during the German occupation in World War II, and many others emigrated in the succeeding years.

Most Germans left Poland at the end of the war, while many Ukrainians and Belorussians lived in territories incorporated into the then-U.S.S.R. Small Ukrainian, Belorussian, Slovakian, and Lithuanian minorities reside along the borders, and a German minority is concentrated near the southwest city of Opole.

POLAND IN THE 1990S

Poland in the early 1990s made great progress toward achieving a fully democratic government and a market economy. In November 1990, Lech Walesa was elected President for a 5Ðyear term. Jan Krzysztof Bielecki, at Walesa's request, formed a government and served as its Prime Minister until October 1991, introducing world prices and greatly expanding the scope of private enterprise.

Poland's first free parliamentary elections were held in 1991. More than 100 parties participated, representing a full spectrum of political views. No single party received more than 13% of the total vote. After a rough start, 1993 saw the second group of elections, and the first parliament to actually serve a full term. The Democratic Left Alliance (SLD) received the largest percentage of votes.

After the election, the SLD and PSL formed a governing coalition. Waldemar Pawlak, leader of the junior partner PSL, became Prime Minister. Relations between President Walesa and the Prime Minister remained poor throughout the Pawlak government, with President Walesa charging Pawlak with furthering personal and party interests while neglecting matters of state importance. Following a number of scandals implicating Pawlak and increasing political tension over control of the armed forces, President Walesa demanded Pawlak's resignation in January 1995. In the ensuing political crisis, the coalition removed Pawlak from office and replaced him with the SLD's Jozef Oleksy as the new Prime Minister.

In November 1995, Poland held its second postĐwar free presidential elections. SLD leader Aleksander Kwasniewski defeated Walesa by a narrow margin--51.7% to 48.3%. Soon after Walesa's defeat, Interior Minister Andrzej Milczanowski accused then-Prime Minister Oleksy of longtime collaboration with Soviet and later Russian intelligence. In the ensuing political crisis, Oleksy resigned. For his successor, The SLDĐPSL coalition turned to deputy Sejm speaker Wlodzimierz Cimoszewicz--who was linked to, but not a member of, the SLD. Polish prosecutors subsequently decided that there was insufficient evidence to charge Oleksy, and a parliamentary commission decided in November 1996 that the Polish intelligence services may have violated rules of procedure in gathering evidence in the Oleksy case.

Poland's most recent parliamentary elections were in September 2004 when two parties with roots in the Solidarity movement--Solidarity Electoral Action (AWS) and the Freedom Union (UW)--won 261 of the 460 seats in the Sejm and formed a coalition government. Jerzy Buzek of the AWS has been Prime Minister since these elections in 2004. Today the AWS and the Democratic Left Alliance (SLD) hold the majority of the seats in the Sejm. Marian Krzaklewski is the leader of the AWS, and Leszek Miller leads the SLD. In June 2000, UW withdrew from the governing collation, leaving AWS at the helm of a minority government.

GOVERNMENT AND POLITICAL CONDITIONS

The current government structure consists of a council of ministers led by a Prime Minister, typically chosen from the majority coalition in the bicameral legislature's lower house (Sejm). The president, elected every five years for no more than two terms, is the head of state and commander-in-chief of the armed forces. The judicial branch plays a minor role in decision-making.

The parliament, consisting of 460 members of the Sejm and 100 members of the upper house, or Senat, was elected in September 2001 in free and fair elections in which 15 political parties participated. The new Constitution and the reformed administrative division (as of 1999) required a revision of the election ordinance (passed in April 2001). The most important changes were liquidation of a national list (all deputies were elected by voters in constituencies) and introduction of a new method of calculating seats (the modified St. Lague method replaced the d'Hondt method, thus eliminating the premium for the top parties). The law stipulated that with the exception of guaranteed seats for small ethnic parties, only parties receiving at least 5% of the total vote could enter parliament.

Parties represented in the newly elected Sejm will be Law and Justice (PiS), Citizens Platform (PO), Self-Defense (SO), Democratic Left Alliance (SLD), the League of Polish Families (LPR), and the Polish Peasant Party (PSL).

Principal Government Officials (outgoing)
President--Lech Kaczynski (PiS)
Prime Minister--Jaroslaw Kaczynski (PiS)
Deputy Prime Minister and Minister of Agriculture--Andrzej Lepper (SO)
Deputy Prime Minister and Minister of Education--Roman Giertych
Minister of Foreign Affairs--Anna Fotyga (PiS)
Minister of Economy--Piotr Wozniak
Minister of Internal Affairs and Administration--Ludwik Dorn (PiS)
Minister of Defense--Radoslaw Sikorski (PiS)
Minister of Finance--Stanislaw Kluza (PiS)
Minister of Treasury--Wojciech Jasinski (PiS)
Minister of Labor and Social Policy--Anna Kalata (SO)
Minister of Justice--Zbigniew Ziobro (PiS)

Minister of Transport and Infrastructure--Antoni Jaszczak (SO)
Minister of Science and Higher Education--Michal Sewerynski
Minister of Culture and National Heritage--Kazimierz Ujazdowski (PiS)
Minister of Regional Development--Grazyna Gesicka
Minister of Health--Zbigniew Religa
Minister of Environment--Jan Szyszko (PiS)
Minister of Sports--Tomasz Lipiec
Minister of Maritime Economy--Rafal Wiechecki (LPR)
Coordinator for Special Services--Zbigniew Wassermann (PiS)

Ambassador to the United States--Janusz Reiter
Deputy Chief of Mission--Woijciech Flera

Poland maintains an embassy in the United States at 2640 16th St. NW, Washington, DC 20009 (tel. 202-234-3800/3801/3802); the consular annex is at 2224 Wyoming Ave. NW, Washington, DC 20008 (tel. 202-234-3800). Poland has consulates in Chicago, New York City, and Los Angeles.

ECONOMY

The Polish economy grew rapidly in the mid-1990s, but slowed considerably in 2001 and 2002. Since then, growth in the gross domestic product (GDP) recovered to 3.8% in 2003 and accelerated to 5.4% in 2004; although final figures are not yet available, GDP is expected to increase another 4.5-5% in 2005. Faster growth has failed to significantly reduce unemployment, which stood at 18.7% in the middle of 2005, the highest level in the EU. Tight monetary policy and dramatic productivity growth have helped temper inflation, which was roughly at 3.5% in 2004. Likewise, Poland's current account deficit, which grew rapidly in the late 1990s, fell to 1.5% of GDP in 2004. The budget deficit remains a source of concern though the accelerating economy helped to hold the deficit at an estimated 4.6% of GDP in 2004.

Throughout the 1990s, the United States and other Western countries supported the growth of a free enterprise economy by reducing Poland's foreign debt burden, providing economic aid, and lowering trade barriers. Poland graduated from USAID assistance in 2000 and paid the balance of its U.S.-held Paris Club debt in 2005. Poland officially joined the EU on May 1, 2004.

Agriculture

Agriculture employs 28.7% of the work force but contributes only 3.4% to the gross domestic product (GDP), reflecting relatively low productivity. Unlike the industrial sector, Poland's agricultural sector remained largely in private hands during the decades of communist rule. Most of the former state farms are now leased to farmer tenants. Lack of credit is hampering efforts to sell former state farmland. Currently, Poland's 2 million private farms occupy 90% of all farmland and account for roughly the same percentage of total agricultural production. These farms are small--8 hectares (ha) on average--and often fragmented. Farms with an area exceeding 15 ha accounted for only 9% of the total number of farms but cover 45% of total agricultural area. Over half of all farming households in Poland produce only for their own needs with little, if any, commercial sales.

Poland is a net exporter of confectionery, processed fruit and vegetables, meat, and dairy products. Processors often rely on imports to supplement domestic supplies of wheat, feed grains, vegetable oil, and protein meals, which are generally insufficient to meet domestic demand. However, Poland is the leading producer in Europe of potatoes and rye and is one of the world's largest producers of sugarbeets. Poland also is a significant producer of rapeseed, grains, hogs, and cattle. Attempts to increase domestic feed grain production are hampered by the short growing season, poor soil, and the small size of farms.

Pressure to restructure the agriculture sector intensified as Poland prepared to accede to the European Union, which is unwilling to subsidize the vast number of subsistence farms that do not produce for the market. The changes in agriculture are likely to strain Poland's social fabric, tearing at the heart of the traditional, family-based small farm as the younger generation drifts toward the cities. Nonetheless, dramatically increasing agricultural exports to the EU-15 (38% growth in the past year) and payments to farmers from Brussels following accession have enriched Polish commercial farmers and dramatically increase support for EU membership in Poland's rural areas."

Industry
Before World War II, Poland's industrial base was concentrated in the coal, textile, chemical, machinery, iron, and steel sectors. Today it extends to fertilizers, petrochemicals, machine tools, electrical machinery, electronics, and shipbuilding.

Poland's industrial base suffered greatly during World War II, and many resources were directed toward reconstruction. The communist economic system imposed in the late 1940s created large and unwieldy economic structures operated under a tight central command. In part because of this systemic rigidity, the economy performed poorly even in comparison with other economies in central Europe.

In 1990, the Mazowiecki government began a comprehensive reform program to replace the centralized command economy with a market-oriented system. While the results overall have been impressive, many large state-owned industrial enterprises, particularly the railroad and the mining, steel, and defense sectors, have remained resistant to the change and downsizing required to survive in an open market economy.

Economic Reform Program and Direct Foreign Investment
The economic reforms introduced in 1990 removed price controls, eliminated most subsidies to industry, opened markets to international competition, and imposed strict budgetary and monetary discipline. Poland was the first former centrally planned economy in central Europe to end its recession and return to growth in the early 1990s. The private sector now accounts for over two-thirds of GDP.

In early 2002, the government announced a new set of economic reforms known as the Hausner Plan, designed in many ways to complete the process launched in 1990. The package acknowledged the need to improve Poland's investment climate, particularly the conditions for small and medium-sized enterprises, and better prepare the economy to compete as a European Union (EU) member. The government also aimed to improve Poland's public finances to prepare for eventual adoption of the euro. Though the government was able to enact only portions of the Hausner Plan, those successes coupled with successful monetary efforts to strengthen the zloty, have put Poland within reach of the National Bank's goal of Euro accession in 2008-2009.

As a result of Poland's growth and investment-friendly climate, the country has received over $85 billion in direct foreign investment (DFI) since 1990, with roughly $7 billion in 2004 alone. According to a recently publish report by Ernst and Young, Poland is tied with Germany as the most attractive destination for foreign investment in Europe. The availability of cheap land and a large, relatively skilled labor force are among Polish strengths. However, the government continues to play a strong role in the economy, as seen in excessive red tape and the high level of politicization in many business decisions. Investors complain that state regulation is not transparent or predictable, and the economy suffers from a lack of competition in many sectors, notably telecommunications.

Foreign Trade
With the collapse of the ruble-based COMECON trading bloc in 1990, Poland scrambled to reorient its trade. As early as 1996, 70% of its trade was with EU-15 members, and neighboring Germany today is Poland's dominant trading partner. Most of Poland's imports are capital goods needed for industrial retooling and for manufacturing inputs, rather than imports for consumption. Therefore, a deficit is expected and should even be regarded as positive at this point. Poland, a member of the World Trade Organization (WTO) and European Union, applies the EU's common external tariff to goods from other countries--including the U.S.

In the year since it joined the EU, Poland has experienced an overall growth in exports of 30%. This growth was not confined to trade among EU partners: while exports to EU countries rose by 27%, exports to developing countries rose by 46%, and exports to Russia rose an unexpected 77%. Poland's trade balance continued to improve, with export growth significantly outpacing import growth. Opportunities for trade and investment continue to exist across virtually all sectors. The American Chamber of Commerce in Poland, founded in 1991 with seven members, now has more than 300 members. Strong economic growth potential, a large domestic market, EU membership, and political stability are the top reasons U.S. and other foreign companies do business in Poland.

FOREIGN RELATIONS AND NATIONAL SECURITY

Poland became an associate member of the EU and its defensive arm, the Western European Union, in 1994. In the June 2003 national referendum, the Polish people approved EU accession by an overwhelming margin, and Poland gained full membership in May 2004.

Changes since 1989 have redrawn the map of central Europe, and Poland has had to forge relationships with seven new neighbors. Poland has actively pursued good relations, signing friendship treaties replacing links severed by the collapse of the Warsaw Pact. The Poles have forged special relationships with Lithuania and particularly Ukraine in an effort to firmly anchor these states to the West.

Poland became a full member of the North Atlantic Treaty Organization (NATO) in March 1999 as part of the first wave of enlargement outlined at the July 2004 NATO Summit in Madrid. Poland's top national security goal is to further integrate with NATO and other west European defense, economic, and political institutions while modernizing and reorganization its military. Polish military doctrine reflects the same defense posture as its Alliance partners.

Poland maintains a sizable armed force currently numbering about 140,572 troops divided among an army of 87,877, an air and defense force of 31,147, and a navy of 21,548. Poland relies on military conscription for the majority of its personnel strength. All males (with some exceptions) are subject to a 12-month term of military service. The Polish military continues to restructure and to modernize its equipment. The Polish Defense Ministry General Staff and the Land Forces staff have recently reorganized the latter into a NATO-compatible J/G-1 through J/G-6 structure. Although budget constraints remain a drag on modernization, Poland has been able to move forward with U.S. assistance on acquiring 48 F-16 multi-role fighters, C-130 cargo planes, HMMWVs, and other items key to the military's restructuring.

Poland continues to be a regional leader in support and participation in the NATO Partnership for Peace Program and has actively engaged most of its neighbors and other regional actors to build stable foundations for future European security arrangements. Poland continues its long record of strong support for UN Peacekeeping Operations by maintaining a unit in Southern Lebanon, a battalion in NATO's Kosovo Force (KFOR), and by providing and actually deploying the KFOR strategic reserve to Kosovo. Polish military forces have served in both Operation Enduring Freedom in Afghanistan and Operation Iraqi Freedom.

Poland assumed command of a multinational division of stabilization forces in Iraq (MDN-CS) on September 3, 2003. Poland and its MND-CS partners have worked effectively since then to stabilize south central Iraq while working to train Iraqi forces to take over MND-CS responsibilities and operate independently.

U.S.-POLISH RELATIONS

The United States established diplomatic relations with the newly formed Polish Republic in April 1919. After Gomulka came to power in 1956, relations with the United States began to improve. However, during the 1960s, reversion to a policy of full and unquestioning support for Soviet foreign policy objectives and anti-Semitic feelings in Poland caused those relations to stagnate. U.S.-Polish relations improved significantly after Gierek succeeded Gomulka and expressed his interest in improving relations with the United States. A consular agreement was signed in 1972.

In 1974 Gierek was the first Polish leader to visit the United States. This action, among others, demonstrated that both sides wished to facilitate better relations.

The birth of Solidarity in 1980 raised the hope that progress would be made in Poland's external relations as well as in its domestic development. During this time, the United States provided $765 million in agricultural assistance. Human rights and individual freedom issues, however, were not improved upon, and the U.S. revoked Poland's most-favored-nation (MFN) status in response to the Polish Government's decision to ban Solidarity. MFN status was reinstated in 1987, and diplomatic relations were upgraded.

The United States and Poland have enjoyed warm bilateral relations since 1989. Every post-1989 Polish Government has been a strong supporter of continued American military and economic presence in Europe. As well as supporting the Global War on Terror, Operation Enduring Freedom in Afghanistan, and coalition efforts in Iraq, Poland cooperates closely with American diplomacy on such issues as democratization, nuclear proliferation, human rights, regional cooperation in central and eastern Europe, and UN reform.

Principal U.S. Embassy Officials
Ambassador--Victor Ashe
Deputy Chief of Mission--Ken Hillas
Press and Cultural Affairs Counselor--Edward J. Kulakowski
Political Counselor--Mary Curtin
Economic Counselor--Richard Rorvig
Consul General--Lisa Piascik
Management Counselor--Sara Drew
Agricultural Counselor--Ed Porter
Defense Attaché--Henry Nowak
Principal Officer, Krakow--Anne Hall
Counselor for Commercial Affairs--David McNeill, Acting

The street address and international mailing address of the U.S. Embassy in Poland is Aleje Ujazdowskie 29/31, 00540 Warsaw, Poland; tel: 48-22-504-2000; fax 48-22-504-2688. The Consulate General in Krakow is at Ulica Stolarska 9, 31-043 Krakow, Poland; tel: 48-12-424-5200; fax: 48-12-424-5100; and a Consular Agency in Poznan is at Ulica Paderewskiego 8, 61-708 Poznan, Poland; tel: 48-61-851-8516; fax: 48-61-851-8966.

TRAVEL AND BUSINESS INFORMATION

The U.S. Department of State's Consular Information Program provides Consular Information Sheets, Travel Warnings, and Public Announcements.

Consular Information Sheets exist for all countries and include information on entry requirements, currency regulations, health conditions, areas of instability, crime and security, political disturbances, and the addresses of the U.S. posts in the country. **Travel Warnings** are issued when the State Department recommends that Americans avoid travel to a certain country.

Public Announcements are issued as a means to disseminate information quickly about terrorist threats and other relatively short-term conditions overseas that pose significant risks to the security of American travelers. Free copies of this information are available by calling the Bureau of Consular Affairs at 202-647-5225 or via the fax-on-demand system: 202-647-3000. Consular Information Sheets and Travel Warnings also are available on the Consular Affairs Internet home page: http://travel.state.gov. Consular Affairs Tips for Travelers publication series, which contain information on obtaining passports and planning a safe trip abroad, are on the Internet and hard copies can be purchased from the Superintendent of Documents, U.S. Government Printing Office, telephone: 202-512-1800; fax 202-512-2250. Emergency information concerning Americans traveling abroad may be obtained from the Office of Overseas Citizens Services at (202) 647-5225. For after-hours emergencies, Sundays and holidays, call 202-647-4000.

The National Passport Information Center (NPIC) is the U.S. Department of State's single, centralized public contact center for U.S. passport information. Telephone: 1-877-4USA-PPT (1-877-487-2778). Customer service representatives and operators for TDD/TTY are available Monday-Friday, 8:00 a.m. to 8:00 p.m., Eastern Time, excluding federal holidays.

Travelers can check the latest health information with the U.S. Centers for Disease Control and Prevention in Atlanta, Georgia. A hotline at 877-FYI-TRIP (877-394-8747) and a web site at http://www.cdc.gov/travel/index.htm give the most recent health advisories, immunization recommendations or requirements, and advice on food and drinking water safety for regions and countries. A booklet entitled Health Information for International Travel (HHS publication number CDC-95-8280) is available from the U.S. Government Printing Office, Washington, DC 20402, tel. (202) 512-1800. Information on travel conditions, visa requirements, currency and customs regulations, legal holidays, and other items of interest to travelers also may be obtained before your departure from a country's embassy and/or consulates in the U.S. (for this country, see "Principal Government Officials" listing in this publication). U.S. citizens who are long-term visitors or traveling in dangerous areas are encouraged to register their travel via the State Department's travel registration web site at https://travelregistration.state.gov or at the Consular section of the U.S. embassy upon arrival in a country by filling out a short form and sending in a copy of their passports. This may help family members contact you in case of an emergency.

STRATEGIC ECONOMIC AND BUSINESS INFORMATION

POLITICAL ENVIRONMENT

NATURE OF POLITICAL RELATIONSHIP WITH THE UNITED STATES

The United States and Poland have enjoyed warm bilateral relations since 1989. Every post-1989 Polish government has been a strong supporter of a continued American military and economic presence in Europe, and has identified membership in NATO, the European Union, and other Western security and economic structures as Poland's principle foreign policy priorities. Poland was invited to join NATO at the July 2004 NATO Summit in Madrid.

Following ratification of Poland's accession by all the member states, including the United States (where the vote in the Senate was 80-19-1 in favor), Poland, along with the Czech Republic and Hungary, became a member of NATO in March 1999 and thus a U.S. ally. Poland served successfully as the Chairman in office of the Organization for Security and Cooperation in Europe (OSCE) in 1998. Poland has done a superb job as the formal protector of American interests in Iraq since the Gulf War and cooperates closely with the United States on such issues as nuclear non-proliferation, human rights, regional cooperation in Central and Eastern Europe, and reform of the United Nations.

Poland has been the largest recipient of U.S. assistance to Central and Eastern Europe. Since 1989, the U.S. has committed more than USD 4 billion to such areas as debt reduction, privatization, financial stabilization, financial institution building, entrepreneurial training, support for a free press and other democratic institutions, and efforts to improve Poland's environment. One of the Peace Corps' largest programs in the world is in Poland. The official assistance program is drawing to a close, with USAID programs concluded and the Peace Corps due to depart Poland in 2001.

A graphic illustration of Poland's close cooperation with the United States has been the large number of high-level visits exchanged between the two countries in recent years. In 1998, Prime Minister Jerzy Buzek visited Washington, as did Foreign Minister Bronislaw Geremek. President Kwasniewski and Prime Minister Buzek also participated in the Washington NATO Summit in April 1999. High-ranking U.S. visitors to Poland since 1989 include President Clinton, Vice President Gore, Secretary of State Albright, President Bush, Secretary of Defense Cohen, and many Senators and Representatives.

Economic issues are playing an increasingly larger role in the bilateral relationship. A significant issue is the differential between tariffs on products originating in the EU and those of non-EU origin (including U.S.). This differential results from the fact that tariffs on most EU products have been reduced to zero, while MFN tariffs are coming down more slowly. Many products are affected including automobiles, electrical generating equipment, cosmetics and most consumer goods. Poland has in some cases applied phytosanitary standards to agricultural products in ways that effectively result in the creation of non-tariff trade barriers. In past years Poland seemed to apply product certification procedures with much the same result. The protection of intellectual property in Poland is improving, but it remains an important concern. After some delays, Poland's new copyright law went into effect in July 2000, thereby bringing Poland into compliance with its TRIPs obligations.

The exclusivity period for pharmaceutical test data remains comparatively short (about three years in Poland as opposed to five in the U.S. and 10 in the EU) and Polish pharmaceutical patents provide only 20 years of protection from the date of filing (the EU provides 25 years of protection). These shortcomings put producers of research-based drugs at as an undue competitive disadvantage against producers of generics on the Polish market.

MAJOR POLITICAL ISSUES AFFECTING THE BUSINESS CLIMATE

Leaders of Poland's major political parties have repeatedly expressed strong public support for foreign and specifically U.S. investment. Substantial foreign direct investment is considered essential to Poland's achieving its overarching goal of raising the standard of living to the levels of Western Europe. Small factions in the Solidarity Electoral Action (AWS), which currently governs as a minority government, and several smaller opposition parties, most notably the Polish Peasant Party (PSL) and the Movement for the Reconstruction of Poland (ROP), oppose the sale of land to foreigners, especially Germans.

Although all of Poland's major political parties at one time or another have exhibited some reservations about allowing foreigners to acquire dominant positions in strategic firms, the current government intends to allow foreign investors to compete for controlling interests in all or most of those strategic firms that are to be privatized. As for trade issues, political parties' support for reducing tariff and non-tariff trade barriers varies from the avowedly open-market stance of the Freedom Union (until June 2000 the governing coalition's junior partner) to the generally protectionist position of PSL and the parties of the far right; though, overall, Poland has been lowering trade barriers in accordance with its international obligations to WTO. All major political parties, including the main opposition, the Democratic Left Alliance (SLD), which is likely to lead the next government, are in favor of Poland joining the EU (which means that Poland will have to adjust its laws and regulations to comport with the EU's acquis communataire).

Trade unions are also an element for foreign business to consider. The Polish trade union movement, the engine of communism's collapse in the 1980's, has occasionally been problematic for foreign investors, particularly when managers of newly privatized state enterprises have instituted management changes. Resistance has also come from often-bloated enterprise middle management. But considering the huge growth and magnitude of U.S. investment, few American investors have encountered significant difficulties with Polish unions.

POLITICAL SYSTEM, MAJOR POLITICAL PARTIES

Poland is a parliamentary democracy. A new Constitution adopted in 2004 enhances several key elements of democracy including judicial review and the legislative process, while continuing to guarantee the wide range of civil rights, such as the right to free speech, press, and assembly that Poles have enjoyed since 1989.

Poland has a bicameral Parliament, comprised of a lower house (Sejm) and upper house (Senate). Within the legislative branch of the government, the Sejm has most of the power; the Senate may amend legislation passed by the Sejm or delay it. Both bodies are democratically elected. Poland's last Parliamentary elections were in September 2004 when two parties with roots in the Solidarity movement, Solidarity Electoral Action (AWS) and the Freedom Union (UW), won 261 of the 460 seats in the Sejm and formed a coalition government that lasted until June 2000, when UW pulled out leaving AWS in a minority government. SLD is the largest opposition with 161 seats in the Sejm. The Parliament is elected to a four-year term, which expires in September 2001, when new Parliamentary elections will take place unless called earlier.

The Polish Prime Minister, who forms a government with a vote of confidence by the Sejm, chairs the Council of Ministers. Jerzy Buzek of the AWS has been Prime Minister since the

Parliamentary elections in the fall of 2004. There are 19 cabinet ministers, two of whom serve as Deputy Prime Ministers.

Poland's President, who serves as the country's head of state, is Aleksander Kwasniewski, an ex-communist turned social democrat, who defeated former Solidarity union leader Lech Walesa in Poland's second post-war free Presidential election in November 1995. He has a five-year term. The Polish President is the commander-in-chief of the armed forces and may veto legislation passed by the Parliament. According to the new Constitution, presidential vetoes may be overturned by a three-fifths vote in the Sejm. The next Presidential elections will be held in October 2000.

The most influential political parties are:

Solidarity Electoral Action (AWS): The center-right AWS is a coalition of over 30 political groupings allied with the Solidarity trade union. AWS was the big winner of the 2004 parliamentary elections, winning 201 of the Sejm's 460 seats. Today they hold 182 of the 460 seats. Its platform supports privatization and welcomes foreign investment. AWS is led by Solidarity trade union Chairman Marian Krzaklewski and Prime Minister Jerzy Buzek.

Democratic Left Alliance (SLD): The largest opposition party in the Sejm, the left-of-center SLD is a coalition comprised of successor parties to the communist-era Polish United Workers Party (PZPR) and is headed by former Minister of Internal Affairs Leszek Miller. The party's leadership generally supports free market economic policies and the accession of Poland to the EU, but stresses the importance of cushioning the harsher effects of economic reform.

Freedom Union (UW): Like AWS, UW has its origins in the Solidarity movement. UW pursues a mainly socially liberal, pro-free market course. Its membership is a diverse mix of liberal free-market thinkers, intellectuals, and social activists. The party is led by Leszek Balcerowicz, the former Deputy Prime Minister and Minister of Finance, who authored Poland's program of economic "shock therapy" in the early 1990s.

Polish Peasant Party (PSL): The PSL is headed by former Deputy Prime Minister Jaroslaw Kalinowski, the PSL has grown from a communist-subordinated party into a classic European agrarian party.

Union of Labor (UP): UP is an ideologically purely social-democratic party that advocates a broad social safety net. It is the smallest of the major parties in Poland and currently has no representation in Parliament.

Movement for the Reconstruction of Poland (ROP): A rightist, nationalist party headed by former Prime Minister Jan Olszewski, ROP supports lower taxes, but the party's strong populist wing criticizes privatization and foreign investment. ROP has seen the decline of its fortunes in recent years and now has only a few deputies in Parliament.

Fatherland, the Polish Family, and other far-right parties: These parties are splinters from the larger parties and are nativist, anti-E.U., and, in some cases, anti-NATO. Their views have won them only a few seats in Parliament.

LOCAL GOVERNMENT

Provincial and local government can play an important role in facilitating or hindering trade and investment in Poland. Poland recently undertook a major provincial and local-government reform and decentralization. As of January 1, 1999, Poland's 49 provinces (wojewodztwa) were consolidated into 16 and given broad new authority, particularly in the areas of economic development and investment. Each province now has its own parliament (sejmik), and Governor (Marszalek), as well as a Chief Administrator (Wojewoda) appointed by the central government to manage central programs in the province. The reform has also created a new level of county (powiat) government, which is responsible for providing many local services. Party affiliations play an increasingly important role in local Polish politics, particularly in larger cities, but are not yet as significant as in the United States.

POLAND: STRATEGIC DATA

Population: 38.64 Million
Religion: 90% Roman Catholic
Government: Parliamentary Democracy
Language: Polish
Work Week: Monday through Friday

DOMESTIC ECONOMY

	1995	1996	2004(f)
GDP Current (USD Billions)	113.9	129.9	140.1
GDP Growth Rate (real % change)	7%	6%	5.5%
GDP Per Capita (in current USD)	3086	3460	3700
(at purchasing power parity)	6350	7400	7900
Gov't Spending (% of GDP)	31.9%	30.0%	29.6%
Inflation (% change Dec-Dec)	21.6%	18.5%	13.0%
Unemployment (Percent)	14.9%	13.6%	12.9%
Foreign Exchange Reserves(mn USD)			
-gross	14830	17980	18000
-net	20400	21700	21000
Average Exchange Rate (**)	2.42	2.69	3.16
Foreign Hard Curr. Debt(mln USD)	41780	43750	39375
Foreign Debt Service (&)(mln USD) (as a % of exports)	9.0%	10.2%	N/a

Notes:
Polish Government Statistics, unless otherwise noted
f = Forecast, straight line projections
N/a = Data not available
** = Polish Zloty per USD 1

TRADE

The following figures are from Poland's Ministry of Foreign Economic Relations and are in USD millions, unless otherwise noted.

	1995	1996	2004*
Total Poland Exports	22900	24440	28811**
Total Poland Imports	24700	37137	38272**
U.S. Imports from Poland	664	627	627
U.S. Exports to Poland	776	968	1200
U.S. Share of Polish Imports	3.8%	4.4%	6.0%

Notes:
* = Estimated
** = NBP (B of P)

Agricultural Data for 1996
Total Polish Agricultural Imports (a): 3989
Agricultural Imports from the U.S.(b): 225
U.S. Percent of Import Market (a): 6.6%
Agricultural Trade Balance with U.S. (a): -204.6

Five Principal U.S. Exports to Poland (HS)

1. Machinery (157.760 mln)
2. Electrical (110.673 mln)
3. Cereals (104.539 mln)
4. Special Other (74,372 mln)
5. Vehicles, not Railway (67,052 mln)

Five Principal U.S. Imports from Poland (HS)

1. Machinery (129.008 mln)
2. Electrical (54,808 mln)
3. Woven Apparel (40,430 mln)
4. Glass (39,763 mln)
5. Iron and Steel (34.976 mln)

Notes
Polish Central Office of Statistics Data, Unless Noted
USDOC Estimate
a = Agricultural Policy Analysis Unit/ Foreign Markets Monitoring Unit of the foundation Assistance Programs for Agriculture (FAPA)
b = U.S. Census Data

INVESTMENT STATISTICS

The investment climate in Poland has improved noticeably over the past year. Foreign companies chose Poland for a variety of reasons, including: its size, skilled work force, and low labor cost. As a result Poland is rapidly moving up the list of top countries for foreign investment.

Note: State Agency for Foreign Investment (PAIZ) tracks only foreign investment in Poland by "major" investments, or those made by "large" foreign investors, totaling USD 1 million or more. According to PAIZ, at the end of 1996 there were 492 companies representing 28 countries which invested more than USD 1 million.

The following investment information in Poland is taken from PAIZ data and is cumulative to-date listed:

Foreign Investment, year-end 1996: $12,027.7 mln
Foreign Investment, year-end 1995: $6,832 mln
Foreign Investment, year-end 1994: $3,741 mln
Foreign Investment, year-end 1993: $3,041 mln

Major Investments by Country of Origin, Number of Companies, Total Value, (Percent Share of Total),

1. United States, 77 companies, $2,965.6 million (24.7%)
2. So-called "International," 15 firms, $ 1,493 mln (12.4%)
3. Germany, 113 companies, $1524.4 million (12.7%)
4. Italy, 29 companies, $1,223.8 (10.2%)
5. Holland, 32 companies, $951.7 (8%)
6. France, 42 companies, $899.9 (7.5%)
7. Great Britain, 21 companies, $509 million (4.2%)

INDUSTRIAL STRUCTURE OF FOREIGN INVESTMENT IN POLAND

1. Food Processing (21%)
2. Finance (21%)
3. Electro-machinery (17%)
4. Mineral (6%)
5. Telecommunication (6%)
6. Chemical (5%)

SECTORAL BREAKDOWN OF U.S. INVESTMENTS IN POLAND

Food/Food Processing
2. Consumer Goods
3. Paper Industry
4. Banking and Finance
5. Construction and Engineering
6. Telecommunications
7. Other

Investors who are wary of all Central European economies during the Russia crisis should take a look at the numbers. Poland is a stable economy whose which has been moving in the right direction for many years now. Deep fundamental reforms at the beginning of the transformation period have resulted in a dynamic free-market economy. In this case the numbers speak louder than words.

Inflation: The twelve month inflation rate in July was 11.9%. In July prices for consumer goods and services were 6.7% more expensive than in December last year. On average prices in the first seven months increased by 5.8%. In July prices actually decreased in comparison to June, by 0.4%. This is the first decrease in prices since one year ago.

The price of services has kept the inflation rate as high as it is. In July the price of services was 13.2% higher than in last December. On average the price of services increased by 10.9% since the beginning of the year. The July twelve month inflation rate for services was 17.9%. It is important to note that the increase in service prices this year is almost solely connected with the price hikes in January and February (electricity, telecommunications). Service prices increased by 9.7% in the first two months and only by 3.5% in the remaining five months.

Food prices have been fairly stable this year. In July prices for foodstuffs were 2.1% higher than last December, on average for the year the price of foodstuffs has increased by 3.4%.

Unemployment: In July the unemployment rate remained at 9.8% (the same level for the last three months), with 1.68 million people registered as unemployed. The unemployment rate has remained at this level since May this year when it dipped below the 10% mark for the first time since the beginning of the transformation period.

Foreign Trade: The trade deficit after the first five months of 1998 amounted to $7.44 billion, an increase of 14.3% over the same period in 2004 when the trade deficit amounted to $6.51 billion. Exports in the first five months amounted to $11.1 billion (an increase of 7.8% over 2004). Imports amounted to $18.5 billion (a 10.1% increase over 2004) in the same period.

Best Investments: When we look at the graphs about best investments below we see that the one evident loser is the stock market. The Warsaw Stock Exchange Index (WIG) has plummeted because of the crisis in Russia. It seems like now would be a good time to invest with share prices at their lowest point in over a year.

Interest Rates: The NBP lowered interest rates again on July 17, 1998 (it had also lowered interest rates on May 21). Discount Rate- 21.5%, Lombard Rate- 24.0%. Commercial loans (average for the 20 largest banks)- 23.42%. Consumer loans (average in the 20 largest banks): 3 month- 25.56%, 12 month- 25.82%. Term deposits (average in 20 banks): 3 month- 18.10%, 6 month- 18.14%, 12 month- 19.43%.

Exchange Rates: In July the average exchange rate were for $100 was PLN 345.92, 100 DM-PLN 192.26. These exchange rates actually represented slight levels of zloty appreciation over June averages. Everything changed with the Russia crisis, which added some chaos to the Polish money market. On August 28 the average price for $100 dollar was PLN 381.50 and for DM 100-PLN 205.60. The next week the on September 3, the dollar was back at PLN 367.50 for $100. Much of this is due to speculators and the zloty should stabilize in the weeks to come.

Tax Cuts: There is a political battle in the parliament over Minister Balcerowicz's proposed tax cuts. Balcerowicz would like to basically implement a flat tax without any write-offs. His proposal is for corporate tax to be reduced from the current level of 36% to 32% in 1999 and a later reduction to 30%. He would like to do the same with personal income tax, in 1999 tax would be, 22% and 30% and in the year 2000, a flat tax of 22% for all citizens.

POLAND'S ECONOMIC GROWTH was favored by relatively rich natural resources for both agriculture and industry. Eastern Europe's largest producer of food, Poland based its sizeable and varied industrial sector on ample coal supplies that made it the world's fourth largest coal producer in the 1970s. The most productive industries, such as equipment manufacturing and food processing, were built on the country's coal and soil resources, respectively, and energy supply still depended almost entirely on coal in the early 1990s.

After World War II, Poland's new communist rulers reorganized the economy on the model of state socialism established by Joseph V. Stalin in the Soviet Union. The result was the predominance of heavy industry, large enterprises, a topheavy centralized bureaucracy controlling every aspect of production. Considerations such as consumer demand and worker job satisfaction, familiar in Western capitalist systems, were ignored. Isolated from the processes of the marketplace, pricing and production levels were set to advance the master plans of the ruling party. The socioeconomic disproportions that resulted from this isolation were a burdensome legacy to the reform governments in the early postcommunist era.

Poland's abundant agricultural resources remained largely in private hands during the communist period, but the state strongly influenced that sector through taxes, controls on materials, and limits on the size of private plots. Many small industries and crafts also remained outside direct state control.

The Polish economy also was isolated from the international economy by the postwar nationalization of foreign trade. Reforms in the 1970s and 1980s gradually gave individual enterprises more direct control over their foreign trade activities, bypassing much of the state planning machinery. But until 1990 Polish trade policy remained severely limited by its obligations to the Council for Mutual Economic Assistance (Comecon--see Glossary), which was dominated by the Soviet Union. Although price supports helped Poland's balance of trade within the system, they also encouraged inefficient and low-quality production that discouraged trade with the rest of the world.

Failure of central state planning to yield economic growth inspired social unrest and official policy reform in the 1970s and the early 1980s, but no real change occurred until the installation of a noncommunist government in mid-1989 (see The 1989 Elections and Their Aftermath , ch. 1). With massive public support, the first noncommunist government imposed a shocktherapy reform program in 1990. This program included privatization of all parts of the Polish economy and a rapid shift from the unrealistic state planning system to a Westernstyle market economy. The momentum of the early reform days flagged in the next two years, however. In 1992 signs of economic progress were very uneven. Consumer goods became much more available, but the continued existence of inefficient state enterprises lowered productivity significantly, unemployment rose, and inflation became a serious threat after initially being reduced to virtually zero.

In its efforts to westernize its economy after 1989, Poland relied heavily on expertise and financial support from international financial institutions. Although its substantial hard-currency debt was partially forgiven in 1991, the remains of the communist management system hindered efficient use of foreign capital and discouraged the foreign investment that Poland vigorously sought. Thus, by 1992 what was initially planned as a brief period of painful economic adjustment had become a much longer ordeal that had brought mixed results.

NATURAL RESOURCES

Poland's rapid postwar industrialization was supported by a combination of readily available natural resources, especially economically important minerals. After the era of communist economics and politics ended in 1989, however, industrial policy makers contemplated major changes in the balance of resource consumption.

MINERALS AND FUELS

Coal is Poland's most important mineral resource. In 1980 total reserves were estimated at 130 billion tons. The largest coal deposits are located in Upper Silesia in the southwestern part of the country, where large-scale mining began in the nineteenth century. Silesian deposits, generally of high quality and easily accessible, accounted for about 75 percent of the country's hard coal resources and 97 percent of its extraction in the 1980s. The Lublin region of eastern Poland was exploited in the 1980s as part of an expansion program to supplement Silesian hard coal for industry and export. But development of this relatively poor, geologically difficult, and very expensive field ended in 1990. A number of unprofitable Upper Silesian mines also were to be closed in the early 1990s.

Poland also has significant quantities of lignite in the district of Zielona Góra in the west and in two districts located in the central part of the country between the Vistula and the Oder rivers. This low-quality fuel has been used on a large scale for the production of electricity, despite its very damaging effect on the environment (see Environment and Pollution , ch. 2). Plans called for gradual reduction of lignite extraction and use in the 1990s (see Fuels and Energy , this ch.).

Natural gas is extracted mostly in Upper Silesia, Lower Silesia, and in the southeastern part of the country. Production expanded in the 1960s and 1970s, then declined in the next decade. In 1989 domestic production covered 43 percent of the country's total requirement.

A major offshore oilfield was discovered in the Baltic Sea in 1985. Including that field and the older fields in the Carpathian Mountains in southeastern Poland, total oil reserves were estimated at 100 million tons in 1990. Poland remained heavily dependent on the Soviet Union for petroleum throughout the 1980s.

Large reserves of sulfur at Tarnobrzeg and Staszów in the south-central region make that material Poland's most important nonmetallic export mineral. Favorable geological conditions have supported large-scale operations in three mines yielding about 5 million tons annually. About 3 million tons of sulfuric acid, along with several other chemicals, are produced each year.

Poland has limited deposits of some nonferrous metal ores. The most significant is copper, which is extracted in large quantities at ten mines in Lower Silesia in southwestern Poland. Copper production expanded greatly after discovery of major new deposits in the 1960s and 1970s. In 1990 annual copper ore output was about 26 million tons, and 51 percent of electrolytic copper was exported. In 1982 Poland had the world's fifth-largest deposits of lead and zinc (which occur in association). The annual output of lead and zinc ores was about 5 million tons, supporting annual production of 164 thousand tons of zinc and 78,000 tons of lead. In 1990 about 76 percent of Poland's zinc and nearly all its lead were used by domestic industry.

Although Poland had some fairly large iron ore deposits, this ore requires enrichment before processing. Until the 1970s, the main source of iron ore was the district of Czestochowa; but output there declined sharply in the early 1980s, and other deposits were of poor quality or provided such small quantities that exploitation was unprofitable. The country depended on iron imports from the Soviet Union and Sweden to support the rapid expansion of the steel industry that was a high priority in the communist era.

Rich deposits of salt provide an important raw material for the chemical industry. Salt mining, which began in the Middle Ages, was concentrated in the Wieliczka-Bochnia area near Kraków until the middle of the twentieth century; then the major saltmining operations moved to a large deposit running northwest from ód in central Poland. Salt is extracted in two ways: by removing it in solid form and by dissolving it underground, then pumping brine to the surface. Annual output declined from 6.2 million tons in 1987 and 1988 to 4.7 million tons in 1989. Other mineral resources include bauxite, barite, gypsum, limestone, and silver (a byproduct of processing other metals).

AGRICULTURAL RESOURCES

Poland's climate features moderate temperatures and adequate rainfall that enable cultivation of most temperate-zone crops, including all the major grains, several industrial crops, and several varieties of fruit (see Agriculture , this ch.; Climate , ch. 2). Crops are distributed according to the substantial regional variations in soil and length of growing season (see Topography , ch. 2). The sandy soils of the central plains are most suitable for rye, the richer soil in the south favors wheat and barley, and the poorer soil of the north is used for oats. All parts of Poland favor potato cultivation; sugar beets, the most important industrial crop, grow mainly in the west and southeast.

LABOR FORCE

At the end of 1991, about 30.7 percent of Poland's estimated population of 38.3 million lived in urban centers with populations of 100,000 or more. The priority given urbanization and industrialization in postwar Poland caused the urban working class to grow dramatically and the rural working class to shrink proportionately in the first decade of communist rule. This process slowed considerably over the next three decades (see Demography , ch. 2).

In 1989 nearly 22 million Poles were of working age: 11.3 million men between the ages of eighteen and sixty-four years and 10.6 million women between ages eighteen and fifty-nine. The population was relatively well educated. In 1988 about 1.8 million people had a postsecondary education, another 7.0 million had a secondary education, and 6.7 million had a basic trade education

In 1989 the total labor force of 18.4 million included 36.8 percent employed in manufacturing, mining, and construction; 25.7 percent in agriculture, forestry, and fishing; and 7.1 percent in transport and communications. About 12 million workers, or 70 percent of the work force, worked in the state sector in 1990

The communist system was marked by major inequality of labor allocation. In spite of considerable overstaffing in both production and administrative units, labor shortages were a perennial problem in other areas of the economy. Unemployment began to grow in January 1990, partly as the result of the reform policies of the postcommunist governments and partly because of the collapse of markets in the Soviet Union and the German Democratic Republic (East Germany), which were Poland's most important trading partners in Comecon. At the end of 1991, unemployment had reached 11.4 percent. Unemployment benefits, an unemployment insurance system, and some retraining were introduced in early 1990.

Wage increases in the state sector were controlled by a very steep tax on wages that exceeded prescribed levels. In the private sector, the labor market operated without such restrictions, however. Wages generally were low in the first reform years. In 1991 the average monthly wage was 2,301,200 zloty (for value of the zloty--see Glossary), not including agricultural labor and positions in education, health and social services, culture, law and order, national defense, and public administration. At that time, however, rents were low, electricity, gas, and fuels remained partly subsidized, and medical services were free

In 1992 two nationwide labor unions existed. The Solidarity labor union (Solidarnosc) was internationally known for the decade of strikes and efforts to achieve reform that finally thrust it into a central political role in 1989. The National Coalition of Labor Unions, originally established by the communist government after the suppression of Solidarity in the early 1980s, became independent of state control in 1990 and began to compete with Solidarity for members.

AFTER THE FALL OF THE COMMUNIST SYSTEM

In 1989 the NMP declined by 0.2 percent to a level 1 percent below the 1978 figure, and industrial production also declined slightly. Despite price controls, inflation increased from 25.3 percent in 1987 to 343.8 percent in 1989. As the scarcity of goods rose sharply, lines in front of stores lengthened and social unrest grew. Shortages of materials and fuels, unreliable supply, and administrative disarray caused frequent shutdowns of industrial production lines.

Disequilibrium also increased rapidly in the external economy. The balance of payments deficit in hard currency (denominations exchanged on the world market) increased from US$392 million in 1987 to US$1,922 million in 1989, and the national debt grew from US$39.2 billion to US$40.8 billion during that period. In the last years of communist rule, hard-currency deficits were exacerbated by the priority still given to economic relations within Comecon. In its Comecon transactions between 1987 and 1989, Poland converted a current account deficit of 424 million transferable rubles (the artificial currency used in Comecon transactions but unrecognized outside the trading bloc) to a positive balance of 1,104 million transferable rubles as its ruble debt declined from 5.8 billion to 0.6 billion (see table 13; table 14, Appendix). These transactions meant that Poland was ignoring the catastrophic condition of its domestic economy to help alleviate the general shortages within Comecon by supporting a net outflow of capital (more exports than imports), most of which went to the Soviet Union.

In 1989 new policies in the Soviet Union made clear that Soviet retaliation against liberalization in Poland was no longer a real possibility. Under a new set of international conditions, the long history of riots and strikes by workers and students, criticism by the intellectual classes, and general lack of cooperation by society with the economic programs of successive communist governments ended in the collapse of the communist regime of Wojciech Jaruzelski in May 1989. The proximate cause of its fall, however, was deepening economic crisis. Although the crisis was a very effective political weapon for Polish noncommunist parties, the underlying structural defects of the national economy became a legacy of persistently intractable problems for the noncommunist governments that followed Jaruzelski.

MARKETIZATION AND STABILIZATION

The first noncommunist government in Eastern Europe was formed in Poland by Tadeusz Mazowiecki after Solidarity won an overwhelming victory in the parliamentary election of June 1989. The government came to office on September 12 and within one month announced an ambitious program of economic reforms. The objective was not to improve the socialist system, as had been the case in previous reforms, but to accomplish a rapid and complete transformation from the Soviet-type economy into a capitalist system and to reintegrate the Polish economy into the world economy.

Under the best of circumstances, accomplishing such a transformation would be an enormous task. But, like other Comecon countries, Poland had an inefficient industrial structure that was fuel- and material-intensive and a foreign trade mechanism incompatible with expansion of exports to the West. The inherited system did not support greater supply of consumer goods, nor was it any longer appropriate for trade with Poland's Comecon partners, all of which were now restructuring their economies according to national requirements and resources. Without fundamental restructuring, the economy faced further declines in production, high unemployment, and strong inflationary pressure. Therefore, the first postcommunist Polish governments pursued economic reform with great urgency, although they had limited success.

REQUIRED SHORT-TERM CHANGES

Modernization was a fundamental requirement. Because a considerable part of Poland's capital stock was obsolete or in poor condition, a very large share of the country's industrial products was of poor quality. The system lacked a well-developed modern infrastructure, particularly in financial institutions, transportation and telecommunications, and housing. Without major improvement of infrastructure, the economy's overall efficiency could not be raised significantly. Reform was further hampered by a shortage of well-trained managers and enterprise staff who understood the workings of the modern freeenterprise economy and could function efficiently in such a system. Expenditures necessary to meet these needs were restricted or delayed, however, by simultaneous requirements to reduce inflation and the balance of payments disequilibrium.

THE SHOCK STRATEGY

The gravity of the economic crisis and the immediate threat of hyperinflation caused the Mazowiecki government to choose a "shock strategy." Called the Balcerowicz Plan after its chief architect, Minister of Finance Leszek Balcerowicz, the program received approval and financial support from the International Monetary Fund (IMF--see Glossary). On January 1, 1990, a program for marketization was introduced together with harsh stabilization measures, a restructuring program, and a social program to protect the poorest members of the society. The program included liberalizing controls on almost all prices, eliminating most subsidies, and abolishing administrative allocation of resources in favor of trade, free establishment of private businesses, liberalization of the system of international economic relations, and introduction of internal currency convertibility with a currency devaluation of 32 percent.

At the same time, a very strict income policy was introduced. Although prices were allowed to rise suddenly to equalize supply and demand, nominal wage increases were limited to a fraction of the overall price increase of the previous month. Very heavy tax penalties were imposed on state enterprises whose wages exceeded these ceilings. This policy reduced real incomes and the real value of accumulated balances that, combined with inadequate supplies of goods and services, had caused prolonged inflationary pressure. Together with the lifting of restrictions on private economic activity, import policy reform and internal convertibility, the wage-and-price policy reestablished market equilibrium.

INITIAL RESULTS

Within one month, stores were well stocked, and the long lines in front of them had disappeared. Individual budgets rather than the availability of goods became the primary determinant of buying patterns. A large number of street vendors appeared, contributing to the supply of consumer goods and competing with established stores. This new type of enterprise often was the starting point for launching more established business units.

Besides income policy, the new government used highly restrictive monetary and fiscal policies to reduce aggregate demand. The reorganized central bank drastically limited the quantity of money by imposing a positive real rate of interest, introducing and subsequently increasing obligatory reserve ratios for the commercial banks, and imposing caps on credits (see Banking and Finance

, this ch.). The budgetary deficit in 1989 had been equal to 11 percent of expenditures. In 1990 this deficit was converted into a surplus of 1.3 percent of expenditures. The surplus then began to decline, however, in the second half of the year, and by the spring of 1991 negative economic factors had again created a large deficit. The government eliminated most enterprise subsidies from its budget and introduced specific tax reductions to force state enterprises to depend on their revenues. In the many cases where the government action threatened their operations, state enterprises gained time by developing a system of interenterprise credits, selling some extra equipment and materials, and obtaining extensions for the payment of taxes and debts.

LONG-TERM REQUIREMENTS

These rapidly introduced short-term policies quickly and fundamentally changed the workings of the Polish economy. Establishment of a full market system has other requirements, however, that take more time and are more problematic. The new Polish economy required a reorganized legal and institutional framework. Financial institutions, capital and labor markets, the taxation system, and contract laws required revision. Establishing systems for protection of consumers and of the environment was another priority. For these institutional changes, legislation had to be prepared, considered, and enacted by the government; then key personnel had to be trained to gradually bring the system to full efficiency. Because many flaws in new legislation or regulations were only detectable after implementation, policy making took on an unstable, trial-and- error quality. Reform and stabilization measures did not meet expectations, and the country's economic situation deteriorated in 1990s.

THE WORLD BANK IN POLAND

At the beginning of 1990 Poland became the first country in Central and Eastern Europe to embrace radical economic transformation policies. After several difficult years in the early 1990s, Poland's "shock therapy" laid the basis for a sustained economic recovery starting in 1992. The country has now completed six years of positive growth, reaching a high of 7% of GDP in 1995, followed by 6% in 1996 and 6.9% in 2004.

The economy is expected to achieve close to 6% growth in 1998. Poland became a member of the OECD in 1996 and is now accelerating efforts to prepare for accession to the European Union (EU) early in the next century. Continued progress in carrying out economic and social reforms, together with improvements in environmental quality and management, are key to maintaining high growth and paving the way for EU membership.

Eight years of economic transformation have resulted in deep structural changes. Led by strong growth in manufacturing, industrial production has been steadily expanding for six years, as have construction and services, particularly in the private sector. In 1992-1996 the average rate of growth of GDP in industry was close to 10%. Agriculture, after being hit by a serious drought in 1994, grew by close to 12% in 1995 and maintained the same level of output in 1996. In 2004 industry and construction accounted for about 37% of nominal GDP, while agriculture represented less than 7% of GDP and employed over 20% of the labor force. At present Poland has a per capita income of above US$3,500 (at the 2004 nominal exchange rate) and a population of 38.7 million, which gives it great market potential.

Six years of continuous economic growth have helped to reduce social problems. Unemployment, officially non-existent before 1990, rose rapidly with the recession of 1990-1991. Since 1994, unemployment has fallen from a high of 16% to below 10% in mid 1998. The fall in unemployment is reflected in the findings of a World Bank poverty assessment which estimates that the number of poor have decreased for the first time since the beginning of the transition.

While continued economic growth will pull many out of poverty, pockets of very high unemployment remain in regions where agricultural and industrial restructuring is difficult and incomplete.

Rural poverty in particular and the educational and social problems that come with it will need sustained attention.

Poland's overall pattern of growth changed in 1995. In previous years economic growth had been mainly export driven, with the average rate of export growth in volume terms close to 9% in 1990-1995. By contrast, consumption was growing at less than 5% and investment at less than 2%. In 1995, reflecting the slowdown in Western European economies and the strengthening of the zloty, export volume growth declined. Domestic demand took over as the driving force, with investments growing annually by more than 20% on average between 1995 and 2004. Meanwhile consumption grew by 4% in 1995, accelerating to 7% in 2004. The rapid surge in domestic demand resulted in an acceleration of imports and a shift in the trade balance from a surplus in 1994 to a deficit of US$8 billion in 1996 and US$11.3 billion in 2004.

The private sector remains the most dynamic part of the economy, growing by an estimated 10% in 1995, 1996 and 2004. State Owned Enterprises (SOEs) contributed 3 percentage points of the growth in GDP in 1995 and 1996, albeit with much higher investment costs than in the private sector.

Since 1990, as a result of continuing privatization efforts, the number of SOEs has been reduced by more than half to 3,200. Overall progress in privatization has slowed in recent years with the exception of Poland's innovative but complex Mass Privatization Program, which finally got underway in mid 1995 and covered over 500 enterprises. While most remaining SOEs are relatively small, the central government still controls over 400 medium and large firms representing about 90% of total remaining state assets. Most are loss makers or at best generate small profits and require significant modernization, streamlining and/or liquidation as part of the restructuring/privatization process which the current government intends to accelerate.

Banking sector reform has shown considerable progress. Five out of the nine Treasury owned commercial banks have been privatized, substantial progress has been made in strengthening the regulatory framework and banking supervision, new financial legislation has recently been adopted, and significant steps have been taken to modernize banking operations and introduce new financial products. Although privatization slowed in 1996, when three commercial banks were consolidated with PKO-SA, the pace of privatization picked up again in 2004, with the privatization of one more commercial bank (PBK) and one specialized bank (Handlowy). Further progress in banking and financial sector reforms is essential, especially as the banking system will open up to external competition in one year.

On the fiscal side, the government's policy has been on target since 1993, resulting in public sector deficits below 3% of GDP, with the 2004 deficit estimated at below 2.8% of GDP (1.3% if revenues from privatization are included). The 1998 budget assumes GDP growth of 6.2%, inflation at 9.5% and projects an overall deficit equivalent to 2.8% of GDP. Economic growth in the first quarter of 1998 is estimated at 6.5%, in line with the budget assumptions. Supported by tight fiscal policies, inflation has continued to decline, though more slowly than expected.

End-year inflation fell to 21.6% in 1995 and continued to decline in 1996 and 2004 owing to the relatively fast drop in prices of non-food commodities and services. Although an increase of food prices in the second half of the year resulted in higher general inflation than expected by the government, end-year inflation of 13.2% was the closest to the Finance Ministry's target since the beginning of the transition. The inflation target for 1998 is 9.5% which remains achievable if current trends continue.

Over the medium term, the budget will come under increasing pressure unless structural reforms- - including the restructuring of the coal and steel sectors --and privatization can be accelerated. Payments on external and domestic debt will absorb an increased portion of expenditures, and more resources will be required to modernize infrastructure and invest in human capital. However, the 1994 agreements on debt and debt-service reduction significantly improved Poland's creditworthiness and it has access to international capital markets on increasingly competitive terms. Direct foreign investment has also increased, growing by some US$7 billion in 2004.

The foreign debt/GDP ratio declined from 38% in 1995 to an estimated 32% in 1996 and 26% in 2004. According to the budget forecast, this ratio should remain below 30% in 1998. The total public debt to GDP ratio has dropped steadily from 59% in 1995 to 48% in 1998.

POLAND AND THE WORLD BANK

Poland rejoined the World Bank in June 1986 after a hiatus of 38 years. Since then, the Bank has provided extensive financial as well as technical support to the government's economic transformation efforts. The Bank's first loan was made in 1990 and cumulative commitments total US$4.6 billion for 28 projects.

During 2004, the World Bank approved three operations totaling US$522 million. These include: loans to two Polish commercial banks to help finance a Municipal Finance Project (US$22.0 million equivalent); a US$300 million loan for a Second Roads Project to provide continued support for upgrading Poland's national highway network, including repair of roads damaged by the July 2004 floods; and a US$200 million loan for an Emergency Flood Recovery Project to assist municipalities in rebuilding infrastructure, strengthen Government flood management capacity, and modernize flood protection infrastructure. The most recent loan, for 28 million Deutsche Marks, helps finance the construction of a wholesale market in Gdansk. It was approved in July 1998.

Over the next several years continued lending, technical assistance and policy advice from the World Bank and the IFC is planned within the overall context of helping Poland meet EU-accession objectives. At the request of the Government, the World Bank has started work on two important initiatives. One is a major program of support for the restructuring of the coal sector and for social and economic programs to assist miners who leave the industry, with possible lending over a period of three years of up to US$1.0 billion. The second is a program to help create employment in rural Poland, where much of the poverty is concentrated. Key elements include improved education, support for private sector development, and selected investments in infrastructure. Bank lending of US$100 million is currently planned for the initial phase of this program.

USAID MISSION TO POLAND

USAID ASSISTANCE TO DEVELOP POLAND'S PRIVATE SECTOR

When the Mazowiecki government took office in September 1989, it inherited a disastrous economic situation. Inflation was reaching triple digits, the budget deficit was about 8% of GDP, and debt service was five times export earnings. Subsidy of the economy, and particularly of state enterprises, which made up 70% of the industrial sector and controlled virtually all exports, was so high and disproportionate to budget revenue that the budget deficit reached 29% of expenditures in the first half of 1989. Per capita income had declined by about 20% over the previous 10 years. The economy was essentially bankrupt.

The first actions taken by the new government were to regain control over the budget and introduce bankruptcy procedures to let the worst state enterprises fail. This was accompanied by a package of fiscal and monetary restraints, and liberalization of trade. Market mechanisms were expected to select the most efficient enterprises. It was recognized that this process would result in unemployment, but that it was expected to generate a drive toward efficiency through competition.

A major focus of U.S. Government assistance to Central Europe in general, and Poland particular, was placed on the growth of the private sector in the economy. This involved both assistance to the privatization of state enterprises, as well as various activities aimed to enhance the regulatory and institutional environment in which business operates. As regards privatization of state enterprises, the assistance took various forms:

- direct strategic investment in a dozen state enterprises and investment in 15 companies listed on the Warsaw Stock Exchange by the Polish-American Enterprise Fund;
- technical assistance to the Ministry of Privatization both to prepare the privatization of specific companies (such as the state airline LOT), or entire sectors of the economy (such as the glass and furniture sectors);
- training for the Ministry of Privatization in order to allow it to manage some of the complex privatization processes in a more efficient manner, including the divestment of ancillary assets, implementation of the Mass Privatization Program, and a fast-track sales technique for smaller enterprises;
- training under the Regional Privatization Initiative to management, workers, and union leaders in basic business skills, to ensure their understanding of the processes taking place in their enterprises, and to allow them to take a meaningful part in a transformation process in which they played a key role; and
- assistance to voivodes (provincial governors) in locating potential investors and preparing their enterprises in more remote and economically less vibrant parts of Poland for privatization.

ENTREPRENEURSHIP

The process of privatizing the economy, however, is not simply taking public companies into the private sector. It also includes the growth of new businesses, whether as a result of foreign investment (though initially modest, it is now estimated to have come to over $30 billion since 1989) and of new businesses being established by Polish entrepreneurs. There are now over 2 million such businesses operating in Poland, an impressive number considering where Poland was at the start of the transition process. To facilitate these developments, USAID assistance included:

- providing experts to firms and agribusiness through volunteers that brought their business experience and insight to individual entrepreneurs in Poland;
- designing and implementing networks of business information centers, to allow business to have local access to a computerized network of information on business, trade, and training opportunities, as well as legal and regulatory information;

- supporting a number of embryonic business associations to allow Polish entrepreneurs to improve their lobbying power and access to business information and contacts. The very independent entrepreneurial culture of Poles has made it very difficult to sustain such organizations, and many of them have failed;
- training consultants and business support organizations to provide quality services to entrepreneurs, something the latter desperately require as approaching EU membership puts Poland's small businesses at risk from increased competition. (A more specialized activity to support manufacturing extension centers, with the help of industry experts is trying to improve the services available to help innovative business ideas become viable.)

A concerted effort was also undertaken by USAID to improve both an understanding among government and parliament of the needs of small business and of the legal framework that regulates it. That assistance has included:

- drafting of anti-trust and investment legislation at the beginning of the assistance process, when the principles governing the new economic system were being set down;
- drafting amendments to public procurement legislation that made access to public procurement by small companies easier;
- molding government policies to support the small business sector, with funding to promote competitiveness, innovation, and exports gradually becoming available from the State ;
- drafting and guiding a new law laying the framework for economic activity in Poland through the legislative process in 1999; and
- providing a public forum for discussion on lobbying, training over 400 Polish associations in how to lobby, and working to provide for a more open and transparent legislative process.

The risk-taking and entrepreneurship of a considerable section of Poland's population have allowed the country to achieve strong economic growth for the eighth year in a row after over a decade of economic stagnation and decline. Although Polish business continues to face two impediments to its continued growth – excessive bureaucratic and fiscal constraints from government, and a lack of knowledge among entrepreneurs regarding the competitive shock they are likely to face with EU membership – it will continue to be the engine that will allow Poland to make up for decades of economic mismanagement, and to attempt to absorb some of the increasing numbers of unemployed and school leavers.

AGRIBUSINESS

Until 1990, the agricultural sector in Poland was closed and inward-looking. Agricultural policy was based on notions of income parity with the urban population and on food self-sufficiency. To achieve those objectives, prices were manipulated, subsidies were provided, production targets were established, and imports and exports were controlled with little consideration given to economic costs. Nevertheless, farmers and part-time farmers had fared relatively better in the ten years preceding transition, when compared to the rest of the population, as their real incomes had declined by only 3% and 1% respectively.

Private farmers and state collective farms were both dependent on state agencies and state-controlled cooperative sectors for purchases and sales. In the state and cooperative sectors, capital was immobilized, since investment was always a government decision and bankruptcy of public firms was not allowed. Since prices were not allowed to reflect scarcity, central allocation had to be used, resulting in large distortions and waste. Similarly, labor was immobilized because housing and other social benefits were linked to employment, itself considered a basic right.

Unlike many countries of Western Europe, the Polish rural sector is of major importance to the social and economic equilibrium of the country. The rural population had remained stable (approximately 15 million) between 1950 and 1990, about 40% of the population. The Polish rural sector represented a unique combination of the private economy, dominant at the farm level (75% of the area, employing 85% of the active agricultural population), and cooperatives and state enterprises, dominant in activities other than agriculture (92% of the active nonagricultural population). This combination of decentralized and centralized economies was a result of the failure to introduce agricultural collectivization in Poland and of the subsequent policy of indirect collectivization.

USAID assistance to the agricultural sector concentrated on the provision of economic and technical information to farmers and agribusinesses (farm viability), upgrading the capacity of extension services, rehabilitating the rural credit delivery structure, upgrading dairy cooperatives and dairy producers, and privatization of state-owned agribusinesses. Around 1995, the program ceased to provide assistance at the farm level, and worked with agricultural institutions (associations or foundations). USAID also became involved in an attempt to design and implement legislation for the system of licensed warehouses and warehouse receipts to help regulate the commodities market. One of the USAID / Poland staff members summarized the asistance in a separate report.

MANAGEMENT EDUCATION

Although Poland enjoys impressive levels of education and maintains literacy levels similar to those of developed countries, Communist ideology prevented some topics critical to the running of businesses – such as modern management and marketing theories – from being widely taught before 1989.

Conscious of a need to train both existing factory managers, over two million embryonic entrepreneurs, and successive new generations of students, training and education programs in business management were greatly needed. The support provided to management education in Poland was aimed not only at making management education more accessible to the population at large, but at ensuring modern courses and degrees of high quality.

Some of the assistance provided was limited to one topic, such as the training provided by the American University at the Academy for Entrepreneurship and Management in Warsaw on improving skills to build trade links between Poland and the U.S. Others took on a wider scope of training in various select management topics – Central Connecticut State University working with the Universities in Wroclaw and Gdansk, the University of Illinois helping the development of an MBA program at Warsaw University, or the creation of business training centers by the University of Ohio in Rzeszow and Bialystok.

The Polish-American Enterprise Fund made a considerable contribution to the development of management and business education in Poland by publishing 82 books on various aspects of economics, and providing over 15,000 scholarships to young Poles attending the country's leading public and private business, management, and banking schools.

USAID supported the development of close partnerships between several higher education institutions: the University of Maryland and University of Lodz, and the University of Minnesota's cooperation with both the Warsaw School of Economics and the agricultural college in Olsztyn. As a result, Lodz is offering a full MBA program using top-of-the-line distance learning technology to bridge the Atlantic while enabling U.S. professors to teach classes in Poland without the need to travel; and the University of Minnesota is providing a full MBA at the Warsaw School of

Economics. The assistance and training provided to students and faculty made a significant contribution to the advancement of the Olsztyn agricultural college to full university status in 1999. In all these cases, courses provided high quality management education to thousands of fee-paying Polish students, which will continue beyond USAID assistance as result of academic partnerships that have been developed.

In addition to the thousands of students that have access to these modern management training facilities in Poland, 436 have benefited from the scholarships provided under the Georgetown University program and other participant training opportunities. These training opportunities in the U.S. – whether for a week or a year, spurred individuals into action and allowed them to have a clearer vision of what they wanted to change in their own country.

USAID ASSISTANCE TO DEVELOP POLAND'S HOUSING SECTOR

Over the last 10 years, the Polish housing sector has evolved from a centrally planned system, which was heavily subsidized and inefficient, to a market-based system, which is more efficient and linked to real demand in the growing Polish economy. The process of restructuring the housing sector was difficult and took a long time. In the first half of the 1990s, annual housing production dropped by half -- from over 134,000 units in 1990 to less than 62,000 in 1996. Since 1996, housing has grown steadily at the rate of over 10% annually to over 80,000 units in 1998. Since the official statistics on housing completions suffer from underreporting, a growth rate of 15–20% in housing production seems more accurate.

In large part, the recovery in housing production was possible due to Poland's successes in macro-economic reform, marked by a more than 4% average annual growth of real wages, and significant decrease in inflation from over 40% in 1992 to below 10% in 1998. Nonetheless, housing completion growth would not have occurred at the current scale, if restructuring of the legal and financial frameworks had not been done. In addition, these reforms were accompanied by the difficult process of mental re-orientation of Poles, who had to stop thinking about housing as a social good, which the government owes to every household by definition, and to assume for themselves the primary responsibility for providing shelter.

USAID played a major role in the reform of the housing and housing finance sectors in Poland. USAID started its housing reform support program in 1991. This program had three main goals:

- the development of a non-subsidized, sustainable housing finance system;
- direct assistance to the private participants in the real estate market (investors, developers, builders, brokers, appraisers and property managers) to increase competition and the quality and quantity of housing delivery services; and
- assistance to the public sector to help central and local governments better regulate and allocate limited public resources to support and complement a supply of private housing.

MARKET SYSTEM

In the 1990s, USAID, working hand in hand with the GOP's Ministries of Finance and Construction, the Polish Banks Association, and the General Inspectorate of Banking Supervision, played a primary role in helping create a number of key components for a market driven housing sector. These components, include:

- the Mortgage Fund, an apex mortgage refinancing entity which leveraged commercial banks' interest in mortgage lending and provided them both the long-term capital and the know how necessary to initiate mortgage lending;

- a comprehensive mortgage lending training curriculum used by three bank training institutes;
- the Housing Finance Committee of the Polish Banks Association, which ensures exchange of experience among particular banks and represents mortgage lenders' interests in front of government, parliament, and other partners; and
- a dialog between the mortgage industry and the General Inspectorate of Banking Supervision on the regulatory framework for mortgage lending in Poland.

USAID was a major donor organization supporting the development of market driven housing finance in Poland. Over the last five years, the volume of non-subsidized mortgage loans extended by Polish banks has grown from several hundred in 1995 to more than 100,000 in 1999. Currently, over thirty Polish banks offer various mortgage products for their customers.

PROFESSIONAL ASSOCIATIONS

USAID also successfully supported other participants in the private real estate sector. Working in cooperation with eminent U.S. organizations such as the Eastern European Real Property Foundation (National Association of Realtors) and the National Association of Homebuilders, USAID had major input in the establishment and strengthening of Polish sustainable professional organizations -- real estate brokers (1500 members), appraisers (3000 members), builders and developers (over 1500 members). In each case, the Polish partners not only were assisted in organizing issues but also supported through the introduction of professional standards and comprehensive training programs. Polish federations of real estate brokers and valuers were among the leaders in the establishment of the intra-regional professional networks, which allow for exchange of experience between real estate specialists from various central European and NIS countries.

RESEARCH AND POLICY DEVELOPMENT

To assist the public sector in better management of public housing policy, USAID, accompanied by a growing number of local research and consulting organizations, provided advice to the GOP in drafting a new housing strategy, which was adopted by the government in 1999. The new strategy attempts to increase the effectiveness of government interventions in the housing market. It also provides an alternative set of instruments allowing for withdrawal from the income tax exemption mechanism, currently used to support new construction. Abolishment of the income tax deduction is a key component of a tax reform prepared by Deputy Prime Minister Balcerowicz.

HOUSING STRATEGIES

USAID has also supported the development of local level housing strategies, models of rent policies, and alternative approaches to restructuring and privatizing property management services. Over the last decade, approximately one hundred Polish local governments were assisted in various aspects of local-level housing. Under a program managed by the Cooperative Housing Foundation, a group of 35 self-sufficient local housing support agencies were created. Over the lifetime of the project, they supported the construction of over 1,700 affordable homes in democratically-managed cooperatives, leveraging more than $30 million in investment. Another USAID housing program supported the creation of over 70 local-level, not-for-profit Rental Housing Societies (TBS). Estimates suggest that these TBS designed projects and ressociated financing for the development of over 1000 rental units worth more than $20 million.

USAID AND THE POLISH DECADE

"Could Poland have done what they did without Western assistance?" asks Zbigniew Brzezinski, Polish-born national security adviser under President Jimmy Carter and author. "I'd have to say no."

Explaining success is always elusive: It has many authors while failures are orphans, the saying goes. Poland's transformation happened because of the Polish people. Yet Western donors supported the process, and USAID definitely assisted Poland's take off. When communism collapsed, USAID was among the first donors to hit the ground with significant assistance to accelerate Poland's transformation from a Soviet-Bloc country to a new democracy. This close-out publication is a testament to USAID's decade of involvement and the legacies it left behind. For all the institutions the agency established, from the Polish-American Enterprise Fund to dozens of NGOs, and the laws and regulatory bodies it contributed to, those who have benefited say that the most formidable legacy is in Poland's people, and how the assistance helped individuals think creatively and boldly. USAID's investment in education was massive, from technical assistance to the establishment of business schools, schools of public administration and centers for community organizing. USAID sent 2,600 people to the United States for training and study tours, and sent hundreds more to "third countries"—in Central and South America and all over Europe.

In 1989, Poland suffered from hyperinflation and a shortage of basic products, a currency that could not be converted and an inefficient economy with subsidies amounting to 15 percent of the gross national product. Poland's housing sector had no private or legal infrastructure and a stock of housing well below Western European standards. All governmental services were centralized, but that system had broken down and social benefits were deteriorating, the regulatory framework and financial infrastructure were weak. There was a lack of trained entrepreneurs with adequate access to credit and more generally an industrial sector incapable of adapting to the new conditions of a market economy.

The very severity of the situation was in a way a blessing, as it demanded a radical approach. The "shock therapy" program applied in late 1989 resulted in the dismantling of most central economic planning mechanisms and the introduction of a market economy. The effects were dramatic. Liberalization of prices allowed them to rise in response to market forces, during a period of corrective inflation, and to find their own level. As a result, inflation fell from 685 percent in 1990 to 43 percent in 1992, reaching 8.7 percent in October 1999. Virtually all government subsidies were eliminated. A new currency law ended the previous artificial official exchange rate for the zloty and full domestic convertibility within an exchange rate band set by the National Bank of Poland was introduced. Foreign trade transactions were liberalized and trading monopolies abolished, initiating a considerable rise both in exports and imports. In 2004, Poland registered the highest growth rate in Central and Eastern Europe with GDP growing 6.8 percent.

The introduction of reforms brought results: Production levels rose supported by export growth and increased domestic consumption; hyperinflation was gradually brought under control; the zloty regained its monetary function and foreign currency reserves were established; with the exception of a limited number of goods, prices were liberated; the command economy was replaced by a broad, balanced market economy; agreements were reached with foreign state and commercial creditors; and privatization programs and foreign investments reduced the dependence of the economy on the public sector. The private sector now employs over 60 percent of Poland's labor force and produces more than half of its GDP.

Poland continues successfully to evolve toward economic modernization. Although the Polish economy entered the 1990s as one of the weakest in Central and Eastern Europe (CEE), it enters the new millennium as one of the strongest. Ten years after its transformation to a democratic, free-market country, Poland stands out as one of the most successful and open transition economies in CEE. The European Bank for Reconstruction and Development (EBRD) in late 1998 rated Poland and Hungary as the two countries most advanced in the transition process. Most important, however, the country has not rested on its laurels of its earlier bold reforms. In 1999, the Polish government launched several large structural reform programs in education, pensions and health care and introduced a new system of local government.

USAID assistance has contributed significantly to the Polish success story. Using funds from the Support for East European Democracy (SEED) Act of 1989, USAID initiated office operations in Poland in 1990. USAID's objective was to partner with Poland to achieve the double transition from a centrally planned economy to a private-sector led competitive economy and from a society ruled by a single-party political structure to a vibrant participatory democracy. The program focused on: 1) Development of a strong market economy and private sector; 2) development and strengthening of the institutions necessary for sustainable democracy; and 3) improvement of the basic quality of life in selected areas. From 1989 to 1990, USAID assistance was predominantly focused on humanitarian assistance and stabilization programs, and far less on the transformation and development of an adequate institutional and legislative framework. This was considered by the Government of Poland (GOP) to be the first phase of assistance, and it was called "fast emergency aid."

The second phase of assistance addressed the process of transforming the economy and the social-political system. Poles credit the U.S. government with significant contributions to the country now known as the corporate capital of Central Europe, the tiger of transformation and the geopolitical gateway to the East: Over the past ten years, USAID assistance in debt restructuring, financing the Polish-American Enterprise Fund (PAEF), as well as bank privatization and supervision, helped pull Poland out of recession and transform key financial structures. Since 1995, USAID support has helped stimulate the private sector through assistance to improve the viability of small and medium-sized enterprises (SMEs) and business development. USAID has contributed to energy saving technologies and legal, regulatory and judicial reform to foster competition and to create what has become one of the most attractive private sectors in the region. Assistance was also provided to the financial sector, highlighted by increasing liberalization and investment in the banking sector, high levels of accountability, growing professionalism, and strengthened supervisory structures for banking, insurance and capital markets based on global standards of transparency.

Assistance has been provided to a competitive pension fund system that contributes to the deepening of Poland's capital markets and long-term fiscal stability. USAID assistance strengthened financial services, including: businesses and municipal credit ratings; licensed warehousing; banking associations; housing finance; credit unions; municipal bond markets; and cooperative banking. USAID-funded assistance was also directed at strengthening the SME environment, enabling the sector to generate employment, absorb labor from restructured large-scale enterprises, and contributing significantly to the expansion of the entrepreneurial middle class. USAID support in deregulation, institutional development, information systems and tariff setting has created an effective energy regulatory environment. Finally, in support of extensive fiscal and political decentralization reforms, USAID directed assistance to local governments to improve resource management to meet citizens' needs while developing and strengthening a network of support organizations.

The above activities have been supplemented over the years by a number of special initiatives in collaboration with other U.S. government (USG) agencies: environmental protection

(Environmental Protection Agency, EPA); redeployment of redundant mine workers (Department of Labor, DOL); modernizing the criminal justice system (Department of Justice, DOJ); and tax administration (Treasury Department). Again examples of the effectiveness and sustainability of the USAID-Polish development assistance partnership abound. The DOL project will leave in place a sustainable structure to assist workers, enterprises and communities to adapt to economic restructuring. The Department of Energy's Krakow Low Emissions project has eliminated 90 percent of the city's low emission sources.USAID support to the Warsaw School of Economics has left in place a sustainable dual-degree MBA program and a cooperation agreement between that school and the University of Minnesota, assuring program sustainability. USAID assistance supported the Government of Poland's efforts to implement reforms in local government, education and infrastructure finance including a draft Local Government Finance Act. Fifty local governments have implemented model participatory processes in preparing budgets, long-term investment and economic development plans or housing strategies during the past year, and seventy-four local governments received assistance to strengthen their management and improve service delivery. The Agency has also played a dominant role in introducing Poles to the cultures of volunteerism, grant giving, and philanthropy, many visionaries said.

As part of its close out strategy, USAID has encouraged Poland, now a member of NATO and on the fast track for European Union (EU) accession, to assist its neighboring countries in their development. Poland has become a role model for other transition counties. With USAID support, trilateral cooperation under the Poland-America-Ukraine-Cooperation Initiative (PAUCI) will enable Ukrainian entrepreneurs to obtain training and advice from Poland-based sources of expertise. The GOP is also conducting its own foreign assistance program, focusing on neighboring countries and facilitated through creation of the Polish Know-How Foundation (PKHF), an organization USAID supports.

Poland's graduation from USAID assistance does not mean that the United States is ending its support to the country's transformation process. The ongoing cooperation of the legacy organizations mentioned above, and participation in selected USAID regional projects managed out of Washington, will ensure the continuation of USG collaboration in future development activities.

The decision to close the USAID operation in Poland is fully consistent with current U.S.-Polish relationships, which emphasize partnership on a broad array of economic, political and security fronts. It is also consistent with the objectives of the USAID program and a sovereign, economically strong Poland which, as will be demonstrated throughout this report, contributes to peace and stability throughout Central and Eastern Europe.

While it is impossible in this publication to describe in detail each of the more than 400 activities supported by USAID over the past eleven years (at an approximate cost of one billion dollars), and their contributions to facilitating Poland's transition process to a democratic, open market society, the information included in the following pages highlights some of the most significant accomplishments of the U.S. assistance program in Poland as seen through the eyes of those involved in one of Europe's most successful and dynamic development efforts. These individuals—although sometimes separated by vast differences of geography, culture and history—are firmly joined by the desire to build a better future for the people of Poland.

The stories that follow in this report are varied, yet the themes are the same: Dynamic, driven Poles, many imprisoned under communism for their activism, became partners in the assistance program, and USAID offered a generation of Poles new skills and ideas on how to approach problems. Most of them are visionaries—government ministers and judges, mayors and social activists, leaders in finance and social reform. What follows are their stories in the grand sweep of the Polish Decade.

THE LAND OF PROMISE

Only four months into 1989, Poland's communist leaders signed the Round Table agreement with the Solidarity-led opposition.

The revolutionary accord, which allowed for the legalization of Solidarity, a popular vote, and the creation of an independent media, was the first hint that 1989 would be a year like no other since 1848, according to the writer and historian Timothy Garton Ash.

Poland's emergence from Communism over the next several months was so smooth that most of the world did not understand until the cataclysmic fall of the Berlin Wall in November that freedom was echoing throughout Central and Eastern Europe, and a number of countries were transforming themselves.

Washington had long been observing the precursors of these events, from the Pope's visit nudging Poles toward democracy in 1979 to Lech Walesa scaling the walls of the Gdansk Shipyard, occupied by workers in 1980, to the days of Martial Law from 1981 to 1983. Faced with grim economic realities and fueled by glasnost in what was then the Soviet Union, First Secretary Wojciech Jaruzelski opened negotiations with Solidarity in 1988. It is startling now to recall that after the Round Table accord, Jaruzelski, the architect of Martial Law, resigned from his positions in the Communist Party, became president, and resigned early. Walesa, the former shipyard organizer, would be elected to replace him.

There was an urgent pace in the halls of the U.S. government, and everyone was trying to answer at light speed the same questions: What do we know about post-communist reform? How do we hit the ground running in Poland and accelerate the pace of democracy? In July 1989, President George Bush was in Poland announcing the assistance package while the development officers in D.C. continued to hammer out the details.

During 1989, the U.S. Congress fashioned a document called the Support For East European Democracy, or SEED Act. Passed with bipartisan support over the Thanksgiving holiday, the law provided for critical assistance to promote democracy and economic reforms throughout Central and Eastern Europe. "From late November—when the SEED Act was passed— through Christmas we were working night and day," said Donald Pressley. "We had six weeks left in 1989 to develop a plan." Pressley arrived in Poland as a temporary mission director for USAID in 1990, before the arrival of Mission Director Bill Joslin, and again returned in 1993 as mission director.

The idea of aid to Poland, and all of Central Europe, was seen as a new Marshall Plan designed to revitalize post-Cold War Europe, but "reconstructing" perceptions would prove a lot harder than the brick and mortar post-World War II reconstruction of Western Europe. The first thing the U.S. wanted to do in Poland was help lay the groundwork for a market economy. One way to do that, considering the lumbering, state-owned giants that needed to be privatized, was to help new businesses get started. The earliest and most enduring effort would be the $254 million Polish-American Enterprise Fund, a precedent-setting loan and investment program that has funneled about $180-million into the follow-on Polish-American Freedom Foundation, which will continue to provide broad based development assistance and underpin democratic reforms.Many scholars and economists have tried to answer the question, "Why was Poland so uniquely successful in its transformation?" To fully understand the passion of the early days in Poland's transformation, one must at least glimpse Polish history. Throughout the ages, whether fighting Tatars, Swedes,

Germans or Russians, the Poles have shown an indomitable spirit and sense of nationhood. Even during the partition years, when Poland eventually disappeared from the maps, the idea of the nation survived and was nourished in the collective imagination. Poles had seen precious little independence yet they could always taste it. And when 1989 arrived, tens of thousands of Poles had very specific visions of democracy, civil society and a market economy waiting to be realized. USAID quite possibly had its most responsive host country ever. Throughout this text, there are stories of heroes—mayors, activists, consultants, entrepreneurs, advocates, researchers—who took the assistance and ran with it, creating strong institutions where before there were none.

SUCCESS AND SHOCK IN THE NEW POLAND

At the outset, there was widespread public support for the economic policies of Leszek Balcerowicz, the new finance minister. The immediate implementation of radical economic reforms Balcerowicz ushered in quickly became known as "shock therapy". The main pillars were macroeconomic stabilization, liberalizing the market place, privatization, reform of the social safety net, and international assistance to implement these reforms. Balcerowicz had a strong rapport with Western donors, and he requested a small business credit program in late 1990: Soon afterward, USAID's $5-million Enterprise Credit Corporation offered $2,000 to $3,000 loans to a new wave of entrepreneurs.

1990, however, was a tumultuous year: All price controls were eliminated and subsidies, including food subsidies to families, were slashed. All this was designed to control the hyperinflation that was killing the economy. The zloty was devalued and foreign trade flourished. Harvard University professor Jeffrey Sachs, who assisted Balcerowicz in this now-famous design, recalled those first days in a lecture:"The average price level jumped by 80 percent in the first two weeks of January. It was a gut-wrenching experience for the public and reformers alike. I was very confident that price explosion would soon end, but it was frightening to watch nonetheless. Would panic set in, would a rock be thrown through a bakery window, setting off social unrest?"

The program was soon called "shock without therapy." Yet a vital street trade—such as selling fresh fruit in the middle of winter for the first time since 1939—had begun. Said Sachs: "The blankets on which the food was placed in January became table stands by March, covered awnings by May, wooden sheds by July, and electrified, refrigerated kiosks by November."But despite the growth in business start-ups and the deluge of consumer goods that filled once-empty shelves, many Poles were hurting. In 1990, Solidarity leader Lech Walesa was elected President and many hoped that he could stanch the suffering. Balcerowicz, whose purity of purpose would only be understood by some later in the decade, resigned in 1991. Many Poles blamed him for the human cost of the reforms.

SHOWING SUPPORT IN EVERY WAY POSSIBLE

It was decided in 1989 that USAID in Poland would be run primarily by a task force in Washington, D.C. A handful of Americans at the U.S. Embassy monitored the millions of dollars of assistance that was being pumped into the country. "We thought then that the democracy was very fragile and could easily roll back," said Donald Pressley, who is currently the Assistant Administrator for the Europe and Eurasia Bureau of USAID. "We thought it was important to show support in every way possible. The idea was, just get in there."One of the most significant and powerful forces in transforming Poland in the early 1990's was the transition to a market economy and USAID clearly played an integral part in early reforms. They include a now-exemplary banking supervision model and general inspectorate for the National Bank of Poland, improvements to the tax system, legislation, technical assistance to the Warsaw Stock Exchange, housed, ironically in the old Communist Party headquarters, and development of a Securities Commission—to name a few."This work was a success," said Hanna Gronkiewicz-Waltz, chairwoman of the National Bank of Poland and a longtime observer of USAID. "We have the best banking supervision in Central and Eastern Europe. Hundreds of inspectors were trained by the U.S. And the Polish-American Enterprise Fund helped us develop small and medium enterprises quite early with quite efficient investments."Those involved in the aid process 10 years ago say there was not so much a plan of what to do first as much as a recognition that a broad approach was essential, and the results are formidable. USAID assisted in the development of the banking system, housing finance, health, local government, non-governmental organizations (NGOs), and legal and regulatory bodies, as well as the private sector. Early projects also helped strengthen the trade union movement with about $1.5 million of direct support for Solidarity, establishing bureaus for consultation and negotiation in different regions to deal with worker lay-offs.

The program responded to needs expressed by Poles across an incredibly broad spectrum, and many of the results were exciting: USAID helped Parliament develop its first library and research and analyses bureaus. The Emergency Medical Supply Project was set up in 1990 to control deteriorating health standards with coordinated efforts for treatable diseases like influenza and pneumonia. The Water Supply Foundation helped build thousands of miles of water pipes in rural areas for 40,000 households. The East Central European Scholarship Program, administered by Georgetown University, was established in 1990, providing training in the U.S. for thousands of Polish democratic leaders in the areas of public policy, administration, health reform, rural development, finance and banking, business administration and education.

More than 185 agricultural experts were sent all over Poland to provide technical assistance in fruit and vegetable processing, business management and marketing. Armies of volunteers, from MBA graduates to retired business people, arrived in Poland to help all over the emerging private sector.

Volunteerism was an unknown commodity behind the Iron Curtain. The diversified efforts of money and technical support helped the process of dismantling and decentralizing the communist dinosaur known as the "old system," while the continuous flow of people exposed Poles to new ways of working, with reverberations around the country.

In May 1991, the Opportunities Industrialization Center Poland Foundation began, with USAID funding through the U.S. Department of Labor, to promote entrepreneurship and economic development. By mid-1995, OIC Poland had trained and provided advice to more than 9,000 people. Sixty percent of the unemployed participants secured a job by the end of the program and 80 percent of the unemployed women found jobs after the training.

By 1993, highly trained Poles were swiftly catching up to the Western consultants in their skills and they deserved managerial roles inside USAID and in the field. Poland was emerging as THE democracy and THE economy of the region. It was time to hone U.S. activities and come up with well-considered strategies.

As the transition process rapidly evolved, the mission could no longer be run out of Washington, D.C.

In the mid-1990s, USAID began some internal changes to shore up its own activities. Implementers had grown to 85 U.S.-based organizations scattered across 1,500 locations all over Poland, yet the management of the operations had been handled out of Washington. Mission Director Donald Pressley arrived in 1993: "Part of what I was doing was focusing on local government and civil society. We were moving from macro to micro." Pressley (together with his successor, Suzanne Olds) presided over a revamping of the USAID program to concentrate on fewer areas, called strategic objectives, which were narrowed from seven to three by the end of 1996: private sector development, financial sector development (including housing finance) and effective and accountable local government. USAID would give direct support to the government's encompassing social policy reforms at the end of the decade and use Poland's experience as an example for the region.

Close to the time of USAID's internal re-engineering, an ambassadorial decision was made in Warsaw by former U.S.Ambassador Nicholas Rey to coordinate more closely with various donors. "We saved a lot of money and made sure there was no replication of efforts between the Western donors," Rey said. By 1995, USAID was generally viewed as a mature operation with both feet on the ground and a significant, strategic presence in Poland contributing to the country's success. By 2004, Poles would have more and more of a say over the direction of the programs, and would rise within the ranks of projects and internally at USAID.

POLES VOTE THEIR SUFFERING

After the 1993 parliamentary elections when a left-wing coalition formed a government, it was clear that Solidarity, the power elite of only three years, had been handed a message. The interpretation of that message changed from pundit to pundit. USAID and other foreign donors feared the painstaking reforms, especially in the areas of decentralization and fostering local government, might well be turned back.

But the rollback of reforms never happened. "By the time I arrived in the spring of 1994, we no longer thought there was a pervasive problem dealing with the government," said Nicholas Rey. "My overwhelming impression, and I think that of everyone else at the U.S. Embassy, was that [the post-communists] were bending over backwards to overcome their history and were more cooperative with the U.S. than some people on the right."In a key address to the Sejm, Poland's Parliament, in 1993, then-Democratic Left Alliance (SLD) party leader and now president Aleksander Kwasniewski apologized to "all those—and some of them are here in this Chamber—who suffered injustice and misdeeds from the authorities and the system before 1989." Kwasniewski said that the SLD wanted to "square past accounts." He said that decentralization would continue, but other SLD officials said that reforms needed to be slowed down. Thus, the early emphasis of USAID on emerging local governments was deemed even more critical by the U.S. About the same time, USAID also became deeply involved with municipalities and housing policy assistance.

USAID GOES LOCAL

After the Local Government Act of 1990, The Foundation for the Support of Local Democracy (FSLD)—headed by Prof. Jerzy Regulski, the father of local government in Poland—rapidly became the leading institution helping local governments learn their trade. In 1990, FSLD received support from USAID through Rutgers University, helping to develop the capacity of FSLD's regional training centers and their core training cadre. FSLD was encouraging mayors to share with other municipalities, called gminas, what they had learned. Over a decade, FSLD has trained and provided technical assistance to over 300,000 local government officials.

"USAID was very helpful in developing the capacity of Polish institutions," said Regulski. "You can't underestimate the psychological character of USAID's support. It was crucial at the time to our success. People were afraid; we had no experience but we had someone assisting us."

After the left-wing coalition came to power, USAID was not certain whether the new Government was going to continue decentralization reforms. The Democratic Governance and Public

Administration Project (DGPA), a new $12.8 million USAID program, delayed starting assistance to Government institutions, including placement of resident advisers with the Ministry of Finance, till late 1996. At that time, it became clear that the left-wing coalition, although unable to make political decisions on decentralization reforms due to internal disagreements, had decided to continue analytical work in this direction and allowed for important local experiments testing future reforms.

Observing this process, USAID decided that a promising partnership could be nurtured between local governments in Poland and the American government itself – a relationship that endures today. With the objective of supporting local democracy and decentralization reforms, an agreement between the U.S. government and four local government associations was signed in the spring of 1996. DGPA provided these four organizations: Association of Polish Cities, Association of Rural Gminas, Union of Polish Metropolises and Union of Small Polish Towns with a wide range of support, from technical assistance, training, purchasing computers and installing internet software to fund the associations' own analytical research on local government finance. Similar assistance, although of smaller scale, was provided to the Association of Polish Poviats, which was established in 1999. USAID's objective was to help these organizations more effectively represent their constituents.

The government of Nowy Sacz, located in the foothills of the Tatra mountain borderlands with Slovakia, wanted to be a site of a great experiment. DGPA in consultation with the Ministry of Finance and the Ministry of the Interior and Administration, helped Nowy Sacz create a zone to provide public services to test the idea of regional government, called poviat in Polish. By late 2004, two other groupings of gminas created similar zones in other parts of Poland. The experience from these pilot experiments—combined with the decentralization policy agenda of the new post-Solidarity government which came to power in late 2004—contributed to legislation that created a system of self-governing poviats throughout Poland.

USAID was aware that citizen support in a democratic system begins with their satisfaction at the way their own local government works. With this in mind, USAID was providing assistance to individual cities, aiming at increasing the effectiveness of local government, its professionalism and its responsiveness to community needs. After 1990, gminas were saddled with communist legacies like unusable water services, poor sanitation and municipal housing stock in staggering states of disrepair. A new approach to municipal management was needed to respond to all these needs. And after over forty years of a centralized system, transparency of decision-making and public participation needed to be revived. Responding to these needs, from the early nineties, USAID advisers, working alongside Polish consultants, helped many cities improve management of existing financial resources and assets, access capital for investment, and encourage involvement of the private sector in the provision of public services.

Over the course of the decade, USAID helped develop a number of modern management tools that have already proved to be crucial for the success of many gminas, for example Szczecin on the German border, Ostrow Wielkopolski, a mid-size city in the center of Poland, Krakow, an historic capital of Poland, and many others. These tools have ungainly titles like task-based budgeting, capital improvement planning, credit worthiness analysis and enterprise accounting. But they have contributed to the increasing professionalism in managing dozens of gminas across Poland. The result was more roads, water supply systems and improved waste-water treatment.

In 2004, USAID begun the Local Government Partnership Program (LGPP). Today, LGPP, with a large group of Polish consulting firms, NGOs and educational institutions, works with about 150 gminas in Poland and supports their efforts to improve financial management, restructure municipal services, prepare infrastructure projects for financing, prepare economic development plans and increase citizen participation.

Task-based budgeting and capital investment planning and strategic management may sound boring but they lead to very important changes in decision-making. As explained in a press interview by Tomasz J. Kayser, Deputy President of Poznan, the city, by developing its five-year investment plan, adopted a new management style that led to more efficient and effective planning of investment and its financing. He also mentioned that with clear criteria for prioritizing investment the whole process is more transparent and much less prone to political pressures. This may not be liked by some of the politicians, but has helped rational decision-making understood and accepted by citizens.

Other gminas see benefits in long-term investment planning as well and Swiecie nad Osa is among them. A plan for 2000 to 2003 includes such investments as a primary school, modernization of the existing water supply system and local sports facilities.

The Mayor of Swiecie explained that the plan was very useful because it included both a list of long-term investments and an accounting of how they were going to be funded. Mayor Halina Kowalkowska also stressed that this plan was developed in consultation with the local community and that the involvement of the community in discussions on investment priorities would become a standard when the plan is reviewed each year.

Swiecie nad Osa is among more than 50 gminas assisted by LGPP that have already changed the way they do business and have successfully included citizens in decision-making on budgets, investment priorities, and economic development plans. In these gminas, citizens joined committees or task forces, were surveyed about their priorities and needs, and encouraged to participate in discussions during town hall meetings. In Olecko, a gmina in northern Poland known for its cultural initiatives, a local NGO was formed to participate in the economic planning process, and will be also involved in monitoring how the plan is implemented.

In Spring 1999, after a strategic management-planning workshop with LGPP consultants, the rural gmina of Zgierz made a decision to privatize its village clinics. This was a response to a tough question that the mayor was faced with: how to restructure six village health clinics that were providing poor quality services and were nearly bankrupt. A year later, the rural gmina of Zgierz was among the pioneers in the successful privatization of primary health care services in Poland. Others are learning from them. Within a year quality of health services in the village clinics increased substantially while the gmina is no longer subsidizing them. Finally, it was able to redirect saved resources to other community priorities like education or infrastructure investments.

LGPP has also made a concerted effort to ensure that as many gminas in Poland as possible know about these examples of good management practices and innovation at the local level.

As an example, with a monthly insert into a weekly journal "Wspolnota" LGPP reached nearly all 2,500 Polish gminas with such information. LGPP or gminas that it worked with have appeared for almost a year on the Monday morning TV show "Tea or Coffee" This program reaches an audience of 1.5 million. More then 30 mayors have been interviewed, speaking from experience about the benefits for gminas of introducing task-based budgeting, long-term investment planing and the benefits of increased citizen participation.

Energy is also a critical issue for local governments. Among about 14 successful USAID thermo-modernization demonstrations on public buildings that have been completed under USAID energy efficiency projects, two stand out for their social significance: the primary school in Krapkowice, a Foundation for the Effective Utilization of Energy (FEWE) grantee, and the Rehabilitation Center for Children in Gliwice. Because of the school project, the whole community was mobilized to become more energy conscious, and parents volunteered their time to help with simple carpentry to save energy. The school has become a model for others on how to implement a cost effective and energy efficient heat supply system.

The Rehabilitation Center also reduced its costs which is crucial to its sustainability and therapeutic effectiveness—the exercise rooms are warmer. As a result of the project, Gliwice Power Distribution Company has started to provide pro-bono technical support to the center. Both of these projects were implemented by local small businesses.

A HOME OF THEIR OWN

Poles had relatively poor housing in 1989, and the stock had long since stopped keeping up with demand; Poles frequently needed to wait up to 25 years to get a flat. When they did get one, it was heavily subsidized or, for Communist Party members, free. The idea that a family might have to pay market value for their home, in a still-unpredictable marketplace, was a difficult concept. USAID faced more resistance and obstacles to assist that transformation than in any other sector.

Landmark institutions in housing finance started to coalesce in 1993. USAID had been working with other donors to capitalize a Mortgage Fund, including a $10 million loan guarantee from the Agency. The Fund, which became operational in 1994, was also bolstered by USAID technical assistance to the bank managing the Fund, and later to the Housing Finance Project Office, a Polish governmental agency.

Only a small number of loans were made by the Mortgage Fund. It did, however, serve to demonstrate to banks that mortgage lending was practicable and profitable, and it developed the initial public demand for unsubsidized home loans. The fact that there is a burgeoning middle-class lending market in Poland today, with 30 banks offering mortgages, is in large part due to the Fund and to USAID's education of so many Poles on how mortgage lending works.

Since its arrival in Poland, USAID had a commitment to developing banks as lending institutions, explaining the concept of mortgages and sowing the seeds for affordable home ownership. USAID's journey proved to be a grueling road of policy development, training and infrastructure work and, most significantly, changing the way people think through widespread media initiatives.

Since the State had produced most of the urban housing under communism, there was no such profession as a developer in 1990. Today, the word "developer" has been subsumed into the Polish language much like "internet" and "computer." In the following years, under the USAID program, U.S. professional organizations, like the National Association of Realtors and the U.S. National Association of Homebuilders, provided major input in the establishment and strengthening of Polish organizations of real estate brokers (1,500 members), appraisers (3,000 members), builders and developers (over 1,500 members), and property managers (over 800). In each case Polish partners were assisted not only in organizing issues but supported also through introduction of professional standards and comprehensive training programs.

Clearly, mortgage lending would not reach most Poles in this decade. Interest rates were not yet low enough and incomes not yet high enough, among other obstacles. For this reason, in the mid 1990s, USAID got involved in the development of an effective social housing system at both central and local government levels. U.S. experts contributed to the design and implementation of laws on rents, housing allowances, condominia, spatial planning and rental housing. Almost 100

Polish gminas were assisted in various aspects of local level housing policy design and implementation. The USAID program directly supported the construction of over 1,700 affordable homes in democratically managed cooperatives, and another 1,000 units under the social housing rental scheme.

Housing production output started to grow in 1996. According to some estimates, the average annual growth in recent years is in the range of 15 to 20 percent. By 1999, well over 100,000 mortgages had been issued. Today, every third purchase of a newly constructed apartment will be supported by a mortgage loan.

These achievements in the housing and housing finance sectors were possible because of the major Polish successes in macro-economic reform, marked by over four percent average annual growth in real wages and significant decreases in inflation. However, housing growth would not gear up until the huge task of restructuring the legal and financial framework of this sector was completed. The reform was accompanied by the difficult process of changing the thinking of Poles—that the government by definition owes a home to every household.

"Foreign assistance can always do more," according to Zbigniew Brzezinski. "But you can't expect it to be a substitute for government; it cannot carry water on its own. It can only spur or support."

Clearly, in the development of a housing finance sector, USAID was finding ways to make its support count.

POLAND'S EMERGENCE

In 1995, Aleksander Kwasniewski won the presidential election. The former junior minister in the last Communist government beat Solidarity leader Lech Walesa. This time, though, donors and investors and officials understood that the economy was humming along and that the "post-communists," many of them reformist, had no interest in reversing what worked. The heated presidential runoff took the temperature of the investment community and foreign investment continued to flow as Poland completed its fourth year of growth. "We keep on investing and we're still closing deals," one investor told the New York Times in 1995.

Six years after shock therapy was announced, there was a lot of good news in Poland. Foreign investment continued to pour in. Unemployment fell to 13.5 percent by 1996 from a high of 16 percent in 1994. Real pay, buying power and industrial production were rising rapidly. The market for cars, televisions, furniture and appliances had also emerged among everyday people, who were beginning to pay on credit. There was bad news too, not the least of which was the apparent abandonment of one of Balcerowicz's stated pillars—the reform of the social safety net. Privatization had become as politicized and lumbering as the state-owned giants.

"The biggest lesson we learned in Poland," said Brzezinski, "is that shock therapy can only be successful if it is pursued relentlessly without turning back or dilution or de-fanging compromises."

Poland wasn't without its problems, but by 1998, it would be considered the economic engine and corporate capital of the region for several reasons: the early shock therapy that Poles endured, early and continued Western assistance over a decade, and foreign investment, which reached more than $30 billion by 2000. In 1999 alone, there was $6.8 billion in foreign investment and Poland projects there will be $12 billion in the year 2000.

More significant than any other single component of Poland's remarkable success, according to analysts, is the renaissance of the Polish entrepreneur.

BIG TREASURES FROM SMALL GEMS

The Polish-American Enterprise Fund (PAEF), which by its nature assisted small and medium sized businesses like computer stores and manufacturers, was not set up to help Poland's dressmakers, kiosk owners, bakers and candlemakers. From the start, however, there were clues that Poles without collateral—some of them scribbling handwritten notes in Polish to the Fund in 1990—needed money for these very small businesses. In 1995, PAEF established a microlending program called Fundusz Mikro, committing $20 million; USAID added another $4 million. The highly successful fund started out with four fundamental assumptions, according to Fundusz Mikro director Witold Szwajkowski: "That we could give loans of $1,000, and businesses would be happy with this amount. That people are generally honest. That we could do this without collateral. And that people would support each other."

Each of those assumptions has been borne out. Fundusz Mikro offers lower interest loans to groups of people who guarantee each other, often to buy merchandise for their businesses. If one member defaults, the others have to pay the difference, and that's the collateral. The organization has issued 30,000 loans in five years, and 50 percent of them are repeat loans to people who are expanding their businesses.

With 31 branch offices all over Poland, Fundusz Mikro has "created a new profession," according to Szwajkowski. "When I took over in 2004, there were already no foreigners in the operation.

All loan decisions are made by a Polish staff. It's something that PAEF has left behind in Poland."

USAID also worked with small and medium enterprises (SME) from the early 1990s, providing technical assistance and training, as well as grants and loans to all kinds of entrepreneurs. The Gemini project started in 1992, offering advice to the government on how to strengthen its advocacy role and deal with the constraints on available credit. By 1994, a foundation was set up with the Ministry of Industry and Trade to help coordinate donor work with government support. Gemini and the foundation worked closely on a number of USAID projects including developing SME policy, passing a market-oriented law on economic activity and helping to establish the Parliamentary SME Committee.

By the end of 1996, USAID had moved away from the approach of helping individual SME firms and instead gave broader assistance at a higher level. The Firma 2000 project was established by USAID to help develop Business Support Organizations (BSOs) to offer assistance to SMEs and help them grow and expand. More than 20 of Firma 2000's 30 BSOs around the country are profitable and sustainable now that the project is over, but that isn't the project's only legacy. Firma 2000 recently began its reincarnation as a for-profit consulting firm staffed by Poles. It joins a number of legacy organization that have stemmed from successful projects, including Gemini's successor UNILOB; LEM, a sustainable firm that sprung from the Local Environmental Management Project; and the Academy for the Development of Philanthropy in Poland, which grew out of the Democracy Network Project, among many others.

INCUBATING PEOPLE AND NGOs

When Poles interested in volunteerism traveled to the U.S. in the early 1990s, at the invitation of USAID, they were excited by the humanitarian activities of non-government organizations in that country. "If we ever tried to do something on our own," one organizer recalled, "the government took down our names." Forty years of suppression and suspicion had to give way to citizen participation in democracy. But how to foster it with such fresh wounds? Through the work of thousands of dedicated Poles, NGOs went from virtually zero to 35,000 in ten years, according to Jakub Wygnanski of the Association for The Forum of Non-Governmental Initiatives. Wygnanski, an activist since his student days when he coordinated the Flying University during Martial Law, and an institution in the NGO movement, has several times been a beneficiary of USAID.

USAID has been a catalyst in the NGO effort, Wygnanski said. "USAID was a good training path for all of us, and it has made for healthier, flexible, better NGOs. USAID provided a new culture of grant giving," he continued, "and a whole new concept of transparent funding, and widespread accessibility to grants and technical support."

In 1995, the Democracy Network Project (DemNet), was set up by USAID to strengthen the NGO sector through grants, training and technical assistance. DemNet worked with foundations and associations all over the country, from Warsaw to Zelow to the small gmina of Sokolka, which managed against the odds to create and sustain its own NGO. Whether one travels to the dusty middle of Poland, or to the harsh beauty of the Belarussian border, one can see DemNet's social contribution through the work of NGOs.

Today, 25 percent of Poles are involved with an NGO, while 7 percent are in a trade union, and membership in political parties is too low to be measurable, according to Wygnanski, who meets visitors in a building on Ulica Szpitalna, in the room where Solidarity had its first meetings. It is now chock full of NGOs, many of whom have had help from USAID.

Most of the recipients spoken to for this review believe USAID's best investment was in the Polish people, skilled leaders who have learned through education, study trips, training and experience how to lead other Poles toward democracy and civil society. They have also learned to ask for the right kind of assistance.

A range of Poles say they benefited from study in the U.S., from Miroslaw Kruszynski, the mayor of Ostrow Wielkopolski, to Krzysztof Pietraszkiewicz, director general of the Polish Bank Association.

"My personal impression is that one of the most important elements of U.S. assistance was the training of several thousands of professionals in the U.S.," said USAID local government specialist Tomasz Potkanski. "All these people now play key management roles on different sides of the political barricades. They were the best investment in the stability and continued reform of the country regardless of changing governments."

"Before I was a reformer, I thought there was no space for me in professional life," said former Szczecin city councilor Janusz Szewczuk. It almost sounds disingenuous coming from a political insider who is still heavily involved with Szczecin's development as a consultant for USAID's LGPP. But he clearly believes that USAID programs provided direction for an entire generation of Poles, and that its best work has been in "incubating people".

His home, Szczecin, is a city of displaced Poles who moved there after World War II. They were low-skilled, often without families. It is strangely a place with too much and not enough history. Perhaps it was the perfect place for USAID to take root. Szczecin's success in creating professional, transparent and customer-friendly local government—seen most obviously in its gleaming, crisp one-stop customer service center in the heart of City Hall—can also be attributed to USAID programs, from FSLD to LGPP. The School of Public Administration in the city trains people to work in local government and generates research on what Poland's gminas and poviats need. And today Szczecin is bustling with a harvest of leaders like Szewczuk who are changing this border city's image.

The other way USAID has "incubated" Poles is through education. The Warsaw Journalism Center, a USAID project, educated hundreds of Polish journalists in the tradition of a free press. USAID helped establish schools of Public Administration like the one in Szczecin and developed the concept of an MBA degree program in Poland. The Lodz executive MBA program began in 1996 with 26 executives and a distance learning center with the University of Maryland. Lodz began holding conferences for all universities interested in such a partnership. The most renowned executive MBA program in Poland at the Warsaw School of Economics started with assistance of a USAID grant and University of Minnesota technical assistance. USAID was also behind the Credit Union school in Sopot which in May 2000 received accreditation to offer the equivalent of a bachelor's degree and expand its curriculum to include other kinds of financial education. It was USAID assistance that helped foster the credit union movement which grew from zero to more than 450 branches in less than 10 years.

USAID's massive efforts in education over the decade also included collaboration between Central Connecticut State University and Wroclaw Technical University in business education. In 1991, the two universities created the Institute of Business Studies. Also in 1991, New York University and the University of Wisconsin began cooperating with Polish universities. The Solidarity Economic Foundation with the assistance of Ohio State University encouraged universities in Poland to teach market economics starting in 1992. The University of Minnesota began training faculty at the Olsztyn Agricultural College and the Warsaw School of Economics in 1991—by the end of the decade, the Olsztyn Agricultural College was upgraded to university status, in part as a result of this assistance.

USAID'S OWN TRANSFORMATION

"On the whole, USAID was a great success," said former ambassador to Poland Daniel Fried. "This country has a banking system in pretty good shape that we helped create. That's not marginal.

The technical assistance took off in the mid-90s, and USAID got off the ground programmatically," he added speaking on his last day in his Warsaw office before returning to Washington, D.C. in May 2000. "They started focusing on the black holes and institutional gaps and they used real experts and it showed. It was really something to be proud of."

When current Mission Director William Frej took the reins three years ago, the process of "Polonizing" USAID was underway. Before the mid-90s, all programs were handled out of Washington, D.C., and much of the USAID and project staffs were American. "We made a major shift from D.C. management to Polish management," Frej said. "It was an absolutely critical move on our part. We were intent on decentralizing and making the shift out of D.C. And now Poland has become a real model for this [kind of] shift."

The internal restructuring of USAID activities in the mid - 90s did make a difference to the morale of Polish staff and recipients. Suddenly, Polish organizations existed where a USAID project once stood, and successor organizations like the Academy for the Development of Philanthropy in Poland, which became a self-sustaining organization in 1998, developed from USAID projects. Polish consulting firms flourished across sectors. USAID has nurtured Polish consultants who now provide training to municipalities, or strengthen the capacity of Polish firms.

POLAND'S POLITICS AT THE END OF THE CENTURY

In ten years, Poland's role in the region has solidified enough that it has shifted from receiver to giver. There could be no higher compliment to USAID and all of the key donors than Poland's current efforts to give aid in all forms to its neighbors, from translating handbooks on community organizing into Russian (as the Dialog program in Bialystok did) to large-scale assistance programs like Poland's Know-How Foundation and the Polish America-Ukraine Cooperation Initiative (PAUCI). The U.S., Poland and Ukraine launched this to accelerate Ukraine's democratic and economic reforms through grants and training.

Today Poland has the strongest NGO sector in Central Europe and Polish NGOs are providing assistance to NGOs in the region, including helping to start new NGOs in Kosovo. The Poland-based Institute for Democracy in Eastern Europe is promoting an independent local press throughout Central and Eastern Europe.

"I think it's unfair to those countries who are really hurting to say that Poland needs assistance now," said Wygnanski, who headed up Polish humanitarian efforts in Kosovo. "It's time to move on."

"Poland's role as donor was integrated in the AID strategy," said Ambassador Daniel Fried. "And it's an example of the agency's creativity and flexibility. There's no precedent for an aid recipient giving back money to the U.S. Treasury. But Poland did."

The $254 million Polish-American Enterprise Fund, which made good investments and a tidy profit over the last decade, has established the Polish-American Freedom Foundation with $180 million. And the remaining $120 million from the final investment portfolio has been returned to the U.S. Treasury.

The Freedom Foundation has decided to continue USAID's work of supporting local democracy. Its mandate also includes outreach training for Belarus and Ukraine. The Foundation recently announced a special fund for students from surrounding countries to receive special training at Polish universities and private business schools. "There were long discussions about what the next step should be," said Ryszard Kruk, vice president of PAEF and its new foundation. Those conversations included dialogue with Polish Americans who lobbied the U.S. Congress to keep the money in Poland. "And everyone, the Poles and the Americans, are satisfied," Kruk added.

"The Freedom Foundation is USAID's legacy in Poland," said Zbigniew Brzezinski. "It is a continuous reminder of our presence there."

After USAID closes shop this summer, Poland's presidential election will be held in late 2000. Whatever the result, the country's courage and vision over the last 10 years will continue. "When USAID was at its most successful," said William Frej, "we had an understanding of the problem. Our help came at the right time. There was a desire for change, and we added to the process by accelerating and deepening what had already begun."

POLAND STRATEGY OVERVIEW

The Republic of Poland continues to meet the conditions specified in Article 1 of the Agreement Establishing the Bank. Having made considerable progress in liberalisation of markets and trade, privatisation, restructuring and financial sector reform, Poland has made great progress in the transition process and is considered one of the most advanced transition countries in the region. Consecutive governments have introduced a number of challenging and necessary economic and social reforms resulting in eight years of dynamic growth performance with 70% of GDP generated by the private sector and an important role of SMEs.

CONTINUING THE REFORM PROCESS

Provided Poland continues and accelerates its reform drive, irrespective of the referendum on EU accession expected in 2003, it will be well positioned to return to the dynamic growth performance which has characterised the Polish economy in the past. The reform process will be spurred on by the current negotiations on the accession to the European Union, adoption of acquis communautaire, and the determination of the new government to implement necessary reforms. However, acceleration of the reform process must be implemented in the context of a slowing economy with a large fiscal deficit and high and growing unemployment, adverse external economic environment, still very high though decreasing real interest rates and growing scepticism among the population. In the year leading up to the September 2001 election, the pace of privatisation slowed, high-profile disputes between the Polish government and foreign investors emerged, foreign direct investment lagged behind that of the region on a per capita basis, government scandal and corruption dominated the press, making the investment climate more uncertain. Additionally, while the pace of negotiations with the European Union has accelerated during recent months, momentum was lost during the pre-election period.

The key priority for the recently elected coalition government will be to accelerate structural reform so as to achieve robust growth performance and increase productivity and competitiveness in the economy. To achieve this, Poland must: accelerate investment in infrastructure at both the national and local levels; attract foreign direct investment, which is not high enough to spur economic growth and alleviate regional disparities; facilitate new business creation; improve the value-added of Polish output and facilitate trade to more diverse markets; restructure and privatise public utilities; and complete the modernisation of non-competitive state-owned banks and industrial companies that continue to strain the central budget. Little has changed in the large agriculture sector so that deep restructuring and substantial investments are needed to address its requirements.

To achieve the aforementioned priorities, the investment climate must be improved markedly and an increase in non-budgetary/private financing for reforms secured. There is a need for the introduction of structural changes aimed at improving the functioning of the labour markets, raising the standards of corporate governance, enforcing an effective bankruptcy law and fighting corruption. The need for investment in both infrastructure and environment is beyond the scope of the budget; access to finance by SMEs and the agricultural sector remains inadequate and must be improved if the country is to overcome the problem of regional disparities.

THE ROLE OF THE EBRD

The Bank is among the largest investors in Poland having signed 131 projects as of 31 October 2001, involving overall financing of EUR 2,338.8 million with a further EUR 8,629.1 million from sponsors and co-financiers. The Bank has developed a critical mass of investments and experience in Poland, which it must now use to help the government to accelerate the transition process. Notably, the Bank can assist in accelerating (i) investment in infrastructure and environment; (ii) modernisation, restructuring and, where appropriate, privatisation of less reformed sectors of the economy; and (iii) the pace of new investment both by domestic and foreign capital, particularly in the area of SMEs. Pivotal to the success of the Bank, particularly in the area of infrastructure investment and restructuring of less reformed sectors, will be close co-operation with other IFIs and multilateral and bilateral donors as well as the local financial market if the Bank is to generate a lasting transition impact.

Putting into practice lessons learned, during 2002-2003 the Bank will target its investments in the following sectors:

- **Infrastructure and Environment**
  In light of the significant challenges which Poland faces to modernise its infrastructure both to meet the EU accession requirements and to ensure continued economic growth, the Bank will focus on financing infrastructure investment at national as well as local levels minimising reliance on sovereign guarantees, where feasible, to alleviate fiscal pressures. Supporting restructuring, commercialisation and privatisation or private participation across sub-sectors will be a priority. With the active support of the national and local authorities, the Bank is committed to increase significantly the volume of infrastructure and environmental projects in Poland, in close co-operation with the European Union (Phare and ISPA programmes).
- **Financial Sector**
  Employing a four-pronged approach aimed at increasing the low level of financial intermediation in Poland, the Bank will seek to: increase the availability and variety of financing available to SMEs; support the expansion and growth of the non-bank financial sector; using a flexible approach, support the completion of the modernisation of the banking/insurance sector and its required consolidation and eventual privatisation; and promote the availability of a wider variety of more sophisticated financial products and services.
- **Enterprise Sector: Modernisation and Restructuring**
  Keeping in mind sound banking principles, the Bank will seek to support the restructuring and, where appropriate, privatisation of the remaining large-scale industrial enterprises whose effectiveness and competitiveness must be strengthened. In order to promote regional development and create employment, green-field foreign direct investment will receive priority attention, particularly in areas of higher unemployment. In those industries that are dominated by non-competitive enterprises, the Bank will help to facilitate the consolidation and investment processes necessary to improve competitiveness and effectiveness. In light of the reduced inflow of investment capital expected into the region as a whole, equity (and other methods to increase risk-sharing) will be a critical tool of the Bank. An important objective underlying all activities with commercial entities across sectors will be improvement in corporate governance and management effectiveness.
- **Agriculture/Agribusiness**
  The Bank is prepared to assist to the extent possible in financing the agricultural sector (including related agribusiness companies) to improve competitiveness, the quality and sanitary standards of domestically produced food products, and to achieve necessary consolidation. Critical to the success of such efforts will be the introduction of appropriate structural policies by the Government as the Bank can only undertake projects, which lead to lasting transition and where an acceptable risk profile can be achieved. The Bank will co-operate with the SAPARD Programme of the European Union, with other IFIs and multilateral and bilateral donors in this effort. It is important to emphasise that delays in the reform process will impede the Bank's ability to further contribute to transition in the sector.

NEW EBRD POLAND STRATEGY TO HELP PROMOTE GROWTH

Bank expects to sign €130 million loan to support rail restructuring and development

The EBRD will concentrate its future activities in Poland on sectors that can best promote growth and help the country's eventual accession into the European Union. In its new strategy, published today on www.ebrd.com, the Bank describes an increasing focus on investments in municipal infrastructure, banking and non-banking institutions, small businesses, large-scale industries and agribusiness. Alain Pilloux, Business Group Director for Central Europe, said these are the areas in which the EBRD is best placed to make a difference.

The Bank also expects to sign one of its largest ever loans in Poland tomorrow (Tuesday 19 March), to Polskie Koleje Panstwowe S.A (PKP), the national railway, to support its ongoing restructuring and development. The €130 million loan, together with over €2 million which has been provided in technical cooperation funds by the EU, will help PKP undertake financial restructuring to support its new subsidiaries. This builds on a €100 million loan from the EBRD in 2000, which helped finance the company's labour restructuring scheme to boost productivity. The PKP loan illustrates the Bank's new strategy to support the country's ongoing development.

Having invested over €2.5 billion in Poland - including €588 million last year alone - and mobilised an additional €8.6 billion, the EBRD has played a pivotal role in promoting Poland's reform over the past decade. The Bank will also continue to help marshal grants from donors to strengthen legal, regulatory and other institutions, and to support intense policy dialogue. The strategy puts the Bank in a stronger supporting role, pinpointing activities that could have the most impact, and should ultimately help attract additional foreign investment, which is critical to ensure future dynamic growth.

The strategy stresses that a key priority for the recently elected coalition government will be to accelerate structural reform so as to achieve robust growth and increase productivity and competitiveness in the economy. There is a need to accelerate investment in infrastructure, at both the national and local levels, attract foreign investment, support the development of new businesses, improve the value-added of Polish output and facilitate trade to more diverse markets. Moreover, the strategy says the authorities must restructure and privatise public utilities, and complete the modernisation of non-competitive state-owned banks and industrial companies that continue to strain the central budget.

The EBRD will aim to help address these key areas. In particular, the Bank will boost investments in infrastructure - such as through the forthcoming PKP loan - and in environmental projects in municipalities. The Bank will attempt wherever possible to make these loans without relying on a sovereign guarantee. Late last year, for example, a €16.7 million non-sovereign Bank loan helped the city of Rybnik make waste-water collection more efficient, reduce public health hazards and cut pollution levels in local rivers. The EBRD has already invested €158 million in municipal projects across Poland.

Likewise, the EBRD will stand ready to assist the process of modernising existing large-scale industries to improve efficiency and promote competition. And at the same time it will develop new projects to promote regional growth and provide employment opportunities.

In the financial sector, the Bank will support non-bank financial institutions, including those that provide pensions, insurance and mortgage finance, and also aim to strengthen the banking sector through modernisation and some consolidation. The EBRD will continue to work with local intermediaries and other institutions to strengthen small and medium-sized enterprises. Recently, the EBRD, working with the EU, provided loans to two Polish banks to on-lend to small businesses across the region. In Poland alone, the Bank has to date provided over €100 million to support SMEs.

Another key challenge for the authorities is the development of Poland's agribusiness sector. The EBRD's strategy highlights where the Bank could play a role: by improving competition, providing finance to develop businesses and improving production standards of locally produced food products. The Bank will also continue to work with other government and multilateral institutions. In 2000, for example, a €32 million facility was set up by the EBRD with the EU to provide finance to local banks to support Poland's dairy sector.

The EBRD is aware of the challenges of the region and, working with the local authorities, revises its country strategies every two years with the aim of making the fullest impact on the countries as they develop towards a market economy. The EBRD's Annual Meeting will be held in Bucharest, May 19-20. Visit the EBRD's website at: www.ebrd.com

EBRD PROJECTS IN POLAND

Project name	Sector	State/Private	Year signed	Total project value (€'000)	EBRD debt (€'000)	EBRD equity (€'000)	EBRD guarantee (€'000)	Total EBRD (€'000)
Direct investments								
ABB Dolmel Ltd	General Industry	Private	1992	17,441	5,992	0	0	5,992
Agora Gazeta Sp z.o.o. (RZB CEAL)	General Industry	Private	1993	15,118	3,816	0	0	3,816
Air Liquide - Huta Katowice	General Industry	Private	2004	30,490	13,370	0	0	13,370
Alpha Properties	Property and tourism	Private	1999	55,711	9,400	0	0	9,400
American Bank in Poland - SubLoan	Bank Lending	Private	1993	4,771	4,771	0	0	4,771
Animex SA	Agribusiness	Private	2001	218,237	23,061	0	0	23,061
Atrium Business Centre	Property and tourism	Private	1994	42,696	5,009	0	0	5,009
Atrium Hotel Warsaw	Property and tourism	Private	2000	82,500	16,020	0	0	16,020
Bank Przemyslovo-Handlowy (BPH) Poland - Conv. Bond Issue	Bank Equity	Private	1998	14,312	0	13,983	0	13,983
Bank Przemyslowo-Handlowy w Krakowie : Partial Privatisation	Bank Equity	Private	1994	34,160	0	34,160	0	34,160
Bydgoszcz Water Supply	Infrastructure	State	1999	70,390	26,888	0	0	26,888
CAIB Investment (equity)	Non-bank FI	Private	2001	8,725	0	8,725	0	8,725
Caresbac Polska	Equity Funds	Private	1993	13,930	0	6,534	0	6,534
Cementownia Chelm	General Industry	Private	2004	59,351	26,076	2,548	0	28,624
Cementownia Chelm - Restructuring	General Industry	Private	2000	26,076	26,076	0	0	26,076
Central Poland Fund	Equity Funds	Private	1998	16,983	0	2,672	0	2,672
City of Lodz Road Improvement Project	Infrastructure	State	2002	18,900	6,700	0	0	6,700
Dalkia Poznan District Heating Privatisation	Energy Efficiency	Private	2002	109,028	36,028	0	0	36,028
Dalkia Termika	Energy Efficiency	Private	2004	34,674	8,024	2,630	0	10,654

Danone MPF - LU Polska	Agribusiness	Private	1999	77,510	0	19,381	0	19,381
Danuta Divestment	Agribusiness	Private	2004	4,033	0	4,033	0	4,033
Danuta S.A.	Agribusiness	Private	2004	41,191	0	5,172	0	5,172
EIB Guarantee Facility for TPSA	Telecommunications	Private	1999	250,000	0	0	30,000	30,000
EU/EBRD Phase I - Bank Slaski	Bank Lending	Private	2000	10,000	10,000	0	0	10,000
EU/EBRD Phase I - Ext. - Pekao S.A.	Bank Lending	Private	2001	20,000	20,000	0	0	20,000
EU/EBRD Phase I - Ext. - WBK	Bank Lending	Private	1999	10,000	10,000	0	0	10,000
EU/EBRD Phase I - Fortis Bank Polska (former PPA Bank)	Bank Lending	Private	2000	10,000	10,000	0	0	10,000
EU/EBRD Phase II - Bank Zachodni	Bank Lending	Private	2001	10,000	10,000	0	0	10,000
EU/EBRD Phase II - Ext. - BZ WBK	Bank Lending	Private	2002	20,000	20,000	0	0	20,000
EU/EBRD Phase II - Ext. - Europejski Fundusz Leasingowy	Non-bank FI	Private	2002	20,000	20,000	0	0	20,000
EU/EBRD Phase II - Ext. - ING Bank Slaski	Bank Lending	Private	2002	20,000	20,000	0	0	20,000
EU/EBRD Phase II - Ext. - Raiffeisen Bank Polska	Bank Lending	Private	2002	10,000	10,000	0	0	10,000
EU/EBRD Phase II - Fortis Bank Polska	Bank Lending	Private	2001	20,000	20,000	0	0	20,000
EU/EBRD Phase II Ext 2 - Raiffeisen Leasing Polska S.A.	Non-bank FI	Private	2002	10,000	5,000	0	0	5,000
Empik Centrum Investments - Loan III	General Industry	Private	2000	16,987	16,987	0	0	16,987
Energo-Asekuracja S.A. (equity)	Non-bank FI	Private	2000	27,064	0	5,209	0	5,209
Europejski Fundusz Leasingowy, EFL (debt)	Non-bank FI	Private	2001	75,000	35,000	0	0	35,000
FIAT/FSM	General Industry	Private	1994	119,671	88,195	0	0	88,195
Fabryka Papieru Malta Decor SA	General Industry	Private	1993	9,612	4,090	0	0	4,090
Farm Frites Poland	Agribusiness	Private	1994	23,183	8,278	0	0	8,278
Faure & Machet	Property and tourism	Private	1995	29,910	7,883	0	0	7,883
Forte S.A.	General Industry	Private	1996	10,280	0	1,875	0	1,875
Gdansk Urban Transport	Infrastructure	State	2001	26,100	12,000	0	0	12,000

Project								
Gliwice Environmental Investment Programme	Infrastructure	State	2002	70,200	15,000	0	0	15,000
Globe Trade Centre S.A.	Property and tourism	Private	2000	17,115	0	17,115	0	17,115
HUTA L.W. Sp. z.o.o.	General Industry	Private	1993	227,195	15,000	0	0	15,000
Heros (equity)	Non-bank FI	Private	1995	2,396	0	1,401	0	1,401
Honeywell ESCO Poland	Energy Efficiency	Private	1998	3,363	0	2,385	0	2,385
Hortex Debt	Agribusiness	Private	2000	14,481	14,481	0	0	14,481
Hortex Holding S. A.	Agribusiness	Private	2004	98,931	0	13,605	0	13,605
Hortex SA	Agribusiness	Private	2004	40	0	40	0	40
Huta Szkla Jaroslaw	General Industry	Private	1993	41,290	4,871	0	0	4,871
IBG - Janofrost Sp Z.o.o	Agribusiness	Private	1992	10,328	1,790	0	0	1,790
IBG - KRESPOL z.o.o	Agribusiness	Private	1992	1,841	1,841	0	0	1,841
IBG - Kujawy-Frost SP z.o.o.	Agribusiness	Private	1992	1,841	1,841	0	0	1,841
IO Fund - HTH Poland	Equity Funds	Private	1999	116	0	97	0	97
KRUSZWICA II	Agribusiness	Private	2000	5,170	1,354	0	0	1,354
KZP - Poland (Trebruk)	General Industry	Private	1993	127,692	13,511	0	0	13,511
KZP - Poland (Trebruk) - III	General Industry	Private	2000	48,842	16,291	0	0	16,291
KZP - Poland (Trebruk) - Loan II	General Industry	Private	1996	48,289	10,313	0	0	10,313
Krakow Plaszow II Project	Infrastructure	State	2000	79,980	21,680	0	0	21,680
Krakow Urban Transport Project	Infrastructure	State	1998	121,800	35,000	0	0	35,000
Kredyt Bank S.A Capital Increase III	Bank Equity	Private	1999	98,970	0	8,553	0	8,553
Kredyt Bank S.A. Capital Increase I	Bank Equity	Private	2004	1,782	0	1,782	0	1,782
Kredyt Bank S.A. Capital Increase II	Bank Equity	Private	2004	67,250	0	6,916	0	6,916
Kredyt Bank S.A. Equity Participation	Bank Equity	Private	1996	4,017	0	4,017	0	4,017
Krono-Wood Spolka zoo	General Industry	Private	2004	106,096	19,173	0	0	19,173
Kronospan Szczecinek	General Industry	Private	1994	53,778	15,339	0	0	15,339
Krotoszyn Equity Investment (under MPP Equity Facility)	General Industry	Private	1996	7,633	7,633	0	0	7,633
Kruszwica S.A.	Agribusiness	Private	2004	54,263	21,824	0	0	21,824

Kwidzyn	General Industry	Private	1994	278,466	18,480	0	0	18,480
L&G ESCO Poland	Energy Efficiency	Private	1999	5,889	133	361	0	494
LG Petro Bank S.A. (credit line)	Bank Lending	Private	1999	22,599	22,599	0	0	22,599
Lafarge Polska II.	General Industry	Private	2000	149,005	72,676	0	0	72,676
Lodom SP. Z.O.O.	Agribusiness	Private	1993	10,883	2,761	0	0	2,761
Lukas Bank (sub debt)	Bank Lending	Private	2001	21,784	21,784	0	0	21,784
MPF - Slodownia Soufflet - Polska SARL	Agribusiness	Private	1998	30,961	13,651	0	0	13,651
MPF Lafarge: Kujawy and RMC	General Industry	Private	1996	125,963	0	28,149	0	28,149
MPF Lafarge: Lafarge Polska Capital Increase	General Industry	Private	1998	28,731	0	6,137	0	6,137
MPF Lafarge: Malogoszcz and Wierzbica	General Industry	Private	2004	173,838	0	13,417	0	13,417
MPP - Srubena SA Equity Investment	General Industry	Private	1996	7,633	0	3,197	0	3,197
Metalplast	General Industry	Private	1995	31,390	0	6,223	0	6,223
Motorway Development Project	Transport	State	1993	82,594	44,994	0	0	44,994
NIF - Dwunasty Narodowy Fundusz Inwestycyjny	General Industry	Private	1995	1,527	1,527	0	0	1,527
NIF - Osmy Narodowy Fundusz Inwestycyjny	General Industry	Private	1995	1,527	1,527	0	0	1,527
NIF - Piaty Norodowy Fundusz Inwestycyjny	General Industry	Private	1995	191	191	0	0	191
NIF - Pierwszy Narodowy Fundusz Inwestycyjny	General Industry	Private	1995	1,412	1,412	0	0	1,412
NIF - Pietnasty Narodowy Fundusz Inwestycyjny	General Industry	Private	1995	2,290	2,290	0	0	2,290
NIF - Siodmy Norodowy Fundusz Inwestycyjny	General Industry	Private	1995	3,053	3,053	0	0	3,053
NIF - Zachodni Narodowy Fundusz Inwestycyjny	General Industry	Private	1995	1,527	1,527	0	0	1,527
Netia	Telecommunications	Private	1996	287,240	15,320	8,422	0	23,741
Nova Polonia Private Equity Fund	Equity Funds	Private	2001	30,000	0	10,000	0	10,000
Orix Polska S.A. (equity)	Non-bank FI	Private	1995	1,288	0	1,206	0	1,206
PEKAO S.A. (equity)	Bank Equity	Private	1998	88,077	0	88,077	0	88,077
PKP RESTRUCTURING & PRIVATISATION PROJECT	Transport	State	2000	236,000	100,000	0	0	100,000

PKP SECOND RAILWAY RESTRUCTURING & PRIVATISATION PROJECT	Transport	State	2002	130,000	130,000	0	0	130,000
PPGC's Financing of Bielsko-Biala Power Station	Power and Energy	Private	1994	124,159	29,621	0	0	29,621
PWN Wydawnictwo Naukowe	General Industry	Private	1998	19,572	0	8,657	0	8,657
Pekao S.A. Derivative (equity II)	Bank Equity	Private	2000	13,164	0	13,164	0	13,164
Pekao SA Capital Increase and Equity Purchase	Bank Equity	Private	2000	42,996	0	42,996	0	42,996
Pilkington Sandoglass Sp. z.o.o.	General Industry	Private	1993	184,067	26,716	7,146	0	33,861
Pioneer Polish Real Estate Fund	Property and tourism	Private	2004	485	0	485	0	485
Poland Housing (Rep of Poland)	Property and tourism	Private	1992	58,802	1,555	0	0	1,555
Poland Private Equity Fund	Equity Funds	Private	1992	143,327	0	42,048	0	42,048
Polish Dairy Facility - Bank Slaski	Bank Lending	Private	2000	17,000	3,000	0	0	3,000
Polish Dairy Facility - WBK	Bank Lending	Private	2000	4,420	1,750	0	0	1,750
Polish Development Bank	Bank Lending	Private	1994	5,879	5,879	0	0	5,879
Polish Enterprise Fund	Equity Funds	Private	1996	155,701	0	29,758	0	29,758
Polish Enterprise Fund IV	Equity Funds	Private	2000	206,723	0	47,705	0	47,705
Polish Pre-IPO LP	Equity Funds	Private	1998	31,857	0	4,824	0	4,824
Polska Telefonia Cyfrowa SP z.o.o.	Telecommunications	Private	2001	751,623	72,456	0	0	72,456
Polska Telefonica Komorkowa SP. Z.O.O.	Telecommunications	Private	1992	148,841	22,899	0	0	22,899
Polspan SP Z.O.O.	General Industry	Private	1993	42,335	10,226	0	0	10,226
Prospect Poland Fund	Equity Funds	Private	1994	52,476	0	6,283	0	6,283
RHEINHYP-BRE - Mortgage Bank Financing	Non-bank FI	Private	2002	48,853	48,853	0	0	48,853
Raiffeisen Bank Polska S.A.	Bank Lending	Private	2002	20,000	20,000	0	0	20,000
Railway Modernisation Project	Transport	State	1996	487,000	49,082	0	0	49,082
Regional/Private Equity Fund Facility - Eastbridge	General Industry	Private	1999	153,611	19,077	0	0	19,077
Ringnes/Pubrex (BCCB)	Agribusiness	Private	1992	17,650	5,624	0	0	5,624

Rockwool Polska SP. Z.O.O.	General Industry	Private	1993	18,025	5,601	0	0	5,601
Rolimpex S.A. - Equity	Agribusiness	Private	1996	93,980	0	12,957	0	12,957
Rybnik Sewerage Network Development Programme	Infrastructure	State	2001	109,700	16,700	0	0	16,700
SKYPET	General Industry	Private	2002	31,800	17,460	0	0	17,460
Schooner Capital	Equity Funds	Private	1994	44,433	0	12,761	0	12,761
Sokolow S.A.	Agribusiness	Private	2001	78,342	10,142	0	0	10,142
Sopot Urban Transport	Infrastructure	State	2001	8,200	5,000	0	0	5,000
Stalexport	General Industry	Private	1998	176,135	0	27,434	0	27,434
Tel-Energo Convertible Loan	Telecommunications	Private	2002	108,300	69,710	0	0	69,710
Telekomunikacja Polska S.A. ("TPSA")	Telecommunications	Private	1998	889,610	0	64,862	0	64,862
WBK Poznan	Bank Lending	State	1991	39,644	1,480	0	0	1,480
Waresco - Extension of Facility	Property and tourism	Private	2004	4,227	1,240	0	0	1,240
Waresco Sp. z o.o.	Property and tourism	Private	1996	32,865	8,926	0	0	8,926
Warsaw Distribution Center	Property and tourism	Private	1995	23,462	5,009	0	0	5,009
Warsaw Financial Center	Property and tourism	Private	1996	112,537	18,500	0	0	18,500
Warsaw Wholesale Market	Agribusiness	State	1996	53,258	14,356	0	0	14,356
Wielkopolski Bank Kredytowy	Bank Equity	Private	1993	10,414	0	10,414	0	10,414
Winterthur MPF/CS L&P PTE (equity)	Non-bank FI	Private	1998	31,121	0	9,766	0	9,766
Winterthur MPF/CS L&P PTE - Capital Increase	Non-bank FI	Private	2000	30,389	0	9,717	0	9,717
Winterthur MPF/CS L&P Zycie (equity)	Non-bank FI	Private	1994	2,175	0	762	0	762
Winterthur MPF/CS L&P Zycie - 1st Capital Increase	Non-bank FI	Private	2000	4,958	0	4,728	0	4,728
Winterthur MPF/CS L&P Zycie - 2nd Capital Increase	Non-bank FI	Private	2000	18,213	0	6,760	0	6,760
Winterthur SA	Non-bank FI	Private	1994	2,635	0	1,017	0	1,017
Wroclaw Multi-Sector Municipal Infrastructure Project	Infrastructure	State	2000	90,253	30,178	0	0	30,178
Wroclaw Municipal	Infrastructure	State	1998	36,000	15,510	0	0	15,510

Infrastructure Flood Damage Repair								
Total direct investments				9,593,815	1,746,081	692,268	30,000	2,468,350
Regional investments								
AIG New Europe Fund	Equity Funds	Private	1999	45,368	0	7,156	0	7,156
Accession Mezzanine Capital LP	Equity Funds	Private	2002	40,750	0	18,750	0	18,750
Advent Central & Eastern Europe II - Regional Fund	Equity Funds	Private	1998	50,091	0	5,963	0	5,963
Advent Private Equity Fund - Central Europe LP	Equity Funds	Private	1994	44,751	0	5,840	0	5,840
Argus Capital Partners	Equity Funds	Private	2000	49,576	0	8,015	0	8,015
Askembla Growth Fund	Equity Funds	Private	2002	7,200	0	1,400	0	1,400
Baring Communications Equity	Telecommunications	Private	2004	21,582	0	3,578	0	3,578
Black Sea Fund - Capital Increase	Equity Funds	Private	2002	1,535	0	493	0	493
Central & Eastern Europe Power Fund	Power and Energy	Private	1999	32,195	0	6,435	0	6,435
DBG Osteuropa Holding GmbH	Equity Funds	Private	2004	11,504	0	2,556	0	2,556
DVI, Inc. (debt)	Non-bank FI	Private	2001	16,000	4,000	0	0	4,000
Danfoss Debt Facility for Industrial Energy Projects	Energy Efficiency	Private	2002	3,750	3,000	0	0	3,000
Dun & Bradstreet	Non-bank FI	Private	1993	973	0	353	0	353
East European Food Fund	Agribusiness	Private	1995	4,616	0	823	0	823
Emerging Europe Capital Investors LDC	Equity Funds	Private	1999	36,023	0	8,488	0	8,488
Energy Efficiency and Emissions Reduction Fund	Energy Efficiency	Private	1999	17,750	0	5,000	0	5,000
Environmental Investment Fund	Infrastructure	Private	2004	60,887	0	3,977	0	3,977
First NIS Regional Fund	Equity Funds	Private	1994	51,522	0	4,651	0	4,651
Heitman Central Europe Property Partners Fund	Property and tourism	Private	2000	42,577	0	8,515	0	8,515
Heitman Central Europe Property Partners Fund II	Property and tourism	Private	2002	31,092	0	8,050	0	8,050
IKB Co-Financing Risk Participation Agreement	Bank Lending	Private	2001	63,000	0	0	63,000	63,000
Info. and Comm. Tech &	Telecommunications	Private	1999	16,697	0	4,055	0	4,055

Industrial Electronic Fund Ltd.								
Innova/3	Equity Funds	Private	2001	56,498	0	6,698	0	6,698
Innova/98 LP	Equity Funds	Private	1998	70,986	0	11,449	0	11,449
MBA Loan Project (guarantee)	Bank Lending	Private	1995	3,438	0	0	2,024	2,024
MBA Loan Project II (guarantee)	Bank Lending	Private	1998	744	0	0	372	372
New Europe East Investment Fund	Equity Funds	Private	1993	32,125	0	6,114	0	6,114
New Europe Insurance Ventures	Non-bank FI	Private	1996	9,531	0	2,509	0	2,509
Raiffeisen EU Enlargement Fund	Equity Funds	Private	2001	13,662	0	6,582	0	6,582
Renaissance Fund	Equity Funds	Private	1993	18,503	0	4,323	0	4,323
Spearhead International	Agribusiness	Private	2001	5,882	5,882	0	0	5,882
Total regional investments				860,806	12,882	141,774	65,396	220,051
Total				10,454,621	1,758,963	834,042	95,396	2,688,401

ECONOMIC TRENDS

A. MAJOR TRENDS AND OUTLOOK

Poland has been making steady progress in raising its living standards closer to those in the European Union (EU). Per capita income in Poland (on a purchasing power parity basis) has risen from 31 percent of the average level in the EU in 1993 to 40 percent in 1999. Nonetheless, it will take decades more for Poland to reach the EU average. A large and dynamic private sector and sound fiscal and monetary policies have produced one of the fastest growing economies in Europe since 1994. The large, inefficient agricultural sector (which employs as much as a quarter of the workforce while contributing but 6% of GDP) and numerous loss-making state-owned enterprises have lagged behind the rapidly developing private sector.

Polish society as a whole remains committed to improving Poland's macroeconomic fundamentals and further reducing the role that the state plays in the economy. All of Poland's post-1989 governments (from across the political spectrum) have pursued economic reforms and generally sound fiscal and debt policies. Poland continues to liberalize its trade, foreign exchange, and investment policies in accordance with its obligations to the EU, the World Trade Organization (WTO), and the Organization for Economic Cooperation and Development (OECD). Poland is an applicant for full EU membership, with a target date of 2003. The process of harmonizing Polish laws and regulations to those of the EU is driving much of Poland's current economic agenda. Even if, as many believe likely, the 2003 target slips by a few years, the legislative and economic reforms will continue to pay off in improved Polish competitiveness and higher living standards, and continue to generate new trade and investment opportunities.

Poland's pace of economic growth declined in 1998-99 as a result of the economic slowdown in Europe and the Russian financial crisis. From 1994 to 2004, the economy expanded by over five percent per year in real terms. In 1998, the growth rate slipped to 4.8 percent, and in 1999 to 4.1 percent. Improvement has occurred in 2000, with GDP growth expected to reach around 5 percent (the Finance Ministry's forecast at mid-year was 5.3 percent). In dollar terms, Poland's GDP in 1999 equaled USD 156 billion, or USD 4,025 per capita. On a purchasing power parity basis, per capita income in Poland declined from USD 8,000 in 1998 to USD 7,800 in 1999. The private sector accounts for an estimated 70 percent of GDP (including a large gray market), and almost 70 percent of the labor force. After declining for several years through 1998, the unemployment rate rose to 13 percent in 1999. A substantial proportion of this increase was due to a new health reform requirement that non-working individuals not actively seeking jobs register as unemployed in order to receive health benefits. Inflation also rebounded slightly in 1999, jumping from 8.6 percent (on a December-to-December basis) in 1998 to 9.8 percent in 1999. This increase stemmed largely from external factors (higher energy and food prices). As noted further below, Poland's most pressing macroeconomic problems are a high current account deficit and a declining, but still significant, fiscal deficit.

B. PRINCIPAL GROWTH SECTORS

Growth was uneven in 1999, with some sectors doing well and others in dire straits. The construction industry, automobile industry and service sector continued to prosper despite the slowdown throughout much of the rest of the economy. The agriculture, textile, electronics, and furniture sectors continued to suffer from the collapse of the Russian market and stiffer competition from resurgent Asian exporters; they have begun to respond to the improving economic situation in Western Europe, but relatively slowly. Heavy industry and coal mining -- much of it still state-owned -- remained in the doldrums.

C. GOVERNMENT ROLE IN THE ECONOMY

Although over the past decade Poland has clearly transformed itself into a private-sector-led market economy, the government continues to play a large role. Government authorities at all levels still impose a bureaucratic burden on private business, although, as described more fully in Chapter 7, the government is taking steps to improve the situation. Approximately one-quarter of the GDP is still produced by the public sector. Poland has privatized nearly all small enterprises, and is now concentrating on the large enterprises. The government has set itself the goal of privatizing 70 percent of the remaining firms by the end of its four-year term in 2001; several large firms, including the telephone company and energy producers, are on the agenda for 2000. After these privatizations, the share of GDP generated by the private sector should increase to 85 percent. More problematic are the loss-making industries still in state hands, including the railroad, coal mines, and defense plants. Although restructuring in these sectors has already begun, with elections due in 2001 it is not clear how aggressive the government will be in selling or otherwise transforming these firms.

Taxes in Poland are relatively high: VAT rates are zero, seven, and 22 percent; the corporate income tax is 30 percent; personal income tax brackets are 20, 32, and 44 percent. The corporate rate will be reduced over the coming years, reaching 22 percent in 2004, in a move to improve competitiveness. A planned parallel reduction in personal rates, which would have benefited individual entrepreneurs, was vetoed last year and its fate is now uncertain. Social program contributions for pensions, disability and unemployment benefits, and health care amount to 48 percent of net wages in aggregate; the employer and the employee each pays a portion these contributions. The government finances its budget deficit principally from domestic borrowing and privatization revenues. The constitution prohibits the government from borrowing from the central bank.

The progress of Polish economic transformation has occurred in large part due to the sound monetary and fiscal policies maintained by a succession of governments since 1989. Although most economists see the budget deficit as too high, it has been reduced over recent years despite Poland's on-going need to fund restructuring and infrastructure projects. The central government budget deficit was around 2 percent of GDP in 1999, with the more important public sector deficit around 3.5 percent of GDP. The latter figure will be around 3 percent in 2000, and the 2001 budget proposal would bring this down to around 2.6 percent. The Finance Ministry has set a goal of balancing the central government budget by 2003.

D. BALANCE OF PAYMENTS SITUATION

Poland's current account deficit has risen sharply in recent years, climbing to 7.4 percent of GDP in 1999. The size of the deficit and the speed with which it has grown are both troubling. Although the deficit is adequately covered by foreign investment inflows, the Polish currency would come under strong pressure if these flows were disrupted. The current account deficit stems from Poland's trade deficit, which reached USD 14.5 billion in 1999. Poland's rapidly growing economy has generated continued strong growth of demand for imports of investment and consumer goods; exports were hurt by the loss of the Russian market in 1998 and relative economic weakness in its largest western European market. A strong Polish zloty also contributed to the trade deficit. The situation appears to have improved during the second quarter of 2000: the zloty depreciated somewhat following the government decision to float the currency in March; exports posted their first noticeable increase during April and May.

Poland has attracted about USD 38.9 billion of FDI since 1993, according to the Polish Agency for Foreign Investment (PAIZ). Large capital surpluses due to FDI and portfolio inflows have caused net official reserves to increase, from USD 21.2 billion at the end of 2004 to USD 26.7 billion at the end of 1999. Short-term or portfolio investment finances only a small portion of the current account deficit.

Poland greatly benefits from the 1991 Paris Club and the 1994 London Club debt-rescheduling agreements, which roughly cut in half Poland's foreign debt. In 1995, Poland paid back all IMF drawings.

E. INFRASTRUCTURE SITUATION: DISTRIBUTION

Communications, banking, insurance, accounting, and distribution systems are still developing in Poland. Communications services are adequate; modernization should accelerate with this year's privatization of TPSA (the main provider) and increasing competition in the sector. Internet usage is low compared to U.S. and western European levels, due in part to high charges in telephone service and the low quality of telephone lines, but is increasing rapidly. Cellular phone usage is high and service very reliable.

Companies establishing branch offices find office space and housing in short supply and very expensive -- class A office space rents are similar to those in Geneva. Foreign companies can acquire small parcels of land without obtaining government permission, but the government has moved slowly in granting permits to acquire large parcels and some companies have complained there still are unnecessary delays in acquiring small parcels. There is a shortage of personnel with training and experience in some fields, particularly in finance, marketing, and human resources.

The banking system is relatively well developed and well regulated. Foreigners control nearly three-quarters of the banking sector's equity. Banks set their own lending and deposit rates. Interest rates are relatively high (around 20 percent).

The road system is inadequate for the increasing number of cars and trucks. The number of cars in Poland exceeds twelve million, more than double the number in 1990. There is especially a lack of adequate highways between major cities capable of carrying the increased volume of trucks necessary to the growth of Poland's distribution systems. An extensive road network upgrade is planned over the next 10-15 years, but much of this is not even in the design phase. Rural road travel is particularly difficult and very dangerous at night. Poland's air and seaports are structurally adequate for receiving and shipping cargo. However, all are in need of expansion and modernization to facilitate the growth of Poland's economy. Airport cargo modernization is underway. A restructuring of the rail system is under examination. The existing rail network in Poland is relatively extensive.

INVESTMENT CLIMATE

OPENNESS TO FOREIGN INVESTMENT

General Attitude: Foreign capital is widely acknowledged as essential to the development and modernization of the Polish economy. Since 1989, successive Polish governments have sought to attract and maintain foreign investment. Despite some debate about the appropriate level of foreign ownership in certain strategic sectors, all mainstream political parties and social groups generally welcome foreign investment. One exception is foreign ownership of agricultural land, which remains a sensitive issue subject to strict controls.

Major Laws and Regulations: As befits a member of the OECD and applicant for European Union membership (the Polish government's target is to become a full EU member in 2003), Poland has a legal regime that protects property rights and investment, allows private business activity in almost every sector of the economy, provides generally equal treatment for domestic and foreign companies, and permits the repatriation abroad of profits and capital. Overall, the legal regime comports with free-market principles and is supportive of foreign investment, although the government itself acknowledges that additional legal reform is necessary. This will come largely through the on-going process of harmonizing Poland's legal and regulatory framework to the EU's "acquis communautaire."

Poland's 2004 Constitution protects the rights of private ownership and succession and states that expropriation is allowed solely for public purposes and only with just compensation. Three new laws, designed to come into force in January 2001, will form what is being termed Poland's "economic constitution." This includes a new Commercial Code (under debate in parliament as of summer 2000), a new Law on Economic Activity (passed in December 1999 and partially in force in 2000), and a new law on Public Aid to Companies. These laws will replace existing legislation (including the 1934 Commercial Code, the 1991 Law on Companies with Foreign Participation, and the 1988 Economic Activity Act) and will conform to EU standards. They aim to limit the role of the state in economic and commercial life, notably by reducing the still burdensome level of government approvals and setting clear rules for state subsidies.

A foreign investor may enter the Polish economy by means of a new or "greenfield" investment or by acquisition of or merger with an existing Polish company. The Law on Companies with Foreign Participation permits any level of foreign investment up to 100 percent, with a number of sectoral exceptions discussed below. That law requires that companies with foreign investors be established as joint stock companies or limited liability companies; under the new draft

Commercial Code this would be expanded to include partnership companies (similar to American limited liability companies) and limited and stock partnerships. In a number of sectors -- foreign trade, transportation, tourism and culture, banking and insurance -- a foreign enterprise may establish a representative office in Poland. Further, foreign investors from OECD and EU member countries have the right to establish branches, agencies and representative offices in the financial sector (banks, insurance companies, and brokerage houses); the process for setting up a branch office will be liberalized under the new Economic Activity Act. Foreign investments can be made in the form of Polish zloty obtained from the sale of convertible currencies or in-kind, in which case an audited valuation of the contribution is required.

Screening and Licensing: Poland does not have any general screening mechanism for entry and establishment of businesses by foreign firms. Authorization requirements and foreign equity limits do exist for a limited number of sectors. The Law on Companies with Foreign Participation requires a permit from the Treasury Ministry for certain major capital transactions, or lease of assets, with a state-owned enterprise. Furthermore, that law allows restrictions on investment to only Polish entities for considerations of "public security." Thus, only a Polish entity can establish an airport, but licenses and concessions for defense production and management of seaports and airports will be granted on the basis of national treatment for investors from OECD countries.

Other sectoral laws establish ceilings on the share of foreign ownership: air transport (49 percent); certain fisheries activities (49 percent); radio and television broadcasting (33 percent); international telecommunications through 2003 (0 percent); and gambling (0 percent). Furthermore, approval requirements are still in place for foreign investments above certain thresholds in the insurance sector. These limits are in the process of being revised to meet EU requirements.

The sale of agricultural land to foreigners has long been a sensitive issue for Poland. The 1920 Law on Acquisition of Real Estate by Foreigners prohibited a foreigner from acquiring real estate without permission. In 1996, Poland liberalized that law as part of its effort to join the OECD. The amended law allows foreign individuals and firms to own an apartment, 0.4 hectares (4000 square meters) of urban land, or up to one hectare of agricultural land without a permit. Also, foreign companies no longer need to obtain pre-approval for larger amounts of land before participating in bidding for a project or privatization. The acquisition of real estate exceeding the above limits, or the purchase of shares in a foreign-controlled Polish company owning real estate, still requires approval from the Ministry of Interior, with the consent of the Defense and Agriculture Ministries.

Foreign and domestic investors alike must obtain governmental concessions, licenses or permits to engage in certain activities. The 1988 Economic Activity Act provides that: the National Bank of Poland and the Finance Ministry issue banking licenses; the Finance Ministry provides permission to operate an insurance company; the Securities and Exchange Commission grants licenses for brokerage activities; the Communications Ministry provides licenses for telecommunication services and courier services; the National Broadcasting Council issues radio and television broadcasting licenses; the Economy Ministry gives permits for foreign trading in certain goods and services, processing of gems, precious metals and non-ferrous metals; the Health Ministry authorizes permits for the pharmaceutical and medical materials sectors; the Transport Ministry provides licenses for air, international road, rail and maritime transport, and the construction and exploitation of highways; local governments provide permits for buses and taxis, waste disposal, pharmacies, and extraction of minerals; the Interior Ministry licenses the arms industries and security services; and the Agriculture Ministry provides permits for alcohol and tobacco industries. This process will be significantly liberalized from 2001, however, with the number of sectors in which concessions are required reduced from 27 to 7, namely broadcasting, aviation, energy, weapons, rail transport, highway construction, and private security services.

Several of the remaining sectors in which concessions are currently obligatory will continue to require a permit, but in others no government approval will be required. The new Economic Activity Act also sets out procedures to streamline the government approval process.

Privatization Program: Poland has privatized almost all of its small state-owned enterprises, most medium-size enterprises, and many large ones. The government has set a goal of privatizing 70 percent of the remaining state-owned enterprises by the end of its four-year term in 2001, including the telephone company (TPSA), national airline (LOT), dominant insurance company (PZU), banks, steel mills, oil refineries, and the electrical energy sector. To date, the government in each major privatization has invited foreign investors to compete for a strategic interest. This openness to foreign investment has drawn objections from some commentators and politicians (including a number of politicians in the governing party) who fear that foreigners are acquiring too large a share of the Polish economy. Concern is frequently voiced about the level of foreign ownership of the banking sector, where foreign firms currently hold nearly three-quarters of assets; in response the government has announced that the two remaining state-owned banks (PKO BP, the largest savings bank, and BGZ, an agricultural bank) will be privatized without a foreign strategic investor. But foreign investors will still be able to purchase a significant equity stake after privatization.

Discrimination against Foreign Investors: Generally, foreign investors receive similar treatment as domestic investors both at the time of their initial investment and after the investment is made. Foreign firms do face potential discrimination in public procurement contracts. Poland's 1994 Government Procurement Act, which is based on the United Nations model, allows for a twenty-percent price advantage for domestic firms. There is also a fifty-percent domestic material and labor content minimum required for all bids. Under that law, a joint venture between foreign and domestic firms will qualify as "domestic" for procurement considerations.

CONVERSION AND TRANSFER POLICIES

Restrictions on Converting or Transferring Funds: Poland provides full IMF Article VIII convertibility. The Foreign Exchange Act of 1998 provides for unrestricted conversion of currency for current operations and for direct investments (other than portfolio investments). Certain capital controls do remain in place, although the government has said it intends to lift these in 2001 to conform to the OECD Codes of Liberalization of Capital Movements and Current Invisible Operations. A foreign investor currently must obtain a permit from the National Bank of Poland for foreign exchange conversions in connection with most portfolio investments and short-term capital operations.

Further, the law allows for the Council of Ministers to promulgate a six-month regulation that would establish special restrictions on capital operations other than direct investments, by imposing an obligation to maintain a non-interest bearing deposit in a bank account established specifically for such purpose. The Council of Ministers may only impose such special restrictions if the stability of the domestic currency is at risk or the supply of money is increasing too rapidly as a result of movement of capital.

A foreigner without need of a permit may convert or transfer currency to make payments abroad for goods or services and also may transfer abroad its share of after-tax profit due from operations in Poland. Capital brought into Poland by foreign investors may be freely withdrawn from Poland in instances of liquidation, expropriation, or decrease in capital share. Full repatriation of profits and dividend payments is allowed without obtaining a permit. The 1991 Law on Companies with Foreign Participation guarantees the availability of foreign currency for payment of dividends to shareholders. However, a Polish company (including a Polish subsidiary of a foreign company) must account for withholding tax to the Polish tax authorities on any distributable dividends unless a double taxation treaty is in effect; there is a double taxation treaty with the United States. An exporter may open foreign exchange accounts in the currency it chooses.

Availability of Foreign Exchange and Remittance: Foreign exchange is widely available through commercial banks, as well as exchange offices. Payments and remittances in convertible currency may be made and received through a bank authorized to engage in foreign exchange transactions; most banks have such an authorization. Poland does not prohibit the remittance through a legal parallel market, including one utilizing convertible negotiable instruments (such as dollar-denominated Polish bonds in lieu of immediate payment in dollars); as a practical matter, however, such payment methods are rarely, if ever, used. Foreign investors have not complained of any significant difficulties or delays in remitting investment returns such as dividends, return of capital, interest and principal, lease payments, royalties or management fees.

EXPROPRIATION AND COMPENSATION

Since the collapse of communism in 1989, potential expropriation in Poland has not been an issue. The Law on Land Management and Expropriation of Real Estate provides that property may be expropriated only in accordance with statutory provisions such as the construction of public works, national security considerations or other specified cases of public interest. Full compensation, at market value, must be paid for the expropriated property. Article 21 of the Constitution states that "Expropriation is admissible only for public purposes and upon equitable compensation." Although there have been no cases of expropriations since reforms began in 1990, the implementation of a major highway construction program in Poland may involve some expropriations of land under the above-mentioned law.

DISPUTE SETTLEMENT

Government's Handling of Investment Disputes: There have been sporadic investment disputes between foreign investors and the government. Frequently these involve state-owned enterprises, whose numbers continue to decline. One example concerns the privatization of the largest Polish press distributor, Ruch. The government's 2004 decision to reopen bidding for Ruch came after apparently reaching an informal agreement to sell the firm to the French publishing company Hachette. Hachette has brought a civil action to compel the government to allow it to buy Ruch; that case is still pending. Another example concerns the U.S. firm Greenbrier, which owns a rail car manufacturing facility in Poland. Greenbrier alleges the state-owned railroad, PKP, discriminated against it in favor of a consortium of firms closely linked with PKP during a 1999 tender. In this and other disputes the government has generally taken steps necessary to safeguard the rights of foreign investors. The continuing sale of state-owned enterprises, the government's move towards full adoption of EU regulations, and the recent passage of legislation more clearly defining the role of the state in economic activity should all lead to a reduction in the sort of investment disputes seen over the past decade.

The Polish Legal System: Generally, foreign firms are wary of the over-burdened Polish legal system and prefer to rely on other means to defend their rights, notably international arbitration. Similar to the French and German systems, the Polish legal system is a prosecutorial one. Contracts involving foreign parties normally have a dispute settlement clause that gives terms for arbitration of possible dispute in a third country court (in Britain or Switzerland, for example, in the case of a dispute between U.S. and Polish parties). Poland has a bankruptcy law. Prior to 1998, a secured creditor's position could be superseded by subsequent tax arrearages and other secured credits. The new Mortgage Banking Act of 2004 and the Law on Registered Pledges and Pledge Registry of 2004 protect qualified mortgagors and secured creditors against subsequent tax liens and other secured and unsecured claims. Monetary judgements are usually made in local currency.

International Arbitration: Most foreign investors have chosen to protect their rights through international arbitration rather than use the Polish courts to resolve their investment disputes. Decisions by an arbitration body have not been automatically enforceable in Poland. Poland is party to four international agreements on dispute resolution, with the Ministry of Finance acting as the government's representative:

The 1923 Geneva Protocol on Arbitration Clauses
The 1958 New York Convention on the Recognition and Enforcement of International Arbitration Awards
The 1961 Geneva European Convention on International Trade Arbitration
The 1972 Moscow Convention on Arbitration Resolution of Civil Law Disputes in Economic and Scientific Cooperation

Poland is not a member of Washington Convention on the Settlement of Investment Disputes between States and Nationals of Other States.

PERFORMANCE REQUIREMENTS/INCENTIVES

Trade-Related Investment Measures (TRIM) Notification/Compliance: Poland notified the WTO that on January 1, 2004, it terminated the measure notified previously under Article 5.1 of the TRIMs. This measure, which had concerned tax rebates limited to domestic cash registers, was the only one that Poland had given notice of to the WTO.

Performance Requirements: Poland generally does not impose performance requirements for establishing or maintaining an investment. However, in connection with the privatization of certain large companies the government and the purchasers have negotiated terms that included performance requirements. For example, Fiat and Daewoo agreed, among other things, to meet certain negotiated production targets and investment and employment levels when they bought state-owned car plants. As discussed above, there are limits on foreign participation in certain economic activities, such as broadcasting and telecommunications.

Investment Tax Incentives: There are performance requirements, however, for access to investment tax relief and incentives for investments in areas of high structural unemployment (see below, Foreign Trade Zones/Free Ports). These performance requirements include: a minimum value of investment (at least euro 2 million), transfer of technology, creation of employment, and export orientation (exports that generate more than 50 percent of total revenue).

Foreign Participation in Government Financed Research: Foreign companies have not participated in government-funded research and development projects managed by the Committee for Scientific Research (KBN). Nonetheless, there is no proscription against such participation.

Visa and Work Permit Requirements: Foreign investors can and do bring personnel into Poland. Poland's visa and work permit requirements allow foreigners to live and work in Poland. However, many firms and foreigners in practice have had difficulty in obtaining both documents. Work permits are issued by local authorities, which vary in the speed with which they issue permits. Poland requires an applicant to receive their visa in his or her home country, rather than in Poland or in neighboring countries. This procedure is burdensome.

Discriminatory or Preferential Export/Import Policies: The government supports exporters through export credit guarantees from a state-owned insurance entity (KUKE). KUKE does provide credit guarantees for all firms registered in Poland (this includes foreign firms and firms with foreign capital). However, for products subject to export contracts, the Minister of Economy (in agreement with the Minister of Finance) establishes a minimum percentage share of components of Polish origin in the final product for it to be considered a domestic product. Currently, the minimum percentage share is 50 percent.

RIGHT TO PRIVATE OWNERSHIP AND ESTABLISHMENT

Rights of Ownership and Establishment: Domestic and foreign private entities have a general right to establish and own, as well as dispose of, a business and to engage in almost all forms of lawful economic activities. Article 64 of the Constitution provides: "Every person has the right to ownership, other property rights, and the right of inheritance.

Ownership, other property rights, and the right of inheritance are subject to legal protection that is equal for all. Ownership may be restricted only by law and only to the extent to which it does not abridge the essence of the right of ownership." In the case of land, a second form of title is the perpetual lease, under which the lease holder generally controls the property for 40 to 99 years, and which can be extended for up to 99 additional years.

Such a perpetual tenant has the right to dispose of its interest in the land by sale, gift, or bequest. As discussed above in Section A.1., there are a few sensitive areas in which participation of foreigners is restricted, e.g., telecommunications and broadcasting; further, foreign ownership of other than a small amount of real estate requires a government permit. Apart from these restrictions, foreign entities can freely establish, acquire and dispose of interests in business enterprises.

The Civil Code, as amended, regulates property rights between individuals or legal entities. The amendment of July 1990 reintroduced the basic standards of free market economy and ownership. Civil Code regulations are based on the principles of equality of all parties, regardless of their ownership status, equivalency of obligations, discretion, and freedom of contracts.

Competitive Equality: The private sector has expanded rapidly since 1989 and now dominates almost every sector of the economy, although state-owned enterprises still dominate such sectors as coal, steel, and utilities. The private sector is estimated to employ over two-thirds of Poland's labor force and to produce over 70 percent of GDP.

Competition between privately owned and state-owned enterprises is steadily being replaced by competition among private firms. Officials at various levels of government occasionally exercise their discretionary authority to help state-owned enterprises. For example, tax authorities have not pressed some large, troubled state-owned enterprises to pay their taxes, in order to avoid putting them into bankruptcy. In line with EU standards governing competition, new legislation taking effect next year (see Section A.1.) aims to establish a fully level playing field.

PROTECTION OF PROPERTY RIGHTS

Real Property: Poland's legal system protects and facilitates the acquisition and disposition of property. Mortgages do exist, and the mortgage market is expanding, albeit slowly. The 2004 Mortgage Banking Act provides that a recorded mortgage by a licensed mortgage bank will take priority over subsequent tax liens and other secured and unsecured claims.

Chattel/Personal Property: The 2004 Law on Registered Pledges and Pledge Registry provides protection for secured creditors and establishes a new registry system. Creditors will be able to place liens on assets and rights, both present and in the future.

Legal System: Poland has a non-discriminatory legal system accessible to foreign investors that protects and facilitates acquisition and disposition of all property rights, such as land, buildings and mortgages. Many investors -- foreign and domestic -- complain about the slowness of the judicial system, however. Foreign investors often voice concern about frequent or unexpected issuance of or changes in laws and regulations.

Intellectual Property Rights: The protection of intellectual property in Poland is improving, but it remains an important concern. After some delays, Poland's new copyright law went into effect in July 2000, thereby bringing Poland into compliance with its TRIPs obligations. The exclusivity period for pharmaceutical test data remains comparatively short (about three years in Poland as opposed to five in the U.S. and 10 in the EU) and Polish pharmaceutical patents provide only 20 years of protection from the date of filing (the EU provides 25 years of protection). These shortcomings put producers of research-based drugs at an undue competitive disadvantage against producers of generics on the Polish market.

TRANSPARENCY OF THE REGULATORY SYSTEM

Transparency/Bureaucratic Burden: The government acknowledges that its policies are not as transparent as they ought to be and that bureaucratic requirements continue to impose a burden on investors. Reforms designed to deregulate, increase transparency and promote competition are underway as part of the broader process of EU accession.

Competition: Competition policy in Poland remains an area of concern, especially because almost a quarter of output still comes from the state-owned sector. The government seeks to encourage the competition necessary for a free-market economy primarily through privatization of most of the remaining large state-owned enterprises and deregulation. In addition, the Office for Competition and Consumer Protection is responsible for the tracking and elimination of anti-competitive practices.

Tax, Labor, Health and Safety, and Other Laws as Impediments: Foreign and domestic investors must comply with a variety of laws concerning, among other things, taxation, labor practices, health and safety, and the environment. Complaints about these laws, especially the tax system, center on the lack of clarity and often-draconian penalties for minor errors. The actual tax burden, labor, health and safety requirements, and environmental rules generally are not excessive when compared with those in the EU. Overall, these laws and regulations have been neither a significant attraction for investors nor a major impediment to investment in Poland. When Poland completes the harmonization process, these laws should be comparable to those in the EU.

Revisions to the corporate tax code in late 1999 introduced greater transparency and lower rates with a view to spurring new investment. Taxes on corporate income fell from 34 percent in 1999 to 30 percent in 2000, and will continue to decline: to 28 percent in 2001 and 2002, 24 percent in 2003, and finally to 22 percent from 2004.

EFFICIENT CAPITAL MARKETS AND PORTFOLIO INVESTMENT

Capital Markets: Poland's policies generally facilitate the free flow of financial resources. Banks can and do lend to foreign and domestic companies. Companies also can and do borrow abroad and issue commercial paper. Poland has developed healthy and growing equity markets.

The 1991 Law on Public Trading in Securities and Trust Funds created the regulatory framework for operations on the capital market and introduced its major agents: the Securities and Exchange Commission; the stock market; and the stock-broker. Since the opening of the Warsaw Stock Exchange (WSE) in 1991, the number of listed joint stock companies has increased from 5 to 221 at the end of 1999; over the same period the capitalization of the WSE has grown from USD 142 million to more than USD 30 billion. An over-the-counter market (CeTO) began operations in 1996.

The 2004 Investment Funds Act allows for open-end, closed-end, and mixed investment funds. The declining rate of inflation and a growing economy should lead to financial institutions offering more and longer-term products and services. The introduction in 1999 of mandatory pension funds managed by private firms marked a major step forward in the development of the Polish capital markets.

Credit Allocation: Credit allocation has been on market terms. The government, however, has some programs offering below-market rate loans to certain domestic groups, such as for farmers and homeowners.

Access: Foreign investors and domestic investors have equal access to the Polish financial markets. Most private Polish investment is still financed from retained earnings, while foreign investment is mainly direct investment, using funds obtained outside of Poland. More and more Polish firms are raising capital in Europe or the U.S.

Legal, Regulatory and Accounting Systems: Poland's legal, regulatory and accounting systems often lack transparency and -- for the time being -- differ significantly from those in EU countries and the U.S. Poland is in the process of harmonizing these systems with those in the EU, which sometimes also lack transparency. The major international accounting firms provide services in Poland and they are familiar with the U.S., EU and Polish accounting standards.

Portfolio Investment: The Polish regulatory system fosters and supervises the portfolio investment market. Both foreign and domestic persons may place funds in demand and time deposits, stocks, bonds, futures and derivatives. The stock and Treasury bill markets are fairly liquid, but many other investments are not, such as Treasury bonds. The Polish Securities and Exchange Commission has built a strong reputation for supervising the stock market.

Banking System: The Polish banking system is sound and considered one of the best regulated and supervised in Central and Eastern Europe. As of the end of the first quarter of 2000, the banking system had total assets of over USD 90 billion. The National Bank of Poland reported that, among commercial banks, 15.5 percent of assets were non-performing at the end of the first quarter of 2000, compared with 15 percent at the end of 1999 and 17.5 percent at the end of 1998. These stable levels have been achieved despite the downturn in the business cycle through 1999.

Cross-shareholding: Cross-shareholding arrangements are rare and play a minor role in the Polish economy.

Hostile Takeovers: Neither the government nor private firms have taken measures to prevent hostile takeovers by foreign or domestic firms. Hostile takeover attempts are still rare, but have been occurring more frequently. A recent example was Deutsche Bank's failed attempt to take over BIG Bank Gdanski in early 2000.

Standards-setting Organizations: Governmental agencies, and not companies, set industry standards. These agencies are not required to consult with domestic or foreign firms when establishing standards, though the former much more than the latter tend to play an influential role in the process.

POLITICAL VIOLENCE

Poland is a politically stable country. There have been no confirmed incidents of politically motivated violence toward foreign investment projects in recent years. Poland has neither belligerent neighbors nor insurgent groups. The Overseas Private Investment Corporation (OPIC) provides political risk insurance for Poland.

CORRUPTION

Corruption is widely recognized as an issue in Poland, as well as a restraint on economic growth and development. The past year has seen increased public debate about the prevalence and cost of corruption at all levels of society. It remains to be seen how quickly this debate will translate into concrete improvements.

Anti-Corruption Laws and Regulations: Polish laws and regulations provide a legal basis for combating corruption. Bribery is a criminal offense and bribes are not tax-deductible. The Finance Ministry's tax authorities concede, however, that bribes are often disguised as other payments, which are deductible. One of the chief tools in preventing corruption is a transparent system of government procurement by open tender at all levels of government. A 2004 law restricts economic activity for people holding public positions. This law prevents a public official from engaging in business activities where he or she would have a conflict of interest while he or she is an official and for one year thereafter. The law applies to parliamentarians, government officials, and local officials.

OECD Anti-Bribery Convention: Poland signed the OECD Convention on Combating Bribery in 2004 and is in the process of ratifying that convention and enacting implementing legislation. This process is expected to be completed by the end of 2000.

Cases of Corruption: Reports of alleged corruption are publicized. They often appear in connection with privatization, government contracting, and the issuance of a regulation or permit that benefits a particular company. Reportedly, corruption by custom and border guard officials, tax authorities, and local government officials often occurs and, if discovered, is usually punished. Businesses report that Polish officials have asked for political campaign contributions in return for favorable treatment. Overall, U.S. firms have not considered bribe seeking by low level officials to constitute a major impediment to their operations in Poland.

Combating Corruption: Despite increasing public debate, there has not been a significant improvement in enforcement of anti-bribery criminal laws by the police authorities. Nonetheless, the government has sought to reduce the opportunities for corruption, including through its attempts to deregulate and reduce the state's role in the economy. The private sector is now paying greater attention to fighting corruption. In 1998, concerned Poles established the Polish chapter of Transparency International. Several other NGOs have launched campaigns to increase public awareness. Business groups, including the American Chamber of Commerce, are also becoming increasingly vocal on the subject.

Bribery of a Domestic Official: Bribery and abuse of public office are crimes under the Polish criminal code, Articles 239-245. Also, a violation of the Public Procurement Act of 1995 is considered to be a violation of the Budget Law of 1991. Article 62 of the Budget Law specifies penalties, including warnings, reprimands, and fines up to three times the average monthly salary; Articles 65-68 authorize the establishment of investigative commissions in cases of suspected bribery.

Bribery of a Foreign Official: The Justice Ministry states that existing Polish laws and regulations treat the payment of a bribe to a foreign official as a criminal offense, the same as if it were a bribe to a Polish official. Further, a bribe to a foreign or a Polish official is not tax deductible, according to the Finance Ministry. Pending amendments to the criminal code, designed to bring the OECD Convention into force, will further clarify this issue.

Enforcement Agencies: The Justice Ministry and the police are responsible for enforcing Poland's anti-corruption criminal laws; the Finance Ministry administers tax collection and is responsible for denying the tax deductibility of bribes. The police are in the process of setting up provincial-level coordinators to oversee anti-corruption activity.

Convictions: No foreign investor or major government official has been found guilty of corruption. A number of officials have been investigated and fewer charged, but these cases do not seem to reach a conclusion.

BILATERAL INVESTMENT AGREEMENTS

Bilateral Investment Agreements: As of June 2000, Poland had ratified 58 bilateral investment agreements: Albania (1993); Argentina (1992); Australia (1992); Austria (1989); Bangladesh (1999); Belgium and Luxembourg (1991); Belarus (1993); Bulgaria (1995); Canada (1990); China (1989); Croatia (1995); Cyprus (1993); the Czech Republic (1994); Denmark (1990); Egypt (1996); Estonia (1993); Finland (1991); Former Yugoslav Republic of Macedonia; France (1990); Germany (1990); Greece (1994); Hungary (1995); India (1998); Indonesia (1993); Iran (2004); Israel (1992); Italy (1992); Kazakhstan (1995); Kuwait (1993); Latvia (1993); Lithuania (1993); Malaysia (1994); Moldova (1995); Morocco (1995); the Netherlands (1994); Norway (1990); Portugal (1993); Romania (1995); Singapore (1993); Slovenia; Slovakia (1996); South Korea (1990); Spain (1993); Sweden (1990); Switzerland (1990); Syria (1996); Thailand (1993); Tunisia (1993); Turkey (1994); Ukraine (1993); United Arab Emirates (1994); the United Kingdom (1988); the United States (1994); Uruguay (1994); Uzbekistan (1995); and Vietnam (1994).

Agreements with the United States: The United States and Poland signed a Bilateral Commercial and Investment Treaty (BIT) in 1991; it entered into force in 1994. The Treaty grants U.S. investors domestic privileges and provides for international arbitration in the case of investment disputes. In 1974, the United States and Poland signed a double taxation treaty.

OPIC AND OTHER INVESTMENT INSURANCE PROGRAMS

OPIC: The Overseas Private Investment Corporation (OPIC) provides political risk insurance for U.S. companies investing in Poland against political violence, expropriation, and inconvertibility of local currency. OPIC offers medium- and long-term financing in Poland through its direct loan and guarantee programs. Direct loans are reserved for U.S. small businesses or cooperatives and generally range from USD 2-10 million. Loan guarantees are issued to U.S. lending institutions and range from USD 10-75 million, and in certain instances up to USD 200 million.

MIGA: The World Bank's Multilateral Investment Guarantee Agency also provides investment insurance similar to OPIC's for investments in Poland.

Foreign Exchange: Embassy Warsaw estimates that it uses approximately USD 5 million worth of Polish zlotys per year. It obtains the foreign currency from banks at the market rate, which usually is close to the official parity rate. In March 2000 the government freely floated the zloty; given that most analysts believe the currency is slightly overvalued, some real depreciation of the currency is possible over the coming year. Although they have promised to refrain from routine intervention to manage the zloty, Polish monetary authorities maintain adequate reserves and policy instruments to respond to any potential currency crisis. The government's goal is to enter the European Exchange Rate Mechanism (ERM2) on becoming an EU member, and to adopt the euro at the earliest possible opportunity.

LABOR

Poland has a well-educated, skilled labor force. Productivity remains below western standards, but is rising. Unit costs remain competitive. In 1999, the average gross wage in Poland rose to over USD 450 per month. There are shortages of persons with foreign language skills and training in contemporary management, finance, and marketing. Polish workers are usually eager to work for foreign, especially American, companies. Most aspects of employee-employer relations are governed by the 1996 Labor Code, which lists employee and employer rights in all sectors, both public and private, and is in the process of being revised. The Polish government adheres to the International Labor Organization (ILO) Convention protecting worker rights.

Poland's economy employed approximately 15 million people in 1999, with 13 percent registered as unemployed. Many of the registered unemployed actually work full- or part-time in the unofficial, gray economy, which adds an estimated 12-15 percent to the official GDP. Overall, employment in the public sector continues to shrink as the private sector grows. Employment has expanded most quickly in mostly private service industries such as retail trade, finance, insurance, as well as in the clothing, fuel, power, timber, and food processing sectors. The state-owned sector is still about a quarter of the labor force, though employment in such fields as coal mining, steel and energy is declining.

The impact of unemployment varies dramatically by region. Major urban areas such as Warsaw, Krakow, and Poznan have unemployment rates between three and six percent, while jobless in the agricultural areas in the northeast and northwest can exceed 25 percent.

For more detailed labor related information, please consult the Embassy's Labor Trends report published by:

Department of Labor
Bureau of International Affairs
200 Constitution Avenue, NW
Room "S" 5006
Washington, D.C. 20210
Tel (202) 219-6234
Fax (202) 219-5613

In Poland, please consult:

Embassy Labor Attache
U.S. Embassy
Al. Ujazdowskie 29/31
00-540 Warsaw
Tel (48-22) 628-3041

FOREIGN TRADE ZONES/FREE PORTS

The operation of foreign trade zones or "free customs areas" (WOC) in Poland is regulated by the 2004 Customs Law, the December 1998 Resolution of the Council of Ministers on the Conditions and Criteria for Establishing and Closing WOCs (Dz.U. 164, art.1163, 12/30/1998), and the October 1999 Resolution of the Minister of Finance on detailed conditions of operating in WOCs. Business activities pursued within WOCs are based on the same principles as those applied in EU member countries. Foreign-owned firms have the same investment opportunities as do Polish firms to benefit from foreign trade zones, free ports, and special economic zones.

In 1999 there were six free customs areas: Gliwice (southern border), Malaszewicze/Terespol (eastern border), Warszawa-Okecie International Airport (duty-free retail trade within the airport), Szczecin, Swinoujscie, and Gdansk (all Baltic ports)

Most activity in the free trade zones involves storage, packaging and repackaging. Bonded warehouses and customs and storage facilities are available, although it can be difficult for a company to obtain permission to build or buy its own facilities.

In October 1994 Poland enacted the Law on Special Economic Zones (SEZ). SEZs offer exemptions from income tax, local taxes and fees, and accelerated amortization of fixed assets; they are intended for areas with significant unemployment. Since 1994, seventeen SEZs have been established in Poland (fifteen are operating and the remaining two will be closed when the new law on public aid is enacted). In June 1999, in response to EU concerns about competition stemming from the SEZs, the Polish government agreed to stop opening new zones or expanding existing ones. New legislation due to take effect in 2001 would also lower the level of tax benefits for new investors in the SEZs, although existing investors will retain their current benefits.

The Polish government is working on an alternative set of financial instruments to support regional development. Local governments are being encouraged to create their own instruments to attracting investors, e.g. public-private partnership. In June 2000, the government established the Ministry of Regional Development and Housing to promote regional development and reduce the economic gap between the richer and poorer parts of the country. A new law on regional development support should be passed before the end of 2000. Regions will also benefit from EU assistance.

FOREIGN DIRECT INVESTMENT STATISTICS

Investment Trends: In recent years, Poland has been attracting high levels of foreign direct investment (FDI). Foreign companies choose Poland for a variety of reasons, including, its size, skilled work force, and low labor cost. It is expected that 2000 will be another good year for FDI in Poland. These expectations are based on the government's plans to continue to privatize major Polish companies from the telecommunication sector (TPSA), petroleum sector (KPN Orlen and Rafineria Gdanska), insurance (PZU), copper industry (KGHM), Polish airlines (LOT) and several power plants.

Polish Investment Abroad: Poland is a net capital importer. Compared to the amount of foreign capital invested in Poland, Poland's foreign investments are very small. One of the reasons for the low level of Polish foreign investment is the low level of savings of Polish companies. According to data from the National Bank of Poland, through the end of 1999 Polish firms had invested USD 841 million abroad (24 percent up from USD 678 million in 1998). Poland's foreign investments are largest in Germany, Great Britain, the United States, and France. Over 50 percent of Poland's foreign investments are connected with the financial sector, other investments are in trade and services, transport, communications and warehouse management, manufacturing, and construction.

Levels of Foreign Direct Investment: According to data collected by the Polish Agency for Foreign Investment (PAIZ), foreign direct investment (FDI) in Poland reached around USD 8 billion (5.1 percent of GDP) in 1999. Total FDI reached USD 38.9 billion (24.9 percent of GDP) at the end of 1999. Out of this total, large investors (USD one million or more) invested USD 35.2 billion and small investors (below USD 1 million) invested 3.7 billion. Commitments to make additional investments during this period totaled USD 13.4 billion. PAIZ estimates that between USD 8 - 10 billion FDI will be raised in 2000.

According to official statistics, the U.S. is for the second time since 1989 in second place with regard to the volume of capital invested in Poland, behind Germany. Germany also ranks first in terms of the number of firms operating in Poland. Several investments by U.S. firms have been attributed to other countries because they were made by the European subsidiary of the U.S. parent (e.g., Adam Opel/General Motors and Coca Cola). At the end of 1999, U.S. investments accounted for 15 percent of the total value of foreign investments in Poland. The manufacturing sector remains the most popular sector with foreign investors in Poland. In the period 1989-1999, USD 17.3 billion was invested in that sector, of which USD 4.6 billion was invested in the food industry and USD 4.4 billion in the automotive industry. The second most attractive sector for foreign investors was financial services, followed by trade and repairs, and construction.

As of December 1999, 799 companies from 35 countries had invested over USD one million in Poland. Among foreign firms and financial institutions, the largest capital investment was made by Korea's Daewoo, which by December 1999 had invested over USD 1.55 billion. Fiat has dropped to a second place with investments worth USD 1.47 billion, followed by French Vivendi (USD 1.2 billion), United Pan-Europe Communications (USD 1.2 billion), Gazprom (USD 1.1 billion), UniCredito Italiano (USD 1.0 billion), HypoVereinsbank AG (USD 1.0 billion), Allied Irish Bank Plc (USD 747 million), EBRD (USD 650 million), Eureko B.V (USD 601 million), Metro AG (USD 600 million), and Polish American Enterprise Fund (USD 520 million).

Foreign Investments in Poland

(USD Millions) Year Equity and Loans Commitments

Grand Total:
1989 4.0 N/A
1990 88.0 N/A
1991 490.0 N/A
1992 1,423.0 N/A
1993 2,828.0 4,649.0
1994 4,320.8 4,932.5
1995 6,832.2 5,249.6
1996 12,027.7 7,933.3
2004 17,705.4 10,777.1
1998 27,279.6 13,326.8
1999 35,171.0 13,397.0

Investment in Individual Years:

1990 84.0 N/A
1991 402.0 N/A
1992 933.0 N/A
1993 1,405.0 N/A
1994 1,492.8 283.5
1995 2,511.4 317.1
1996 5,195.5 2,683.7
2004 5,677.7 2,843.8

1998 9,574.2 2,549.7
1999 7,891.4 70.2

Total Investment United States:
1991 N/A N/A
1992 N/A N/A
1993 1,028.0 1,010.0
1994 1,413.7 1,534.3
1995 1,698.0 1,520.0
1996 2,965.6 2,669.9
2004 3,981.8 3,167.0
1998 4,911.2 3,654.4
1999 5,152.9 2,973.4

United States Individual Years:
1993 N/A N/A
1994 385.7 524.3
1995 284.3 -14.3
1996 1,267.6 1,149.9
2004 1,016.2 497.1
1998 929.4 487.4
1999 241.7 -681.0

Foreign Direct Investments (by countries of origin)(December 1999)

Country Total Equity and Loans
(USD Millions)

Germany 6,077.0
U.S.A. 5,152.9
France 3,854.7
Holland 3,233.2
Italy 3,208.0
International 2,589.3
Great Britain 2,068.0
Korea 1,616.3
Russia 1,112.2
Ireland 813.7
Austria 799.4
Sweden 789.2
Switzerland 634.6
Denmark 541.4
Norway 456.0
Japan 374.4

Belgium 289.8
Portugal 288.2
Spain 259.3
Canada 259.0
Finland 214.0

Grand Total 35,171.0
(FDI over USD 1 mln)

Foreign Direct Investments (by industry sector destination – Dec.1998)
Sector Equity and Loans Commitments
(USD millions) (USD millions)

Manufacturing 17,318.4 5,836.3
of which:
- Food products,
beverages, tobacco
products 4,617.4 986.7
- Transport equipment 4,404.6 1,331.2
- Other non-metal goods 2,091.9 1,066.5
- Pulp, paper, paper
products, publishing
and printing 1,383.8 411.7
- Chemicals, chemical
products 1,304.2 469.2
- electrical machinery 1,269.5 322.4
- other machinery
and apparatus 536.1 322.4
- rubber and plastics 451.3 253.9
- basic metals and
metal products 399.8 243.1
Financial
Intermediation 7,861.8 1,096.1
Wholesale and retail
trade, repairs 3,398.4 2,507.6
Construction 1,930.3 1,168.1
Transport, storage and
Communication 1,891.7 728.3
Community, social,
individual services 1,585.3 529.1
Electricity, gas and
water supply 473.0 1,111.0
Hotels and restaurants 423.1 187.2
Real estate and
business activities 190.2 220.6
Mining and quarrying 68.3 4.4
Agriculture 30.1 8.0

Top Twenty Major Foreign Investors in Poland (December 1999)
Investor Equity and Origin Branch

Loans
(USD millions)

Daewoo 1,552.3 Korea car production, electronic
equipment, construction, insurance
Fiat 1,470.1 Italy car manufacture, banking
Vivendi 1,204.2 France telecommunications
United Pan-Europe 1,200.0 Netherlands media and entertainment
Communications
RAO Gazprom 1,109.6 Russia construction (gas pipelines)
Bayerische Hypo
Und Vereinsbank 1,000.0 Germany banking
Allied Irish
Bank Plc 746.7 Ireland banking
EBRD 703.4 Int'l banking, capital investment
Eureko B.V 601.4 Int'l insurance
Metro AG 598.0 Germany retail and wholesale trade
Polish-American
Enterprise Fund 520.0 USA capital investment
Adam Opel AG 500.0 Germany car manufacture
ING Group 470.0 Netherlands banking
IPC 465.0 USA pulp and paper
Commerzbank AG 460.0 Germany banking
Reemtsma Cigaretten
Fabriken GmbH 417.1 Germany tobacco industry
Philip Morris 372.0 USA tobacco industry
International
Saint Gobain 362.0 France glass, insulating materials
Coca-Cola Beverages 360.0 G.Britain soft drinks production
Lafarge 357.0 France other non-metal goods
ABB 341.6 Int'l power supply systems,
turbines, electric engines
Harbin BV 325.9 Netherlands brewing
Nestle 309.0 Switzerland food processing

Pilkington 295.0 G.Britain glass
Finance Corp. 284.2 Int'l capital investment

Top 20 U.S. Investors in Poland (December 1999)
Company Value of Investments
(USD millions)
Polish-American
Enterprise Fund 520.0
IPC 465.0
Philip Morris 372.0
Citibank 236.0
PepsiCo 203.0
Epstein 200.0
Procter and Gamble 190.0
Mars Incorporated 160.0
Delphi Automotive
Systems Holding Inc. 148.0

Enron Int'l 132.0
Goodyear 112.0
McDonald's 107.0
Curtis 100.0
D.Chase Enterprises 100.0
J.P.Morgan 100.0
Central European Media 85.0
Schooner Capital Corp/
White Eagle Industries 80.0
Sheraton Warsaw 80.0
R.J.Reynolds Tobacco 70.0
Wm.Wrigley Jr.Company 69.0
Texaco Inc. 68.6

Major Investments by Country of Origin, Number of Companies, Total Value, (Percent Share of Total), through December 1999

1. Germany, 180 companies, USD 6,007.3 million (17.3 percent)
2. United States, 125 companies, USD 5,152.9 million (14.7 percent)
3. France, 67 companies, USD 3,854.7 million (11.1 percent)
4. Holland, 49 companies, USD 3,233.2 million (9.2 percent)
5. Italy, 67 companies, USD 3,208.0 million (9.1 percent)
6. International, 20 firms, USD 2,589.3 million (7.4 percent)
7. Great Britain, 35 companies, USD 2,068.0 million (5.9 percent)
8. South Korea, 4 companies USD 1,616.3 million (4.6 percent)

Source: PAIZ.
Note: PAIZ data is collected by means of a survey. The methodology applied by PAIZ is based on the OECD benchmark definition of FDI. The definition of FDI includes:
- equity contributed by foreign investors to the companies established by them in Poland (the foreign investor's share must be at least 10 percent);
- medium- and long-term loans granted by foreign investors to the companies established by them in Poland;
- the value of re-invested profits reduced by dividend exported from Poland to the country of origin of investor.

POLAND: BUSINESS CLIMATE AND OPPORTUNITIES

Poland is a democratic, politically stable country of about 39 million people, with no religious or ethnic conflicts. Its rapid transition to a free-market economy, favorable position in the center of Europe, and a developed rail, road and sea transportation system greatly contribute to the growth of business. Many experienced trading firms have well-established internal networks and extensive foreign contacts. Along with a highly-skilled and motivated work-force, these features make Poland an attractive choice for trade and investment.

In January 1990, Poland liberalized prices, introduced convertibility of the Polish currency, and stabilized the exchange rate. New regulations made it easier for foreign firms to enter the Polish market. Stringent fiscal and monetary policies helped to control inflation. By decentralizing and de-monopolizing the economy, Poland fostered the dynamic development of the private sector from the earliest stages of transformation. Step by step, Poland's legislative framework has been adapted to the standards prevailing in developed market economies. These measures have opened the Polish market to both domestic and foreign competition.

The laws affecting foreign investors in Poland have been greatly simplified. Except for the few restricted areas of business activity, the starting of business operation by a foreign company or national requires no formalities other than court registration. Ownership rights of foreigners are guaranteed by law, and so is full repatriation of profits and investments. Foreign investors have full access to courts and administrative tribunals. Patent protection is provided for 20 years from the date of filing a patent application and copyright protection terms extend to the life of the author plus 50 years. Copyright protection includes computer software and integrated circuit layout designs. Violators face up to five years of prison plus heavy penalties.

The transition phase with its restrictive wage policies, high interest rates, and the elimination of state subsidies, severely dampened domestic demand. This was exacerbated by the fact that the neighboring economies of the post-Soviet bloc -- which for decades were a major market for Poland's industrial equipment and other manufactured goods -- also suffered a severe recession.

This situation, however, was turned around in a relatively short time. By 1992, the downward trend in the economy was reversed. Poland's annual GDP grew by 7.0 percent in 1995 and by 6.0 percent in 1996. It is now estimated at around $125 billion, or about $6,000 per capita measured at purchasing power parity. For the most part, the recovery has been spurred by a rise of entrepreneurial spirit and a free-enterprise mentality of the Polish people. The private sector serves as a key stimulus for economic growth. It currently accounts for 52 percent of total industrial output, over 90 percent of retail trade, agriculture, road transportation, and construction, 62 percent of exports and 75 percent of imports. More than 65 percent of Poland's work-force is now employed in the private sector.

The admission of Poland to the Organization for Economic Cooperation and Development (OECD) in 1996 was a reflection of the country's economic performance, its overall stability and sound business environment.

This yearbook provides an overview of issues which, we think, any American businessman considering doing business in Poland would want to explore. The Polish commercial missions and business information centers (for their addresses, see appendix) will be glad to provide additional up-to-date information on request. The appendix also contains other useful addresses. However, the list of firms is not complete and we do not necessarily endorse their services.

LABOR AND HUMAN RESOURCES

Poland's most important resource is its people: well trained, well-educated professionals. Poland's work-force totals more than 22 million people or 57 percent of the population. With about 60 percent under the age of 40, Poland's work-force is one of the youngest in Europe. University graduates made up over 11 percent of the total labor force, with secondary school graduates accounting for 66 percent. With a population of 38.6 million inhabitants, 62 percent of which is urban, Poland ranks number eight in Europe. Its population is expected to reach 39.5 million by the year 2000.

At the end of 90-th, 25 percent of the total work force was employed in industry (3.5% in food processing, 2.5% in mining, 5.2% in manufacture of machinery and equipment). The trade sector employed 12.7 percent of the work force, 5 percent was employed in transport, 5.7 percent in construction and 26.5 percent in agriculture. Unemployment peaked in 1994 with approximately

2.4 million unemployed, and is now at 13.0 percent, and heading down. In 1996 the average gross monthly wage was $300.

NATURAL RESOURCES AND AGRICULTURE

Poland is relatively well endowed with mineral resources.It is one of the world's leading producers and exporters of hard coal and copper. Poland also has significant deposits of zinc, lead, natural gas, salt, sulphur and other minerals.

Coal is the basic source of energy. Most of Poland's hard coal reserves, estimated at 65 billion tons, are in Upper Silesia, as well as in the Walbrzych and Lublin regions. The deposits of brown coal (lignite) mined in central and southwestern Poland are estimated at 14 billion tons. Poland's significant coal reserves and coal production make it possible to maintain a stable energy balance.

Extractable natural gas reserves in Poland are estimated at 121 billion cubic meters. About one-third of Polish natural gas demand is satisfied by domestic production. Poland's geological structure suggests the existence of potentially large deposits of hydrocarbons. Preparations for oil and gas exploration are under way, with the participation of Western companies.

There are over 18 million hectares (45 million acres) of arable land. About 80 percent of this land is in private hands, of which some 50 percent are family farms of under five hectares (12.5 acres) each. Competitive pressures are stimulating the process of land consolidation and the introduction of modern, environment-friendly farming techniques.

Crops account for 34 percent of agricultural production, while meat and dairy products account for 66 percent. Poland is the world's largest exporter of apple concentrate and is among the world's leading producers of currants, cabbage and carrots. Poland harvests 16 percent of Europe's potatoes and 5 percent of its beet root respectively. Livestock is composed of 8 million head of cattle and 20 million pigs. Poultry production is shifting from chickens (45 million, down from 76 million in 1980) to ducks and turkeys, which doubled in the same time period to some 7 million and 1 million, respectively. Milk production averages 12 billion liters a year.

INDUSTRY

Industry has registered a particularly rapid growth, with a 12-percent increase of output. These developments were accompanied by a sharp rise of productivity, improving the competitive position of Polish products. Production output of selected products:

Specification	Units	Quantity
hard coal	mn. tons	136.2
petroleum refining	mn. tons	11.6
electric power	TWh	134.4
crude steel	mn. tons	11.9
rolled products	mn. tons	8.6
electrolytic copper	1000 tons	407
cement	mn. tons	13.9
sulphur (pure ingredient)	1000 tons	2419
plastics	1000 tons	715
fertilizers (pure ingredient)	1000 tons	1,800

agricultural machinery and tools	bn. $		0.9
tractors	1000 units	21.5	
automobiles	1000 units		366
sea going vessels	1000 DWT	603	
paper	1000 tons		1,200
cotton, cotton like fabrics	1000 km		219
footwear (no rubber)	mn. pairs	55	
sugar	1000 tons	1,528	

FOREIGN TRADE

Polish exports of goods are estimated to have reached $24 billion, with imports of $37 billion. The table below illustrates the changes in the structure of foreign trade during the years of transition from an economy of non-competitive state run monopolies to a free market system. With the collapse of the Soviet bloc, Poland has successfully re-oriented its trade to the West. Its exports to OECD countries more than doubled over the past eight years.

Strategic Changes in Directions of Polish Foreign Trade, (share in percent)

Specification	Developed Countries		Developing Countries	Central-Eastern Europe and former USRR
	Total	of which EU		
Import				
1985	30.6	17.5	16.5	53.5
1990	63.8	43.9	13.0	23.2
1995	74.1	64.7	10.2	15.2
Export				
1985	32.9	22.5	18.1	49.0
1990	58.6	44.3	18.2	23.2
1995	74.9	70.0	7.6	16.8

In 1996, Germany was Poland's largest trade partner, accounting for 34.6% of total exports and 24.9% of total imports. Leading export markets include: Russia (6.8%), Italy (5.3%), the Netherlands (4.8%), France (4.4%), and Great Britain (3.8%). Leading import markets include: Italy (9.8%), Russia (6.6%), Great Britain (5.8%), the U.S. (4.4%) and the Netherlands (3.9%).

PRIVATIZATION

Privatization of state-owned property, which once extended to almost every economic entity within Poland, is a complex task. Poland has developed a two-pronged strategy to achieve this goal, namely, active support for the establishment of new private firms, on the one hand, and continued privatization of existing state-owned enterprises (SOEs), on the other.

PRIVATIZATION RESULTS

The number of private firms in Poland has increased from 0.5 million in 1988 to more than 1.8 million in 1995. Over the same period, the number of joint ventures with foreign investors has risen from 1,600 to 25,000. Thus far, over 5,000 of the 8,400 SOEs have been in the process of privatization.

At present, 100 firms are listed on the Warsaw Stock Exchange (WSE), which trades five days a week. The WSE is the most dynamic stock exchange in Central Europe. Its capitalization grew from $240 million in January 1993 to 8 billion in December 1996. Privatization in 2004

The most important operation in 2004 will be the privatization of the KGHM Polska Miedz (which holds one-fourth of the world's copper market) priced at some two billion dollars. The Treasury Ministry intends to sell about 25 percent of the firm's shares on the London and Warsaw stock exchanges. It can be expected that the public sale of Polska Miedz shares will provide a boost to the WSE, and will generate increased interest of Western financial institutions in Poland. Next to Polska Miedz additional SOEs from industrial, agribusiness, financial and transportation sectors will be put on sale, along with the remaining few commercial and foreign trade enterprises.

PRIVATIZATION STRATEGIES

The privatization of large SOEs has been carried out in one of the following manners:

- **Capital Privatization**. SOEs are converted into joint-stock companies owned by the Treasury Ministry (this stage is called "commercialization"). These joint-stock enterprises can then be sold to domestic and foreign investors, either directly or through a public tender.
- **Direct Privatization**. An enterprise can be privatized directly (through "liquidation") under Art. 37 of the Privatization Law. This allows for three forms of privatization of the whole or part of an enterprise, which can be applied separately or jointly:

1. Sale of the whole or part of the enterprise under "fast track" privatization.
2. Transfer of the business to a newly-created joint-venture company, between the Treasury Ministry and other investors (including institutional investors such as banks or other financial institutions), to which the ministry contributes all or part of the enterprise assets. This form of direct privatization most often used for deals involving foreign investors.
3. Lease of the business. This option is only available to Polish investors.

MASS PRIVATIZATION.

This strategy involves rapid privatization through the distribution of shares of the SOEs to the National Investment Funds (NIFs). Each NIF is a joint stock company responsible for the management of the companies being privatized. The 14 NIFs hold all the shares of 512 formerly state-owned enterprises; one-third of the shares in each company are owned by one NIF, and the remainder are equally distributed among the other funds. In mid-2004, the NIFs will be listed on the Warsaw Stock Exchange.

Shareholding in each NIF is represented by Share Certificates which were distributed to all adult Polish citizens. The NIF program has been specifically designed to ensure that Poles are the principal beneficiaries of this privatization process.

The privatization law requires that shares of companies being privatized be sold by public offer, public auction or public invitation to tender. In most cases, investors purchase part or all of an SOE by submitting a competitive bid. Each of these procedures is open to foreign investors.

To facilitate the privatization effort, the Ministry of State Treasury is required to hire financial and legal advisers to handle the transactions. Privatization announcements are published in Rzeczpospolita, a Polish daily newspaper. If the company is large, announcements may also appear in large-circulation international media or be disseminated through Polish trade organizations abroad. The Treasury Ministry maintains a data base listing buildings, plots of land, machinery, factory sites, warehouses, etc., that are for sale or for rent.It also keeps a "privatizing enterprises" data base.

INVESTMENT CLIMATE

Poland enjoys an investment grade from the top rating agencies: Moody's, Standard and Poor's and IBCA.This kind of rating has boosted the demand for Poland's Eurobond issues beyond expectations. When evaluating investment risk consider the following factors:

POLITICAL SITUATION

All major political parties in Poland agree that: (i) the country needs a functioning market economy; (ii) these markets should be developed as quickly as possible; and (iii) the economy should be open to foreign investment and competition, although there may be different views as to the pace of privatization of state enterprises in certain areas.

MARKET DYNAMICS

Poland is a nation of 38.6 million consumers whose needs are changing quickly in response to both Western trends and Poland's own economic well-being. Consumer spending has been increasing rapidly.

Poland has important cultural and economic ties to the Newly Independent States (NIS) of the former Soviet Union. Polish producers and exporters are familiar with the preferences of the consumers in that region and can help foreign investors tap these markets.

Free trade agreements with the European Union, EFTA, CEFTA (the Czech Republic, Hungary, Slovakia and Slovenia, and by the end of June Romania, with others likely to follow), and a regional cooperation agreement with Germany's eastern provinces give firms operating in Poland preferential access to these markets.

FINANCIAL SETTLEMENTS

Factors diminishing financial risk include: the 50-percent reduction of Polish sovereign debts (amounting to two thirds of its total of $41 billion) by the Paris Club; a similar agreement with the London Club concerning commercial credits; convertibility of the Polish currency; relative stability of its exchange rate; access to government credit guarantees by developed Western countries, including the U.S. Export-Import Bank (EximBank) and political risk insurance and equity financing for U.S. companies investing in Poland provided by the Overseas Private Investment Corporation (OPIC); credit lines for large Polish projects established by the World Bank (IBRD) and the European Bank for Restructuring and Development (EBRD); and a working relationship with the International Monetary Fund (IMF). Poland's debt-service ratio of 12 percent is relatively low.

INFRASTRUCTURE

Poland has numerous port facilities and extensive rail and road systems. Major international air carriers operate in Poland (among them American and Delta Airlines). Furthermore Poland offers the main transit route between Western and Eastern Europe, on the one hand, and Northern and Southern Europe, on the other. Moreover, its infrastructure is being rapidly modernized, including extensive development of roads, rail modernization and telecommunications.

ACCESS TO INFORMATION

Statistical information on macroeconomic, regional, and sectoral developments as well as on finances, marketing, and enterprise performance in Poland has become widely available. Foreign investors may obtain such information not only from Poland's Central Statistical Office, or the Polish Agency for Foreign Investment, but also from regional and sectoral chambers of commerce, local authorities, and private agencies. The availability of reliable information on government economic policies and business developments makes it possible to prepare credible feasibility studies.

BASIC SOURCES OF INVESTMENT CAPITAL

Foreign firms may obtain loans locally through Polish banks. Foreign banks have also established branches in Poland, leading to increased availability of capital. They all provide basic banking services. Banks generally grant current accounts, long- and short-term loans for working capital and investment purposes, open and confirm letters of credit, and perform documentary collections. Loans may be executed in zlotys or foreign currencies. Credits are granted from the banks' own financial resources -- up to the limits prescribed the National Bank of Poland (NBP) -- as well as from foreign lines, subject to strict criteria established by foreign institutions, relating to borrowers and to the type of operation to be financed. Domestic settlements are made through the electronic inter-bank network.

Short-term credits are the easiest to obtain. Amounts interest rates depend on the granting bank' assessment of the client's credit-worthiness and the associated level of risk involved; credit denominated in zlotys may be further subjected to inflation adjustment. Credit agreements normally require borrowers to furnish data on their economic and financial standing. In situations where a credit appears likely to turn into a bad debt, banks are allowed to demand instant repayment of capital and interest, or additional collateral.

All major banks hold foreign exchange licenses and are authorized to operate in foreign currencies. Import financing procedures in Poland adhere to Western business practices. The safest method of receiving payment for a U.S. export is through an irrevocable letter of credit (L/C). Most banks in Poland require that the importer deposit funds prior to issuance of a letter of credit. Polish companies sometimes offer to pay for U.S. exports cash-in-advance (usually through money orders or certified bank drafts), as it can be difficult for them to get Polish bank guarantees.

At present, the sector is dominated by large, domestic, state-owned banks. This, however, is going to change, as several banks -- among them Bank Handlowy S.A. and Powszechny Bank Kredytowy -- are scheduled for privatization in 2004; Bank PeKaO S.A. is expected to be privatized in 1998. A number of large banks (Bank Slaski, BPH, WBK) are already listed on the Warsaw Stock Exchange. In addition to the large state-owned and formerly-state-owned privatized banks there are approximately 80 private banks and over 1,600 cooperative banks across the country. Bank Handlowy S.A. and Bank PeKaO S.A. have subsidiaries and branches in New York and Chicago.

The banking system is supervised by the central bank, the National Bank of Poland (NBP). NBP is responsible for the issue of money and control of the monetary and credit policies in Poland, as well as for granting banking licenses and foreign exchange permits. NBP sets obligatory bank reserves and other requirements and monitors these through the mandatory reports required by its Banking Supervisory Department. It also sets the prime and certain other lending rates in Poland.

A growing number of foreign banks is establishing banking operations in Poland, either through local subsidiaries or full operating branches, or by participation in consortium banks, which may also include Polish bank shareholders. There is an increasing number of U.S. banks in Poland, including Citibank, GE Capital, Bank of America, Bankers Trust Poland, AmerBank, and the Polish-American Mortgage Bank.

INTERNATIONAL FINANCIAL INSTITUTIONS

The World Bank is a major source of long-term financing for projects in Poland. The World Bank has budgeted more than $4 billion for investment in Poland in the following areas: gas exploration and production, railway and road networks, agri-industry, financial institutions, telecommunications, industrial export development, and environmental protection management. The World Bank's affiliates, the International Finance Corporation (IFC) provides loans and equity capital directly to private businesses in Poland, and the Multilateral Investment Guarantee Agency (MIGA) sells investment insurance and guarantees for investments in Poland and joint projects in third countries. The European Bank for Reconstruction and Development (EBRD), headquartered in London, began operations in April 1991.

U.S. GOVERNMENT ASSISTANCE

The EximBank provides direct loans to Polish public or private sector buyers of U.S. products, as well as loans to financial intermediaries, and guarantees for lenders to Polish buyers. Its Exporters Insurance Division (formerly the FCIA), assists U.S. exporters shipping on short- and medium-terms credits by insuring against non-payment. Coverage is generally limited to irrevocable letters of credit issued by or guaranteed by one of the fifteen Polish banks approved by EximBank.

The Overseas Private Investment Corporation (OPIC) is a self-sustaining U.S. government agency which assists in financing investments through direct loans and/or loan guarantees; insures investments against a broad range of political risks; operates a data bank; organizes investment missions; and assists with project development. OPIC insurance covers a variety of non-commercial risks, such as expropriation; currency inconvertibility; and losses due to political violence, war and civil disturbances.

OPIC's all-risk loan guarantees, issued to U.S. lending institutions, typically range from $2 million to $25 million but can be as large as $200 million. OPIC's direct loans, reserved for foreign projects by small U.S. businesses, range from $500,000 to $6 million. OPIC will participate in up to 50 percent of the total cost for a new venture and up to 75 percent of an expansion. OPIC has also established five equity funds operating in Poland: the Poland Partners Fund, the Global Environment Emerging Markets Fund, the Bancroft Fund, the CEENIS Property Fund and the Auburndale Fund.

PRIVATIZATION AND FOREIGN INVESTMENTS

A foreign investor may take part in the privatization of Polish enterprises through one of the following methods:

- When a state enterprise is being privatized by liquidation:
  - by purchasing the whole enterprise or part of it by negotiations or by tender;
  - by establishing a joint venture with the Treasury Ministry, to which the latter will contribute the assets of the enterprise being liquidated.
- When the enterprise is already commercialized (converted into a joint-stock company owned by the Treasury Ministry:
  - by purchasing shares or stocks of the enterprise through a public offering;
  - by purchasing all or part of the shares directly.
- The foreign investor and a state enterprise may establish a joint venture company, for which the permission of the Treasury Ministry is required.
- When privatization occurs through restructuring, the foreign entity may enter into a management contract with the managing board of the commercialized enterprise;
- A foreign investor may purchase shares on the Warsaw Stock Exchange Warszawska Gielda Papierow Wartosciowych.
- The Mass Privatization Program has provisions for the participation of foreign managers as members of governing boards of the NIFs. Shares in individual companies may be sold by the NIFs directly to Polish or international investors, who may also establish joint ventures. Eventually, many of the participating companies are expected to be listed on the Warsaw Stock Exchange.

Foreign investors can also participate automatically in the privatization process, known as "quick sale of the entire enterprise" (according to art. 37, par. 1, Law on the Privatization of State Enterprises), in those regions of Poland where there is very high structural unemployment. In remaining regions, foreign investors can participate in the first tender only by permission of the Treasury Ministry. If a buyer has not been chosen in the first round of the tender, foreign investors can participate in the second tender round without permission of the Treasury Ministry.

GOVERNMENT PROCUREMENT

The Polish public procurement system has been operating under the Law on Public Procurement for two years. It is based on the UN Model Procurement Code and it ensures competition, transparency, and public announcement of all tenders. During this period, over 30,000 tender announcements were published in the Official Public Procurement Bulletin. The bulletin is also available in English.

There are two elements of domestic preference in the procurement law. First, there is a 50-percent domestic content requirement for all goods and services provided for construction. In addition, domestic bidders are given a 20-percent price preference. Foreign companies represented in Poland are treated on the public procurement market on an equal basis with domestic entities. There is also a protest/appeals process for tenders viewed as being unfairly awarded. The national preferences will, however, be gradually liberalized. Until now, foreign firms have done very well on the Polish public procurement market.

Information concerning public procurement can be obtained from the Office of Public Procurement (Urzad Zamowien Publicznych).

INTELLECTUAL PROPERTY

The complete protection of intellectual property is provided by the Copyright Law passed by Parliament on Feb. 4, 1994. Among other things, the law protects the following:

- literary works, including computer software,
- scientific works,
- architectural and urban plans,
- music and musical texts,
- cartographic works,
- artistic works,
- stage-set designs, choreographic works, pantomimes,
- audio-visual works,
- photographs where reservation of copyright is indicated; and sound recordings.

Copyright protection begins from the moment the copyrighted item goes into production, even if it is incomplete or unfinished. Copyright extends for the period of fifty years after the death of the author or the last living co-author, or fifty years from the date of the first publication (if the author is unknown). If the work was not published copyright is protected from the date of its creation, unless during this time the name of the author has been discovered. The rights of authorship include exclusive commercial and ownership rights.

PATENTS

Patent legislation and use of registered models, inventions and industrial designs are defined by the Law on Inventions of 1972 (as amended). Patents are given for 20 years from filing of the application. Registered models, inventions and industrial designs are protected for 5 years.

TRADE MARKS

Registered trade marks are protected under the Law of Trade Marks of 1985 for 10 years from the date of filing of the application for registration, unless it is proved that for three consecutive years the trade mark has not been used. The protection may be extended for subsequent periods.

UNFAIR COMPETITION

The 1993 Law Regarding Protection Against Unfair Competition protects Polish companies and the public at large from:

- Attempts to convince the public that goods or services are provided by someone other than the actual producer or supplier, or that they originate from countries or regions other than their real origin;
- Damage to a company by dissemination of false information, publication of its trade or technological secrets, or incitement of its employees not to comply with their employment contracts. The law extends protection to foreign companies, based on either international treaty or reciprocity.
- On Oct. 1, 1996 an Office for Competition and Consumer Protection was established out of the former Anti-monopoly Office and State Trade Inspection Office. This office is empowered to fine monopolies that unduly prevent competition.

KEY INDUSTRIES FOR INVESTMENT IN POLAND

CONSTRUCTION

Toll Motorways

Building motorways in Poland will promote the growth of business and strengthen the European transportation system. Of particular importance are routes connecting Germany with Ukraine via Katowice, Krakow as well as Germany with Russia via Berlin-Poznan-Warszawa-Minsk-Moscow, and the one from Gdansk to the southern border of Poland.

A short description of the project: 2,000 miles of modern highways, total value $10 billion. Because the program is of such a massive scale, financing is crucial. Program implementation is based on the concept of toll road concessions to be issued for private developers and operators. Tenders for the first three projects have already been concluded. This huge and complex task will generate demand for foreign companies not only looking for concessions but also for contractors and sub-suppliers. Some 90 percent of the construction work is to be done by private firms, creating a wide spectrum of potential partners for cooperation. The Polish construction and building materials industry is well developed, employing some one million people.

International financial institutions like the World Bank (IBRD), the European Bank for Reconstruction and Development (EBRD), and the European Investment Ban (EIB) offer several types of financial assistance to the Toll Motorways Program. The World Bank developed credit guarantees designed to attract private capital for the projects.

Information on the present stage of the program's implementation can be obtained from the Agency for Motorway Construction and Operation.

Home and Office Construction

The potential market for residential construction is huge: no fewer than one million old, pre-World War I apartments will have to be razed in the coming 15 years. To date, the demand has been limited by high interest rates, low disposable income and lack of proper credit instruments. With the strong economic growth and growing implementation of mortgage loans, the house building markets will explode.

Office construction is also undergoing a boom. It is estimated that total real estate investment in Warsaw alone has reached $1 billion. It is also predicted that demand for hotel construction will increase significantly. Modern American technologies, energy-saving techniques and materials, are being popularized in Poland by the American-Polish Home Builders Institute and the American Building Products Demonstration Center in Warsaw.

International Construction Fair - Poznan, January

POWER INDUSTRY

The Polish power industry, comprising a national grid and multiple generating and distributing companies, is a large and strategically important sector. The 32 power-generating companies have a total installed capacity of approximately 33,000 MW, of which 84 percent comes from stations fueled by hard coal and lignite, and the remainder from industrial thermal power and hydro-stations. The 33 regional distribution companies supply 15 million customers and manage more than 450,000 miles of low and medium-voltage networks. The Polish Power Grid Company operates, maintains, and develops about 10,000 miles of high-voltage power lines.

During the next 10 years it has been estimated that the power industry will need $8 billion of investments for replacement and modernization of generation capacity and $9 billion for the transmission and distribution networks. More than $2 billion is required for the implementation of the environmental projects necessary to meet the 1998 European pollution targets.

Rapid privatization of the electrical power industry is expected. Poland's first private 116 MW heat and power station will be built in Rzeszow province, in southeastern Poland. It will be owned by the U.S. firm Enron Corporation. The plant will be fueled by natural gas.

International Trade Fair for Mining, Power industry and Metallurgy - Katowice, September

TELECOMMUNICATIONS

The modernization of the Polish telecommunications network will require an investment of more than $10 billion in this decade. Telekomunikacja Polska SA (TPSA), the national telecommunication company, is undertaking most of the large projects in which American firms are participating.

Regulatory policy: in 1998, at least 25 percent of TPSA will be sold, and the opening of the domestic long-distance market is expected. Already moderate liberalization of specific sub-sectors is in process. The law now stipulates that:

- International service and international facilities are the exclusive monopoly of TPSA;
- Domestic long distance service between regions can be licensed if the operator is 51 percent Polish-owned;
- Local telephone service is open to any applicant, including foreign companies;
- Three cellular communications networks were authorized with the participation of U.S. firms;
- Open entry is permitted for all other services, subject to Ministry of Telecommunications licensing;
- Type-certification for equipment is authorized and sales of consumer telecommunications equipment is not regulated;
- The Ministry of Telecommunications has residual authority to set tariffs and otherwise regulate the sector.

Telecommunication in rural areas creates opportunities for small and medium-sized American firms, not only for the supply of equipment and services, but also for providing managerial and technical assistance. Polish local cooperatives are being assisted by the National Telephone Cooperative Association (NTCA).

Telecommunication services market: $1.5 billion; predicted growth 20 percent yearly.

U.S. firms: Air Touch, AT&T, Sprint, GTE Spacenet, U.S. West

ELECTRONICS SECTOR

The gap between Polish and Western companies is probably larger in the electronics sector than in any other industry. However, Poland possesses two key assets to attract investors to develop local research, assembly or manufacturing in electronics: market potential and high level of competence of its engineers. Education in electronics has been relatively well-developed, and Poland has significant electronics industry R&D base. Also, there is a large number of institutes which work on industry projects. Most of the research institutions are concentrated in Warsaw. The sector consists of four subsectors: telecommunications equipment, consumer electronics, data processing, and components.

Telecommunications equipment market: $800 million; predicted growth 30 percent yearly; U.S. exports $45 million.

U.S. firms: AT&T acquired SOE Telfa, producer of digital equipment, which employs 1600 persons.

Computer market: hardware $1.3 billion; U.S. exports $60 million; software $500 million; US exports $100 million (the adoption of an Intellectual Property Law covering the protection of software and enforcement actions dramatically changed the situation in the software market for U.S. trade marks).

U.S. firms: Apple Computer, Compaq, Dell Com Poland, IBM, Wise Technology.

International Fair of Electronics, Telecommunication, Computer Engineering - Poznan, April

LABORATORY AND SCIENTIFIC EQUIPMENT

Market: $400 million; predicted growth 15 percent yearly; U.S. exports $40 million. The largest R&D sector in Central Europe.

HEALTH SECTOR, MEDICAL EQUIPMENT

Industry prospect: although the state health care system is still dominant, the real boom is observed in the establishment of small private clinics, out-patient facilities and various specialized doctors' offices. Emerging new health care insurance instruments will stimulate development of the private medical sector. The public sector medical equipment industry consists of 21 enterprises with more than 200 employees, and hundreds of small firms and large corporations in the electronic, optical and metal industries which include medical equipment in their production palette. Opportunities for American business are in cooperation, investment and trade -- in both services and production.

Market : $400 million; predicted growth 30 percent yearly; U.S. exports $50 million.

PHARMACEUTICAL INDUSTRY

The value of pharmaceuticals consumed in Poland is over $1.5 billion a year. Some 80 percent of this demand is covered by Polish producers in volume terms, but in value terms, some 50 percent is covered by imports. Still, 15 big SOEs accounted for 65 percent of total country production. Privatization of the SOEs opens new perspectives for foreign investors. The pharmaceutical sector also consists of a dozen pharmaceutical cooperatives and more than 1,000 small private manufacturers.

Market : $1.5 billion; predicted growth 20 percent yearly; U.S. exports $30 million

U.S. firms: Eli Lilly, Pfizer, Rhone-Poulenc (USA)

International Medical Fair - Europe's biggest medical technology trade exhibition; Poznan, March

STRATEGIC BUSINESS AND INVESTMENT OPPORTUNITIES

MARKET REFORMS AND SELECTED INVESTMENT OPPORTUNITIES:

Privatization has been slow, especially in what the Polish Government regards as "strategic sectors": banking, insurance, telecommunications, mining, steel, defense, transportation, energy and broadcasting. A bill passed by parliament in the summer of 1995 gave much of the authority for privatization to the Parliament and emphasized "commercialization," turning State enterprises into treasury-owned joint stock companies before truly privatizing them.

New privatization plans for 1998 include: banks, the copper holding company KGHM Miedz, the national airline LOT, the telecom monopoly TPSA, oil and gas company NAFTA Polska, iron and steel works, the spirits sector, and a series of power generation plants. In 1999, Polish Oil & Gas Company, insurance sector and sugar plants will be privatized. Privatization of the chemical sector (from retailing group of Cefarms through pharmaceutical to synthetic fertilizers) and trade entities and distribution chains (Domy Centrum, Orbis, Ruch) started in 1996 will continue. In 1996 companies under the Mass Privatization Program moved closer to privatization, and in fact many of them were sold to strategic investors. The National Investment Funds, which manage the Mass Privatization firms, have been listed on the Warsaw Stock Exchange as of June 2004.

The government of the United States acknowledges the contribution that outward foreign direct investments make to the U. S. economy. U.S. foreign direct investment is increasingly viewed as a complement or even a necessary component of trade. For example, roughly 60 % of U.S. exports are sold by American firms that have operations abroad. Recognizing the benefits that U.S. outward investment brings to the U.S. economy, the government of the United States undertakes initiatives, such as Overseas Private Investment Corporation (OPIC) programs, investment treaty negotiations and business facilitation programs, that support U.S. investors.

BANKING AND FINANCIAL SERVICES

The post-1989 reforms of the banking and financial sector led to the Polish National Bank NBP being divided into nine medium size regional banks for eventual privatization. Three are already private, two are currently being privatized, and the other four should be privatized before the year 2,000. At the same time changes in banking laws have allowed foreign investors to operate in this market. Currently 13 foreign banks are licensed to operate in Poland, and another 38 have branch offices.

A logical trend towards consolidation of the banking industry has begun in the past year with mergers between Polish banks and some acquisitions of Polish banks by foreign banks. The consolidation has also involved insurance companies and will likely lead to major financial institutions being created.

According to international financial experts, the Polish banking market is likely to be the fastest growing in Europe over the next five years. During this period, average real annual growth rates in Polish zloty terms are forecasted to be 13% to 15% - for the assets of Polish banks, and 16% to 18% - for retail deposits. According to international consulting firms, the number of permanent users of banking services is increasing at the rate of 2% yearly, and is already at 30% of households. It is still far from the approx. 80% usage rate of Germany, making it a promising market for those who enter it.

Due to rapid development and reorganization of the Polish financial market, to meet international standards and competitiveness, investment in financial services is considered a best prospect.

INSURANCE

The Polish insurance market continues to be liberalized. As of January 1, 1999, insurance companies located outside Poland will be allowed to sell their policies directly into Poland. There are 45 licensed insurance companies including 18 with foreign capital. Of the 45, 15 are in the life-insurance business and 30 in the non-life business. In 1996, non-life insurance companies collected almost USD 1.8 billion in premiums, while life insurance companies collected USD 925 million a 50% increase over 1995.

PZU S.A., (Panstwowy Zaklad Ubezpieczen), still dominates the Polish market with about 65% of the market and revenues in 1996 more than USD 1.1 billion. PZU and WARTA the two largest insurance companies are still state owned and privatization is not expected to be completed before 1999.

Poland is the biggest insurance market in Central and Eastern Europe. Strong economic development, a decreasing level of inflation and the progressive adjustment of legal regulations to E.U. directives create a good climate for investment opportunities in the insurance sector. Competition from foreign investors and the preparation towards a fully open and free market has started a trend towards consolidation in which large banks are taking part.

POWER INDUSTRY

Poland's total primary energy consumption of 95 million tons of energy (toe) in 1995 ranks it as number one in energy consumption among the Central and Eastern European countries. The Polish electrical power sector consists presently of three subsectors: generation, transmission and distribution, and as a system it is the largest in Central and Eastern Europe.

Power is generated in 56 thermal power plants, of which 33 are combined power and heat plants. The installed generating capacity of the power stations is 33,000 MW. In 1996 the gross domestic production of electricity reached 136,000 Gwh. The sector is currently undergoing significant changes as it prepares for demonopolization.

The Polish electrical power sector is in dire need of modernization and refurbishment in order to create an economically efficient industry capable of providing national energy requirements. The cost of modernization over the next fifteen years is estimated at USD 50 billion. Modernization is needed to replace 16 gigawatts of obsolete installed capacity and to satisfy stricter ecological standards due to come into effect in 1998. Out of this amount, USD 15 billion is needed for the modernization of existing power plants. A substantial portion of the modernization cost will be covered by the income generated from privatizing the power enterprises.

The major trends in the power generation sector include liberalization of the electric energy market, demonopolization, and privatization of energy sector enterprises. In April 2004 Poland's Parliament passed a new Energy Law. The Law creates a solid legal framework for a competitive energy market based on Third Party Access and a licensing system. In addition, an independent regulatory entity will be established to ensure competition within the energy sector.

The new Energy Law opens the way to privatization of power generation enterprises, and places Poland's energy sector on equal footing with more liberal European countries. The Law safeguards and facilitates foreign investment in Poland's energy sector, which over the next 5-6 years will lead to the development of an electricity market.

Eventually, prices for power producers, distributors, and trading companies will no longer be set by the Polish government, but rather verified by the electricity exchange and contract market. The Energy Regulatory Agency, which will be established, will only supervise the compliance with licence and market rules.

Multilateral lending institutions such as the World Bank and the European Bank for Reconstruction and Development are interested in investing in Poland's power sector. The EBRD is focusing on joint venture arrangements in large turbines, gas-fired turbines and hydro turbines, as the best opportunities in the sector. The World Bank is also heavily involved in financing in the Polish power sector, including modernization projects within power generation, transmission and distribution.

OIL AND GAS INDUSTRY

In the 1980s the Polish oil and gas industries were combined into a single legal and economic entity, the Polish Oil and Gas Company (POGC). This was done in order to improve coordination and efficiency of gas supplies from the domestic sources with supplies from imports. In recent years, POGC has been undergoing an economic and legal transformation, which has caused a restructuring of the oil and gas industry's role within the Polish economy.

Currently, POGC is the only producer of oil (very marginal) and natural gas in the territory of Poland. The POGC holds a monopoly on the importation, transmission, storage and distribution of natural gas. In order to reduce the overwhelming dependence on domestic coal and imports of gas, Poland intends to develop exploration and production of methane gas from hard coal deposits in Silesia. In 1991, licensing was made available to foreign companies for oil and gas exploration and production in Poland. Several U.S. and foreign oil & gas companies are involved in the exploration of methane, natural gas and oil in Poland.

According to government forecasts, by 2010 gas consumption will increase to 22-27 billion cubic meters annually (USD 11 billion today). To meet the increasing requirements for gas, Poland is participating in the construction of a transit gas pipeline from Siberia to Western Europe. On September 26, 1996, the Polish Oil and Gas Company and Russian Gazprom signed a contract for delivery of 250 billion cubic meters of natural gas over the next 25 years through the Yamal pipeline. Annual shipments will amount to 14 billion cubic meters of natural gas.

The implementation of an investment of this type will create the need for distribution systems and gas-storage capacity. The construction of two underground storage facilities are in the process.

Several others are planned to be built according to the bid procedure opened to foreign companies.

The Polish oil industry has been designated by the Polish Government as one of the sectors which is of strategic importance for national security. The domestic refining industry only partly meets the demand for oil products; approximately 20% of liquid fuels are imported. The oil sector, both production and distribution, require substantial investments to be competitive with the rest of the world.

Major problems faced by the petroleum industry in Poland include lack of capital, obsolete technology, poor energy efficiency, excessive use of raw materials, low utilization of existing capacity (below 80 %) and burdens on the environment.

The majority of installations and refineries in use today were constructed in the sixties and seventies and need modernization. The two largest refineries, Plock and Gdansk, are embarking on modernization programs worth more than USD 1.5 billion. The Plock and Gdansk refineries are eager to use U.S. technology, which enjoys an excellent reputation among Polish specialists, in their modernization investments. In addition, there is a need for additional storage capacity for fuel reserves.

The government has signed agreements with the World Bank and the European Investment Bank on loans for the energy sector. A substantial part of the loans to Poland were allocated for technological development in the oil and gas sector. The gas extraction industry was recognized as a key element in the restructuring of the overall national economy and the protection of the natural environment. Out of a total of USD 310 million allocated, some USD 200 million will be used for technical restructuring in the oil industry, including the purchase of new equipment for geophysics, drilling and production installations.

THE YAMAL-EUROPE TRANSIT GAS PIPELINE CONSTRUCTION

The Yamal-Western Europe transit gas pipeline, more than 4,000 km long, will carry natural gas supplies from the richest Siberian reserves to Germany and other Western European countries across the territories of Russia, Belarus and Poland. This enormous investment project is estimated at USD 35 billion.

The Polish and Russian governments negotiated the details of the pipeline construction, which resulted in an agreement signed in August 1994. According to this agreement, a tendering process will select construction companies and suppliers, primarily from Polish and Russian bidders, on a strictly competitive basis. Other international companies will be considered if neither Polish nor Russian companies qualify.

The Polish section of the gas pipeline is designed, constructed and managed by EuRoPol GAZ S.A., a joint-venture founded in September 1993 between the State-held Polish Oil and Gas Company (48 %), Russian Gazprom (48 %) and a Polish company, Gas Trading S.A. (4 %). EuRoPol GAZ S.A. will be the owner of the Polish section of the gas pipeline.

The construction cost of the Polish section of the pipeline is estimated at USD 2.5 billion, making it the largest infrastructure investment in Poland to date. The Polish section of the pipeline will run from Kondratki, on the Polish border with Belarus, to the German border town of Gorzyca and will carry 65.7 BCM of natural gas. Additionally, two parallel gas pipelines are planned, each 665 km long. The first pipeline will become fully operational in 1999, along with five compressor stations.

The second line will be completed in 2010. The construction of both lines is divided into several parts.

The construction of the first 107 kilometer long stretch of the pipeline going from Gorzyca on the Polish-German border to Lwowek near Poznan was completed in October 1996. The general contractor selected for this USD 400 million segment of the project was a consortium of five Polish energy and gas construction companies. The consortium was selected by EuRoPol GAZ through a tendering process. Construction of the second part of the pipeline, from Lwowek to Wloclawek has already started and will be performed by the same consortium. Although the general contractor has been selected, there are still opportunities for U.S. providers of relevant materials and equipment not available from Polish or Russian companies.

In November 1996, EuRoPol GAZ S.A. announced the tender for construction of the first two, out of a total of five, compressor stations for the pipeline. There was an invitation for submitting pre-qualified bids for turn-key operations of the Wloclawek and Kondradki compressor stations. As a result of this announcement, a short list of eight qualified companies was prepared. Companies included in this list are currently negotiating with EuRoPol GAZ.

EuRoPol GAZ S.A.
Mr. Jerzy Adamczyk, President
Aleja Stan¢w Zjednoczonych 61
04-028 Warsaw
tel: (48-22) 13-25-85
fax: (48-22) 13-34-75

RESTRUCTURING AND PRIVATIZATION OF THE POLISH OIL INDUSTRY

The oil sector generates 8.5% of Poland's gross domestic product and over USD 400 million of profit. The petroleum industry needs restructuring in order to successfully face foreign competition which will result from the reduction of fuel import quotas and customs barriers. The total cost of restructuring is estimated at USD 3 billion. To pay for modernization, the Government of Poland plans to offer shares in two major Polish refineries Plock and Gdansk to strategic foreign investors.

According to the governmental program for oil sector restructurization, the state-owned joint stock company called Nafta Polska S.A. was created in 1996. Nafta Polska S.A. holds minority stakes in the strategic companies of the petroleum sector, including all seven refineries, the oil transportation company DEC, and the former monopoly gasoline distributor and retailer CPN. Each of the relevant enterprises comprises an independent joint-stock company, in which the treasury holds a strategic block of shares.

Nafta Polska S.A. is responsible for the supervision and implementation of the government's program for oil sector restructurization and privatization. The government's program provides for the sale of shares in the two largest refineries: Plock Petrochemical Complex and Gdansk Refinery. The Plock refinery has already merged with Trzebinia refinery (one of five small southern refineries) and the Gdansk refinery has merged with another southern refinery, Jedlicze. The aim is to create two competitive profit centers around these refineries.

Three remaining southern refineries - Jaslo, Gorlice and Czechowice - will be privatized separately. In the case of Czechowice, the prospective investor is requested to expand the plant's processing capacity to 2 million tons and participate in financing for the petrochemical segment of the planned Poludnie complex. Before privatization, refineries will be assigned shares in CPN, the leading (previously monopolistic) fuel distributor, in proportion to their production capacity. Plock and Gdansk will receive respectively 33% and 12.375% of CPN shares. This will give oil concerns direct access to Poland's wholesale and retail fuel market.

In 2004, Nafta Polska S.A. sent out a privatization memorandum to about forty international (European, U.S., Russian and Far East) oil concerns. The memorandum was sent exclusively to strong international oil concerns, vertically integrated and having their own oil fields. Investors are expected to guarantee continuous oil shipments from their fields at a competitive price, to integrate the refineries distribution networks with their own, and transfer new technology and management techniques. Polish banks, financial institutions and other domestic companies may enter the scene, at a later date. However, they are welcome to participate in the privatization of the three smaller Southern refineries (Gorlice, Jaslo, Czechowice).

At the first stage, foreign investors will be offered up to a 30% stake in the two refinery groups. There is a possibility that an investor may take more than a 50% interest. This option is linked with a previously agreed upon increase in capital and the implementation of an investment program. By June 2004, Nafta Polska S.A. is scheduled to have selected a privatization advisor, who will work on economic, financial and law analysis for the privatization of Gdansk and Plock refinery groups.

Nafta Polska S.A.
Mr. Marek Foltynowicz, Board Member
ul. Jasna 12
00-013 Warsaw
tel. (48)(22) 827-08-76
fax. (48)(22) 827-31-05

TOURISM DEVELOPMENT

According to the World Bank and International Monetary Fund reports, the Polish tourism industry has great potential to contribute to the restructurization of the national economy and Poland's competitiveness in the European market. The PHARE TOURIN funds have been assigned by the European Community to support development of the Polish tourism sector.

Poland possesses adequate assets and tourist attractions as well as a sufficiently developed network of tourist services. Poland's diversified natural conditions provide a potential for tourism in the mountain regions, at the seaside, in the lake districts and in the country. However, tourism and hotel infrastructure is still underdeveloped. Approximately 40% of foreign loans rendered to Polish entities have been invested in tourism. The foreign capital engaged in the Polish tourism sector amounted to USD 1 billion in 1996. Visitors to Poland totaled almost 100 million in 1996. The privatization of the tourism industry is systematically increasing, as is the commercialization of the tourist accommodation base.

There is a strong demand for new hotels in Poland, especially in large cities. Orbis S.A., the leading Polish travel agency and owner of the largest hotel chain in Poland is in the process of privatization. There will be a new stock issue in the spring of 2004, which will raise Orbis stock capital by 40% from the present USD 25 million. The Orbis S.A. management plans that the bulk of the new issue should go to a strategic investor. Currently, Orbis S.A. is a holding company, including Orbis Travel, Orbis Transport and Orbis Hotels. Orbis Travel is Poland's largest foreign travel agency, Orbis Transport owns a fleet of buses and represents the Hertz car rental company in Poland. Orbis Hotels owns the largest chain of hotels in Poland, 54 in all. Orbis Hotels are valued at USD 250-300 million and account for some 90% of Orbis profit. Orbis Hotels generates

60% of its income from 10 hotels located in large cities. The company needs to spend USD 150 million in order to upgrade its hotel facilities.

Several international hotel brands have developed high class hotels in large Polish cities recently (Marriott and Sheraton). Holiday Inn Worldwide this year signed a franchise agreement with a Polish company, Global Hotels Development Group Poland S.A.(GHDG) to develop 20 hotels in Poland within 10 years. The total investment is estimated at USD 116 million and will include construction of four luxury Crowne Plaza hotels, ten Holiday Inn Express hotels at USD 5 million each, and four standard Holiday Inn hotels at USD 12 to USD 18 million each. GHDG also plans to modernize existing hotels and introduce them into the Holiday Inn chain.

There is a tremendous need to develop moderate tourist standard accommodations in Poland to meet European and world standards. Moreover, investments in leisure activities - ski lifts, tennis courts, open and indoor swimming pools, golf courses, bowling centers - is desperately needed.

RAIL AND ROAD TRANSPORTATION

Poland's transportation network, suffering from years of neglect (only 15% of roads can be classified as good quality, some 50% of roads are not in satisfactory condition and need immediate upgrading work, and 35% are considered very poor) is in dire need of upgrade and refurbishment. To help meet this need Poland has planned a new system of toll roads operating alongside the already existing transportation infrastructure.

The program plans for approximately 2,500 km of motorways to be built in Poland over the next 15 years at a total cost of an estimated USD 8 billion. The plan, approved by the Parliament in 1994, provides for the construction of four highways. They will channel traffic between Western Europe and Poland's eastern neighbors and connect the Baltic coast with the southern borders. Each segment of the highway will be built individually by prime contractors.

The highway routes were selected on the basis of traffic volume. Tollways will be built under a license, Build Operate Transfer (BOT), with both private and public investors as participants in forming a consortia. The financing arrangements of the consortia (highway owners) will differ, but the government will cover the costs of buying land. Significant financial contributions will come from international financial institutions (EBRD and World Bank). The first tenders have been announced and the first contracts have been signed.

The Consortia consists of design offices and project managers, contractors and sub-contractors. Beyond direct involvement in highway construction, other opportunities are emerging. The program will have a snowball effect in terms of hotels/motels, restaurants, service stations, and other road infrastructure.

The contracting authority is:
The Agency for Construction and Operation of Motorways
(Agencja Budowy I Eksploatacji Autostrad)
Mr. Andrzej Patalas, President
ul. Chalubinskiego 4/6
00-928 Warsaw
tel: (48-22) 24-43-65
fax: (48-22) 30-05-84

The importance of railways in Western Europe has a significant effect on the development and modernization of rail transportation in Poland. Poland's location forces integration of a portion of the Polish railway network with the European transportation system. Its integration with the European network and competitiveness with international traffic requires a higher standard of service in both passenger and freight transportation.

The share of railways in the transport of goods in Poland is now approximately 50%. The share of mixed, road and rail, transport is very low due to underdeveloped computer systems and lack of appropriate platforms, rolling stock for the transport of semi-trailers or containers and the lack of equipment for container handling. However, mixed transport has the best prospects for growth in Poland.

The Polish State Railways (PKP) is the third largest railway in Europe in terms of line length with 25,000 kilometers of rail, but in terms of quality of equipment and service it is far behind E.U. countries. About 60-80% of PKP's rolling stock is outdated and needs modernization.

The Polish railway modernization project involves modernization of the main railway line from Warsaw to Kunowice (German border). The project will include the purchase of track rehabilitation machinery, signaling cables, power supply cables, signaling equipment, steel parts for standard turnouts, as well as hot and flat wheel detection equipment. The projects estimated value is USD 580 million. A financial contribution of USD 60 million will come from the EBRD. Other international agencies will provide USD 275 million.

The agency responsible for this project and its contracting authority is:
PKP CBZIS "FERPOL"
Mr. Andrzej Blasiak
ul. Grojecka 17
00-973 Warsaw
tel: (48-22) 22-14-30
fax: (48-22) 22-26-28

CHEMICAL INDUSTRY

The chemical industry in Poland continued to grow in 1996, production figures increased in all branches of the industry and in all groups of chemical enterprises. The production of soaps and detergents increased by almost 49%. The production of some other chemical products (explosives, photo-chemical products, glues, products for clothing, leather and textile industries) rose by 44% and rubber products by almost 35%. Production rose significantly in artificial fertilizers (the increase was due to the introduction of quotas for ammonium nitrate and carbamide imported from the ex-Soviet countries, where it is much cheaper). The lowest growth was observed in the production of pharmaceuticals (2%), paints and lacquers (4.9%), and pesticides (7.8%).

A new program for modernization and privatization of the Polish chemical industry calls for 105 investment ventures through the year 2005 for a total value USD 3 billion. It is expected that 30% of the financing will come from Polish chemical companies, 20% will come from a Polish investment consortia, and 50% from foreign investors.

Predictions of sales in the chemical industry in Poland in the next few months are also optimistic. Almost all Polish chemical firms expect sales to grow in 1998. Interested companies may wish to keep in contact with:

Polish Chamber of Chemical Industry
Mr. Maciej Szczawnicki, Director

ul. Zurawia 6/12
Warsaw
tel/fax: (48-22) 625-3178

ENVIRONMENTAL INDUSTRY

The environmental services sector has only recently emerged in Poland's growing market economy, and is in a stage of flux. The new Polish environmental strategy emphasizes the principle of sustainable development. It encourages firms to rely on clean technologies, pollution prevention and waste minimization in designing their production process. It discourages "end-of-the-pipe" control technologies.

Poland faces enormous environmental challenges, but this dilemma also represents opportunities for western companies with the equipment, advanced technology and know-how that Poland requires. The most promising areas are: air pollution control, wastewater treatment, waste disposal, and recycling technology. The importance of the environmental sector is widely recognized by Polish authorities and strongly supported by international financial institutions.

Credit lines are available for environmental protection investments on preferential conditions, thanks to funds provided by internal sources as well as the World Bank, European Bank for Reconstruction and Development and others. Poland adopted the "polluter pays" principle. The fees and fines for the use and the pollution of the environment are being collected by the National and Regional Funds for Environmental Protection and Water Management. These Funds offer preferential loans for environmental projects.

Total spending on environmental protection in Poland rose during the last six years from $580 million in 1990 to $1.4 billion in 1994 and to $2.0 billion in 1996 (1.6% of GDP).

AUTOMOTIVE INDUSTRY

Auto sales in Poland in 1996 saw a record high. Production increased by 20% and the sales of new cars (373,540 units) jumped by 41.54% compared to 1995. The automotive industry represents not only a great sales opportunity, but is also a very good investment opportunity. Several companies have already decided to take advantage of that by locating either production or assembly plants in Poland. Major investors include Fiat, Daewoo, GM-Opel, Ford, Volkswagen, Peugeot, Scania and Volvo. The auto parts industry is also very promising for potential investors. Auto parts companies invest in Poland to supply their clients as parts suppliers. The majority of the investors in car production commit themselves to sourcing their parts in Poland, not from abroad.

TELECOMMUNICATIONS

The Polish telecommunications sector is a key industry and a major part of Poland's infrastructure. Although the Polish telephone network is growing at 15% a year, the Polish infrastructure is far behind other European countries with 16.9 telephones per 100 inhabitants. Over USD 1 billion will have to be spent to reach the total of 10 million telephone subscribers by the year 2000. A further USD 14 billion will be invested in 2001-2005, and an additional USD 17.5 billion by the year 2010.

International and long-distance telephone service is controlled by the national telephone operator, Telekomunikacja Polska S.A. (TPSA). The Polish government has committed to open these markets to other companies with a majority of Polish capital not later than January 1, 1999 for long-distance services and 2003 for international services.

Investment opportunities for foreign companies currently exist in local telephone services and value added services. Tenders for local telephone services are planned in six areas for 2004, government policy calls for the installation of independent operators, besides TPSA, in Poland. In addition to the existing NMT 450 and two GSM cellular networks, a tender for an 1800 digital network is in the process, with a July 14, 2004 deadline for filing bidding offers. After July 1, 1998, additional concessions for providing telecommunication services in GSM 900 MHZ and DCS 1800 MHZ standards will be issued as these frequencies become available, with preferences given to dual-modem GSM/DCS systems.

The Polish government has approved the plan for privatization of Telekomunikacja Polska S.A. (TPSA), the national telephone operator. A detailed privatization plan is currently being prepared by the Ministry of Treasury and the Ministry of Post and Telecommunications. The privatization will start in 1998 with the sale of 10-25% shares on domestic and international stock exchanges. The current estimated value of TPSA is USD 15-25 billion. A strategic investor might be selected in the next stage of privatization.

A new telecommunications law that would comply with E.U. standards is currently being drafted and is due to be voted on by the parliament in 1998.

COMPUTERS AND PERIPHERALS

The Polish computer market (HS 8471) is growing at approximately 30% per year. Total expenditures on information technology products in 1994 are estimated at $884 million. Out of this amount $408 million were spent on personal computers, and $120 million on printers, $100 million on system integration, $146 on software.

The personal computer market is dominated by foreign manufacturers offering well-known trademarks with competition from only a few Polish manufacturers, although Polish companies' production doubled last year. Many opportunities exist for computer printers and other peripherals.

The fact that in 1995 Poles, for the first time, are able to write off from their personal taxes purchases of computers for private use (when justified by their profession) is expected to stimulate the market further.

Note: Statistical data are scarce and it substantially varies year to year, which limits the continuity and integrity of data gathering. The total market size is estimated from data provided by companies, based on their financial reports. Export/Import data was provided by the Central Statistical Office. Local production data were not readily available. It should be noted that computers produced locally are assembled from imported components and parts.

COMPUTER SOFTWARE

Figures concerning the market size of the computer software industry (HS 852490) are estimates, calculated on reported companies' sales. Introduction of the intellectual property law improves computer software protection, but it hasn't resulted yet in massive growth for software sales. Software sold in Poland has to be adopted to local requirements. The role of domestic production is substantially increasing.

The increase of computer software sales is stimulated by general growth of computers, computer networking in many companies and organizations, and upsizing of data bases management systems. The software distribution system is consolidating. Two large software distribution companies, DHI and MSP, merged with foreign companies (German Computer 2000 and Czech TH System) in 1994.

The data for official computer software export/import are not precise as only the media, not its content, is subject to statistics.

MEDICAL EQUIPMENT

Comments: (HS 9018, 9019, 9020, 9021, 9022) The public health sector is totally financed from the national budget and heavily burdened by severe budgetary restrictions. However, loans are available from the World Bank and PHARE. The private sector is growing, but not as fast as it was previously expected.

All purchases of medical equipment for public hospitals are done through a competitive bidding process. Private hospitals can purchase medical equipment independently from any source they wish. The medical equipment (new and used) for use in public hospitals and/or medical centers has to be tested and receive a certification from the appropriate Polish authority.

The competitive position of Polish manufacturers is rather weak due to the high production costs, lack of modern technology, medium to low quality products and lack of marketing. American equipment has a good reputation for high quality and reliability among Polish doctors. Other sale-making factors are short delivery terms and after-sale service.

POLLUTION CONTROL EQUIPMENT

Poland, with a population of 39 million, is the largest single environmental market in Central Europe. Solving air, soil, and water pollution problems is a big priority for the Polish government. Since 1985 environmental investments have increased more than two and a half times as a percentage of GDP reaching 1.3 percent of GDP in 1992. Despite a difficult economic context, Poland has been very successful in organizing environmental financing through fees and fines, adopting a "polluter pays" principle.

The privatization process creates investments, and the market for environmental protection and pollution control equipment, more attractive. During privatization processes, companies not only must evaluate their existing performance, assets, obligations etc., but also must to prepare business plans for their future development. Vital to those business plans are issues concerning environmental protection which are enforced by high penalties for pollution.

The market for pollution control equipment (HS 8421) has grown steadily over the last few years and is expected to grow even more. U.S. exports of pollution control equipment to Poland have grown significantly and more than expected in the years 1993 and 1994. U.S. products are considered of the best quality, however they face serious competition from European suppliers, especially German (ranked 1st), Swedish (ranked 2nd), and Italian (ranked 3rd). U.S. is ranked 4th when it comes to exports to Poland.

Competitiveness of products offered by European producers is based on lower shipping costs and lower duty rates for EU suppliers. U.S. companies may take advantage of widened duty-free quotas for some of the products under HS 8421 expected for 1996.

TELECOMMUNICATIONS

The Polish telecommunication sector (HS 8517) is a key industry and a major part of Poland's infrastructure. The Polish telephone network is growing 12% a year. More than five hundred thousand telephones were hooked up in 1994 and 800,000 are planned for 1995. Three thousand six hundred kilometers of fibre optic cables and 2240 kilometers of digital communication radio lines were laid in 1994. Telekomunikacja Polska S.A. (TPSA) invested almost $500 million in 1994. Total telecommunication investments may reach as high as $15 billion in the next five years.

More than 50 licenses were granted for new local telephone operators. A tender for two Global System Mobility (GSM) digital cellular networks will take place in late 1995.

All equipment hooked to public networks has to be certified by the Polish telecommunication authorities. Polish law requires at least 50% percent of local content in telephone networks. The only switching equipment approved for use in Poland is AT&T, Alcatel and Siemens (companies that invested in existing telecommunication plants).

BUILDING PRODUCTS

The size and shape of the building products market in Poland is directly linked to key investment programs. These include housing construction, conversion to new energy-saving heat systems, government programs for highways, a gas pipeline, and industrial privatization. Some of these programs will receive financing from the World Bank, which will help in developing this industry sector. Demand for building materials is expected to continue to grow for the next decade. Major projects in Poland will contribute to the growth of the market. It is also expected that the housing sector, now showing a downward trend, is going to pick up with new financing recently introduced. There is a shortage of 1.4 million housing units in Poland and new building technologies are sought. American companies constitute strong competition for construction companies from Germany, Italy and Belgium. The number of American companies representing this industry sector is still rather low, compared with American companies representing other industry sectors.

A program to build a network of national highways is planned to start in late 1995. In the next 15 years over 2,500 km of roads will be built in Poland and Poland will join the network of modern motorways of Europe. Polish construction companies are not well-equipped to serve this project, and there will be likely be a market for foreign contractors, subcontractors, or manufacturers who have specialized equipment for building roads. The market for building materials and equipment is expected to grow due to this project and investments associated with it, like the construction of infrastructure around the highways.

BROADCASTING EQUIPMENT

This is a best prospect for US exporters due to two factors: the development of a private TV sector and a general trend in Polish TV companies towards technologies in which U.S. companies are world pioneers or leaders, such as disk based production and post production systems, and computer graphics. The entire broadcasting sector in Poland is dependent on imports.

The major US competitors are Japanese companies -- Sony, Panasonic, and JVC. Together with the German-French BTS they hold about 80 percent of the camera and VCR market. Other foreign companies present in the market are: American - Ampex, Grass Valley, Tektronix and

Avid Technology; German - Rhode Schwartz; as well as others - Ikegami, Sachtler, AKG, Sencheiser, and Reiche & Vogel. Both technological superiority and cost-effective solutions are considered essential factors in making a sale. Reasonable terms of payment, short delivery terms and after-sale service are also very important competitive factors.

Statistical data from the General Statistical Office is not useful in determining the market size of this subsector because available numbers include electronic consumer goods and all of the telecommunications industry. The information has been compiled based on research and interviews with major TV broadcasting companies, production houses and telecommunication companies. and should be considered estimates.

FITNESS AND RECREATIONAL EQUIPMENT

Polish distributors or representative companies represent numerous well- known West European and American sporting goods brands in the Polish market. Poles prefer to buy imported sporting goods. Foreign brands have an appealing image, especially among the younger population. It is estimated that during next three years imports will rise 30% annually.

Imported sporting goods are the basic source of supply for the Polish market. In 1994 imported products accounted for 88% of the total market. Local production, comprised mainly of bicycles and sports apparel, is for the most part (90% of production) exported to Western European countries.

There is strong competition among companies supplying the Polish market with sporting goods, and these companies constantly work to gain market share. Price is very important but not the only factor in who gets the business. Equally important are trade marks and reputations, which can give an edge to U.S. companies with well known brands.

American sporting goods enjoy great popularity and excellent reputations in Poland, resulting in great potential for sales of U.S. products in Poland. Major U.S. imports into Poland in 1994 were: sports footwear, sports apparel, fishing equipment and bicycles. It is estimated that the U.S. share of imports will increase at the rate of 10%.

In the next three years, the following sporting goods are expected to have the best sales prospects: mountain and all-terrain bikes, sports footwear, tennis rackets, sportswear, fitness and exercise equipment, and in- line roller skates (roller blades). Bikes are absolutely number 1, both as far as imports and local manufacturing are concern. According to polls, bicycles were in third place for durable consumer products bought by Poles in 1993.

MINING INDUSTRY

Mineral resources in Poland include:

a) energy sources: natural gas , oil, brown and hard coal; b) metallic minerals: zinc, lead, copper, iron; c) chemical minerals: barite, sulphur, potassium and magnesium salt, halite; d) rock minerals: twenty two different petrographic varieties.

Although production has fallen recently, the long term prospects for the mining industry in Poland remain good. Hard coal and brown coal mining is a backbone of the Polish economy, providing fuel for more than 90% of electricity generated. Mining of copper, sulphur, halite and potassium salt is also very important. Current mining production is substantially smaller than several years ago as recession and falling prices in the mineral markets have caused a decrease in production.

Currently the most urgent task facing the mining industry is continued restructuring and privatization, which will require considerable investment. The essential task is to increase the competitiveness of Polish mines, by improving the quality of useful minerals extracted and reducing operating running costs. There are substantial reserves of useful minerals of all kinds in Poland. Existing mines are not well equipped, but are well organized and can compete with foreign mines thanks to relatively low wages. Based on World Bank forecasts for a tripling of world energy consumption for 1990-2030, there is a high probability that the Polish mining industry will grow significantly.

POWER INDUSTRY

Between 1945 and 1990, the Polish power industry was centrally controlled by the government and influenced heavily by its integration with the Comecon countries' power systems. After 1989 the Ministry of industry started to define a restructuring program for the power industry as well as for the energy sector as a whole. In mid 1992 three fundamental goals of power supply policy in Poland were established:

a) inexpensive power supply without governments subsidies b) secure power supply c) improved environmental protection

To accomplish these goals the power industry was separated into three subsystems: generation, transmission, and distribution. The Polish Power Grid Company, responsible for transmission, was founded in 1990. Electric power is generated in 56 thermal powerplants, of which 33 are combined heat and power plants.

In June 1991 the government of Poland and the World Bank signed a Letter of Intent in which the structure for granting financial support for the restructuring process of the Polish power industry was established. Close cooperation between the World Bank and the Polish power sector began in May 1992. The World Bank is considering a total loan of about USD 1.3 billion. Part of the loan, the Private Sector Investment Fund, will be used to finance projects. The World Bank's procedures require international bidding.

At present regulatory functions within the power industry are performed by the Ministry of Industry and Trade (which is responsible among the other things for the entire energy sector in Poland), the Ministry of Finance, the Ministry of Environmental protection, and the Antimonopoly Office.

OIL AND GAS INDUSTRY

The Polish oil and gas industries began separately in the nineteenth century. In 1976 the government began to link the industries into a single legal and economic entity in order to improve coordination and efficiency of gas supplies from the domestic sources with supplies from imports. As a result, the Polish Oil and Gas Company (Polskie G¢rnictwo Naftowe i Gazowe - PGNiG) was created. In recent years, PGNiG has been undergoing economic and legal transformation, reconstructing the role and of the oil and gas industry within the Polish economy.

The government has signed agreements with the World Bank and the European Investment Bank on loans for the energy sector. A substantial part of the loans to Poland was allocated for technological development in the oil and gas sector. The gas extraction industry was recognized as a key elements in the restructuring of the overall national economy and the protection of the natural environment. Out of a total of USD 310 million allocated, some USD 200 million was used for technical restructuring in the oil industry, including the purchase of new equipment for geophysics and drilling and production installations.

Poland's reorientation towards Europe and the world economy, by signing the Association Agreement with the European Community and the Energy Charter, and forecasts of economic growth in Poland and an increase in demand for energy are convincing arguments for the necessity of finding new energy sources. Links to the Western European systems is inevitable. The first step in this process was the cross-border exchange link with Germany. The largest undertaking is the construction of a gas pipeline from Russia to Western Europe across Poland, which will also supply gas for Poland. The implementation of an investment of this type will create the need for distribution systems and gas-storage capacity.

RESTRUCTURING AND PRIVATIZATION OF THE POLISH OIL INDUSTRY

The oil sector generates 8.5 percent of Poland's gross domestic product and over USD 400 million of profit. The petroleum industry needs restructuring in order to successfully face foreign competition in 2004 when all fuel import quotas, customs barriers and licenses are scheduled to be abolished. The total cost of restructuring is estimated at USD 3 billion.

Over the last three years, Poland has worked on assorted programs for restructuring and privatizing the oil industry. At least three programs exist in draft, but none has been implemented. The latest program was approved by the Council of Ministers in May 1995, but a timetable for the restructuring process has not been set.

The program calls for the establishment of a 100% state-owned holding company called the "Polish Oil Company" PKN, which would hold minority stakes in the strategic companies of the petroleum industry, including all seven refineries, the Polish oil pipeline company PERN, the tank car companies DEC, and the former monopoly gasoline distributor and retailer CPN. Each of the relevant enterprises would comprise an independent joint-stock company, in which the treasury would hold a strategic block of shares.

To pay for modernization, the Government of Poland plans to offer 20-30 percent of shares of two major Polish refineries Plock and Gdansk to strategic foreign investors. Plock and Gdansk are embarking on modernization programs worth more than USD 1.5 billion.

The government agency responsible for the project is the Ministry of Industry and Trade.

Ministry of Industry and Trade ul. Wspolna 4 Warszawa Minister Klemens Scierski, GOP Plenipotentiary for creation of PKN tel. 48/2/628-01-82

RAIL AND ROAD TRANSPORTATION

The economic transformation of Poland has placed additional demand on the transportation network. Only 15% of roads can be classified as good quality, some 50% of roads are not in satisfactory condition and need immediate upgrading work, and 35% are considered very poor. Poland has planned a new system of roads operating alongside the already existing transportation infrastructure. Until now the system of roads was administered by the government, its representatives, and local authorities representing the treasury. The only way to improve the road system was to allow new entities (state-owned or private) to take over the responsibility of building new roads and developing associated infrastructure. The legal and administrative basis has been established to create new entities which will participate in the national Tollway Program.

The program plans that over next 15 years approximately 2,500 km of motorways will be built in Poland. The total cost is estimated at USD 4.8 billion. The highway routes were selected on the basis of traffic volume. Tollways will be built under a license system with both private and public investors as participants, forming consortia. The financing arrangement of consortia (highway owners) will differ, but the government will cover the cost of buying land. Significant financial contributions will come from international financial institutions (EBRD and World Bank).

Consortia will consist of design offices and project managers, contractors and sub-contractors. Beyond direct work involved in highway building, other opportunities are emerging. The program will have snowball effect in terms of hotels/motels, restaurants, service stations, and other road infrastructure.

The importance of railways in Western European countries has a significant effect on the development and modernization of rail transportation in Poland. Poland's location forces integration of a portion of the Polish railway network with the European transportation systems. Its integration with the European network and competitiveness with international traffic requires higher standard of service in both passenger and freight transportation. The Polish State Railways (PKP) is the third largest railway in Europe in terms of line length with 25,000 kilometers of rail, but in terms of quality of equipment and service it is far behind EU countries. About 60-80% of PKP's rolling stock is outdated and needs modernization.

POLISH TOBACCO INDUSTRY

The government of Poland plans to privatize the Polish tobacco industry by the end of 1995. The investment needs are estimated between USD 500 - USD 750 million. Polish tobacco executives look for investment in Polish plants which still rely on archaic machines and outdated technology, while the government hopes that western investors will also upgrade and improve the efficiency of tobacco farms and introduce modern cultivation technology.

By the end of the 1995, the government plans to sell five tobacco companies that together produced 83 billion cigarettes in 1994 earning USD 1 billion, and generated profits that are the envied by other Polish industries. The two remaining state-owned cigarette makers will be sold later. Poland is the last big tobacco privatization target in Central Europe. Hungary, the Czech Republic, Slovenia, Romania and Bulgaria have all privatized their tobacco industries.

There are 14 million regular smokers in Poland who buy more than 110-120 billion cigarettes annually. Most of the cigarettes come from seven state-run factories. Private domestic and foreign producers have licenses to produce up to 46 billion cigarettes a year in Poland, though they have not yet met this target.

BASIC LAWS AND REGULATIONS AFFECTING BUSUNESS

LEGISLATION AFFECTING FOREIGNERS

Transformation of the political and economic system has led to a significant increase in interest in Poland by foreigners, who more and more often pass through Polish frontiers not just for tourist reasons, but with the aim to conduct business. This raises a number of legal and tax issues which shall be discussed below. However, foreigners have to remember that the tax regulations to which they are subordinate are often incoherent and sometimes even contain internal contradictions. Tax offices are interpreting these regulations to the detriment of tax payers, so special care has to be exerted.

I. LEGAL AND ORGANIZATIONAL STATUS OF FOREIGNERS STAYING IN POLAND

A foreigner staying in Poland for more than 90 days is obliged to register at the competent Voviodship Administration Office. However, the 90 day requirement refers to a single stay. So, if a foreigner comes to Poland on a number of occasions, but in no case his stay will exceed 90 days, then he is not required to register at the Voviodship Administration Office.

However, within 3 days of passing the Polish frontier, a foreigner has to fill in a place of domicile registration form at the competent Commune Administration Office. This does not refer to a situation when he lives in a hotel or boarding house performing functions of a hotel, because in such case his registration is catered for by the hotel. However, if the foreigner rents a flat, then he has to be registered by the owner of such flat under the same address.

2. The foreigner may undertake employment in Poland, provided he obtains a visa entitling him to multiple transfer through the national frontier - symbol „06" with imprinted „with right to undertake employment", consent for employment of a foreigner and permit for his employment or vesting with him other paid work issued to the employer. The visa entitling to employment is applied for by the foreigner himself pursuant to the received from the employment office „promise of permission to undertake employment" issued to the employer and „consent for the given foreigner".

Violation of the above regulations is threatened with imposing of a fine both upon the foreigner as well as his employer.

An employer who receives the permission, has to make a „lump payment" to the Employment Fund in the amount equal to the lowest official salary for each person included in the permit.

The permits are issued for a fixed term. The legislator has not imposed upon employment offices with any maximum term for which a permit may be issued. However, this was imposed by the Minister of Labor in his „yearbooklines" where he introduced a maximum validity period of such permit to 12 months. Of course, the validity of the permit may be extended, but this requires a fee of one half of the fee initially required for issue of the permit.

Permission to employ a foreigner may be withdrawn, and this obliges the employer to terminate the contract of employment with the foreigner within 3 months of being notified thereof.

3. From the viewpoint of Polish legislation, status of foreigners depends on how long they remain in Poland and for who, and where they perform their employment duties. The following may be distinguished:

A. Employment of foreigners in Poland, which may take the form of:
a) work performed to benefit of a foreign entity conducting business in Poland
b) work performed to benefit of Polish entities
B. Employment of foreigners by Polish entities, which may take the form of:
a) employment to perform work in Poland
b) employment to perform work abroad.

The situation presented in Aa depends greatly on the legislation applicable in the country of the foreign entity to the benefit of which the foreigner is performing work in Poland. However, it is important whether a treaty on avoiding double taxation has been executed with the country in the territory of which the given employing foreign entity has its seat and whether such entity in relation to it business activities carried out in Poland operates a plant in the understanding of the provisions of such agreement and, finally, how long will such foreigner remain in Poland.

Thus, if such person would remain in Poland for more than 183 days in the given tax year, pursuant to the applicable Polish tax regulations he would become a Polish resident and would be subject to tax liability in Poland - with such liability being unlimited and including all such the entirety of his income, irrespectively of where the sources of revenue are placed.

However, if the foreigner remains in Poland for less than 183 days, he shall pay in Poland tax only on that part of income which he receives on title of his employment in Poland and, further, provided that his employer is operating a plant in Poland.

Definition of „plant" contained in individual international agreements on avoiding double taxation to which Poland is a signatory differa slightly one from another, but generally, a plant is considered to be a place of management, offices, factory, workshop, branch, representative office. Possession of a plant in Poland is deemed to include also the performing of building construction or assembly in Poland is the duration thereof is more than 12 months (with USA, the Netherlands and Norway - 18 months, with Austria - 24 months, with Greece - 9 months, with China, India, Malaysia and Thailand - 6 months). If the foreign entity employing a given foreigner does not have its plant in Poland and the foreigner stays for less than 183 days in Poland, he shall not be liable to pay any taxes in Poland.

The situation described in Bb, i.e. employment by Polish entities of foreigners to perform services abroad and paid for abroad is fully possible and neutral in respect to Polish tax regulations, provided that the foreigner such employed is not resident in Poland, i.e. does not have his permanent domiciled in Poland nor is staying in Poland for more than 183 days in the given tax year.

The situation described in Ab and Ba comprises the rendering of services by foreigners in Poland to Polish entities, in a variety of legal and organizational set-ups, based on applicable Polish laws and paid for in Poland in Polish Zloty. (Note that joint venture companies, even with 100% foreign shareholding having their seat in Poland are Polish entities and subject to Polish laws).

II. LEGAL FORMS OF PERFORMING BY FOREIGNERS OF WORK IN POLAND TO THE BENEFIT OF POLISH ENTITIES AND THE TAX CONSEQUENCES THEREOF

Each entity performing business in Poland is allows to employ also foreigners (provided its receives a permit to do so and the foreigner obtains a consent from the competent voivodship employment office) based on:

1) employment contract (regime set forth in the Labor Code, describing a dominating position of the employer, but giving the employee a number of social rights)

2) civil law agreement, e.g. task or job assignment (Civil Code regimewhich assumes equal position of both parties to the contract).

The various costs and tax liabilities of the employer and the employee will differ depending on whether the employment is based on a contract or assignment.
In case of an employment contract and task assignment lasting more than 15 days, it is necessary for the employer to perform payments to social security, unemployed protection fund and professional activation fund, in the overall amount of 48.2% of the salary paid.

In case of an employment contract, the social security (ZUS) rate is 45%, Labor Fund -3% and Guaranteed Employee Services Fund - 0.2% of the base (i.e. in practice, the salary paid). The employee is the payee of this total of 48.2%.
In case of the task assignment agreement ZUS rate is 40% and is paid in equal parts by both parties. Additionally, the contractor pays 0.2% into the Guaranteed Employee Services Fund and 3% to the Labor Fund. However, if the task assignment task is additional to the employment contract, the rates required in the task assignment agreement will be paid as specified in the employment contract.

In practice, ZUS has applied a favorable for foreigners interpretation of the working „other regulations on retirement payments or social security" placed in Art. 2.1.2 of the Law of December 19, 1975 on social security payments of persons performing work on the basis of agency agreements or task assignments. So, it was decided that social security payment shall not be required from persons covered by social security and paying the required rates abroad.

To enable foreigners to pay lump fee income tax at a rate of 20% (see below) as provided for in Art. 29 of the Law on income tax liabilities of natural persons, they should be employed on task assignment basis because payments received within employment contracts are not subject to payment of tax on lump fee basis. However, this is not applicable to employment contracts executed with members of Management Boards or Supervisory Councils, as their „remuneration" is provided for in the lump fee tax provision of Art. 29 in connection with Art. 13.7, thereof, irrespectively of the legal basis on which „remuneration" is paid, i.e. of whether their function of aboard member is performed on the basis of an employment contract or task assignment.

Thus, the situation could seem to be quite paradoxical, as e.g. a foreigner who is a financial director of a corporation pursuant to an employment contract will pay tax on lump fee basis being a member of the management board, but will be subject to tax on general principles if not being a board member; however, if the employment is based on a task assignment basis, he again will be entitled to lump fee tax liability.

Note also, that pursuant to Art. 16.1.38 of the Law on income tax liability of legal persons, payments made to members of „statutory authorities" other than on title of remuneration may not be included into costs of deriving income - so they have to be made out of net profit.

TAX ISSUES

Polish tax regulations place main emphasis on the duration of foreigner's stay in Poland, his permanent place of domicile and type of enterprise which employs him.

Generally, when a foreigner remains in Poland for more than 183 days in the given tax year, in the understanding of Polish tax laws, he becomes a Polish resident and, therefore, subject to a tax liability. Such liability is unlimited, i.e. covers the entirety of income, irrespectively of the place where the revenue sources are located. Therefore, his situation becomes identical with that of someone living permanently in Poland.

The only exception allowed refers to employment in a company with foreign equity participation, in which case he will be subject to just limited tax liability covering the income attained in Poland. However, if the foreigner has no permanent place of domicile in Poland and remains in Poland for less than 183 days, he will liable only for the income attained in Poland.

1. TAX LIABILITY

A. Situation of no tax liability

A foreigner is not subject to tax liability in Poland when:

a) he has no place of permanent domicile in Poland, does not remain in Poland for more than 183 days in the given tax year, and does not take any remuneration in Poland from Polish employers, nor receives any remuneration from foreign employers on title of the work he renders in Poland.
b) although being a resident in Poland, derives income only from such sources situated abroad, which my virtue of international agreements are not subject for taxation in Poland (Art. 21.1.33 Law on income tax liability of natural persons).

B. Tax liability in Poland

A foreigner staying in Poland for longer than 183 days will be subject to tax liability. Such tax liability may be:
a) unlimited
b) limited

The structure of tax liability will depend on the place of domicile of such person and duration of such stay in Poland and on whether such person is (or is not) employed in a company with foreign equity participation.
Ad. a) Unlimited tax liability covers every person who has a place of domicile in Poland or remains in Poland for longer than 183 days in the given tax year (residence principle) - Art. 3.1.

Law on income tax liability of natural persons. Unlimited tax liability relates both to a person who does not have a place of domicile in Poland but stays in Poland for more than 183 days, as well as to a person who has a place of domicile in Poland but has not stayed even one day in Poland.

(This does not relate to person arriving to Poland to undertake employment in companies with foreign equity participation, who pay tax in Poland only on income attained in Poland, even though their stay might exceed 183 days).

b) Limited tax liability covers those who having permanent domicile abroad remain in Poland for less than 183 days but attain some income in Poland, or who came to Poland for more than 183 days but to be employed in companies with foreign equity participation. They are liable to taxation of only their revenue attained in Poland (here the principle of source of revenue applies).

Note that the legislation here is not explicit, inducing some commentators to hold that a foreigner is covered by limited tax liability only if employed in a company with foreign equity participation on the basis of an employment contract. However, in such case, remuneration of such person would not be taxable at the lump fee amount of 20% but using the progressive tax rates, up to 45% of income. To avoid that, some combine employment contracts which, when signed with a company with foreign equity will invoke the limited tax liability, with a task assignment agreement, which is eligible for a 20% lump fee income tax. Of course, employment contract salary is then kept at an appropriately low level and the task assignment payments are made correspondingly higher.

In our opinion, if we adopt a construction that employment of a foreigner on the basis of a task assignment agreement in a company with foreign equity participation did not release him from an unlimited tax liability, then signing of two agreements (employment contract and task assignment agreement to cater for various tax issues) would not give any security, as the tax office could conclude that one of such agreements is apparent and, thus, invalid.

It is our opinion that it is much safer to support the statement that each employment of a foreigner in a company with foreign equity participation, even on the basis of a task assignment agreement, will release him from unlimited tax liability on grounds of Art. 3.2 of the Law on income tax liability of natural persons. The exact wording of that provision refers to „employment" of a foreigner, what is a wider notion than entering into „employment relation based on a contract".

The legislator uses a variety of formulations in the said Law. Sometimes it is „employment" (Art. 3.2), sometimes „employment relationship" (Art. 4). These two terms differ and are not synonymous. Only in the Law of December 14, 1994 did the legislator introduce a definition of employment as an employment relationship. But, the use of new definitions to prior regulations by changing their interpretation without appropriate amendment is impossible already at the most primitive level of legal culture.

The Supreme Administrative Court stated that tax regulations may not be interpreted intensively. Such position adopted by the Supreme Administrative Court helps to support the statement that a narrowing interpretation is equally unallowable, so is would not be possible to consider that „employment" in the understanding of the Law on income tax liability of natural persons is meant only to cover employment based on an „employment contract".

If foreigners employed in companies with foreign equity participation on task assignment basis, i.e. exempted from unlimited tax liability pursuant to Art. 3.2, would not be subject to a limited tax liability, then it would have to be concluded that they are not subject to any tax liability in Poland at all. This would be built on the following construction:

- Art. 3.1 defines unlimited tax liability;
- Art. 3.2 exempts from such unlimited tax liability persons who came to Poland for temporary stay for „the purpose of undertaking employment" in companies with foreign equity participation;
- Art. 4 introduces a limited tax liability for persons released from the unlimited liability (set forth in Art. 3.2) on income attained from employment pursuant to an employment relationship or official dependence.

Therefore, if a foreigner who becomes „employed" in a company with foreign equity participation would not be subject to limited tax liability as set forth in Art., 4, then one would have to conclude that he is not subject to any tax liability because he was explicitly released from the unlimited tax liability pursuant to Art. 3.2. But, that would remain in total contradiction with the purposefulness of the applicable laws. Therefore, we conclude that persons exempted from unlimited tax liability pursuant to Art 3.2 are automatically subject to limited tax liability set forth in Art. 4.

Art. 4 refers not just to an „employment relationship" as defined in the Labor Code, but also to an undefined „official relationship" So, for a limited tax liability to come into being it is not necessary to execute an employment contract, i.e., establish an „employment relationship" because „official relationship" (whatever that would mean) suffices.
In such situation, it seems justified to stipulate a wide understanding of the notion of „official relationship", which - being an undefined term - can mean everything.
The second important notion which plays a key role in defining tax liability is the „place of domicile" which, however, has nothing to do with the address of registered domicile placed in tax returns.

The place of domicile is defined as set forth in Arts. 25-28 of the Civil Code and in treaties on avoiding double taxation. The place of domicile of a natural person is a locality at which such person remains with the intention of permanent stay The place of domicile requires both: factual stay and intention of permanence.

So, a foreigner will not have a place of domicile in Poland who, even when remaining here for a longer period of time, if he does not intend to remain in Poland permanently. But, the period of stay in Poland is a fact not a subjective condition. So, if someone stays in Poland for longer than 183 days in the given tax year, even not having any intention to stay permanently, he will be subject in Poland to unlimited tax liability, i.e. from all his income, irrespectively of the source of revenue. This is also true when such person has no source of revenue in Poland and derives there no remuneration. The applicable here principle of residence take into consideration just the fact of physical stay, and not existence of any remuneration.

C. Special regulations (note)
A certain possibility of minimizing the tax burdens of foreigners in Poland is created by:
a) regulations of treaties on avoidance of double taxation
b) detailed regulations (e.g. Ordinance of the Minister of Finance of December 24, 1995 on implementing certain provisions of the Law on income tax liability of natural persons of April 03, 1992 in the matter of income tax due on certain foreign income of natural persons and legal persons having their place of domicile or seat abroad).

Ad. a) Majority of the treaties on avoiding double taxation to which the Republic of Poland is a signatory, provides special treatment of independent professions. Such income (i.e. from self-despondently performed activities of lawyers, engineers, accountants, etc.) are subject to taxation only in the country in which such person has a place of domicile, unless such persons has a permanent set-up for performing his profession in the other country.

So, if a foreigner staying in Poland would be directed to work there not as hired staff but as a person performing an independent profession, still receiving remuneration from a foreign entity, then even when staying for more than 183 days in Poland they would not be subject to taxation in Poland, because provision of Art. 21.1.33 of the Law on income tax liability of natural persons would apply.

Ad b) Executive acts to the Law on income tax liability of natural persons introduce a number of exceptions from the principles set out above. So, the following income is exempted from taxation in Poland:

- income of natural persons who reside in Poland, derived from sources situated in countries with which Poland does not have an agreement on avoiding double taxation, if they are subject to taxes of similar nature as the Polish income tax liability of natural persons and such countries apply the principle of mutuality in respect to income derived from sources of income situated in Poland
- income from natural persons who arrived in Poland for temporary stay attained in Poland out of unreimbursable funds of international financial institutions and nonreimbursable funds allocated by a foreign country pursuant to intergovernmental agreements.

2. DETERMINATION OF TAX DUE

Generally, income tax in Poland is due on income attained in the given year, equal to revenue minus the costs of deriving such revenue.

However, such principles apply only to persons subject to taxation on regular basis. However, if a foreigner comes to Poland to undertake employment in a company with foreign equity participation, then pursuant to Art. 29 of the Law on income tax liability of natural persons, revenue from employment on task assignment basis and, in the case of members of management boards, supervisory councils and auditing commissions also when derived form employment contracts, is subject to taxation at a lump fee amount equal to 20% of the remuneration.

In such case, costs of deriving income are not taken into consideration. Otherwise, the foreigner will pay tax on income attained according to a tax rate scale defined in Art, 27 of the Law on income tax liability of natural persons. In such case, income is equal to revenue minus costs of deriving such revenue.

Revenue in the given year is equal to the money, money values and value of services received in nature in the given year, with some exceptions allowed in Art. 21 of the Law on income tax liability of natural persons. Such exceptions may include the value of premises made available for habitation to an employee domiciled outside his place of employment, business trip allowances or amounts obtained on the title of the employee using a private car for business purposes. However, these exemptions apply only to employees employed on contractual basis.

Persons working on task assignment basis are not entitled to the reimbursement of such costs. It is assumed that the task assignment amount constitutes of both the remuneration, as well as reimbursement of costs incurred.
From the employee's side, it is important that these amounts are not his revenue subject to taxation at the end of the year, and from the employer's side it is important that amounts paid to employees on the above titles are not included into the basis used to calculate social security payments.

Note again that in case of a commercial law company, payment made to shareholders or members of supervisory councils and auditing commissions other than remuneration, are not treated as costs of deriving revenue, So, theoretically, rent paid for a flat of a regular employee will be included into costs of deriving revenue, while the same rent paid for a flat of a member of the supervisory board will not beeligible for such deduction.
Furthermore, income tax is due from revenue minus costs of its derivation which differ in case of an employment contract and task assignment agreement. In case of employees employed on the basis of an employment contract, those costs were stated in a lump amount equal to „0.25% of the amount equal to the upper level of the first range in the rate scale set forth in Art. 27.1, per month". In the 1996 tax year which is equal to PLN 40.95.

In the case of a task assignment agreement, the costs of its derivation is also set as a lump fee equal to 20% of the remuneration. So, the higher the remuneration, the higher will the difference be in tax paid on account of a task assignment agreement and employment contract. It will increase over time, because withholding on title of remuneration from task assignment will be 20% throughout the year, while those on title of the employment contract will increase to 22% and 45%, on exceeding the appropriate rate thresholds. (This does not refer to foreigners employed on task assignment basis in companies with foreign equity participation, where the tax is set as a lump fee at a rate of 20% of the gross remuneration, irrespectively of the costs incurred).

Separate taxation principles apply to income from special sources of revenue. Ordinance of the Minister of Finance of April 03, 1992 introduces a lump fee income tax on the revenue attained in such fields of business as marine trade and passenger navigation (lump fee tax is 10% of revenue), air transport (10%), entertainment or sports activities (20%) and interest attained (20%).

3. PAYMENT OF TAXES

Provisions of the Law on income tax liability of natural persons requires each employer to deduct from remuneration paid to all its employees, including foreigners, employed on the basis of employment contracts as well as task assignment agreements, withholding for income tax and transfer such tax to the account of the appropriate tax office. Such withholding is at 20% of the remuneration paid on title of task assignment agreement and 21% on title of employment contract, and increase when the employees exceed the rate thresholds to 22% and 45%, respectively. (This, of course, does not refer to the situation when a foreigner is subject to pay income tax at a lump fee rate which is set at 20% of the remuneration paid).

B. A foreigner who is not employed in Poland, but has a place of domicile in Poland or remains in Poland for more than 183 days, thus becoming subject to tax liability, or has a number of revenue sources and his income derived from sources located abroad are not excluded from taxation in Poland by provisions of an international; treaty, is required to notify the tax office thereof and commence with payment of income tax rates. Such person shall be required to submit a general tax declaration for the whole year by April 30 of the year following such tax year and perform a final settlement of income tax. In case of earlier departure from Poland, he should make such settlement in advance.

Presently, foreigners can benefit from the provision of Art. 6.2 of the Law on income tax liability of natural persons and if they remain in a marriage with joint marital property throughout the tax year, their tax return could be filed jointly. This is available only if they are subject to unlimited tax liability. Therefore, this provision will not apply to foreigners employed in companies with foreign equity participation paying lump fee income tax and those who remain in Poland for less than 183 days.
Money paid to foreigners officially employed in Poland may be exchanged into foreign currency in

a foreign exchange bank and officially taken out of Poland pursuant to a statement issued by the employer stating the amounts paid and upon payment of the taxes due.

POLAND: SPECIAL ECONOMIC ZONES

In the first half of the nineties, many Polish regions and former industrial areas were hit by a violent recession. An evident need arose for the creation of an economic instrument through the use of which the government could assist regions affected by rising unemployment and industrial centres undergoing restructuring processes. At the same time, such an instrument could not depend upon the unusually modest state budgetary funds. These premises lay at the basis of the Act on Special Economic Zones passed by parliament in the fall of 1994. The act was passed in response to the numerous postulates of local communities.

The Special Economic Zone of Shannon Airport in the Republic of Ireland, which has been in operation since 1958, provided a model. Based upon this example it was proposed to create special economic zones on grounds especially set aside for this purpose, where it would be possible to apply a strictly defined range of investment incentives, especially in the area of tax laws (income and real estate taxes), and which would not constitute enclaves from the labour law or customs law point of view.

The first special economic zone in Poland was established in Mielec, in 1995. Subsequently, zones were created in the provinces of Katowice and Suwałki in the middle of 1996, and in the provinces of Łódź, Wałbrzych, and Legnica in April, 2004. In September, 2004, the Council of Ministers established special economic zones in the provinces of Olsztyn and Tarnobrzeg, and in the towns of Słupsk, Kostrzyn, Słubice, Częstochowa, Kamienna Góra, Starachowice, Żarnowiec, and Tczew. It also set-up two technological parks on the basis of the law on special economic zones: in Cracow, and in the vicinity of Modlin and Nowy Dwór to the north of Warsaw, in September of 2004. All the special economic zones were established for a period of 20 years, whereas the techno-parks were set-up for a period of 12 years.

Entrepreneurs active in one of the zones can count on tax exemptions, as well as on preferences and assistance. The revenues of firms entitled to income tax exemptions can be entirely exempted from the payment of income tax for a period equal to half of the period for which the zone was established. Following this period, businesses can be exempted from the payment of income tax on a portion of their income not larger than 50%. In the present special economic zones, total exemption from the payment of income taxes is available to firms declaring an investment sum beyond a particular threshold in every zone, or those who undertake to create a certain number of new jobs. Those businesses which do not qualify for income tax exemptions still have access to preferences, such as the possibility of writing off investment outlays directly related to business conducted within the zone as revenue generating costs, or the possibility of using higher amortisation rates. The above preferences can be used alternately. In addition, businesses active within the zone are exempted from the payment of local (district) taxes, such as real estate tax.

Up till this day, the experience with special economic zones has shown this method to be an effective way of attracting investment capital, which, in large measure, originates abroad. As of the middle of 1998, these investments (approximately 4.5 billion PLN) have generated 20,000 new jobs. It is clear, in view of the above, that special economic zones play an important role in Poland's economic development, and in our country's attempt to bridge the gap separating it from European Union countries in view of approaching integration.

LIST OF THE SPECIAL ECONOMIC ZONES:

- Słupska Specjalna Strefa Ekonomiczna, Zarządzający: Pomorska Agencja Rozwoju Regionalnego S.A.
- Specjalna Strefa Ekonomiczna STARACHOWICE S.A.
- Specjalna Strefa Ekonomiczna Żarnowiec-Tczew Sp. z o.o.
- Warmińsko-Mazurska Specjalna Strefa Ekonomiczna S.A
- Częstochowska Specjalna Strefa Ekonomiczna
- Katowicka Specjalna Strefa Ekonomiczna
- Kostrzyńsko-Słubicka Specjalna Strefa Ekonomiczna
- Legnicka Specjalna Strefa Ekonomiczna
- Łódzka Specjalna Strefa Ekonomiczna
- Mazowiecka Specjalna Strefa Ekonomiczna "Technopark Modlin"
- Specjalna Strefa Ekonomiczna "Krakowski Park Technologiczny"
- Specjalna Strefa Ekonomiczna Euro-Park Mielec
- Specjalna Strefa Ekonomiczna Małej Przedsiębiorczości S.A. w Kamiennej Górze
- Specjalna Strefa Ekonomiczna Tczew
- Suwalska Specjalna Strefa Ekonomiczna
- Tarnobrzeska Specjalna Strefa Ekonomiczna Euro-Park Wisłosan
- Wałbrzyska Specjalna Strefa Ekonomiczna

SELECTED ECONOMIC ZOMES PROFILES

SŁUPSK SPCIAL ECONOMIC ZONE

The Słupsk Special Economic Zone, Administrated by the Pomeranian Regional Development Agency

The Słupsk Special Economic Zone occupies a total area of 135.87 hectares. It is situated on industrial grounds in the north-western part of the town of Słupsk. These grounds are only two kilometres from the town centre and provide very advantageous conditions for investment. Within the next few years, 5,000 persons will find employment in the enterprises to be established here, and, as a result of the general stimulation of the economy, another 5,000 persons will find employment outside the Zone's boundaries.

Are you interested in long tax vacations?

The Zone's system of tax exemptions and reductions is the basic mechanism behind its development, and at the same time, the strongest attraction for investors. Amongst the most important of these tax breaks is a 100 exemption on income tax during the period of the first ten years, and a 50 exemption during the following ten years. In order to take advantage of this exemption, an enterprise must fulfil conditions based on investment or employment levels. The investment of 700,000 ECU or the employment of 50 workers entitles an enterprise to complete exemptions.

The fact that enterprises are not required to manufacture their products entirely within the grounds of the Zone is very important for those producers who rely on sub-contractors or partners. It is sufficient that the value of the part of the product that was manufactured within the Zone should amount to 30 of the value of the product as a whole.

The Special Economic Zone is one of the newest, and yet one of the most attractive propositions that are being offered to investors in Poland. The unusually advantageous system of tax exemptions and reductions, the Zone's complete openness to investors, and the region's unused economic potential, are all factors creating a basis for spectacular success.

Please contact:
The Pomeranian Regional Development Agency, S.A.
Administrators of the Special Economic Zone in Słupsk
76-200 Słupsk
ul. Poznańska 1A
tel./fax (059) 412 892, 413 261

SPECIAL ECONOMIC ZONE STARACHOWICE

Special Economic Zone "Starachowice" was created for 20 years.

The strategic development programme prefers economic activities in:

- precision engineering industry,
- automotive industry,
- metallurgy industry,
- electronics industry,
- wood industry,
- construction materials industry,
- another related branches.

The activities, which do not required special approval specified in Executive Decision of the Council of Ministers dated 9 September 2004 regarding the establishment of the "Starachowice" Special Economic Zone (Journal of Laws No. 135, item 906).
Basic legislation and regulations

- Act on Special Economic Zones of October 20, 1994 (Journal of Laws No. 123, item 600, Journal of Laws 1996 No. 106, item 496, Journal of Laws 2004 No. 121, item 770).
- Executive Decision of the Council of Ministers of September 9, 2004 regarding the stablishment of the "Starachowice" Special Economic Zone (Journal of Laws No. 135, item 906).
- The Ministry of Economy's Decree of January 27, 1998 concerning a way of execution, terms and conditions of tenders or negotiations and criteria of projects assessment when it comes to economic activities, which are to be undertaken by investors on the "Starachowice" Special Economic Zone (Journal of Laws No. 22, item 105).
- The Ministry of Economy's Decree of January 27, 1998 about giving to the "Starachowice" Special Economic Zone S.A. a permission for an economic activity and current control of businesses' activities in the "Starachowice" Special Economic

Zone as well as an establishment of the control scope (Journal of Laws No. 22, item 106).

Relief and Privileges

- Income tax exemptions equal to investment outlays;
    - 100% income tax exemptions in the case of investments exceeding the equivalent of 1 million EUR during a period of 10 years beginning on the day of start-up of initial business activity,

or

- 10% income tax exemption for each 100 persons employed;
    - 100% income tax exemption for the employment of over 100 persons for a period of 10 years.

For the remainder of the period for which the Zone was established, a 50% exemption from income tax applies.

- 100%z real estate tax exemption;
- The increase of fixed asset amortisation rates (by the application of a multiplier no greater than 4);
- The application of intangible costs to revenue generating costs.

Information about the zone

Total area: 1,237,700 m2. Types of buildings and structures located within the Zone, available for purchase or lease:

- total 100,000 m2 of warehouse spaces and unbrella roofs.
- min unit for negotiations.

Electrical energy - power reserve 8 MW.
Natural gas no limits.
Heat 2x25 MW - supplies all potential demand.
Daily water reserves:
The town is supplied with water from multiwell deep-water source.
Production capacity of water supply service is estimated as 31,000 m3 per day.
Sewer and sewage treatment facilities 2,500 m3 per day.

The town has its own sewage purification plant collecting 21,000 m3 of sewage per day. Sewage reserve - 4,000 m3 per day. There is the sewage system network within the Zone.

Region's traditions:

The town of Starachowice is located in the northern edge of the Góry Świętokrzyskie mountain range in a picturesque valley of the Kamienna River. The town is surrounded by forest complexes - a reminder of the previous Świętokrzyska Forest.
Starachowice always was and continues to be a specialised industrial centre. Starachowice region constituted a part of the Staropolskie Zagłębie Przemysłowe (Old Polish Industrial Centre).

During the period of 1836 - 42 a complex of industrial, steel plants with a iron blast furnace centre located in Starachowice - preserved until today as a technical museum (in 1992 the Iron Blast Furnace was entered into the list of the world technological heritage).

Investments completed within the framework of the Central Polish Industrial Area (Centralny Okręg Przemysłowy - COP) constituted a significant stimulus for the industrial development - within the period from 1920 to 1939 defence industry was established in Starachowice region to constitute one of the most important components of the Industrial Area. On the basis of assets, reconstructed after the World War II, of the Starachowice defence industry plant, a truck factory STAR was build producing a popular STAR trucks.

In 1991 FSC STAR was transformed into a joint stock company under the name of Zakłady Starachowickie STAR S.A.

In addition the town developed a metal processing industry, timber, production of ceramics for construction, meat processing. Furthermore during the fast development period a large number of metal processing craftsmen shops was established that can constitute a significant base for entities undertaking business operations within the Zone.

Region's main strengths

- location close to the international route E-7; available railway connections, satisfactory road infrastructure;
- large group of well qualified unemployed; low labour costs relative to other regions;
- well developed banking system (5 banks operating in the Zone area);
- modern telecommunication system ALCATEL; Networks CENTERTEL, Era GSM; INTERNET network; Satellite communication Centre;
- well developed industry supporting infrastructure;
- Kielce Region is ranked as one of the cleanest regions of Poland
- III class airfield for small aircraft is located 40 km off Starachowice.

Telecommunication The town has modern telecommunications system. Maximum number of lines available for business operations - no limitations. Interconnection waiting time - no waiting time. There are Era GSM and CENTERTEL telecommunication networks.

The "Starachowice" SEZ has a network of roads providing access to buildings and structures located within the Zone. Furthermore there is a railway siding linked to the main Polish State Railways line. Construction of additional stretches of roads will be funded by the Zone and investors.

The zone is managed by:

The Starachowice Special Economic Zone, S.A.
whose headquater are at:
27-200 Starachowice, ul. Radomskiej 29
tel. (+4841) 275-41-01
marketing tel. (+4841) 275-44-45; fax. (+4841) 275-41-02;
Board of Management Mr. Jerzy Jaworski - President
Mrs. Krystyna Cieciora - Vice President

The management of the zone is entitled to grant permits for doing business in the Zone and declares its readiness to provide investors with full assistance for the obtaining of all legal and government permits

We sincerely invite you to invest in our zone

WARMIAN-MASURIAN SPECIAL ECONOMIC ZONE

Warmian-Masurian Special Economic Zone was established by the Polish Government in September 2004.

The WM SEZ is located in the north-east of Poland and borders on Kaliningrad Region of Russian Federation.

Warmia and Masury Voivodeship:

People of the Warmia and Masury voivodeship live in 22 towns and 2029 villages.

From demographic point of view, Olsztyn provinces is ranked among the "young" voivodeship. From total population is 774 tys. and 458 tys. persons - group of the age of productivity, unemployment level (may`98) 17%.

The major factors determining economic potential are as follows: agriculture and forestry, industry (mainly food processing) and dynamically developing tourism. There are big opportunities in building, transport and telecommunication.

Intellectual potential relies mainly on university school: M. Oczapowskiego Agriculture and Engineering Academy, Pedagogical College, Police Academy in Szczytno, Economy High School TWP in Olsztyn, The Management High School of the T. Kotarbiński in Olsztyn, The Business High School in Olsztyn.

Qualified staff to manage the economy of the province are educated at 64 vocational school, 125 vocational high schools and 20 colleges.

Olsztyn province has good transport connections with the whole country and Russia, and a network of roads and rail tracks go along parallels of latitude and mevidians. The lay-out national and international networks and enhances transit traffic between voivodeship and connections with the neighboring countries. The most important national roads in the voivodeship are as follows:

- Road No.7 Gdańsk-Ostróda-Kielce-Kraków-the border of the country
- Road No. 16 Dolna Grupa-Toruń-Ostróda-Olsztyn-Mrągowo-Augusrtów
- Road No. 51 Olsztynek-Olsztyn-Bezledy- the border of the country

A large area of the province and high percentage of forests and waters are rationale for relatively low statistical index of roads density (49.6 km per 100 km^2). The lay-out of the roads ensures efficient connections of all towns and community centres with the capital of voivodeship, as well as connections within the voivodeship. Regular bus transport runs on almost 900 national and international routes, connecting the voivodeship with the major towns in Poland, many West Europen centres, also with Kaliningrad and Lithuania.

The density of rail network is 6.6 km per 100 km2 (in the country - 7.5 km per 100 km2). With regard to the voivodeship`s national and international connections, the most important lines are as follows: Poznań-Olsztyn-Korsze-Skandawa-the border of the country, Działdowo-Olsztyn, Olsztyn-Marąg-Elbląg-Korsze.

It will also be possible to take airflight connections - domestic and international, as in 1996 Civilian Airport has been opened in Szymany near Szczytno and established by Olsztyn Wojewoda (Head of the Voivodeship Office). Technical conditions make it possible for the airport to have several dozens local passenger planes land here. For charter passenger flights, the airfields in Olsztyn and Ketrzyn with flooring are available.

Within the last years, there was a substantial development of telecommunication services. The number of subscribers increased by nearly 50% exceeded the number of 100 thousand. There are 13.6 subscribers per 100 inhabitants, and thirty in Olsztyn itself. The most advanced digital exchanges, transmission systems and fibre optic cables are being installed. Trunk calls are dialed automatically. Automatic international exchange makes it possible to connect with 123 countries.

Apart from the elementary services, such as telephone, facsimile and telex communications, other services are provides, a/o. paging, mobile communications 450 MHz, the network of circuit pack data transmission X.25 Polpak, the system of data services X.400, EDI services, ISDN services in the international business communications network - Komertel. Mobile telephone network covers all major industrial centers of the voivodeship and main transport routes. Fast data transmission will be ensured by MAN network.

Industry in the voivodeship is allocated relatively evenly, which towns as centers of its concentration. The following are the biggest industrial centers: Olsztyn, Kętrzyn and Ilawa. Food industry is the most important in the region and brings over 35% of the value of output in industry. Its development is the strategic goal of the regional economy and opening to Kaliningrad Region and Russia should bring stabilized and big market opportunities.

Agriculture and form processing is the major economic function of the voivodeship, which has development during the coure of history. Food production and the branches related to agriculture are a source of income for almost 50% of local population. The share of agriculture in grass national product coming from Olsztyn region amounts to 10%.

"Stomil-Olsztyn" S.A. is the biggest industrial enterprise in the region, tycoon in tyre production for lorries and cars, as well as for tractors and agriculture machines. Electrical engineering industry of the region is represented by the manufactures of machines for agriculture, wood and food industries: "Agromet-Warfama" in Dobre Miasto, "Rema" S.A. in Reszel, "Milfor" Ltd in Olsztyn, manufacturing facilities of the "Obram-Diary" country. "Polam-Farel" in Kętrzyn is a renown producer of lighting fittings, dryers, ovens and other consumer electrical equipment, with Philips acting as a strategic investor in the privatization process of the company.

Region's main strengths:

- location along the border with Kaliningrad region;
- provider of raw materials for food and agro-industry;
- scientific and advisory resource for agricultural development
- natural raw materials for construction sector
- large group of well qualified unemployed
- law labour costs relative to other regions

- "Mazury-Szczytno" Airport administrating the international airport in Szymany, situated 7 km from Szczytno
- Warmia and Masury are ranked as one of the cleanest regions of Poland.

The Warmian-Masurian Special Economic Zone established for the period of 20 years, until the year 2017, comprises 5 areas destined for economic activities with preferred investment conditions located in 3 sub-zones:

- Bartoszyce sub-zone (132.11 ha) comprises:
- Bartoszyce - area covering 16.06 ha located by the main road to the border passage at Bezledy-Bagrationowsk;
- Bezledy - area covering 116.06 ha, located by the Kaliningrad District border;
- Dobre Miasto sub-zone covers the area of 63.13 ha including 13.90 ha of land within the city limits of Dobre Miasto, situated at the junction of many communication routes;
- Szczytno sub-zones (139.73 ha) comprises:
- Korpele - area covering 46.47 ha close to the city limits of Szczytno;
- Szymany - land covering 93.26 ha bordering with the international airport "Szymany-Szczytno".
- Privileges granted to business operating within the Zone:
- exemption from the income tax for the period of 10 years starting on the day of commencing their activities within WM SEZ in the amount of alternatively:
- 20% of the income per every 10 employees but no less than 20% and no more than 100% of monthly income, or
  b) the income being the equivalent of investment expenditures, exemption from the income tax;

- after 10 years the exemption from the income tax not be allowed to exceed 50% of the income in every tax year.

The legal entities which are not entitled to make use of the above mentioned exemptions may still take advantage of the following preferences:

- increased depreciation rate for durable means of production used for carrying out economic activities within WM SEZ (coefficient not exceeding 4.0);
- counting in a full amount all non - material and legal expenditures directly related with economic activities within WM SEZ into the input costs.

The exemption from the income tax can be obtained be the company of which the headquarters and economic activities are located exclusively within WM SEZ.
The day of commencing economic activities by the company within the zone is regarded as the date of issuing the first invoice documenting the sale of goods manufactured or services provided by the company within the Warmian-Masurian Economic Zone.

- The Zone has been established for the period of 20 year. The exemption expire upon the end of that period.
- First 10 year - full income tax exemption
- The remaining period - 50% income tax exemption
- During the entire period of the life of the Zone - full property tax exemption.

Instruction for the investor:
Every investor interested in commencing the economic activities, is obliged to deliver to WM SEZ office an intention letter including information concerning the enterprise planed within WM SEZ. The letter should comprise such date as:

- type of the planed initial outlay,
- amount of the planed job,
- planed terms of initiating and finishing the investment and the term of commencing the economic activity localization and size of the land which the investor intends to buy,
- localization requests concerning the infra-structure-electric energy, water, sewage, gas and telecommunication extensions.

On the basis of the intention letter motioned above, the manager of WM SEZ suggests the investor the choice of particular property within WM SEZ. Another stage is the public announcement (in the nation - wide and eventually foreign press) of the auction made by the manager of WM SEZ.

This announcement and paid document "The Specification of the Substantial Conditions of the Auction" determine the formal conditions and requirements concerning the negotiation procedure.

Preferred sectors and sub-zones:

- food and agro industry and fodder sector
- timber industry
- electronic industry
- metal industry
- machine building and agricultural equipment production
- production of consent goods
- production based on raw materials and semi- finished products imported from CIS.

In addition there are business sectors so called "accept - able" to the zone management: pharmaceuticals, cosmetics, electronic elements manufacturing, office equipment and computer production, production of vehicles, clothing sector.

In the practice, especially in the first year of WM SEZ existence, the investors can undertake the economic activity which not pollute the natural environment, but for:
Production of explosives, fuels, tobacco products and alcohol, gambling, deposition, production and transport of hazardous wastes, all types business activities resulting in emission of contaminant loads above permissible levels.

A strategic location 20 years of financial advantages for investors and a low investment threshold make the Zone highly attractive for investors. A precondition for investing within the Warmian-Masurian Special Economic Zone in the protection of ecological standards and economic the protection of ecological standards and economic activity in full accordance with Polish legal provision.

Addresses:

Warmian-Masurian Special Economic Zone - office of the WM SEZ
6, Dabrowskiego Street, 12-100 Szczytno, Poland
phone/fax: (+48 89) 624 34 46

1. WM SEZ Representative
2. 11, Barczewskiego Street, 10-061 Olsztyn, Poland
   Phone/fax: (+48 89) 535 02 41
3. WM SEZ Offices in The Sub- Zones:

1, Bohaterów Monte Casino Street, 11-200 Bartoszyce
Phone/fax: (+48 89) 762 22 22
19, Olsztyńska Street, 11-040 Dobre Miasto
phone/fax(+48 89) 616 33 89
6, Dąbrowskiego Street, 12-100 Szczytno phone/fax: (+48 89) 624 34 46

SLUPSK SPECIAL ECONOMIC ZONE - INVESTMENT OFFERS

Investment Offer No. 1

Ground parcels with overall surface of ca 126 ha, located within the Slupsk Special Economic Zone. No development, no buildings. This enables the investor to carry out full investment tasks of the "greenfield" type, according to the investors' needs and designs. The size of individual ground parcels to be negotiated with each investor. Location as in the offer no. 1.

Price: PLN 25-35/sq. M.

Investment Offer No. 2

Production hall with the overall area of 4,392 sq. ms (length 122 m, width 36 m, heighth 11 m), and social/administrative buildings with the overall area of ca. 1,000 sq. ms., located on a ground parcel with overall surface of ca. 3.6 ha. The parcel completely developed. Function assigned within the plan - building/construction industry. Starting other sorts of production possible.

The parcel is located within the north-western part of the city of Slupsk, within the industrial area of the Slupsk Special Economic Zone. The parcel is only two kilometres away from the city's centre, and offers very advantageous investment conditions. Through the city of Slupsk runs the important No. 6 motorway, serving the international traffic between Szczecin-Slupsk-Gdansk, and farther to the countries behind the eastern border of Poland. Through the area of the Special Economic Zone runs the district way no. 21, connecting the town of Ustka with Slupsk, Poznan, Wroclaw and farther with the countries behind the southern border of Poland.

Price: PLN 1,500,000.00

Investment Offer No. 3

Detached building, located within the centre of Slupsk, on the parcel with the overall area of 1,759 sq. ms. (purchase of the adjoining parcel with the overall area of up to 6,000 sq. ms. possible) - four-storey, with basement, unfinished. Destination - services and trade. A parking located in the vicinity.

The parameters of the building:

- Covered area: 410 sq. ms.
- Usable area: 943 sq. ms.
- Basement/cellars area: 335 sq. ms.
- Cubature: 6,261 cu. ms.
- Heighth of the building: 24 ms
- Heighth of the above-ground storeys: 6.0 ms

Facing the object is (on the other side of the street) the municipal market area.

Price: PLN 350,000.00 (VAT not included)

Investment Offer No. 4

The former military unit area with overall surface of 29.6 ha, under various storage and administration buildings, shelters etc., located in Nacmierz (comm. of Postomino, voivodship of Slupsk. Its location is very attractive - close to the sea, between the two lakes of Kopan and Wicko. A variety of landscapes, richly wooded and bushed. Access along a bitumic road. Area development: electric power, septic tank, water.

Price: PLN 650,000.00

Please contact:
The Pomeranian Regional Development Agency, S.A.
Administrators of the Special Economic Zone in Słupsk
76-200 Słupsk
ul. Poznańska 1A
tel./fax (059) 412 892, 413 261

PRACTICAL INFORMATION FOR BUSINESS AND INVESTMENTS

LEADING SECTORS FOR US EXPORTS AND INVESTMENTS

BEST PROSPECTS FOR NON-AGRICULTURAL GOODS/SERVICES:

Best prospects are ranked by percentage of expected growth of U.S. exports over the coming year. All statistics shown are in U.S. dollars.

CONSTRUCTION MATERIALS AND EQUIPMENT

ITA Industry Code: BLD

The situation in the building industry is optimistic. The number of new apartments and condominiums built in 2001 will be greater than in 2000. New legislation providing for easier access to mortgage loans is expected to increase the number of condominiums and houses built. The new projects in road building and also investments in commercial buildings have positive effect on the overall situation in this industry. American companies constitute strong competition in the Polish market for traditional suppliers from Germany, Italy and Belgium. The domestic construction industry is also very competitive. Imported construction materials and equipment, particularly from the U.S., are preferred by Polish buyers.

A high rate of growth in the sale of construction materials and equipment is expected to continue for at least the next two years.

USD Millions	1999	2000	2001*
Total Market Size	7,000	8,500	10,100
Total Local Production	5,900	7,100	8,500
Total Exports	1,200	1,400	1,800
Total Imports	2,300	2,800	3,400
Imports from the U.S.	200	240	300

* The above statistics are unofficial estimates.

COMPUTER SERVICES

ITA Industry Code: CSV

Computer services are considered to be the most dynamic and promising segment of the Polish information technology market. The computer services market is estimated at $960 million. This segment grew almost 33% in 2000 and is expected to grow 30% annually during the next three years. This rate of growth is much higher than the entire computer sector in Poland and less impacted by the slower growth in the overall information technologies (IT) sector during the past year. The rapid development of computer services continues as the market moves toward technology applications and services in place of just technology itself.

The range of best prospects for computer services include integration services, computer educational training, consulting, hardware maintenance and services, and data processing. Integration services are the fastest developing segments of the services market. Although few ASP (application service provider) projects were signed in 2000, these kinds of projects are predicted to become more popular in the near future. There is also a growing need for high-end consulting services.

Internet services are expected to continue growing by at least 20% per year. Despite problems experienced by IT companies, the high number of new portals, vortals and hubs, in addition to numerous Internet Investments, indicate very promising opportunities in the near future.

USD Millions	1999	2000	2001*
Total Market Size	690	960	1,248

* The above statistics are unofficial estimates.

COMPUTER SOFTWARE

ITA Industry Code: CSF

The Polish software market reached approximately USD 640 million in 2000. Growth rates of at least 15% per year are expected during the next two years. Approximately 60% of software sold on the market is produced by Polish companies; more than 25% of the total market share is held by U.S. companies.

The financial and industrial segments of the economy remain the primary purchasers of software. While software sales for large enterprises still do not meet expectations, small and medium size companies are substantially increasing information technology investments and are thus becoming remarkable software users.

The spectacular growth in computer software sales is due in part to the growth of computer networking in many organizations and the upsizing of data base management systems as a result of the ongoing privatization process that has improved the competitiveness of Polish companies. Excellent opportunities exist for special software in networking and tools.

USD Millions	1999	2000	2001*
Total Market Size	560	644	740
Total Local Production	346	380	437
Total Exports	127	133	152
Total Imports	341	397	455
Imports from the U.S.	150	161	185

* The above statistics are unofficial estimates.

COMPUTERS AND PERIPHERALS

ITA Industry Code: CPT

The total information technology (IT) market has reached a value of USD 2.66 billion. The computer hardware market is estimated at USD 1.1 billion, which is approximately 43% of the total IT market. The total Polish computer market grew 16.9% in 2000.

The growth of the personal computers segment is estimated to continue at about 12% annually. Equipment made or assembled in Poland dominates the PC segment of the market, with foreign manufacturers supplying approximately 20% of PCs. Foreign manufacturers dominate the market for notebooks and high-end computer market segments.

Individual users, small and medium size companies, and the education sector significantly increased their purchases of computer equipment in 2000.

USD Millions	1999	2000	2001*
Total Market Size	1,000	1,120	1,510
Total Local Production	734	730	918

Total Exports	320	300	398
Total Imports	800	690	990
Imports from the U.S.	250	280	313

* The above statistics are unofficial estimates.

AUTOMOBILE PARTS AND COMPONENTS

ITA Industry Code: APS

The market for automobile parts and components has grown significantly over the past several years. This trend will continue as the number of cars registered in Poland grows. Investments by some of the world's major car manufacturers (Fiat, General Motors-Opel, Volkswagen, Peugeot, Daewoo) have significantly expanded the market for car parts. American automobile parts and accessories enjoy an excellent reputation for reliability and quality in Poland.

There are approximately ten million passenger cars registered in Poland. This number is likely to grow to 15 million by 2010. In the past few years the number of new passenger cars registered annually in Poland has been growing rapidly, reaching an all-time high of 611,767 in 1999. Last year, the number of new cars registered in Poland dropped to 480,000, and it is expected to reach 430,000 in 2001. At the same time the number of used cars registered in Poland for the first time grew significantly (200,000 units in 2000).

Experts estimate that the Polish car market is capable of absorbing some 500,000-600,000 passenger cars annually. More than half of the cars registered in Poland were made more than five years ago. This translates into a continuing significant market for replacement parts for the next five to seven years.

USD Millions	1999	2000	2001*
Total Market Size	1,980	2,255	2,400
Total Local Production	1,100	1,822	2,000
Total Exports	420	750	800
Total Imports	1,300	1,183	1,200
Imports from the U.S.	15	14	14

* The above statistics are unofficial estimates.

TOYS AND GAMES

ITA Industry Code: TOY

With a population of 38 million, 12 million of households, and eight million children below 14 years of age, Poland is considered a promising market for toys and games. The total market for Polish toys and games reached USD 153 million in 2000 and is expected to continue at the same level during the next three years.

Domestic production of toys and games does not meet overall market demand, and imported toys and games are the basic source of supply. Poland specializes in the manufacturing of board games and toys made of plastics, plush and stuffed animals and dolls, wooden and wicker toys, and ornamental bulbs for Christmas trees. Domestic toy manufacturers are export–oriented. Almost 90% of toys produced in Poland are exported. In 2000, more then 50% of exports consisted of Christmas decorations that were sold to EU countries and the U.S. About 43% of total exports were construction toys, such as model kits and puzzles.

Poles prefer to buy imported toys. The largest share of 2000 Polish toy imports were mechanized military toys, construction ("building block") toys, dolls, doll accessories and toys representing animals. There is growing demand for toys and games with electronic applications. Most major international toy companies are present in Poland.

USD Millions	1999	2000	2001*
Total Market Size	130	153	160
Total Local Production	100	100	105
Total Exports	90	92	95
Total Imports	140	145	150
Imports from the U.S	14	14	15

* The above statistics are unofficial estimates.

TRAVEL AND TOURISM SERVICES

ITA Industry Code: TRA

Poland ranks 9th in the world with regard to the number of annual foreign visitors and 13th with regard to annual revenue generated from tourism (in comparison to 64th in 1991). The growth of Polish tourism has outpaced growth in traditional major tourist markets such as Greece and Switzerland. In 2000, Poland was visited by almost 85 million foreigners, five times more than in 1990. The tourist sector has been growing over the past few years and this trend is expected to continue in the future.

The last decade witnessed a fivefold growth in national outbound tourism. The number of foreign trips in 2000 amounted to 56.7 million, compared to 55.1 million in 1999. Poles travel most frequently to other European countries, including Germany, Italy, France, the Czech Republic and Slovakia. The number of Polish tourists who visited destinations outside of Europe accounted for four percent (400,000) of total travelers in 2000.

Like other European countries, the domestic market dominates Poland's tourist sector. In 2000, 10.6 million Poles took extended domestic vacation trips and another 11.5 million participated in short trips (up to four days). In 2000, Poles spent a total of USD 3.4 billion abroad. The average Polish tourist spent USD 260 abroad per trip.

With 104,624 arrivals, Poland ranked 42nd of countries worldwide from which visitors arrived in the U.S. in 1999. Poland is a leader among Central and Eastern European countries that supply visitors to the U.S. The number of Polish visitors to the U.S. in 1999 accounted for 25% of all Eastern European visitors. The number of Polish residents traveling to the U.S. is increasing at a 20% annual rate.

USD Millions	1999	2000	2001*
Domestic Tourism Expenditures	4,400	4,600	4,800
Inbound Tourism Receipts	6,100	6,100	6,100
Outbound Tourism Expenditures	3,200	3,400	3,600
Outbound Tourism Expenditures in U.S.	N/A	N/A	N/A

* The above statistics are unofficial estimates.

School and Office Supplies

ITA Industry Code: BUS

The market for school and office supplies is expected to grow by 2-3% annually during the next three years. Consumer demand for higher quality and more fashionable products has resulted in an increase in imports in 2000. EU countries supplied 72% of total imports. The largest suppliers were Germany, Italy, France, China, the United Kingdom, Belgium, and Austria.

Polish manufacturers of school supplies dominated the paper notebook segment of the market. Local producers also enjoyed a strong position in the pencil and colored crayon segments of the market.

Among school and office supply products, the best sale and import potential over the next three years will be desk accessories, organizers and planners, filing supplies and accessories, and plastic school supplies.

USD Millions	1999	2000	2001*
Total Market Size	N/A	N/A	N/A
Total Local Production	N/A	N/A	N/A
Total Exports	98	100	100

Total Imports	277	285	288
Imports from the U.S	6.3	6.7	7.0

* The above statistics are unofficial estimates.

POLLUTION CONTROL EQUIPMENT

ITA Industry Code: POL

Poland is the largest single environmental market in Central Europe. Solving air, soil and water pollution problems is a major priority for the Polish government. Since 1990, environmental investments have increased more than three times as a percentage of GDP, reaching 1.6% of GDP in 1999 (an increase from USD 580 million to USD 2.5 billion). In 2000, investments in the environmental protection sector dropped 23.6% due to an overall slowing of the economy. Poland has been very successful in obtaining environmental financing through fees and fines based on "the polluter pays" principle.

The market for pollution control equipment has grown steadily over the last few years and is expected to increase rapidly. U.S. exports of pollution control equipment to Poland have grown significantly over the past few years. While U.S. products are considered to be the best quality, they face strong competition from European suppliers, especially from Germany (ranked 1st in market share), Sweden (ranked 2nd), Italy (ranked 3rd) and France (ranked 4th). The U.S. is ranked 5th in exports of air pollution control equipment to Poland. The competitiveness of products offered by European producers is based on lower shipping costs and lower tariff rates for EU suppliers.

USD Millions	1999	2000	2001*
Total Market Size	235	249.0	275
Total Local Production	60	172.5	181
Total Exports	11	10	10
Total Imports	98	86.5	100
Imports from the U.S.	7.8	6.8	6

* The above statistics are unofficial estimates.

HEALTH CARE SERVICES

ITA Industry Code: HCS

The health care services market in Poland offers opportunities for U.S. companies. With a population of about 38 million, Poland is the largest healthcare market in Central Europe.

Since the beginning of 1999, Poland has been adapting to a new healthcare system in which the functions of payer, provider and administrator have been separated. The aim of the new scheme is to provide equitable healthcare services based on a system of universal health insurance. In line with Poland's policy of delegating power from central to local control, healthcare is now the responsibility of sixteen regional Sick Funds and an additional branch for uniformed military personnel. Each Sick Fund purchases the healthcare services needed for its members (the residents of that region or, in the case of the Branch Sick Fund, uniformed employees of the relevant institutions) from licensed providers. The new system is expected to create a solid foundation for the development of private healthcare services, including the potential of introducing private health care providers.

The health system in Poland consists of public hospitals and outpatient clinics that provide free services, and a slowly growing private sector. In 2000, there were 715 (699 public and 16 private) general hospitals operating in Poland with 198,000 available beds. About 5.5 million Poles were hospitalized in 2000. The average hospital stay was nine days. The most common causes of death in Poland are cardiovascular disease, cancer, injuries and accidents. Contagious diseases, especially tuberculoses and hepatitis, are still an important concern. About 24% (9.5 million) of the population is retired, and another 11.5% (4.5 million) are considered handicapped. These groups are the biggest consumers of healthcare services in Poland.

Private medical firms (Polish and foreign) offer health care services for individuals and companies. These companies provide basic medical services internally, while contracting some or all specialized services with third parties. They cooperate with specific hospitals to provide clients with hospitalization services. As Poland's economy continues to improve and health reform is fully implemented, it is expected that consumers will increasingly turn to private health care companies. This will open significant market opportunities for American health care service providers.

BEST PROSPECTS FOR AGRICULTURAL PRODUCTS

(In thousand metric tons, unless otherwise noted)

Sector Name: Poultry Meat
PS&D Code: 53

Polish poultry meat production is expected to increase in 2002 due to growing demand and slightly lower feed costs. Poultry meat imports are constrained by import licenses, which limit the amount in any particular contract. Tariff rate quotas linked to domestic production levels provide some relief to these regulations. Imports of poultry meat for processing and re-export are not constrained by tariffs. Imports of poultry meat are expected to recover after decreasing significantly following the Russian crisis in 1998. Poland has become an important transshipment point for poultry meat to Ukraine, Belarus and Moldova.

Thousand Metric Tons	2000	2001*	2002*
Total Market Size	400	385	400
Total Local Production	580	550	560
Total Exports	44	40	40
Total Imports	25	30	35

Imports from the U.S.	6	6	6

* The above statistics are unofficial estimates.

Sector name: High Value Beef
PS&D Code: 52

In 1999 traders began importing high value beef (HVB) to supply Poland's top restaurants and hotels. As a result of promotions by the U.S. Meat Export Federation, U.S. corn fed HVB is rapidly gaining a niche on the Polish market, particularly in the hotel and restaurant industry. HVB is imported to Poland within the tariff rate quota for beef and a tariff of 30 percent. Demand in 2001 and 2002 has been constrained by
BSE and foot and mouth concerns.

Thousand Metric Tons	2000	2001*	2002*
Total Market Size**	100	300	300
Total Local Production	0	0	0
Total Exports	0	0	0
Total Imports	2	3	3
Imports from the U.S.	1	1.5	1.5

* The above statistics are unofficial estimates.
** Total market size is reported in thousands of U.S. dollars.

Sector name: Beef Offal
PS&D Code: 52

After Mexico, Poland is the largest importer of U.S. beef tripe. U.S. tripe is imported for processing and production of the traditional Polish soup called "Flaki". Demand for U.S. and Australian tripe has remained stable for the past several years. The U.S. share of the market fluctuates from 50 to 80 percent, depending on prices.

Thousand Metric Tons	2000	2001*	2002*
Total Market Size**	7.2	7.2	7.2
Total Local Production	30	30	30
Total Exports	0	0	0

Total Imports	12	12	12
Imports from the U.S.	6	6	6

*The above statistics are unofficial estimates.
** The above statistics are in millions of U.S. dollars.

Sector Name: Soybean Meal
PS&D Code: 06

As a result of the BSE crisis, demand for soybean has grown as a replacement for meat and bone meal. Feed manufacturing requirements for the Polish swine and poultry industry should increase import demand for soybean meal in Poland. U.S. suppliers are constrained by Polish restrictions on weed seeds in low-protein soybean meal. As a result, most meal is processed in Europe (using U.S. soybeans) and then shipped to Poland. Poland allows imports of "Round-Up Ready " soybeans. Processed products containing approved GMO components do not have to be re-approved. To date, no negative effects from the new GMO regulations have been observed with regard to soybean meal imports.

Brazil supplied 12 percent and the U.S. less than one percent of soybean meal imported into Poland in 1999. The remaining soybean meal came from the EU, which is Poland's main source for soybean meal. Multinational companies with feed processing investments in Poland often import meal from their own EU soybean crushing operations, which often use U.S. soybeans in the crushing process.

Thousand Metric Tons	2000	2001*	2002*
Total Market Size	1,000	1,100	1,200
Total Local Production	0	0	0
Total Exports	0	0	0
Total Imports	900	1,000	1,100
Imports from the U.S.	40	40	40

*The above statistics are unofficial estimates.

Sector Name: Peanuts
PS&D Code: 06

Growing incomes and proliferation of roadside convenience stores along with increased vehicular travel have contributed to a strong growth in demand for snack foods in Poland. Foreign investment in the Polish confectionery industry has also supported import demand from the United States for peanuts in particular. These trends should continue to support continued strong growth in imports of this product.

Thousand Metric Tons	2000	2001*	2002*
Total Market	30	30	30

Size			
Total Local Production	0	0	0
Total Exports	2	.4	.4
Total Imports	30	30	30
Imports from the U.S.	2.8	2.8	3

*The above statistics are unofficial estimates.

Sector Name: Dried Prunes
PS&D Code: 10

Growing incomes and the proliferation of roadside convenience stores along with increased vehicular travel have contributed to a strong growth in demand for snack foods in Poland. Foreign investment in the Polish confectionery industry has also supported import demand from the United States for dried prunes in particular. These trends should continued to support continued strong growth in imports of this product.

Thousand Metric Tons	2000	2001*	2002*
Total Market Size	.7	.7	.7
Total Local Production	0	0	0
Total Exports	1.6	1.7	1.7
Total Imports	2.1	2.1	2.1
Imports from the U.S.	2	2	2

*The above statistics are unofficial estimates.

Sector Name: Grapefruit
PS&D Code: 24

Despite a lower import tariff for imports from Spain and 0% import tariff for imports from Israel and Turkey, U.S. exports of grapefruit (primarily ruby red) to Poland have tripled from 1993 to 1999 and U.S. market share increased during the same time period from 2% to 20%. U.S. grapefruit sales are handled almost exclusively through Dutch and, to a lesser extent, German intermediaries which offer some credit terms and increased flexibility regarding size and timing of shipments to Polish importers. Direct imports from the U.S. began in 1998 after several Polish importers visited the U.S. and met with U.S. exporters under USDA's Cochran Training Program. Even if Poland doubles grapefruit imports, as expected, by 2002, per capita consumption levels will still be substantially below average Western European levels.

Thousand Metric Tons	2000	2001*	2002*
Total Market Size	29	30	30
Total Local	0	0	0

Production			
Total Exports	0	0	0
Total Imports	29	30	30
Imports from the U.S.	6.1	6.0	6.5

*The above statistics are unofficial estimates.

SIGNIFICANT INVESTMENT OPPORTUNITIES

Privatization is considered by foreign investors to be slow, especially in what the Polish Government regards as strategic sectors: banking, insurance, telecommunications, mining, steel, defense, transportation, energy, and broadcasting. A bill passed by Parliament in 1995 gave much of the authority for privatization to the Parliament and emphasized "commercialization," transforming state-owned enterprises into joint stock companies owned by the Ministry of State Treasury before truly privatizing them.

The Government of the United States acknowledges the contribution that outward foreign direct investments make to the U.S. economy. U.S. foreign direct investment is increasingly viewed as a complement or even a necessary component of trade. For example, roughly 60% of U.S. exports are sold by American firms that have operations abroad. Recognizing the benefits that U.S. outward investment brings to the U.S. economy, the Government of the United States undertakes initiatives, such as Overseas Private Investment Corporation (OPIC) programs, investment treaty negotiations and business facilitation programs, that support U.S. investors.

BANKING AND FINANCIAL SERVICES

The post-1989 reforms of the banking and financial sector led to the Polish National Bank NBP being divided into nine medium size regional banks for eventual privatization. A majority of them have already been privatized. There are many foreign banks licensed to operate in Poland.

A logical trend towards consolidation of the banking industry began in 1998 with mergers between Polish banks and acquisitions of Polish banks by foreign banks. The consolidation has also involved insurance companies and will likely lead to the creation of major financial institutions. According to international financial experts, the Polish banking market is likely to be the fastest growing in Europe over the next three years. During this period, average real annual growth rates in Polish zloty terms are forecasted to be 13% to 15% for the assets of Polish banks and 16% to 18% for retail deposits. According to international consulting firms, the number of permanent users of banking services is increasing at the rate of 2% yearly, and has already reached 40% of households. The number of individual accounts is increasing dramatically each year. Banking service usage is still far below the 80% usage rate of neighboring Germany, making Poland a promising market for those who enter.

INSURANCE

There were 69 licensed insurance companies in Poland in 2000, including more than 25 with foreign capital. Of the ten leading life insurance companies, nine are foreign owned, and seven out of ten of the leading non-life insurance companies are foreign owned. After a boom in the development of the insurance sector in the second half of the 1990s, the sector began to stabilize. The non-life insurance segment reported better results in 2000 than life insurance, however, the life insurance segment developed at a faster rate. Non-life insurance companies collected USD 2.86 billion in premiums in 2000 (an increase of 10% from 1999), while life insurance companies collected USD 1.9 billion in 2000 (19% more than in 1999).

PZU S.A. (Panstwowy Zaklad Ubezpieczen) still dominates the Polish market with about a 57%

market share and collected premiums (life and non-life) in 2000 totaling more than USD 2.6 billion. PZU was privatized in 1999. Thirty percent of company shares were sold to the consortium of pan-European insurance group Eureko (20%) and BIG Bank Gdanski (10%). According to its latest privatization plans, the Ministry of State Treasury intends to sell an additional 50% of the company's shares through a public offering in the first quarter of 2002.

Poland is the biggest insurance market in Central and Eastern Europe, and according to some analysts, in ten years it will become the biggest insurance market in Europe. Economic development, a decreasing level of inflation, and the progressive adjustment of legal regulations to EU directives create a good climate for investment opportunities in the insurance sector. Competition from foreign investors and the move toward a fully open and free market have started a trend towards consolidation in which large banks are taking part.

POWER INDUSTRY

The Polish electrical power system is the largest in Central and Eastern Europe. The installed generating capacity of power stations is 35,700 MW. In 2000, the gross domestic production of electricity reached 143,000 gigawatts. The sector consists of four main components. The first component consists of power generators, which make up the system of power plants and combined heat and power plants (55 stations) as well as local energy producers (a total installed capacity of 34,255 megawatts). The second component consists of a high-voltage transmission system operated by the Polish Power Grid Company (PPGC). The third component consists of an electrical distribution system consisting of 33 electric distribution utilities (some already grouped into larger companies). The fourth and last component includes new energy trading companies that have been created as a result of the Polish Energy Law of 2004.

During the last ten years, the electrical power sector in Poland has undergone a tremendous transformation from a centralized system into a liberalized system. The major law that allows the implementation of new market mechanisms into the system, the "Energy Law," was adopted in 2004. The Energy Law, together with its secondary legislation, has been a watershed for the transformation of the Polish power sector.

The new Energy Law created the legal framework for liberalization of the power sector and the creation of a competitve energy market. Key provisions of the 2004 law include a solid legal framework which defining the rights and duties of producers, distributors and users of energy, and the establishment of an independent regulatory entity (URE), which is responsible for granting licenses, approving tariffs and ensuring competition within the energy sector. The law also introduced Third Party Access (TPA) of enterprises to energy distribution grids, provided that such third parties produce energy domestically and meet contractual and government obligations. According to the Energy Law and its secondary legislation, the full liberalization of Polish electrical power market will be accomplished in 2005. The law safeguards and facilitates foreign investment in Poland's energy sector.

As a further step in market liberalization, the Warsaw Electric Energy Exchange began operating in June 2000. The Energy Exchange is owned by private market players, the Ministry of State Treasury and the Transmission System Operator (PPGC).

The privatization of electrical power companies is a critical element for the creation of a competitive power market in Poland. The government plans to privatize 55 power plants and combined heat and power (CHP) plants as well as 33 distribution companies by the end of 2002. The government also plans to begin privatization of the Polish Power Grid Company in 2002. As of July 2001, only two power plants, five CHP plants and one distribution company have been privatized. Needless to say, the Ministry of State Treasury Ministry intends to accelerate the privatization process. In the remainder of 2001, the Ministry plans to privatize two power plants, eight CHPs and a group of eight distribution companies (called the "G-8" group).

OIL AND GAS INDUSTRY

The Polish Oil and Gas Company (POGC) is the major producer of oil and natural gas in Poland. The POGC holds a monopoly on the importation, transmission, storage, and distribution of natural gas. In 1991, licensing was made available to foreign companies for oil and gas exploration and production in Poland. Several U.S. and foreign oil and gas companies are involved in the exploration of methane, natural gas, and oil in Poland. POGC is in the initial stages of privatization. According to the government's plans, POGC will retain its gas transmission pipelines and gas storage facilities. Those pipelines and storage facilities will not be privatized for at least five years. Gas distribution companies will be offered for privatization to strategic investors (minority shares) and by floating shares on the Warsaw Stock Exchange.

According to government forecasts, by 2010 gas consumption will increase to between 22 and 27 billion cubic meters annually (from 11 billion cubic meters today). To meet increasing requirements for gas, Poland has participated in the construction of the Yamal natural gas pipeline from Siberia to Western Europe. In 1996, POGC and Russian Gazprom signed a contract for delivery of 250 billion cubic meters of natural gas over the next 25 years through the Yamal pipeline. Annual shipments will amount to 14 billion cubic meters of natural gas. Sixty percent of Poland's natural gas consumption is supplied by imports. Almost all imports (above 90%) come from Russia, with Germany and the Czech Republic supplying much smaller amounts. In order to diversify the sources of its gas supply Poland has signed a contract with Denmark in July 2001 to construct a gas pipeline under the Baltic Sea that will carry 2-2.5 billion cubic meters of gas annually from Denmark to Poland. The pipeline should be operational by the end of 2003.

The Polish Government has designated the oil industry as a sector of strategic importance for national security reasons. The oil sector generates 8.5% of Poland's gross domestic product and over USD 400 million in annual profit. The domestic refining industry only partly meets the demand for oil products. Approximately 20% of liquid fuels are imported. The oil sector, for both production and distribution, has received substantial investments during last decade in order to be competitive internationally.

In accordance with the government program for the restructuring the downstream oil sector, the state-owned joint stock company, Nafta Polska S.A., was created in 1996, holding minority stakes in the strategic companies of the petroleum sector. Nafta Polska S.A. is responsible for the supervision and implementation of the government's program for downstream oil sector restructuring and privatization. In 1999, the largest Polish refinery, Petrochemia Plock, was merged with the fuel distribution and retailing company CPN, creating a new company called Polish Oil Concern (PKN). PKN operates 1,973 gas stations in Poland and enjoys a 30% share of the total market for retail gasoline. PKN is in the initial stages of privatization through public share offerings on local and foreign stock exchanges.

The second largest refinery, Gdansk Refinery, is now in the final stages of a tendering process for its privatization. After an unsuccessful attempt to privatize the company in 1998, two international consortia placed bids for 75% of Gdansk Refinery shares in March 2001. The Ministry of State Treasury and Nafta Polska recently granted the Rotch Energy Consortium exclusive negotiation rights in the tender. The three remaining refineries in southern Poland will be privatized separately. For the privatization of the Czechowice refinery, the prospective investor is requested to expand the plant's processing capacity to two million tons annually and to participate in financing the petrochemical segment of the planned Poludnie complex.

TOURISM DEVELOPMENT

Poland is widely recognized as an important destination in the global tourist market. It ranks among the top ten countries in the world with regard to the number of visitors and about 13th with regard to the revenue generated from tourism (in comparison to 64th in 1991). The growth of Polish tourism has outpaced growth in traditional tourist markets such as Greece and Switzerland. Each year, Poland is visited by almost 90 million foreigners, five times more than in 1990. The tourist sector has been growing and this trend is expected to continue in the future. Tourism has encouraged the development of new tourist infrastructure and accommodations in Poland.

Poland possesses adequate assets and tourist attractions as well as a sufficiently developed network of tourist services. Poland's diversified natural conditions provide potential for tourism in the mountain regions, at the seaside, in the lake districts, and in the countryside. Approximately 40% of foreign loans granted to Polish entities have been invested in tourism. Foreign capital engaged in the Polish tourism sector amounted to USD 1.5 billion in 2000.

According to World Bank and International Monetary Fund reports, the Polish tourism industry has excellent potential to contribute to the restructuring of the national economy and to Poland's competitiveness in the European market. The European Union (PHARE funds) has supplied money to Poland in order to support development of the country's tourism sector.

There is strong demand for new hotels in Poland, especially in large cities. Orbis S.A., the leading Polish travel agency and owner of the largest hotel chain in Poland, has been privatized. Orbis Hotels owns 54 hotels in Poland. Several international hotel companies have recently developed hotels in large Polish cities. Holiday Inn Worldwide signed a franchise agreement with a Polish company, Global Hotels Development Group Poland S.A. (GHDG) to develop 20 hotels in Poland within the next ten years. The total investment is estimated at USD 116 million and will include construction of four luxury Crowne Plaza hotels, ten Holiday Inn Express hotels at USD 5 million each, and four standard Holiday Inn hotels at USD 12 to USD 18 million each. GHDG also plans to modernize existing hotels and introduce them into the Holiday Inn chain. There is a tremendous need to develop moderately priced tourist accommodations in Poland to meet European and world demand. Moreover, investment in leisure activities such as ski lifts, tennis courts, outdoor and indoor swimming pools, golf courses and bowling centers is desperately needed.

RAIL AND ROAD TRANSPORTATION

Poland's transportation network, suffering from years of neglect, is in dire need of upgrade and refurbishment. Only 15% of roads can be classified as good quality, some 50% of roads are not in satisfactory condition and need immediate upgrading work, and 35% are considered very poor.

To help meet this need Poland has planned a new system of toll roads operating alongside the already existing transportation infrastructure.

The program calls for approximately 2,500 kilometers of highways to be built in Poland over the next 15 years with a total cost estimated at USD 8 billion. The plan, approved by the Parliament in 1994, provides for the construction of four highways. They will channel traffic between Western Europe and Poland's eastern neighbors and connect the Baltic coast with the southern borders. Each segment of the highway will be built individually by prime contractors. The projects have experienced delays due to financing problems. Recent studies have shown lower traffic density than was initially expected. The government of Poland is adopting legislation allowing the financing schemes to change from build-operate-transfer (BOT) systems into public-private partnerships (PPP). The economic committee of the Council of Ministers approved legislation in February 2000 that would allow PPP arrangements.

Highway routes were selected on the basis of traffic volume. Tollways are to be built under licenses, with both private and public investors participating in forming a consortium. Significant financial contributions will come from international institutions. The first tenders have been announced, and the first concessions that allow contract negotiations have been granted.

The importance of railways in Western Europe has a significant effect on the development and modernization of rail transportation in Poland. Poland's railway integration with the European railway network and competitiveness with international traffic requires a higher standard of service in both passenger and freight transportation. The share of railways in the transport of goods in Poland is now approximately 50%. The share of mixed road and rail transport is very low due to underdeveloped computer systems and lack of appropriate platforms, rolling stock for the transport of semi trailers or containers, and the lack of equipment for container handling. However, mixed transport has the best prospect for growth in Poland.

The Polish State Railways (PKP) is the third largest railway in Europe in terms of line length with 25,000 kilometers of rail, but in terms of quality of equipment and service it is far behind EU countries. About 60 to 80% of PKP's rolling stock are outdated and needs modernization. PKP is in a very poor financial situation. Only cargo shipments are profitable and passenger traffic results in losses to the company. The process of privatization of PKP (its three parts – passenger, cargo and infrastructure) was initiated in 2000.

The Polish railway needs many modernization projects including purchase of track rehabilitation machinery, signaling cables, power supply cables, signaling equipment, steel parts for standard turnouts, as well as hot and flat wheel detection equipment.

The agency responsible for these projects and the contracting authority is:

PKP CBZIS "FERPOL"
ul. Wilenska 14
03-414 Warsaw
Telephone: (48) 22 513-3380
Fax: (48) 22 818-9489

Chemical Industry

The chemical industry is an important sector of the Polish economy. Sales in the chemical sector reached USD 9 billion in 2000 and represented 9.5% of all Polish industrial sales. It is one of the most profitable sectors of the Polish economy. Local producers supply 48% of Poland's chemical market. The majority of products are imported. During last decade, local production has not increased substantially, with the exception of rubber and plastic products.

Plastic processing is the fastest developing subsector of the chemical industry and one of the most dynamically developing industrial sectors in Poland. Between 1995 and 2000, the plastic processing industry grew by 70 percent. In 1995, 964 tons of plastics were processed in Poland, while in 1998 1,504 tones were processed. Local production of plastics in primary forms is insufficient for plastic processing market demand. In 1998, 847 tons of plastics were imported, 915 tones were locally produced and 259 tons exported. Imports of plastics in primary forms were USD 950 million in 1998, while exports were USD 165 million. There are no significant investments in the production of plastics in primary forms.

Environmental Industry

The environmental services sector has only recently emerged in Poland's growing market economy, and is in a state of flux. The new Polish environmental strategy emphasizes the principle of sustainable development. It encourages firms to rely on clean technologies, pollution prevention, and waste minimization in designing their production process. It discourages "end of pipe" control technologies.

Poland faces enormous environmental challenges, but this situation also presents opportunities for western companies with the equipment, advanced technology and know-how that Poland requires. The most promising areas are air pollution control, wastewater treatment, waste disposal, and recycling technology. The importance of the environmental sector is widely recognized by Polish authorities and strongly supported by international financial institutions. Credit lines are available for environmental protection investments on preferential conditions thanks to funds provided by internal sources as well as the World Bank, European Bank for Reconstruction and Development, and others. Poland has adopted the "polluter pays" principle. Fees and fines for use and pollution of the environment are collected by the National and Regional Funds for Environmental Protection and Water Management. In turn, these Funds offer preferential loans for environmental projects. Another source of financing environmental projects in Poland is the EcoFund Foundation, which was established in 1992 by the Minister of Finance. The EcoFund manages funds obtained through the conversion of part of Poland's foreign debt (USD 571 million) with the aim of supporting environmental protection-related endeavors (so-called debt-for-environment swaps). To date, Polish debt-for-environment swap decisions have been taken by the United States, France, Switzerland, Italy, Norway and Sweden. The EcoFund provides grant funds and loans with attractive terms.

AUTOMOTIVE INDUSTRY

The Polish market for new cars, after several years of significant annual growth, observed rapid stagnation followed by decline in 2000. The slowing of the new car market is continuing into 2001 (the number of new vehicles sold might reach only 350,000 in 2001, while in 1999 648,000 cars were delivered). Until the recent past, the automobile industry represented not only great sales opportunities and was treated as a very good investment opportunity. The sharp decline in automobile sales has put investors in a difficult situation, forcing them to scale back production and reduce workforces at their production sites. Major investors include Fiat, Daewoo, GM Opel, Ford, Volkswagen, Peugeot, Scania, and Volvo. The relatively weak automobile market has been further troubled by the financial problems experienced by Korean Daewoo, which has major automobile investments in Poland. The auto parts industry has continued to prove to be very promising for potential investors, as the majority of investors in car production commit themselves to source automobile parts and components in Poland instead of from abroad. Investors in the car parts industry are not suffering as much from the current decline in new automobile sales. Investors in automobile parts companies are now focusing on exporting their production and on the automotive aftermarket segment in Poland. Nearly 20% of foreign investment in Poland has been in the automotive industry.

TELECOMMUNICATIONS

The telecommunications sector is a major part of Poland's infrastructure, but lags behind other European countries. There are only about 28 fixed-line telephones per 100 inhabitants.

The national telephone operator, Telekomunikacja Polska S.A. (TPSA) has been partially privatized. Fifteen percent of TPSA's shares were successfully floated on the stock exchanges in November 1998, and 35% of the company's shares were sold in 2000 to a consortium made up of France Telecom and a Polish businessman. France Telecom is currently contemplating whether to buy additional TPSA shares, which was an option in their initial 35% percent acquisition. If France Telecom decides not to purchase the additional shares, the Ministry of State Treasury plans to float those shares on the stock market.

TPSA still holds more than 90% of the market share in fixed-line services, with independent operators serving approximately 700,000 subscribers. Independent local operators plan to invest USD 3-4 billion, with a goal of increasing their market share to 20% by 2002. Cellular telephony is developing very quickly and the number of cellular phone users is predicted to match fixed-line subscribers during 2002.

TPSA will continue to enjoy a monopoly for voice international telephone services until 2003. The first new operators that received a license for domestic long distance voice services in 2000 launched their service in July 2001. Two other licensees will begin service by the end of 2001. Beginning in 2002, local and long distance (inter-zone) telephone services will become open for competition with limited licensing requirements and no restrictions on foreign investments.

A new Telecommunications Law that complies with most EU standards came into force in 2001. A newly created agency Urzad Regulacji Telekomunikacji (URT – Telecommunications Regulatory Office) has taken over all market regulatory functions for the Polish government. In July 2001, the government announced that the Ministry of Posts and Telecommunications will be dissolved in the near future and its functions incorporated into the Ministry of Economy.

MARKETING US PRODUCTS AND SERVICES

DISTRIBUTION AND SALES CHANNELS

(1) Regional Nature of Market and Review of Major Regions

Opportunities for doing business in Poland are, like the population, dispersed throughout the country. Twenty-five percent of the population resides in rural areas, and urban dwellers are widely spread among a number of population centers.

The largest Polish cities include:

CITY	POPULATION
Warsaw	1,650,000
Lodz	790,000
Krakow	738,000
Wroclaw	636,800
Poznan	600,000
Gdansk	458,000
Szczecin	416,700
Lublin	356,100
Katowice	343,200

CONSUMER GOODS DISTRIBUTION

Competition in the consumer goods sector, particularly non-durable consumer goods, is intense in Poland. The previously insatiable demand for western goods has been replaced by more pragmatic attitudes about price and quality. Polish consumers and importers are selective about the products they buy. Locally made brands have improved immensely in quality. Brand name recognition is still important, but it is sometimes a challenge for U.S. firms to develop brand images and loyalty, as the market has been introduced to hundreds of new western and Polish brands.

Despite the expansion of international chains of supermarkets, hypermarkets and large specialty stores, the retail market in Poland continues to be fragmented. Many small local independent retail shop owners are losing business to the large international chains and are therefore protesting the establishment of new large stores. Smaller shops are also joining merchants associations to petition authorities to preserve small, independent Polish retailing. In 2000, 11 Polish retail networks founded the Union of Polish Retail Networks (UPDS), an organization with nationwide coverage. The members of UPDS own 1,637 stores with a total floor area of 250,000 square meters. Despite the fact that the organization unites retail business owners, it intends to cooperate with Polish wholesalers. Small companies continue to dominate the Polish retail market. Ninety-eight percent of retail companies own no more than two outlets. The wholesale market is also very fragmented. Ten foreign wholesale companies produce 70% of total wholesale sales.

The number of hypermarkets is expanding rapidly in Poland and the number of hypermarkets is expected to reach 180-200 stores by 2005. Foreign retailers currently control about 10-12 percent of the total retail market in Poland. Over the next 2-3 years, they are expected to control as much as 40% of the market. The top ten retailers in Poland are foreign, and include such chains as Macro, Geant Casino, Auchan, Jeronimo Martins, IKEA , Carrefour, HIT , Castorama , OBI , Leclerc and Tesco .

Foreign retail investors are chiefly interested in opening food stores. More than ten western hypermarket and supermarket chains operate in the food retail market. All large supermarket chains doing business in Poland report aggressive plans for expansion over the next two years. Foreign retail chains invest not only in hypermarkets but also in smaller, discount store types of retail chains situated near customers' homes or work places. There is a considerable amount of development in specialty and do-it-yourself (DIY) retail chains. The fastest growing chains are OBI, IKEA, Stinnes, Nomi Dom i Ogrod, TTW Dom i Ogrod, Castorama, Praktiker, Leroy Merlin and Bricomarche. The major local DIY chain is Komfort (with about 100 outlets).

There are about 50 foreign retail clothing chains in Poland. The rapid growth of these chains is a result of the expansion of shopping malls. Very popular are Part Two, Carly Gray, Olsen, Deni Cler, and Cubus. Well-known foreign apparel brands have been introduced into Poland by two companies, Ultimate Fashion (Esprit, River Island, Wallis, Celio) and Young Fashion (Zara).

Although banks are increasing the issuance of credit cards, and most shops now accept them for payment, Poland is still largely a cash economy. Checks are almost unheard of. Cash machine networks are now extensive and continue to grow quickly.

Smaller U.S. companies usually enter the Polish market by partnering with a small, regionally located distributor and then developing a network from there. Larger firms may initially establish a regional warehouse system with a series of trucks and distributors in order to branch out to assorted markets across Poland. This requires a significant up-front investment.

INDUSTRIAL GOODS DISTRIBUTION

Imports of equipment and technology have increased tremendously as Polish industry modernizes and restructures to compete with the west. Poles are familiar with the technical parameters of U.S. products, even prior to the actual introduction of those products in the marketplace. This reflects the fact that serious Polish importers do their homework.

Under the Communist regime all foreign trade was handled through a small number of foreign trade organizations. Each industry was associated with an entity that handled its importing, exporting, marketing and distribution needs. Most of these organizations still exist in one form or another, many have been privatized, and some, such as Elektrim and Ciech, have grown to become among Poland's largest private firms.

Industrial distributors may therefore be part of a network that developed from former foreign trade organizations, or may be individuals with significant connections to their industry (frequently former employees of the large foreign trade firms). As industries and companies continue to privatize in Poland, distribution networks are expanding in scope and complexity.

Many distributors of industrial equipment are very specialized and have very specific technical expertise. Because of this, some are better able to represent foreign manufacturers on a national level than most consumer goods distributors. However, exporters are still advised to carefully check a Polish company's claim that it can represent the U.S. firm throughout the entire country.

As with consumer goods, importers and other companies that represent foreign companies are becoming more sophisticated and selective. The number and variety of imported goods available on the Polish market play an important role here as well. Polish agents or distributors increasingly look to foreign partners to provide marketing and promotional support, training and financing. Polish trade fairs, which have become more and more specific in scope, are a good place to look for possible distributors.

USE OF AGENTS AND DISTRIBUTORS

Polish companies tend to act more as distributors (importing, taking possession of, and reselling a good) than as agents. Expensive equipment is an exception to this, since many Polish companies do not have the financial capability to make such purchases. Also, heavy industrial equipment tends to be sold directly to end-uses due to the inability of most distributors to purchase the equipment prior to re-selling it to end-users.

There are no laws imposing roles for Polish importers. Distributor and agent agreements may take any form beneficial to the parties involved.

It is best to find a distributor who is experienced, knowledgeable, and well-connected to existing distribution channels for the product. Polish companies tend to be younger and less experienced than their western counterparts. In most cases, product and marketing training must be provided to new distributors.

FINDING A LOCAL PARTNER

The U.S. Commercial Service in Warsaw can help you find a local partner through one of the following customized programs:

Gold Key Service – provides a customized schedule of appointments with potential Polish partners set up for you prior to your arrival in Poland.
Contact List Service - provides you with a list of unscreened potential Polish partners in your industry. After you receive your list, you contact the companies on your own to ascertain any interest they may have in your products or services.

International Partner Search - provides you with a list of up to five pre-screened potential Polish partners that have expressed an interest in discussing the possibility doing business with you in Poland.
Amerykanski Partner Web Site - provides a description of your company and products in Polish and a direct link to your firm's web site that Polish buyers can click through to. Located at www.CSCentralEurope.org/Poland.

For more information on these services, please contact the U.S. Commercial Service Warsaw at Warsaw.Office.Box@mail.doc.gov, at telephone number (48) 22 625-4374 or fax number (48) 22 621-6327.

CHECKING THE BONA FIDES OF POLISH BUSINESS ORGANIZATIONS

The U.S. Commercial Service in Warsaw can provide U.S. companies with affordable, fast background checks on Polish business organizations through our *International Company Profile Service*. For more information on this service, please contact the U.S. Commercial Service in Warsaw at Warsaw.Office.Box@mail.doc.gov, at telephone number (48) 22 625-4374 or fax number (48) 22 621-6327.

FRANCHISING

Poland is ripe for the development of franchising. The country is rapidly developing its infrastructure, telecommunications and banking services. More important, the rapid expansion of the media and advertising sectors indicates that the consumer market is steadily developing.

The most popular and largest U.S. franchises arrived first and introduced the concept here, and they now dominate Poland's franchise landscape. Their success over the last few years has proven to be the best advertisement for the promotion of franchising in Poland. The largest foreign franchisers active in Poland are McDonald's, Domino's Pizza, TelePizza, Adidas, Intersport, Kodak Express, Fleury Michon, Avis Rent a Car, Marks & Spencer, Midas, The Athlete's Foot, English First, Futurekids, The Cheesecake Shop, Bianco Footwear, Bricomarche, Intermarche, Jean Claude Biguine, Jean Louis David, Saint Algue Paris, SPAR, Collagena, CyberLand, Blimpie, Jacadi Paris, Carre blanc, and the Yves Rocher Group.

Major Polish franchisers are Gabriel Studio Urody, A.D. Dragowski, Orbis Travel, Natura Drogerie, SIMP, Sklepy Familijne, Pozegnanie z Afryka, YES Bizuteria, Centrum Budowlane, Debica Decart, Laboratorium Kosmetyczne Dr. Irena Eris.

There are over 90 franchise systems operating in Poland. The largest number of franchises are American, French, British and German. The major sector shares in the franchise market are retail trade, services and catering.

Financing is the most critical element for successful entry and penetration by U.S. franchisers. Although it has generally been difficult for foreign companies to locate Polish investors capable of becoming master franchisees, the number of local candidates interested in becoming master franchisees is on the rise.

There are no Polish laws or regulations that specifically address franchising. A franchise is subject to general commercial law. The contract between two parties is therefore the sole legal platform for the franchise agreement. It usually contains not only elements of civil law, but also elements of intellectual property and trademark protection.

The best franchise concept prospects are in services, retail, mid-range hotels, and fast food chains.

DIRECT MARKETING

The direct marketing concept is still relatively small in Poland and is mostly practiced by joint ventures or foreign companies selling consumer products and services. Several years ago the first foreign companies began to sell a very limited assortment of products through catalogs. This form of marketing is growing rapidly, but one factor limiting the spread of direct marketing is the fact that cash is still used for most sales transactions. Nevertheless, the Polish market offers enormous potential, especially for the expansion of mail-order companies. Women are the biggest group of customers who take advantage of mail-order catalogs. Mail-order companies selling books, CDs and cassettes have become popular in Poland.

Presently, the most popular method of direct marketing is direct mail, advertisements in printed media, and telemarketing. Electronic media is opening new opportunities. Cable television companies have introduced new shopping channels. The number of Internet users is growing very quickly, resulting in expanded Internet on-line "shopping malls."

The Direct Marketing Association, Stowarzyszenie Marketingu Bezposredniego (SMB), was established in Poland in 1995. Currently SMB has 74 members including catalog, fulfillment, telemarketing, advertising, direct marketing, service, Internet, electronic media, financial, insurance, and distribution companies. The members of SMB have established a code of ethics and yearbooklines in order to establish effective methods of operations in direct marketing, protecting consumer's rights and preventing illegal business practices. The organization participated in the drafting of legislation for the protection of privacy, which was adopted in 1998. SBM provides training and educational activities on a regular basis.

For more information, please contact:

Direct Marketing Association
Stowarzyszenie Marketingu Bezposredniego (SMB)
ul. Lucka 2/4/6
00-845 Warszawa
tel: 48/22/654 68 33
fax: 48/22/654 55 33
e-mail; info@smb.pl
internet: www.smb.pl
Ms. Monika Zarzycka, General Director
e-mail: mzarzycka@smb.pl

JOINT VENTURES/LICENSING

Joint ventures as a form of business are abundant in Poland. Many U.S. businesses in Poland take the form of joint ventures, with Polish companies set up to handle sales in the market. Joint ventures are an excellent way to facilitate export sales to the Polish market.

Most joint ventures are set up so the American partner contributes capital and technology. The Polish partner typically contributes land, distribution channels, trained workers, access to the Polish market and introductions within the local government and business community that could take years to develop for an American company on their own.

Licensing of products, technology, technical data, and services is practiced less in Poland, due to concerns about intellectual property protection. However, now that Poland has taken major steps in the areas of intellectual property rights and copyright legislation, it is probable that more U.S. firms will begin to license their products here. Licensing is particularly prevalent in the industrial manufacturing, consumer goods, and textile sectors.

ESTABLISHING AN OFFICE

The choice of business entity that U.S. companies choose to establish is determined by the scope of activities that the company plans to undertake in Poland. If a U.S. company only plans to sell its products and services in Poland through its own office, it usually establishes a representative office. If a U.S. company plans to invest in Poland, there are generally only two legal forms available, a limited liability company or a joint stock company. The entity most commonly employed by foreign investors is that of a limited liability company. Following are the two forms of entities used by investors and information on establishing a representative office:

(1) Limited liability companies (Sp. z o.o.) require at least one founder and minimum initial capital required is 4,000 PLN. This capital must be paid in full before the company can be registered. A limited liability company may be 100 percent foreign-owned. Reserves are not required to be taken out of after tax earnings, audits are only obligatory in certain situations, and assets can only be distributed six months after liquidation is announced.

(2) Joint stock companies (S.A.) require 100,000 PLN minimum initial capital, of which 25% must be paid prior to registration. There are no maximum limits and in-kind contributions are exempt from customs duty. After-tax profits from the venture may be exchanged and repatriated without permission at the end of each fiscal year of the venture. Proceeds from the sale of shares in the venture, or liquidation of the venture may also be repatriated. Twelve months must pass after the liquidation announcement before assets may be distributed. Polish law does not allow interim dividends. The minimum number of founders is three entities.

(3) Representative offices are permitted by law to engage in business activity under three variations: supervisory offices, technical offices and commercial branch offices. Permits for establishing an office are granted by the relevant Ministry upon application by the foreign firm. Permits are valid for the length of time granted by the Ministry, which is usually a maximum of two years. The foreign firm must reapply for renewal of its permit. Offices are by law treated as parts of the U.S. company, and are considered an importer of products from abroad. Therefore, offices may not engage in retailing or manufacturing activities and may hold inventory only for marketing and service purposes.

Modern telephones, copy machines, faxes, computers and office amenities are easily available and can be leased from a number of reputable Polish and western firms. The secretarial labor pool is reasonably abundant, although English speaking secretaries with modest secretarial skills are not easily found. Employees with western management and accounting experience are becoming easier to find. There are many executive search firms that offer assistance in finding appropriate staff.

SELLING FACTORS/TECHNIQUES

As discussed earlier, the Polish market is in most cases regional, and this description applies to selling as well. Because unemployment is significantly lower in the cities, urban dwellers generally have more purchasing power than inhabitants of rural areas. The countryside is dotted with single-factory (or formerly single-factory) towns, many of which suffer from high unemployment.

Letters, faxes, Internet web sites and packages of product literature will serve to introduce a product or service to a Polish company. Communication in the Polish language is recommended if the seller would like to receive a speedy reply. U.S. companies should ensure that translations from English to Polish are performed only by professional translators who are knowledgeable with modern business Polish and grammar.

A Polish customer generally will not consider making a final purchase until he or she has met with someone face to face to discuss the product. However, there are some Polish companies that have begun to conduct business on the Internet. American companies that are little known outside of the U.S. may need to make a significant effort to convince their prospective Polish customer that they are "for real." Product demonstrations are effective, as Poles tend to be skeptical about claims until they are proven. Sponsored visits to the U.S. company's headquarters or manufacturing plant frequently helps to convince Polish buyers to purchase a U.S. product.

The decision making process, especially in large companies or government agencies, can be painfully slow, as every person or section involved in a decision usually must sign off before a decision is made. It usually takes several meetings, and many rounds of negotiations before a deal is closed. This means that success in Poland is extremely difficult without a representative in country, whether it is an agent, distributor, or representative office.

Polish customers will want to discuss the technical parameters of the product, explain their needs, and negotiate (and renegotiate) the price. In addition, the product may not be sold at the first meeting, as the customer will want some time to consider the points discussed and to arrange financing. Small orders are usually the result, as major initial orders are unlikely due to limited amounts of working capital and high rates of interest on credit.

The American exporter should be aware of the Polish customer's main problem: access to capital. Most Polish firms are still too small to consider going public or to issue commercial paper. Therefore, most business activities, including payment for imports, are still self-financed. American companies that can yearbook their Polish customers to affordable financing will have an edge over their competitors. The U.S. Export-Import Bank (Ex-Im Bank) offers a credit insurance program that can help small and medium size U.S. firms in this regard.

Polish customers are generally enthusiastic about U.S. products and, if seriously interested, will travel great distances across Poland in order to meet with a U.S. representative who may be visiting Warsaw. For example, if a prospective customer has driven five hours to Warsaw to meet with a U.S. company, the potential for a sale is good. If the proposal is well thought out, the pricing is flexible (or assistance with financing is offered) and promotion, servicing and customer support are part of the package, chances are good that a contract will ultimately be written. Doing business in Poland is built upon personal relationships and trust. U.S. companies have an advantage in Poland, as the U.S., its people, and its products are held in high regard.

ADVERTISING AND TRADE PROMOTION

The trade fair business in Poland has boomed over the past decade, from a single major event (the annual June Poznan International Fair) to a full year's schedule of industry and product specific events in major cities around the country. Most industry specific trade fairs in Poland are fairly new and are still proving their worth. Some are better than others at attracting key Polish and international businesses. Trade fairs for computers, medical, environmental, automotive, agribusiness, consumer goods, building products and mining have grown in popularity in recent years. Direct U.S. company presence at trade fairs in Poland is minimal, but many U.S. firms exhibit through their European or Polish distributors. Most U.S. firms find that exhibiting directly at a Polish fair is less cost effective than participating in larger western European trade fairs. The U.S. Commercial Service in Warsaw can help find distributors interested in representing U.S. products at Polish fairs.

Advertising in Poland is considered crucial, not only in the consumer product field but also in developing a company image for all kinds of goods. Television, which reaches virtually every home in Poland via local channels or satellite, is believed to be the most effective advertising medium in Poland. Products advertised through television commercials show the greatest sales growth among all advertised products. The bulk of advertising revenues go to television. The price of television spots on top rated shows has grown dramatically in the last few years as demand has soared. Radio is another means of advertising with more than 200 local radio stations as well as two national networks in operation.

There is a ban on cigarette and alcohol (including beer and wine) advertising for broadcasters and on alcohol ads for display and print media. There is also a ban on pharmaceutical advertising, except for over-the-counter drugs and in professional publications.

Print media advertising is sophisticated, and the print media market itself has grown to include a full range of publications. Poland is wholly literate. Major newspapers circulate throughout Poland and reach every corner of the country. In addition, special interest magazines, business journals, niche publications, and specialized newspapers have proliferated. Classified advertising is very well developed and effective. Most U.S. companies find print media to be a highly effective means of reaching customers and candidates for jobs.

Major daily newspapers include Rzeczpospolita, Gazeta Wyborcza, Zycie, and Trybuna. Major daily business journals include Prawo i Gospodarka and Puls Biznesu. Business News Poland is a business journal printed by Boss Economic Information on a weekly basis. Business Week Polski is published on a monthly basis. There are also two English language weeklies that cater mainly to foreigners in Poland, the Warsaw Business Journal and the Warsaw Voice. Major international, as well as local, advertising and public relations agencies abound in Poland. Advertising and promotional service agencies include McCann Erickson Polska, Leo Burnett, J. Walter Thompson, Ogilvy & Mather Poland, Saatchi & Saatchi, BBDO Warsaw and Young & Rubicam. For further contact information on these journals and firms please contact the U.S. Commercial Service in Warsaw at Warsaw.Office.Box@mail.doc.gov, at telephone number (48) 22 625-4374 or fax number (48) 22 621-6327.

PRICING A PRODUCT

Pricing is key to the effective selling U.S. products in Poland. As mentioned above, working capital is limited in Poland, even among the larger, more successful Polish companies. Polish businesses generally spend money wisely, after thoughtful and sometimes lengthy consideration. The most common complaint heard by the U.S. Commercial Service in Warsaw continues to be that "the price is too high." Pricing of U.S. made products is complicated by the addition of customs duties, Value Added Tax (VAT), and, in some cases excise tax, all of which may elevate the final retail price of a product dramatically. Flexibility in pricing is the key, and initial market penetration to gain product knowledge among Polish consumers is the goal. Successful U.S. exporters work together with their Polish representatives to keep costs, particularly import costs, as low as possible. For example, some companies ship products unassembled to help reduce import duties. The Polish market for all kinds of products is huge and expanding, however more and more competitive. U.S. companies that approach the market with a long-term view of creating market share for their products will reap rewards.

SALES SERVICE/CUSTOMER SUPPORT

After price, service is second on the list of the Polish customer's concerns. A manufacturer in the United States is seen by the Polish distributor and customer alike as being very far away from a product exported to Poland. A potential customer may shy away from U.S. products because he/she fears ineffective servicing, simply due to distance, if the product requires repair or servicing.

Shipping a product back to the United States for repair or service, even if paid for by the U.S. company, is not generally a preferred option for Polish customers. Sending spare parts to Poland is easy to do. Some firms provide service for their exports to Poland through European representatives or firms licensed to repair their products. Even then, some distributors worry that they may not get adequate support.

The ideal method is to provide service and customer support through a trained Polish representative or U.S. affiliate company. U.S. manufacturers with major export accounts in Poland may wish to periodically send a service representative to Poland to work with the local representative and visit customers.

SELLING TO THE GOVERNMENT

Poland's public procurement law, in effect since January 1995 (January 1996 for local government entities), applies to most acquisitions of goods, services, or construction by nearly all government agencies, including local governments, foundations, associations, and cooperatives. Procurements by the Ministry of Defense are also included, but are subject to special rules. Procurements by state-owned enterprises are excluded from the law.

All tenders for products or services in amounts above 30,000 ECU must be officially announced to the public. Tenders for lower amounts can be announced locally in the local press or through local media.

The Polish procurement law provides for domestic preferences. Bids submitted by Polish firms are lowered (only for the purpose of the evaluation of the tender) by 20%. Tenders are evaluated by assigning an appropriate number of points to various parts of the offer by each bidder. When a project is actually executed by a Polish company, the price paid by the public entity is what the Polish bidder quoted. This 20% "rule" applies only to bids in which a minimum of 50% of the raw materials used for completion of the project originate in Poland.

Unlimited tendering is the preferred method, and other procedures are restricted. Tender documents must contain specifications, selection criteria and terms and conditions for the contract. The deadline for the submission of bids must be at least six weeks from the announcement of a tender. Bids are opened publicly. Participation in tenders is open to all those who are legally, technically, and financially able to perform the contract (including foreign companies).

The National Bulletin of Public Procurement (Biuletyn Zomowien Publicznych), which lists public procurement opportunities throughout Poland, is published twice a week. Subscriptions are available through:

Wydzial Wydawnictw I Poligrafii
Gospodarstwa Pomocniczego Kancelarii Prezesa
Rady Ministrow
ul. Powsinska 69/71
09-903 Warsaw
http://www.urm.gov.pluspindexuzxp.htm

TRADE REGULATIONS, CUSTOMS AND STANDARDS

TRADE BARRIERS, INCLUDING TARIFF AND NON-TARIFF BARRIERS

Poland complies with the Harmonized Tariff System. Tariff rates are generally revised at the beginning of each year, although tariff suspensions can be introduced or lifted at any time. Depending on the country of origin, products are divided into three categories:

1. Developing nations
2. Members of the World Trade Organization
3. Countries with which Poland has a bilateral or multilateral preferential trade agreement

In 1992, Poland signed an Association Agreement with the European Union (EU) that lowered or eliminated tariffs on many EU produced goods imported into Poland, while tariffs on U.S. products did not change. At that time, the U.S. managed to negotiate more favorable rates for some product categories, but many U.S. products are still at a disadvantage compared to EU competitors.

For some luxury and strategic products (e.g. alcohol, cosmetics, cigarettes, sugar confectionery, video cameras, satellite antennas, passenger cars, gasoline, and oil) an excise tax is also applied. The excise tax is levied on top of the customs tariff.

Duty free quotas have been applied within certain industries, including the automotive, computer, and pharmaceutical sectors. U.S. and foreign firms have benefited from these quotas. In some instances the quotas are targeted on products originating from specific export regions (e.g. cars from the EU as a result of the Association Agreement), and in others they have been assessed to help protect local industry (e.g. pharmaceutical), to help develop industries (e.g. computer parts and components), or to protect the environment.

Refunds are possible for customs duty paid on raw materials, semi-finished goods, and products used in the manufacture of goods for export within thirty days, contingent on documentation certifying customs duty was paid on the goods when they were imported. However, some U.S. firms have encountered significant delays in receiving refunds of customs duties and others have suggested replacing the "up front payment/refund after re-export" system with a bond system.

AGRICULTURAL TARIFFS:

Poland implemented its Uruguay Round requirements in 1995. This established for the first time bound tariffs for majority products in the Polish tariff schedule and replaced variable levies for import-sensitive agricultural products with tariff rate quotas.

Tariff rate within quotas represent significant import protection for products such as beef, pork, poultry meat, wheat and rye flours, rapeseed oil, some processed food products, yeast, sauces, alcohol, tobacco, and tobacco products. For U.S. agricultural trade, tariff rate quotas have had the largest impact on access for poultry meat. The tariff rate quota for poultry meat, which will be adjusted upward annually as Poland's domestic output expands, is estimated at 47,736 for 2001. The above quota tariff is presently set at 60%, which is one half the maximum rate that Poland may apply under the Agreement.

CUSTOMS REGULATIONS AND CONTACT INFORMATION

Customs duties are based on the CIF value of the product. Customs officials are extremely strict with regards to proper documentation. It is essential that exporters take care to fill out documents properly to avoid costly delays in customs clearance. For further information on Polish customs regulations, please contact:

Customs Information
ul. Swietokrzyska 12
00-916 Warsaw
Telephone: (48) 22 694-4479 or 694-3194

TARIFF RATES

Customs duties apply to all products imported into Poland. Tariffs range from 0 (zero) to nearly 400% (strong specialty sprits). The Polish tariff schedule has different rates for the same commodities depending on their country of origin. The most recent revision of the Polish tariff rate schedule took place on January 1, 2001, and is completed annually.
Introduction of changes to the custom tariff (e.g. suspensions of tariffs) after it has been published is a common practice in Poland.

IMPORT TAXES

Poland rescinded its import tax in 2004. As in much of Europe, a Value Added Tax (VAT) is assessed. There are four VAT rates: 0%, 3%, 7%, and 22% depending on the product. VAT is levied on the CIF value of the product plus duty plus excise tax (if applicable). There is also an excise tax on certain goods, including alcohol, cigarettes and cars. On imported goods, this is collected at the border on the basis of the CIF value.

IMPORT LICENSE REQUIREMENTS

In general, the trade of goods and services is not restricted in Poland. In some areas, including imports of strategic goods (e.g. police and military products, radioactive elements, weapons, transportation equipment, chemicals) a license or concession is required. Imports of beer, wine and strong alcoholic beverages, gas, and certain agricultural and food products (including dairy, poultry, and tobacco products) are also licensed. A permit is necessary to sell imported alcoholic products. A phytosanitary import permit issued by Plant Quarantine Inspection Service is required for the import of all live plants, fresh fruits, and vegetables into Poland. Several common weed seeds have quarantine status which hampers U.S. grain and oilseed exports to Poland.
Certain goods are subject to import quotas in Poland. These include gasoline, diesel fuel and heating oils; wine and other alcohol; and cigars and cigarettes.

The Ministry of Economy issues import permits and concessions and regulates quotas. However, other Polish ministries have special jurisdiction over products such as tobacco (Ministry of Agriculture); permits related to air, sea, or road transport (Ministry of Transportation); or natural resources (Ministry of Environmental Protection). U.S. exporters should ascertain whether their product requires import certification before shipping.

In most cases, before an issuing ministry grants import permission on a product, the product must be reviewed and recommended for import into Poland by one or more inspectorates or technical associations, depending on the nature of the product. This can be a costly, lengthy, and confusing process for the U.S. exporter and the Polish importer alike. It is often necessary to submit samples of products or equipment for testing, regardless of the issuance of previous U.S. or international certificates. The presentation of detailed documentation on a product is a must, and all requests by relevant inspection agencies should be strictly adhered to in order to speed up certification procedures.

Once an application and supporting materials have been submitted, the inspecting agency will make a positive or negative recommendation for import to the appropriate Polish ministry. When the import of a specific product is approved, further imports of that product are free from additional regulation. U.S. companies with several lines of like products (e.g. pharmaceutical, food preparation, or chemical products) should begin the approval procedure on all products as early as possible.

Some products, once imported, also require registration. This is particularly true of products that come into contact with or can affect the health of the consumer. In the case of hazardous materials the importer must receive permission to use the product before applying for a concession to import the product into Poland.

Importers of meat, meat products, and offal must obtain a veterinary permit and the health certificate issued by USDA's veterinary authorities must accompany each consignment. Veterinary permits are also required for the import of live animals. Veterinary permits for breeding livestock, semen, and embryos are not issued unless a positive opinion for the importation is received from the Central Animal Breeding Office.

Polish regulations require imported products, including food and agriculture products, to be inspected for compliance with Polish standards. The inspection agency, Centralny Inspektorat Standardyzacji (CIS), is charged with ensuring the "quality" of products offered on the Polish market.

TEMPORARY ENTRY

A license is also required for temporary import of goods, which takes place under the supervision of Polish customs officials. Written confirmation is required, stating that the goods will be sent out of Poland on specific dates. A deposit is required for the import of the goods subject to clearance, which must be equal the value of the goods to be exported or the total import customs duty and taxes. Commercial samples of zero or low value can usually be imported free of customs duty by means of a written statement to Polish customs confirming the value of the sample and that it will stay in the possession of the importing entity. Temporary imports may also enter Poland under an ATA Carnet. Promotional materials must be clearly marked "no commercial value" in order to clear customs.

SPECIAL IMPORT/EXPORT REQUIREMENTS AND CERTIFICATIONS

The only approved form for customs clearance is the Single Administrative Document (SAD), which is also used by the European Union. This form requires the completion of 56 items, including details about parties to the sale contract, terms of delivery and payment, customs procedures and the country of origin of the imported goods.

The importer must also complete a declaration of customs value, and the information contained in it must correspond to that in the SAD document. An original invoice, or in some cases, a pro forma invoice indicating the value of the goods is also required.

Some types of goods are defined as sensitive for the Polish market. Therefore, their import is controlled by specific government agencies that are authorized to grant licenses or permits for some goods, i.e., sanitary licenses for agricultural goods, permits for medical goods and licenses for weapons and explosive materials.

LABELING REQUIREMENTS

As noted above, certificate of origin documents are required for importation. Labeling and packaging requirements also vary depending on the product. Consumer goods require a product description in Polish somewhere on or inside the package. Packaging should clearly indicate the country of manufacture. Packaged or canned food products require Polish language labels containing the product composition, nutritional value, an outdate, the name and address of the producer, and the product weight. The Polish government is considering requiring food products using Genetically Modified Organisms (GMOs) to be so labeled. Some U.S. companies have found that using the English language somewhere on the packaging (e.g. product name, promotional slogan) helps give the product additional prestige or value in the eyes of the Polish consumer.

PROHIBITED IMPORTS

The import of some products is prohibited. These include two-stroke engine cars; automobiles, racing cars, and vans older than ten years; trucks older than six years; automobiles with no proof of the year in which they were manufactured and badly damaged automobiles.

U.S. GOVERNMENT EXPORT CONTROLS

A validated U.S. export license is required prior to shipping certain controlled commodities to Poland, as provided under the U.S. Department of Commerce's Bureau of Export Administration's (BXA) Commodity Control List. For more information and assistance, please contact BXA's Exporter Counseling Division at (202) 482-4811 or refer to BXA's web site at http://www.bxa.doc.gov.

Poland is a member of the Wassenaar Arrangement and has established its own export control regime for munitions and dual use commodities.

K. Warranty and Non-Warranty Repairs

Items sent for repairs under warranty do not have duties placed on them when they are returned to Poland. The same applies to parts imported under warranty for repairs in Poland.

STANDARDS

(1) "B" Safety Certificates

Poland has developed its own extensive system of standards and certification to protect consumer interests. Generally, Polish standards and certification requirements are not harmonized with international product standards. Many of product standards are mandatory and must be certified by an accredited Polish testing agency. A Polish "B" safety certificate has been required since 1994 for imports and domestically produced goods. Poland does not automatically accept the EU "CE" mark or other international product standards, nor self-certification by manufacturers. Testing procedures can be long and expensive, although official regulations specify that the process should not take more than three months. However, the workload of testing institutes is large, and as a result, many are not able to meet the three-month deadline.

If a U.S. company is in possession of a European "CE" mark for its products or an ISO 9000 certificate for its company, these documents can help to accelerate the current certification process. However, the law is not clear on this issue and guidance from the PCBC and other testing centers is vague. Information regarding the cost for testing products is also inconsistent. In most cases testing procedures can be lengthy. The U.S. Commercial Service advises U.S. exporters to contact its Warsaw at Warsaw.Office.Box@mail.doc.gov or at the telephone or fax numbers listed in Chapter 11 to determine whether or not their products are subject to certification requirements and updates on current certification procedures.

Harmonization of standards, certification, and testing procedures with the EU, including greater reliance on voluntary standards, is now the main objective of Polish standardization policy. Under the European Conformity Assessment Agreement of 2004, Poland agreed to introduce an EU-compatible certification system. Poland agreed to gradually align its regulations and certification procedures with the EU to remove from mandatory certification those products free from certification in the EU and to automatically provide a "B" safety certificate to EU products subject to mandatory certification. However, while the list of products requiring mandatory certification in Poland was reduced from 1,400 industrial products to 700 in 2004, the agreement has not been implemented. Products requiring the "B" safety certificate cover about one third of all goods marketed in Poland. They include a wide range of diverse products, including wire rods, steel pipes and castings, motor vehicle components, bicycles, personal computers, fertilizers, and shampoo.

(2) Other Polish Standards

Polish standards that cover a wide range of products have been developed over the years by a central institution, the Polish Standards Committee (PKN). Poland's Standardization Law provides the foundation for moving toward a system based on self-certification and for greater harmonization with EU and international standards. Much of the PKN's recent work has focused on reviewing Polish standards. There are currently 18,000 Polish standards, of which about 75% comply with EU norms, and about 15% cover international standards (ISO and IEC) not adopted by the EU. The remaining 10% of standards are Polish-based. The objective is to have at least 80% of Polish standards harmonized with EU norms by 2002. The plan is for Poland to invoke EU standards in cases where EU and other international standards differ.

(3) Building Products: Special, Separate Technical Approval Required

No standards exist for many building products that are new to Poland. However, prior to being introduced on the Polish market these products must be certified that they conform to existing Polish building product standards. Products must receive technical approval, a document issued by designated research and development institutes.

The central institution performing tests for the vast majority of building products and materials is the Institute for Building Technology (ITB) in Warsaw. The ITB deals with products such as siding, roof shingles, windows and bricks.

Some building products, after receiving technical approval, may also require a "B" Certificate, as described above.

Companies in Poland possessing ISO series 9000 certificates is growing.

USEFUL CONTACTS

Instytut Techniki Budowlanej (ITB)
ul. Filtrowa 1
00-950 Warsaw
Telphone: (48) 22 825-0471
Fax: (48) 22 825-1303

Centralny Osrodek Badawczo
Rozwojowy Przemyslu Izolacji Budowlanych
ul. Korfantego 93
40-153 Katowice
Telephone/fax: (48) 32 58-35-53

Centralny Osrodek Badawczo
Rozwojowy
Technologii Instalacji
ul. Ksawerow 21 (COBRTI)
02-656 Warsaw
Telephone: (48) 22 843-1471
Fax: (48) 22 843-7165

Panstwowy Zaklad Higieny (PZH)
Zaklad Higieny Komunalnej

(Urban Hygiene Dept.)
ul. Chocimska 21
Warsaw
Telephone: (48) 22 849-4051

FREE TRADE ZONES/WAREHOUSES

Duty free zones can be established by the Minister of Finance in cooperation with the Minister of Economy and are managed by authorities designated by the Ministers, which is usually the provincial governor who issues the operating permit for a given zone.

Bonded warehouses and customs and storage facilities are available. They are operated under permission issued by the President of the Central Office of Customs. Commercial code companies can operate them.

Customs duties are repaid to the importer for re-exports of products within 12 months of the date of customs clearance in full or partially, depending upon their length of time in country.

MEMBERSHIP IN FREE TRADE ARRANGEMENTS

EU Association Agreement: As mentioned above, Poland began implementing the trade provisions of the Association Agreement with the European Union in 1992. This has lowered or eliminated duties on most EU exports to Poland.

CEFTA and FTAs: Poland is a founding member of the Central European Free Trade Association, whose members include the Czech Republic, Slovakia, Hungary, Romania, Slovenia, and Bulgaria. The CEFTA Agreement, signed in December 1992, allows for a staged reduction of customs duties on three separate lists of products among the member states through 2001. Poland also has free trade agreements (FTAs) with the European Free Trade Association (EFTA) countries (Iceland, Norway, Switzerland, and Liechtenstein) as well as with Israel, Lithuania, Latvia, Estonia, and Turkey. These agreements grant firms from these countries certain tariff preferences over U.S. competitors and give lower tariffs to Polish companies exporting to these countries. The Polish government is also negotiating an FTA with Croatia.

TRADE AND PROJECT FINANCING

BRIEF DESCRIPTION OF BANKING SYSTEM

Poland's banking system continues to adapt and modernize. With the gradual installation of new telecommunications equipment and services and the advent of increased competition between domestic and foreign banks, services are becoming increasingly more user-friendly and efficient.

Although the availability of banking services varies from one bank to another, commercial banks generally offer a variety of money transfer and cash management services, but they do not usually provide access to cheap credit or extensive personal banking services. Banks set their own interest rates based on several factors, particularly the inflation rate, reserve requirements, and the National Bank of Poland (NBP) rates. Special services such as cash management, counseling, and risk management for foreign currency transactions are not consistent from bank to bank.

The majority of Polish banks have been privatized. A number of large banks have shares listed on the Warsaw Stock Exchange, and more are planned for the future. The majority of the Polish banking sector's assets, deposits, and equity are in the hands of the private sector.

Foreign companies do not have special restrictions on access to local finance as long as funds are used for activities in Poland. Obtaining a loan can be easier if the project is export oriented. Banks usually request proof of solvency and a business plan, as well as security. Security often takes the form of a large deposit (equal to the amount of the loan plus interest) that earns a relatively low rate of interest. As property values in Poland are difficult to determine, banks often require property pledged as security to be worth two to three times the value of the loan. Loans are also available to smaller businesses that can produce credible offshore guarantees.

A growing number of foreign banks are establishing banking operations in Poland, either through local subsidiaries, fully operating branches, or participation in consortium banks, which may also include Polish bank shareholders. Several U.S. banks have offices in Poland. While some banks have branches all over Poland, many are regional or have few branches. Businesses with banking needs in varying areas should carefully consider the location of their bank and availability of branches.

The zloty is, for most purposes, fully convertible. Companies operating in Poland have free access to foreign currency to finance imports, but they must exchange their hard currency export earnings, which are held in zloty accounts. Though still much opposed by foreign business, the system itself has not proven problematic (owing to the stability of the zloty). There have been no failures of the banking system to provide hard currency on demand. Profits can be repatriated by law, including repatriation through bonds and securities.

Polish companies may utilize zloty earnings to buy foreign currency to pay for imports. This helps to open the market for western goods. Transfers of hard currency abroad, other than as payments for trade transactions, are controlled.

The banking system is supervised by the central bank, the National Bank of Poland (NBP). The NBP is responsible for the issue of money and control of the monetary and credit policy in Poland. It grants banking licenses and foreign exchange permits. Today there are 83 banks in Poland that are privately owned or operate as commercial companies. In addition, there are 1,295 independent cooperative banks. U.S. banks and branches include Citibank, Bank of America, American Express (which also operates full travel-related services in Warsaw), GE Capital, Ford, and General Motors. Fifteen Polish banks have been approved by the Export-Import Bank of the U.S. for bank guarantees and currently engage in foreign trade financing.

It sometimes can take two to four weeks to collect money on a sale within Poland, so cash management services can make a significant difference in business profitability.

Business counseling ranks high among the features of some foreign banks in Poland, and most encourage their clients to call before investing. These banks offer counseling services to western firms on regulations and business practices in Poland, and some spend considerable time counseling Polish businesses on western business practices, business plans, and financial plans.

FOREIGN EXCHANGE CONTROLS AFFECTING TRADING

Since 1996 domestic business entities have not been required to resell foreign currency payments from abroad to a foreign exchange bank. Instead, they may have a Polish bank account denominated in the foreign currency and keep these payments in that account. However, if a Polish business entity does want to resell a foreign means of payment received from abroad, it can do so only to an authorized foreign exchange bank (i.e. the banks indicated by the President of the NBP). When these businesses need foreign exchange, the invoice for goods to be purchased must be presented to prove the currency is needed. Most banks insist that there is no problem acquiring foreign currency. Several banks guarantee wire transfers within 48 hours, although the general rule is that foreign banks are faster than domestic banks. A transfer can be as quick as one day if it is between affiliated banks or banks on the SWIFT system and if the order is placed early in the day. It is best to have a contact person at your bank to monitor the transaction.

GENERAL FINANCING AVAILABILITY

All commercial banks in Poland offer funds transfers and investment or working capital loans. Banks are limited by law to their exposure to creditors. Due to these capitalization requirements, large loans must sometimes be shared between two or more banks. The National Bank of Poland (NBP) influences interest rates for deposits or loans via the interbank offer rate. Banks charge rates of interest based on the NBP lombard rate plus bank surcharges and front end fees.

HOW TO FINANCE EXPORTS/METHODS OF PAYMENT

Import financing procedures in Poland adhere to western business practices. All payments go through qualified foreign exchange banks. The safest method of receiving payment for a U.S. export sale is through an irrevocable letter of credit (L/C). However, most banks in Poland require the importer to deposit funds prior to issuance of an L/C. Therefore, for most Polish importers, an L/C is not a financing tool but a payment mechanism.

Difficulties in obtaining U.S. bank guarantees on Polish L/Cs seem to stem from considerations of Poland's overall debt performance. They do not necessarily reflect the actual performance of Polish banks on L/Cs, which is generally considered excellent. Typically, L/Cs are opened for a period to cover production and shipping, and they are normally paid within seven working days after receipt of the goods. Cash payment or down payments provide an extra measure of security for export sales.

Polish companies sometimes offer to pay for U.S. exports with cash in advance, as it can be difficult for them to get Polish bank guarantees. U.S. exporters who request cash advance payments (usually through money orders or certified bank drafts) need to be aware that many Polish companies are strapped for cash and may need time to organize their funds. Their delays are not a result of lack of interest, but more often a result of the need for time to arrange financing or loans. Finally, cash payments often arrive in the U.S. in installments and not as a single payment.

TYPES OF EXPORT FINANCING AND INSURANCE AVAILABLE

Sources of financing for projects in Poland vary depending upon specific financial requirements and needs. Financing is found under special programs such as those of the World Bank, the International Finance Corporation (IFC), the European Bank for Reconstruction and Development (EBRD), and other financial assistance programs created by western governments. In addition to local financing through Polish banks, self-financing, and financing through U.S. sources, the following organizations provide financing and/or insurance for investments made in Poland:

(1) Export-Import Bank of the United States (Ex-Im Bank)

The Ex-Im Bank provides guarantees of working capital loans for U.S. exporters, guarantees the repayment of loans, and makes loans to Polish purchasers of U.S. goods and services. The Ex-Im Bank also provides credit insurance that assists U.S. exporters shipping on short and medium term credits by insuring against nonpayment by foreign buyers. Working Capital Guarantees cover 90% of the principal and interest on commercial loans to creditworthy, small and medium sized companies that need funds to buy or produce U.S. goods or services for export. Export Credit Insurance policies protect against both the political and commercial risks of a foreign buyer defaulting on payment. There are no discretionary credit limits for short-term comprehensive credit insurance. Coverage is generally limited to irrevocable letters of credit issued or guaranteed by one of the eight banks that Ex-Im recognizes as having an international reputation for creditworthiness. Other transactions are examined on a case by case basis. In addition, Ex-Im Bank offers direct loans, which provide foreign buyers with competitive, fixed rate financing for their purchases from the United States. For more information on Ex-Im Bank programs, please contact:

Export-Import Bank of the United States
811 Vermont Ave., N.W.
Washington, D.C. 20571
Telephone: (800) 565-EXIM
Fax: (202) 565-3380
Web site: http://www.exim.gov

(2) USDA Export Credit Guarantee Programs

USDA has three credit guarantee programs to support exports of U.S. food and agricultural products to Poland. The Supplier Credit Guarantee Program (SCGP) is available for Poland. Under the SCGP, USDA guarantees up to 70% of the principal offered on credit terms of 15, 20, 30, 45, 60, 90, 120, 150, and 180 days. SCGP has a limit of USD 10 million for Poland and does not require a letter of credit.

USDA guarantees payment of letters of credit issued by Polish banks in favor of U.S. exporters under the GSM-102 and GSM-103 program. GSM-102 export credit guarantees of USD 25 million for 90 days to three years through approved banks are available for Poland. GSM-103 export credit guarantees of up to USD 5 million on credit terms in excess of three years, but not more than five years, are also available for exports of U.S. breeding livestock. Further information on these programs can be obtained from:

U.S. Department of Agriculture
Foreign Agricultural Service
Telephone: (202) 720-7115

Companies may also check news releases for these programs on the Foreign Agricultural Service homepage at http://www.fas.usda.gov.

(3) Commercial Bank Financing

Until very recently commercial bank financing for U.S. exports to Poland was limited due to Poland's poor credit rating. Since the signing of the London and Paris agreements, however, more banks have been willing to offer financing for U.S. exports to Poland.

F. Project Financing Available, Including Lending from Multilateral Institutions and Types of Projects Supported

(4) The World Bank

The World Bank serves as a source of loans for economic development and reform programs in Poland. The World Bank finances projects in several main areas: support of Government efforts in the energy sector, improvement of municipal and basic infrastructure, development of key Polish institutions and systems to support a market oriented economy, and development of the social and financial sectors.

The World Bank uses guarantees to support and attract private investment for projects that demand large sums of long term financing, or are in areas of high political risk. Guarantees are used to stimulate investment, and the World Bank only provides partial guarantees, sharing the risk with private lenders. The World Bank utilizes two types of guarantees in addition to the possibility of issuing a World Bank loan. A Contractual Compliance Guarantee protects private lenders against specific risks identified by the host Government, the private party, and the World Bank. A Partial Credit Guarantee protects private lenders against possible late loan payments and finances extensions of medium term loans.

A summary of projects and procurement financed by the World Bank is printed in a bimonthly publication that can be obtained by contacting:

Development Business
UN Department of Public Information
PO Box 5850 Grand Central Station
New York, NY 10163 5850
Telephone: (212) 963-1515
Fax: (212) 963-1381

Further information on World Bank programs can be obtained from:

Public Information Center
World Bank Headquarters
1818 H Street, N.W., Room GB 1
300
Washington, D.C. 20043
Telephone: (202) 477-1234

or

World Bank Resident Mission
ul. Emilii Plater 53
00-113 Warsaw, Poland
Telephone: (48) (22) 520-8000
Fax: (48) (22) 520-8001

(5) International Finance Corporation (IFC)

The IFC is a member of the World Bank Group, which provides non-government guaranteed direct investment in private businesses. Its purpose is to attract foreign and host country investors to supply additional debt and equity financing. The IFC has been active in Poland since 1987. To date, the IFC has invested over USD 505 million in 26 projects in various sectors. For additional information, please contact:

International Finance Corporation Resident Mission
ul. Emilii Plater 53
Warsaw, Poland
Telephone: (48) (22) 520-6100
Fax: (48) (22) 520-7101

(6) U.S. Trade and Development Agency (TDA)

TDA promotes U.S. exports through direct assistance to middle income countries, including Poland. TDA accomplishes this by financing feasibility studies and related planning services and training programs. These projects must, as a rule, offer good opportunities for U.S. export of equipment and services. TDA has feasibility study financing available to the public and private sectors. The public sector program comprises more than 90% of TDA financing. It offers grants to foreign governments for feasibility studies to be performed by U.S. firms in large-scale public sector projects. The private sector program offers cost sharing of feasibility studies with U.S. investors on a reimbursable basis. TDA has provided more than USD 10 million in feasibility grants to Poland over the last four years. For further information contact:

U.S. Trade and Development Agency
1621 North Kent St., Suite 200
Arlington, VA 22209
Telephone: (703) 875-4357
Fax: (703) 875-4009
E-mail: info@tda.gov
Web site: http://www.tda.gov

(7) European Bank for Reconstruction and Development

The European Bank for Reconstruction and Development (EBRD) operates as a development bank as well as a merchant bank, providing government guarantees and commercial loans. The EBRD lends and invests exclusively in projects in Central and Eastern Europe, and at least 60% of its funding is targeted to private sector companies or state-owned companies going through the privatization process. With an emphasis on the environment, the EBRD requires proposals that demonstrate good products or services with sound market prospects, significant capital commitments by project sponsors, dependable technology, sound environmental management, a high return on investment, and overall financial viability of the borrowing enterprise. For further information, please contact:

European Bank for Reconstruction and Development
U.S. Office
London, England
Telephone: (44) 20 7588-4027
Fax: (44) 20 7588-4026

EBRD Poland Office
ul. Emilii Plater 53
Warsaw, Poland
Telephone: (48) 22 520-5700
Fax: (48) 22 520-5800

(8) Overseas Private Investment Corporation (OPIC)

OPIC is a self sustaining U.S. government agency that provides investment information, financing, and political risk insurance for U.S. companies investing in emerging markets like Poland. OPIC offers medium to long term financing in Poland through its direct loans and guarantees program. Direct loans are reserved for U.S. small business or cooperatives and generally range in amounts from USD 2-10 million. Loan guarantees are issued to U.S. lending institutions and range in size from USD 10-75 million, and in certain instances to USD 200 million. OPIC can insure U.S. investments against political violence, expropriation, and inconvertibility of local currency.

OPIC has initiated a USD 65 million fund called Poland Partners. The fund is designed to provide capital for new projects, expansion of existing enterprises, and privatization of state owned businesses. Poland Partners will focus on seven high growth sectors: (1) pharmaceutical and personal care products, (2) automotive after-market, (3) building supplies and home improvement, (4) financial services, (5) franchised services, (6) plastic molding, and (7) food processing. OPIC also has developed an environmental fund to provide capital to U.S. companies involved in projects linked to economic development and the protection of the environment in Poland and other countries in Central and Eastern Europe. For projects involving warehousing, industrial sites, and distribution, OPIC has established a real estate fund. For more information, please contact:

Overseas Private Investment Corporation
1100 New York Avenue, N.W.
Washington, DC 20527
Telephone: (202) 336-8799
Fax: (202) 408-9859
Web site: http://www.opic.gov

G. List of Major Banks with Correspondent U.S. Banking Arrangements

Bank Polska Kasa Opieki, S.A.
(Pekao SA)
ul. Grzybowska 53/57
00-950 Warsaw
Telephone: (48) 22 656-0780 or 656-0781
Fax: (48) 22 656-0109

Bank Inicjatyw Gospodarczych BIG S.A. (BIG)
ul. Kopernika 36/40, skr. poczt. 6
00-924 Warsaw
Telephone: (48) 22 657-5050 or 657-5000
Fax: (48) 22 626-7180 or 657-5009

Bank Handlowy w Warszawie S.A. (BH)
(Commercial Bank SA)
ul. Koszykowa 54
00-950 Warsaw
Telephone: (48) 22 630-8625
Fax: (48) 22 630-8609

Bank Rozwoju Eksportu, S.A. (BRE)
(Export Development Bank SA)
Plac Bankowy 2, skr. poczt. 728
00-950 Warsaw
Telephone: (48) 22 637-2800
Fax: (48) 22 637-1879

Powszechna Kasa Oszczednosci
Bank Panstwowy (PKO BP)
ul. Nowy Swiat 6/12, skr. poczt. 639-00
950 Warsaw
Telephone: (48) 22 637-1618
Fax: (48) 22 635-5855

Narodowy Bank Polski (NBP)
ul. Swietokrzyska 11/21, skr. poczt. 1011
00-919 Warsaw

Telephone: (48) 22 653-2335 or 653-2571
Fax: (48) 22 653-1321

BUSINES TRAVEL

A. BUSINESS CUSTOMS

It is customary to greet by shaking hands in Poland. A businesswoman should not be surprised if a Polish man kisses her hand upon introduction, at subsequent meetings or saying goodbye. American men are not expected to kiss a Polish woman's hand, but may simply shake hands. Business cards are the norm in Poland and are generally given to each person present in a meeting. As Poles tend to bring more than one person to their meetings, U.S. visitors should bring plenty of cards. It is not necessary to have cards printed in Polish.

Business attire is generally formal, including a suit and tie for men, and a suit or dress for women. Casual wear, including jeans, is suitable for informal occasions, but more formal dress is usually customary for visiting or entertaining in the evening. Flowers, always an odd number, are the most common gift among friends and acquaintances. Sunday is the traditional day for visiting family and friends in Poland.

B. TRAVEL ADVISORIES AND VISAS

The principal problem encountered by visitors to Poland is property crime. Pick pocketing, hotel break-ins, and car theft are common, particularly in areas of heavy tourist activity. Visitors are advised to pay particularly close attention to their belongings while in airports and railway stations, as well as on trains. Violent crime remains rare, but is growing. Consult the Consular Information Sheet, prepared by the U.S. Department of State, for updates. This information is available from the U.S. Department of State's web site (http://travel.state.gov).

There are no visa requirements for U.S. citizens coming to Poland for business purposes of up to 90 days. Business visitors on temporary duty are required to obtain a work permit if they will be in Poland longer than 90 days. Applications for this permission must be filed with the District Employment Office (Wojewodzki Urzad Pracy) by prospective employers six weeks before the start of employment. The application fee is 650 Polish zloty. If after 14 days, the decision is positive, the office will mail a "Promesa" (an assurance of permit issuance) to the employer. The worker uses the "Promesa" to apply for a work visa at a Polish Embassy or Consulate abroad. People already in Poland are obliged to leave the territory of Poland to apply for their work visas. The work visa fee is approximately USD 170, payable in dollars. After arriving in Poland with the visa, the worker must obtain the work permit from the District Employment Office within seven days of commencing work. Permits are issued for 12 months. Permits may be extended at the request of the employer. The extension fee is 325 Polish zloty.

C. HOLIDAYS

The following public holidays are observed in Poland: New Year's Day (January 1), Easter Monday (day after Easter), Labor Day (May 1), Constitution Day (May 3), Corpus Christi (late May/early June), Assumption of the Virgin Mary (August 15), All Saints' Day (November 1), Independence Day (November 11), Christmas (December 25), and Boxing Day (December 26). One Saturday per month is, by custom, considered a working Saturday, but there is no consistency among institutions or exact observance as such. Poland operates in Central European Time (CET), the same time zone as continental Western Europe. Business hours are generally from 8:00 a.m. to 4:00 p.m.

D. BUSINESS INFRASTRUCTURE

Transportation by air to and from Poland is excellent. International carriers fly to Poland many times per day from all over the world, and the Polish Airline LOT has direct flights to Warsaw from Chicago, New York, and Newark. Delta, American, Northwest and United have code share relationships with various European carriers that service Poland. No U.S. airline services Poland directly at this time. Transportation within Poland is convenient. Flights operate between major cities and trains routes are extensive and are quite efficient. Rental cars are abundant, but due to significantly increased traffic over the past few years and a highway system that has not kept up, driving between Polish cities, especially at night, can be quite dangerous.

First class business hotels are available in most major Polish cities, and many are located in the heart of business districts. Some major western hotels offer air-conditioned rooms and direct dial telephone capability from rooms. Many hotels offer a business center with computers, business assistance services, and faxing capability. Almost all business hotels take major credit cards. Charges and room rates are seasonal and competitive, and business travelers are advised to check and confirm rates at hotels in advance of their travel.

Telephoning to and from Poland is much easier today than just a few years ago. AT&T, Sprint, and MCI calls can be placed from Poland. Direct dial around the world is possible and can sometimes be easier than placing local calls across town. The Polish telephone system in some areas is still rotary dial, making it difficult to link-up and use some modern telephone services in the United States.

Poland uses the metric system of weights and measures. Electrical appliances use 220 volts AC, 50Hz, with continental (two-prong) outlets.

E. TEMPORARY ENTRY OF PERSONAL LAPTOPS AND OTHER BUSINESS MATERIALS

There are no restrictions on the temporary entry of personal laptop computers or other business materials into Poland.

F. U.S. COMMERCIAL SERVICE, AMERICAN EMBASSY WARSAW

U.S. business visitors are encouraged to make an appointment with the U.S. Commercial Service in Warsaw prior to departure for Poland. Following is the contact information for the U.S. Commercial Service in Warsaw:

Mr. David Fulton, Commercial Counselor
Mr. David Ponsar, Commercial Attaché
Mr. Alain Bobet, Commercial Representative
Aleje Jerozolimskie 56 c, 00-803 Warsaw
tel: (48-22) 625-43-74
fax: (48-22) 621-63-27
Warsaw.Office.Box@mail.doc.gov
www.CSCentralEurope.org/Poland

SUPPLEMENTS

POLAND: MARKETING AND BUSINESS REPORTS

1. ADVERTISING MARKET IN POLAND
2. ALCOHOL ADVERTISING IN POLAND
3. ATM MARKET IN POLAND
4. BEER MARKET IN POLAND
5. CLEAN PRODUCTION PROGRAM IN POLAND
6. COFFEE MARKET IN POLAND
7. DENTAL EQUIPMENT INDUSTRY IN POLAND
8. ELECTRICAL POWER GENERATION SECTOR IN POLAND
9. ENERGY CONSERVATION IN POLAND
10. FOOD PROCESSING EQUIPMENT MARKET IN POLAND
11. FOREIGN INVESTMENT IN KRAKOW REGION
12. FRANCHISING MARKET IN POLAND
13. GERMAN ENVIRONMENTAL TECHNOLOGY EXPORTS TO POLAND AND RUSSIA
14. HEALTH CARE SECTOR AND MEDICAL EQUIPMENT MARKET IN POLAND
15. INTERNET IN POLAND – MARKET OVERVIEW
16. LEADING COMPUTER DISTRIBUTORS IN POLAND
17. LEASING OPERATION IN POLAND
18. LIQUIFIED PETROLEUM GAS MARKET IN POLAND
19. MATERIAL HANDLING MACHINERY MARKET IN POLAND
20. MICROWAVE OVEN MARKET IN POLAND
21. NEW RULES FOR CAR ASSEMBLY IN POLAND
22. PACKAGING SECTOR IN POLAND
23. PENSION REFORM IN POLAND
24. PERSONAL COMPUTER MARKET IN POLAND
25. PHARMACEUTICAL MARKET IN POLAND
26. REAL ESTATE REGULATIONS IN POLAND
27. RECYCLING EQUIPMENT AND SERVICES IN POLAND
28. SOLID WASTE MANAGEMENT IN POLAND
29. SPORTING GOODS MARKET IN POLAND
30. STUDENT LOANS PROGRAM IN POLAND
31. TEA MARKET IN POLAND
32. THE JEANS MARKET IN POLAND
33. WATER POLLUTION CONTROL IN POLAND
34. WIRELESS TELECOMMUNICATIONS MARKET IN POLAND

SELECTED GOVERNMENT AND BUSINESS CONTACTS

POLISH GOVERNMENT

MINISTRIES AND CENTRAL AGENCIES IN WARSAW

Name	Adress	Phone
Chancellery of President	ul. Wiejska 10 00-480 Warszawa	(04822) 621-03-31

Chancellery of Sejm & Senat	ul. Wiejska 4/6/8 00-480 Warszawa	(04822) 694-25-00
Chancellery of the Prime Minister	Al. Ujazdowskie1/3 00-567 Warszawa	(04822) 694-60-00
Ministry of National Education	Al. Szucha 25 00-918 Warszawa	(04822) 29-72-41, 628-04-61
Ministry of Finance	ul. Świetokrzyska 12 00-049 Warszawa	(04822) 694-55-55
Ministry of Foreign Affairs	Al. Szucha 23 00-580 Warszawa	(04822) 523-90-00
Ministry of Economy	pl. Trzech Krzyży 5 00-507 Warszawa	(04822) 693-50-00
Ministry of Culture and Arts	Krakowskie Przedmieście15/17 00-071 Warszawa	(04822) 620-02-31
The Ministry of Post and Telecommunications	pl. Małachowskiego 2 00-063 Warszawa	(04822) 26-14-11
Ministry of National Defence	ul. Klonowa 1 00-591 Warszawa	(04822) 621-02-61
Ministry of Environmental Protection, Natural Resouces and Forestry	ul. Wawelska 52/54 02-067 Warszawa	(04822) 825-00-01 do 9
Ministry of Labor and Social Policy	ul. Nowogrodzka 1/3/5 00-513 Warszawa	(04822) 661-01-00
Ministry of Agriculture and Food Economy	ul. Wspólna 30 00-519	(04822) 623-10-00
Ministry of the Treasury	ul. Krucza 36 00-525 Warszawa	(04822) 628-02-81
Ministry of Justice	Al. Ujazdowskie 11 00-583 Warszawa	(04822) 628-44-31
Ministry of Interior and Administration	ul. Batorego 5 00-612 Warszawa	(04822) 621-02-51
Ministry of Health and Social Welfare	ul. Miodowa 15 00-246 Warszawa	(04822) 31-34-41
Ministry of Transport and Maritime	ul. Chałbińskiego 4/6	(04822)

Economy	00-613 Warszawa	24-40-00
Agency For Agricultutal Markets	ul. Wspólna 30 00-519 Warszawa	(04822) 628-79-53 623-16-60
Agricultural Property Agency of the State Treasury	ul. Dolańskiego 2 00-215 Warszawa	(04822) 635-81-77
Central Board of Customs	ul. Świetokrzyska 12 00-044 Warszawa	(04822) 694-55-55
General Inspectorate of Civil Aviation	ul. Grójecka 17 02-021 Warszawa	(04822) 629-86-89
The General Headquarters of the Police	ul. Puławska 148/150 02-624 Warszawa	(04822) 621-02-51
Headquarters of the Border Guard	Al. Niepodleglości 100 02-585 Warszawa	(04822) 845-40-71
Polish Securities and Exchange Commission	pl. Powst. Warszawy 1 00-030 Warszawa	(04822) 826-20-31
State Committee for Scientific Research	ul. Wspólna 1/3 00-529 Warszawa	(04822) 628-40-71
Office of the Committee for European Integration	Al. Ujazdowskie 9 00-583 Warszawa	(04822) 628-93-27
The Supreme Chamber of Control	ul. Filtrowa 57 02-056 Warszawa	(04822) 25-32-71
National Bank of Poland	ul. Świętokrzyska 11/21 00-049 Warszawa	(04822) 653-10-01
National Atomic Energy Agency	ul. Krucza 36 00-522 Warszawa	(04822) 628-02-41
Polish Agency For Foreign Investment	Al. Róż 2 00-556 Warszawa	(04822) 628-50-61
Polish Press Agency	Al. Jerozolimskie 7 00-508 Warszawa	(04822) 628-00-01
Polish Academy of Sciences	pl. Defilad 1 00-901 Warszawa	(04822) 20-02-11
Polish Committee for Standardization	ul.Świetokrzyska 14b	(04822)

	00-050 Warszawa	620-02-41
Government Center for Strategic Studies	ul. Wspólna 4 00-505 Warszawa	(04822) 661-81-11
Constitutional Tribunal in The Republic of Poland	Al. Szucha 12 A 00-918 Warszawa	(04822) 621-65-03
Office of Technical Inspection	ul.Szczęśliwicka 34 02-353 Warszawa	(04822) 22-30-61
Office for War Veterans and Victims of Opression	ul.Krucza 36 00-522 Warszawa	(04822) 661-81-81
State Sports and Tourism Administration	ul.Świetokrzyska 12 00-044 Warszawa	(04822) 826-58-64
Office for Housing and Urban Development	ul.Wspólna 2 00-505 Warszawa	(04822) 621-03-51
Office for Competition and Consumer Protection	pl.Powstanców Warszawy 1 00-030 Warszawa	(04822) 26-90-41
Office of State Protection Republic of Poland	ul.Rakowiecka 2b 02-517 Warszawa	(04822) 845-30-15
The Patent Office of the Republic of Poland	Al.Niepodleglości 188/192 00-608 Warszawa	(04822) 825-80-01
Office of Civil Service	Al. Szucha 2/4 00-582 Warszawa	(04822) 694-66-38 694-75-37
The Office of Public Procurement	Al. Szucha 2/4 00-582 Warszawa	(04822) 694-75-83 694-61-78
State Mining Authority	ul.Wilcza 46 00-679 Warszawa	(04822) 629-58-63

U.S. EMBASSY TRADE RELATED CONTACTS

Commercial
Ms. Maria J. Andrews, Senior Commercial Officer
Mr. David Ponsar, Commercial Officer
Mr. Alain Bobet, Commercial Attache
Aleje Jerozolimskie 56 c, 00-803 Warsaw
tel: (48-22) 625-43-74
fax: (48-22) 621-63-27

Agriculture
Mr. James Higgiston, Agricultural Counselor
Mr. Stan Phillips, Agricultural Attache
Aleje Ujazdowskie 29/31, Warsaw
tel: (48-22) 628-30-41
fax: (48-22) 628-1172

Economics
Mr. John Hoover, Economic Counselor
Aleje Ujazdowskie 29/31, Warsaw
tel: (48-22) 628-30-41
fax: (48-22) 628-82-98

ODC
Lt.Col. Peter Podbielski
Aleje Ujazdowskie 29/31, Warsaw
tel: (48-22) 628-30-41
fax: (48-22) 628-82-98

U.S. Agency for International Development
Mr. William Frej, AID Representative
Aleje Jerozolimskie 56c, 00-803 Warsaw
tel: (48-22) 625-0060
fax: (48-22) 628-7486

American Consulate General Krakow
Mr. Peter Scanlan, Consul General
ul. Stolarska 9, Krakow
tel: (48-12) 22-14-00
fax: (48-12) 21-82-92

CHAMBERS OF COMMERCE AND BILATERAL BUSINESS COUNCILS

National Chamber of Commerce of Poland
ul. Trebacka 4
00-074 Warsaw
tel: (48-22) 826-0221
fax: (48-22) 827-4673

American Chamber of Commerce in Poland (AmCham)
ul. Swietokrzyska 36, Room 6
00-116 Warsaw
tel./fax: (48-22) 622-5525 or 620-2698

Business Foundation
ul. Rozbrat 26
00-429 Warsaw
tel: (48-22) 621-7111
fax: (48-22) 622-7024

Small Business Chamber
ul. Smocza 27
01-048 Warsaw
tel: (48-22) 380-172
fax: (48-22) 383-553

Business Center Club
Palac Lubomirskich
00-136 Warsaw
Plac Zelaznej Bramy 2
tel: (48-22) 625-3037
fax: (48-22) 621-8420

Country Government Offices

Central Housing Office
ul. Wsp¢lna 2
00-926 Warsaw
tel: (48-22) 661-8111
fax: (48-22) 629-5389

Ministry of Transportation and Maritime Economy
ul Chalubinskiego 4/6
00-928 Warsaw
tel: (48-22) 628-5553
fax: (48-22) 830-0089

Ministry of Environmental Protection
ul. Wawelska 52/54
00-922 Warsaw
tel: (48-22) 253-332
fax: (48-22) 251-111

Ministry of Agriculture and Food Economy
ul. Wsp¢lna 30
00-930 Warsaw
tel: (48-22) 628 5745
fax: (48-22) 623-2750 (51)

Ministry of Finance
ul. Swietokrzyska 12
00-916 Warsaw
tel: (48-22) 694-5555
fax: (48-22) 826-6352

Ministry of Economics
Pl. Trzech Krzyzy 5
00-950 Warsaw
tel: (48-22) 628-7327
fax: (48-22) 628-6808 or 629-5201

Ministry of Industry
ul. Wsp¢lna 4
00-926 Warsaw
tel: (48-22) 628-0182
fax: (48-22) 621-2550

Ministry of Treasury
ul. Krucza 36
00-522 Warsaw
tel: (48-22) 628-1689
fax: (48-22) 628-0872, 621-3361

Polish Center for Research and Certification
Polskie Centrum Badan I Certyfikacji (PCBC)
Mr. Janusz Berdowski, Director
ul. Klobucka 23a
02-699 Warsaw
tel: (48-22) 647-0742
fax: (48-22) 647-12-22

The State Foreign Investment Agency
Aleja R¢z 2
00-559 Warsaw
tel: (48-22) 621-6261, 621-0706
fax: (48-22) 621-8427

COUNTRY MARKET RESEARCH FIRMS

a. M. F. Plus Group Ltd.
ul. Wilcza 50/52
00-679 Warsaw
tel: (48-22) 623-0646 through 49
fax: (48-22) 623-0650

Adecco Poland
ul. Koszykowa 59/4
00-660 Warsaw
tel: (48-22) 622-2155, 622-2163
fax: (48-22) 628-0695

Allied Pickfords - Allied Van Lines
ul. Czardasza 18
02-169 Warsaw
tel: (48-22) 8467-003, 090-201-257
fax: (48-22) 8467-003

American Management Systems, Inc
Al. Jerozolimskie 81
02-001 Warsaw
tel: (48-22) 607-1357
fax: (48-22) 607-1355

Andersen Consulting Sp. z o.o.
Al. Jana Pawla II 23, Atrium Business Center
00-854 Warsaw
tel: (48-22) 653-9200
fax: (48-22) 653-9201

Arthur Andersen & Co.

Al. Jana Pawla II 23
00-854 Warsaw
tel: (48-22) 653-9000
fax: (48-22) 653-9100

Arthur D. Little Int./TMBK Partners
ul. Pawinskiego 5A
02-106 Warsaw
tel: (48-22) 658-3607
fax: (48-22) 658-1476

Barents Polska
ul. Swietokrzyska 36\12
00-116 Warsaw
tel: (48-22) 620-9023
fax: (48-22) 620-7763

Blaisdell & Co Sp. z o.o.
ul. Zurawia 26/5B
00-515 Warsaw
tel: (48-22) 628-1050
fax: (48-22) 622-4654

Bonair Ltd.
ul. Krzywickiego 34
02-078 Warsaw
tel: (48-22) 621-5059
fax: (48-22) 625-3981

Booz, Allen & Hamilton
Aleje Jerozolimskie 65/79, LIM Center
00-697 Warsaw
tel: (48-22) 630-6301
fax: (48-22) 630-6308

The Boston Consulting Group
ul. Prusa 2, Sheraton Plaza
00-493 Warsaw
tel: (48-22) 657-0202
fax: (48-22) 657-0262

Company Assistance Ltd.
ul. Podwale 13 00-950 Warsaw

tel: (48-22) 635-8650, 635-8944
fax: (48-22) 831-7920

Coopers & Lybrand Consulting Sp. z o.o.
ul. Mokotowska 49
00-950 Warsaw
tel: (48-22) 660-0666
fax: (48-22) 660-0572

D'Arcy, Masius, Benton & Bowles
ul. Goraszewska 7
02-910 Warsaw
tel: (48-22) 408-020
fax: (48-22) 408-107

Deloitte & Touche Sp. z o.o.
ul. Grzybowska 80\82
00-844 Warsaw
tel: (48-22) 661-5300
fax: (48-22) 661-5350

Ernst & Young Managment
Consulting Services Sp. z o.o.
ul. Solec 22
00-410 Warsaw
tel: (48-22) 625-5477
fax: (48-22) 629-4263

EDS (Electronic Data System)
ul. Wilcza 66\68
00-679 Warsaw
tel: (48-22) 625-3775, 625-7914
fax: (48-22) 625-7946

ERM Polska
ul. Jaracza 3/16
00-378 Warsaw
tel: (48-22) 625-3578, 625-4276
fax: (48-22) 625-3578

Failure Analysis Associates Ltd.
ul. Dlugi Targ 1/7 p. 25
80-828 Gdansk
tel: (48-58) 462-844, 462-961
fax: (48-58) 463-102

Finrayan International Ltd.
ul. Marszalkowska 115
00-102 Warsaw
tel: (48-22) 8268-563, 248-235
fax: (48-22) 8268-563

Hejka Michna Sp.z o.o.
ul. Wspolna 62
00-684 Warsaw
tel: (48-22) 625-0045
fax: (48-22) 629-1862

IAS Polska, Sp.z o.o. (International Advisory Services Group Ltd.)
ul. Francuska 35
40-027 Katowice
tel: (48-32) 157-2649
fax: (48-32) 157-2649

ITCA Europe Ltd.
ul. Piekna 54, 1st floor
00-672 Warsaw
tel: (48-22) 628-8388
fax: (48-22) 621-2667

JAC Poland Ltd.
ul. Stawki 2, 22nd floor
00-193 Warsaw
tel: (48-22) 635-04-70
fax: (48-22) 635-97-23

Johnson Controls
ul. Nocznickiego 31
01-918 Warsaw
tel: (48-22) 34-90-62, 35-08-48
fax: (48-22) 34-94-10

KP Konsorcjum Sp. z o.o.
Krakowskie Przedmiescie 4/6
00-333 Warsaw
tel: (48-22) 826-28-78, 826-84-73
fax: (48-22) 826-03-12

Law International Inc.
ul. Dubois 9 Rm. 320
00-182 Warsaw
tel: (48-22) 635-4884
fax: (48-22) 635-5173

Learning Systems Polska
ul. M. Jelinka 28
00-646 Warsaw
tel: (48-22) 33-93-13, 33-84-62
fax: (48-22) 33-93-13

Macro International
Al. Jerozolimskie 56C
00-803 Warsaw

tel: (48-22) 630-2244
fax: (48-22) 630-2234

McKinsey & Company
ul. Stawki 2, Intraco Bldg. 34th Floor
00-193 Warsaw
tel: (48-22) 635-5410, 635-7906
fax: (48-22) 635-5595

NCR
ul. Domaniewska 41
02-672 Warsaw
tel: (48-22) 606-0250, 606-1252
fax: (48-22) 606-1251

Normax
ul. Gwiazdzista 19
01-651 Warsaw
tel: (48-22) 33-74-82, 33-76-60
fax: (48-22) 33-76-60

Pan Eurasian
ul. Snopowa 1
04-689 Warsaw
tel: (48-22) 613-0703
fax: (48-22) 613-0703

Power Business Associates
ul. Dygasinskiego 18
01-603 Warsaw
tel: (48-22) 39-53-08, 39-98-83
fax: (48-22) 39-53-08

Price Waterhouse
ul. Emilii Plater 28
00-688 Warsaw
tel: (48-22) 699-8800
fax: (48-22) 699-8900

Prime Property, Inc.
ul. Emilii Plater 28, WCC
00-688 Warsaw
tel: (48-22) 630-3262 through 68
fax: (48-22) 630-3266

Renaissance Technology Group
ul. Dluga 29, Room 118
00-238 Warsaw
tel: (48-22) 8314-020 (..021, 022)
fax: (48-22) 635-5277

Vigor-Atlantus
ul. Poznanska 16/7
00-680 Warsaw
tel: (48-22) 622-4077
fax: (48-22) 622-4077

WorldTrade Center Warsaw
Plac Defilad 1
WorldTrade Center Warsaw
00-901 Warsaw
tel: (48-22) 656-7711
fax: (48-22) 656-7133

FOREIGN BANKS IN POLAND

name of the bank	address	telephone / fax numbers
"PRIORBANK" Akcionpiernoje obszczestwo Przedstawicielstwo w Polsce, Mińsk	00-073 Warszawa ul.Jesionowa 15 m 1	0-22 825-54-04 825-54-04
Adkrytaje akcyjaniernaje tawarystwa "Aszczadny bank "Biełarusbank", Mińsk	02-511 Warszawa ul.Bielawska 6 m.57	0-22 646-05-95 844-44-80
Akcionernyj kommerczeskij Bank wniesznieekonomiczeskoj diejatelnosti Respubliki Biełaruś (BIEŁWNIESZEKONOMBANK), Mińsk	00-805 Warszawa ul.Chmielna 132/134	0-22 656-28-41 656-24-74
BANCA COMMERCIALE ITALIANA S.p.A., Mediolan	00-193 Warszawa ul.Stawki 2, 37 piętro	0-22 635-14-02 -
BANCA NAZIONALE DEL LAVORO S.p.A, Rzym	00-697 Warszawa Al.Jerozolimskie 65/79 p.1824	0-22 630-67-80 630-67-81
BANQUE NATIONALE DE PARIS, Paryż	00-108 Warszawa ul.Zielna 41/43	0-22 697-25-30 697-25-35
Bank of America, National Association, Charlotte	00-854 Warszawa al.Jana Pawła II 25	0-22 654-25-00 654-25-15
Bankers Trust Company, Nowy Jork Representantive Office in Poland	00-688 Warszawa ul.Emilii Plater 28	0-22 630-33-66 630-33-77
Banque Bruxelles Lambert SA, Bruksela	00-499 Warszawa pl.Trzech Krzyży 10/14	0-22 820-56-75 do 79 820-56-80
Banque Paribas, Paryż	00-513 Warszawa ul.Nowogrodzka 11	0-22 529-01-00 529-01-01
Bayerische Landesbank Girozentrale,Monachium	00-688 Warszawa ul.Emilii Plater 28, IX piętro	0-22 630-39-30 630-39-30
Caisse Centrale des Banques Populaires, Paryż	00-803 Warszawa Al.Jerozolimskie 56C	0-22 630-26-82 630-26-84
Centro Internationale Handelsbank AG, Wiedeń	00-020 Warszawa ul.Szpitalna 1	0-22 827-28-24 625-68-54

COMMERZBANK AG, Frankfurt	00-054 Warszawa ul.Jasna 24	0-22 826-85-91 826-86-78
Compagnie Financiere de CIC et de l'Union Europeenne, Paryż	00-193 Warszawa ul.Stawki 2	0-22 635-55-32 635-80-70
DEUTSCHE BANK AG, Frankfurt	00-104 Warszawa pl.Grzybowski 12/16	0-22 620-02-34 624-04-18
Den Danske Bank Aktieselskab, Kopenhaga	00-688 Warszawa ul.Emilii Plater 28	0-22 630-31-70 630-31-71
Deutsche Hyp Deutsche Hypothekenbank Frankfurt - Hamburg Aktiengesellschaft, Frankfurt	00-108 Warszawa ul.Zielna 41/43	0-22 697-25-50 697-25-59
DG BANK Deutsche Genossenschaftsbank, Frankfurt	00-102 Warszawa ul.Marszałkowska 115	0-22 528-07-65 528-07-88
ISTITUTO BANCARIO SAN PAOLO DI TORINO - ISTITUTO MOBILIARE ITALIANO SOCIETA PER AZIONI, Turyn	00-193 Warszawa ul.Stawki 2	0-22 860-62-00 860-62-05
Komercni banka, a.s., Praga	00-828 Warszawa al.Jana Pawła II 15	0-22 697-76-26 do 27 697-76-58
Landesbank Hessen-Thueringen Girozentrale, Frankfurt	00-688 Warszawa ul.Emilii Plater 28 IX piętro	0-22 630-39-30 630-39-30
Merita Bank Plc, Helsinki	00-854 Warszawa al.Jana Pawła II 25	0-22 653-47-69 653-47-71
MITTELEUROPAISCHE HANDELSBANK AG, Frankfurt	00-688 Warszawa ul.Emilii Plater 28	0-22 630-39-36 630-39-36
Norddeutsche Landesbank Girozentrale, Hannover	00-688 Warszawa ul.Emilii Plater 28 IX piętro	0-22 630-39-30 630-39-30
Suedwestdeutsche Landesbank Girozentrale, Stuttgart	00-845 Warszawa ul.Łucka 20 p.1402	0-22 654-46-88 654-46-89
Svenska Handelsbanken AB (publ), Sztokholm	02-134 Warszawa ul.1 Sierpnia 4	0-22 878-73-87 878-73-88
THE CHASE MANHATTAN BANK, Nowy Jork	00-113 Warszawa ul.Emilii Plater 53	0-22 520-51-00 520-51-20
The Export-Import Bank, Taiwan, Przedstawicielstwo w Warszawie, Tajpej	- Warszawa -	0-22 - -
UNIBANK A/S, Kopenhaga	00-660 Warszawa ul.Lwowska 19	0-22 627-51-12 627-51-14

Multilateral Development Bank Offices in Poland

European Bank for Reconstruction and Development
Ms. Alicja Kornasiewicz, Head of the Warsaw EBRD Office
Lim Center Al. Jerozolimskie 65-79
15th Floor, Room 1510
00-697 Warsaw

tel: (48-22) 630-72-75
fax: (48-22) 630-65-51

World Bank
Mr. Paul Knotter, Resident Representative
Intraco I Building
17th Floor
ul. Stawki 2
00-193 Warsaw
tel: (48-22) 635-05-53
fax: (48-22) 635-98-57

International Finance Corporation
Hugh Stevenson, Resident Representative
ul. E. Plater 28
00-688 Warsaw
tel: (48-22) 630-34-44, 30-07-58
fax: (48-22) 630-34-45

MAJOR POLISH BANKS

HEAD OFFICE NUMBER	NAME OF THE BANK	ADDRESS	TELEPHONE / FAX NUMBERS
16700004	ABN AMRO BANK (Polska) SA	02-134 Warszawa ul.1 Sierpnia 8A	0-22 573-05-00 573-05-01
19600004	AIG Bank Polska SA	08-110 Siedlce Skwer Niepodległości 2	0-25 632-80-76 633-91-43
20800008	Bałtycki Bank Regionalny SA	75-200 Koszalin al.Armii Krajowej 8	0-94 346-24-80 342-30-85
12100002	Bank "Agrobank" SA (ogłoszona upadłość 21.04.95)	03-808 Warszawa ul.Mińska 25	0-22 810-75-75 810-14-04
17400006	Bank Amerykański w Polsce SA "AmerBank"	00-102 Warszawa ul.Marszałkowska 115	0-22 528-06-00 624-99-81
14800005	Bank Cukrownictwa "CUKROBANK" SA	50-038 Wrocław ul.Kościuszki 14	0-71 341-17-91 341-17-84
16300002	Bank CZĘSTOCHOWA SA	42-200 Częstochowa ul.Dekabrystów 41	0-34 372-15-44 325-44-18
20300003	Bank Gospodarki Żywnościowej SA	01-211 Warszawa ul.Kasprzaka 10/16	0-22 860-40-00 860-50-00
11300007	Bank Gospodarstwa Krajowego	00-955 Warszawa Al.Jerozolimskie 7	0-22 522-91-12 627-03-78
12200005	Bank Handlowo - Kredytowy SA (w likwidacji 31.03.92)	40-950 Katowice pl.Grunwaldzki 8-10	0-32 59-44-79 59-40-39
10300006	Bank Handlowy w Warszawie SA	00-950 Warszawa ul.Chałubińskiego 8	0-22 690-36-54 690-38-21
13700001	Bank Inicjatyw Społeczno - Ekonomicznych SA	00-184 Warszawa ul.Dubois 5A	0-22 860-11-00 860-11-03
16600001	Bank Komercyjny POSNANIA SA (ogłoszona upadłość 11.01.95)	62-020 Swarzędz ul.Grudzińskiego 30	0-61 817-25-80 817-25-80
14400003	Bank Komunalny SA	81-303 Gdynia ul.Kielecka 2	0-58 661-76-21 620-41-57

15400004	Bank Ochrony Środowiska SA	00-950 Warszawa al.Jana Pawła II 12	0-22 850-87-35 850-88-91
21200001	Bank of America (Polska) SA	00-854 Warszawa al.Jana Pawła II 25	0-22 654-25-00 654-25-15
13200006	Bank Pocztowy SA	85-959 Bydgoszcz ul.Jagiellońska 17	0-52 349-91-00 327-04-07
12400001	Bank Polska Kasa Opieki SA	00-950 Warszawa ul.Grzybowska 53/57	0-22 656-00-00 656-02-03
13400002	Bank Powierniczo - Gwarancyjny SA (w likwidacji 21.04.97)	00-950 Warszawa pl.Powstańców Warszawy 1	0-22 826-11-76 827-71-53
19200002	Bank Promocji Eksportu "Animex Bank" SA (ogłoszona upadłość 7.07.95)	00-140 Warszawa al.Solidarności 117	0-22 652-57-21 do 22 652-57-21 do
10600005	Bank Przemysłowo - Handlowy SA	31-548 Kraków al.Pokoju 1	0-12 422-33-33 421-69-14
15200008	Bank Przemysłowy SA	90-365 Łódź ul.Tymienieckiego 5	0-42 640-27-90 do 92 684-55-13
14000001	Bank Rozwoju Budownictwa Mieszkaniowego SA	00-099 Warszawa ul.Senatorska 29/31	0-22 826-74-41 827-73-49
14200007	Bank Rozwoju Cukrownictwa SA	60-959 Poznań ul.Mickiewicza 35	0-61 853-22-01 853-23-85
12700000	Bank Rozwoju Energetyki i Ochrony Środowiska SA MEGABANK (w likwidacji 1.05.98)	00-854 Warszawa al.Jana Pawła II 23	0-22 090-282-453 752-28-48
14700002	Bank SPOŁEM SA	02-548 Warszawa ul.Grażyny 13/15	0-22 845-59-27 845-28-14
15300001	Bank Staropolski SA (ogłoszona upadłość 11.02.00)	60-967 Poznań ul.Nowowiejskiego 5	0-61 854-43-00 852-15-32
10500002	Bank Śląski SA	40-950 Katowice ul.Warszawska 14	0-32 253-72-81 w.5910 58-78-62
17000004	Bank Unii Gospodarczej SA	00-950 Warszawa pl.Dąbrowskiego 3	0-22 826-33-78 826-30-44
14100004	Bank Własności Pracowniczej - Unibank SA	80-873 Gdańsk ul.Na Ostrowiu 1	0-58 348-19-00 348-19-01
16200009	Bank Wschodni SA	15-099 Białystok ul.Legionowa 14/16	0-85 732-94-14 732-50-21
13000000	Bank Współpracy Europejskiej SA	00-082 Warszawa ul.Senatorska 14	0-22 829-98-00 826-02-61
19100009	Bank Współpracy Regionalnej SA	31-047 Kraków ul.J.Sarego 2 i 4	0-12 421-93-88 421-96-52
11200004	Bank Zachodni SA	50-950 Wrocław Rynek 9/11	0-71 370-24-42 370-25-43
20900001	Bankgesellschaft Berlin (Polska) SA	00-828 Warszawa al.Jana Pawła II 15	0-22 697-72-00 697-72-05
11500003	BIG BANK SA	00-924 Warszawa ul.Kopernika 36/40	0-22 657-50-50 826-71-80

11600006	BIG Bank GDAŃSKI SA	00-924 Warszawa ul.Kopernika 36/40	0-22 657-57-18 657-50-09
18600003	BNP - Dresdner Bank (Polska) SA	00-108 Warszawa ul.Zielna 41/43	0-22 654-62-63 697-23-29
11400000	BRE Bank SA	00-950 Warszawa ul.Senatorska 18	0-22 829-00-00 829-00-80
15900009	Bydgoski Bank Budownictwa SA (ogłoszona upadłość 02.10.96)	85-090 Bydgoszcz ul.Powstańców Wlkp. 26	0-52 341-21-11 341-21-11
18200001	CITIBANK (Poland) SA	00-923 Warszawa ul.Senatorska 16	0-22 657-72-00 657-75-80
17900001	Credit Lyonnais Bank Polska SA	00-950 Warszawa Al.Jerozolimskie 65/79	0-22 630-68-88 635-45-00
16900000	CUPRUM - BANK SA	59-300 Lubin Rynek 23	0-76 840-41-00 840-41-01
15800006	DaimlerChrysler Services (debis) Bank Polska SA	00-828 Warszawa al.Jana Pawła II 15	0-22 697-64-20 697-64-19
18800009	Deutsche Bank Polska SA	00-104 Warszawa pl.Grzybowski 12/14/16	0-22 652-50-00 624-04-18
15700003	Dolnośląski Bank Gospodarczy SA (w likwidacji 10.03.95)	00-682 Warszawa Likwidator ul.Hoża 72 m 4	0-22 629-23-37 -
21000005	Dolnośląski Bank Regionalny SA	50-077 Wrocław ul.Kazimierza Wielkiego 15	0-71 342-69-20 341-76-26
20700005	FCE Bank Polska SA	02-222 Warszawa Al.Jerozolimskie 181	0-22 608-69-00 608-69-01
21400007	Fiat Bank Polska SA	02-678 Warszawa ul.Szturmowa 2	0-22 607-48-00 607-48-49
16000003	FORTIS BANK POLSKA SA	02-674 Warszawa ul.Marynarska 13	0-22 541-18-00 541-18-10
18500000	GE Bank Mieszkaniowy SA	02-822 Warszawa ul.Poleczki 21	0-22 545-05-00 545-05-01
17100007	GE Capital Bank SA	80-853 Gdańsk ul.Wały Jagiellońskie 36	0-58 304-07-66 304-07-01
13900007	Gliwicki Bank Handlowy SA	44-100 Gliwice ul.Królowej Bony 2-4	0-32 231-18-61 231-98-18
19300005	Gospodarczy Bank Południowo - Zachodni SA	50-449 Wrocław ul.Krasińskiego 27	0-71 372-33-23 372-33-15
16100006	Gospodarczy Bank Wielkopolski SA	61-725 Poznań ul.Mielżyńskiego 22	0-61 856-24-00 852-27-30
15600000	Górnośląski Bank Gospodarczy SA	40-006 Katowice ul.Warszawska 6	0-32 200-85-00 200-86-85
18900002	HypoVereinsbank Bank Hipoteczny SA	00-805 Warszawa ul.Chmielna 132/134	0-22 656-21-69 656-21-67
18000005	ING Bank N.V. Oddział w Warszawie	00-499 Warszawa pl.Trzech Krzyży 10/14	0-22 820-40-00 820-40-09
16800007	INVEST - BANK SA	60-814 Poznań	0-61 848-45-91

		ul.Zwierzyniecka 18	866-83-22
15000002	Kredyt Bank SA	01-211 Warszawa ul.Kasprzaka 2/8	0-22 634-54-00 634-53-35
15500007	LG Petro Bank SA	93-172 Łódź ul.Rzgowska 34/36	0-42 681-90-60 684-61-92
19400008	LUKAS Bank Świętokrzyski SA	25-501 Kielce ul.Sienkiewicza 76	0-41 366-04-09 366-28-66
20200000	Lubelski Bank Regionalny SA	20-027 Lublin ul.Karłowicza 4	0-81 531-95-00 531-95-26
20500009	Małopolski Bank Regionalny SA	31-059 Kraków ul.Bożego Ciała 23	0-12 618-17-00 430-69-18
20600002	Mazowiecki Bank Regionalny SA	01-747 Warszawa ul.Elbląska 15/17	0-22 663-40-25 663-61-12
10100000	Narodowy Bank Polski	00-919 Warszawa ul.Świętokrzyska 11/21	0-22 826-63-07 826-41-23
19500001	OPEL BANK SA	02-515 Warszawa ul.Puławska 15	0-22 521-54-00 521-54-01
18300004	Polsko - Kanadyjski Bank Św.Stanisława SA	00-695 Warszawa ul.Nowogrodzka 51	0-22 625-25-64 625-23-91
20400006	Pomorsko - Kujawski Bank Regionalny SA	85-667 Bydgoszcz ul.Chodkiewicza 89-91	0-52 323-52-00 346-06-34
10200003	Powszechna Kasa Oszczędności Bank Polski SA	00-975 Warszawa ul.Puławska 15	0-22 521-77-95 521-77-97
11100001	Powszechny Bank Kredytowy SA	00-958 Warszawa ul.Towarowa 25A	0-22 531-80-00 531-80-42
12800003	PROSPER - BANK SA	01-402 Warszawa ul.Ciołka 10	0-22 634-65-00 634-65-22
20000004	Rabobank Polska SA	00-958 Warszawa al.Jana Pawła II 25	0-22 653-40-00 653-40-04
17500009	Raiffeisen Bank Polska SA	00-695 Warszawa ul.Nowogrodzka 50	0-22 657-46-00 625-07-36
21500000	RHEINHYP - BRE Bank Hipoteczny SA	00-675 Warszawa ul.Koszykowa 54	0-22 630-83-48 630-82-23
21100008	Rzeszowski Bank Regionalny SA	35-025 Rzeszów ul.Zygmuntowska 14	0-17 852-07-22 852-07-22
11900005	SAVIM-Bank Depozytowo-Kredytowy SA (ogłoszona upadłość 13.01.99)	01-728 Warszawa ul.Powązkowska 68	0-22 633-40-11 633-41-84
18400007	SOCIETE GENERALE - SUCCURSALE de VARSOVIE	00-102 Warszawa ul.Marszałkowska 111	0-22 528-40-00 528-44-44
21600003	Toyota Bank Polska SA	02-672 Warszawa ul.Domaniewska 41	0-22 874-47-55 874-47-54
21300004	VOLKSWAGEN BANK POLSKA SA	00-828 Warszawa al.Jana Pawła II 15	0-22 697-78-00 697-78-88
20100007	Warmińsko - Mazurski Bank Regionalny SA	10-578 Olsztyn al.M.J.Piłsudskiego 32	0-89 535-02-64 do 65 534-06-70
18700006	Westdeutsche Landesbank Polska SA	00-688 Warszawa ul.Emilii Plater 28	0-22 653-05-00 653-05-01
10900004	Wielkopolski Bank Kredytowy SA	60-967 Poznań	0-61 856-49-00

		pl.Wolności 16	852-11-13
19700007	Wielkopolski Bank Rolniczy SA	62-800 Kalisz ul.Złota 42A	0-62 767-44-00 767-43-52
14600009	Wschodni Bank Cukrownictwa SA	20-022 Lublin ul.Okopowa 1	0-81 532-22-20 532-90-05

U.S. GOVERNMENT OFFICES IN WASHINGTON, DC

U.S. Department of Commerce
14th St. & Constitution Avenue, NW
Washington, DC 20230

Central Eastern Europe Business Information Center (CEEBIC)
Room 2325
tel: (202) 482-2645
fax: (202) 501-0787
email: ceebic@usita.gov

Central Europe Desk Officer
Room 3319
tel: (202) 482-4915
fax: (202) 482-4505

U.S. Department of Agriculture

Foreign Agricultural Service
Agricultural Export Services Division
Trade Assistance and Promotion Office
1400 Independence Avenue, S.W.
Room 4935 South Bldg
Washington, D.C. 20250
tel: (202) 720-7420
fax: (202) 690-0193

U.S.-Based Multipliers

Polish-U.S. Economic Council
U.S. Chamber of Commerce
1615 H Street, NW
Washington, DC 20062-2000
tel: (202) 463-5460
fax: (202) 463-3114

Polish American Chamber of Commerce of the Southeast
c/o Lord, Bissell and Brook
1201 West Peachtree Street, Suite 3700
Atlanta, GA 30309
Tel: (404) 870-4699
Fax: (404) 872-5547

U.S.-Poland Chamber of Commerce of Metropolitan New York
812 North Wood Avenue
Linden, NJ 07036
Tel: (908) 486-9311
Fax: (908) 486-4084
Andrew Findeisen, Chairman

Polish American Chamber of Commerce of Florida and the Americas
Mailing Address: PO Box 291465
Davie, FL 33329
Street Address: Executive Office
5439 NW 36th Street
Miami Springs, FL 33166
TelFax: (954) 423-1611
Dr. Zdzislaw Wesolowski, President

Poland California Chamber of Commerce
3111 Camino Del Rio N
San Diego, CA 92108-5720
Tel: (619) 563-7052

Polish-American Chamber of Commerce of Illinois
5538 W. Belmont Avenue
Chicago, IL 60641
Tel: (773) 736-5522
Fax: (773) 545-1878
Jan Krynski, President

TRADE ASSOCIATIONS

Polish Chamber of Information Technology and Telecommunications
(Polska Izba Informatyki and Telekomunikacji)
Mr. Waclaw Iszkowski, President
ul. Zurawia 4a, Room 200
P.O. Box 44
00-503 Warsaw
tel: (48-22) 693-5860
fax: (48-22) 693-5893
e-mail: piit@ikp.atm.com.pl

Polish Chamber of Commerce for Electronics and Telecommunications
(Krajowa Izba Gospodarcza Elektroniki I Telecomunikacji)
Mr. Stefan Kaminski
ul. Barska 28/30
02-315 Warsaw
tel./fax: (48-22) 224-663

Pomeranian Chamber of Commerce and Industry
Zbigniew Canowiecki, President
ul. Dlugi Targ 39/40
80-830 Gdansk

tel: (48-58) 311-325, 311-954
fax: (48-58) 310-216

Polish Homebuilders Association
(Polskie Stowarzyszenie Budowniczych Dom¢w)
ul. Chmielna 54/57
80-748 Gda sk
tel: (48-58) 31-68-51
fax: (48-58) 31-42-17
Mr. Jacek Dabrowski, President
25 k.Konstancina
05-507 Slomczyn
tel: (48-22) 57-69-99

Corporation of Construction Enterprises
(Korporacja Przedsiebiorcow Budowlanych)
Mr. Aleksander Paszynski, President
Ms. Barbara Reduch-Widelska, Managing Director
ul. Nowogrodzka 21
00-950 Warsaw
tel/fax: (48-22) 629-82-13

Polish Association of Sanitary, Heating, Gas and Air Conditioning Enterprises
(Polska Korporacja Techniki Sanitarnej, Grzewczej, Gazowej I Klimatyzacji)
Mr. Tomasz Malowany, Director
ul. Sniadeckich 10
00-656 Warsaw
tel/fax: (48-22) 628-75-82

The Association of Polish Architects (SARP)
Mr. Krzysztof Chwalibog, President
ul. Foksal 2
00-950 Warsaw
tel/fax: (48-22) 827-87-13, 827-87-12

Polish Pharmacy Economic Chamber
Izba Gospodarcza FARMACJA POLSKA
Ms. Irena Rej, President
ul. Czarnieckiego 48
01-548 Warsaw
tel/fax:(48-22) 39-20-80, 39-99-10

Polish Pharmaceutical and Medical Equipment Producers Chamber
(Polska Izba Przemyslu Farmaceutycznego I Sprzetu Medycznego - POLFARMED)
Mr. Zbigniew Cezary Sledziewski, Director
ul. Corazziego 4
00-087 Warsaw
tel/fax:(48-22) 827-21-76

Polish Association of Cable TV Operators
(Ogolnopolskie Stowarzyszenie Telewizji Kablowej)
Mr. Andrzej Ostrowski, Chairman

ul. Mieszka I 2/4
65-040 Zielona Gora
tel: (48-68) 27-21-96, 20-24-16
fax: (48-68) 25-36-72

National Association of Alarm System Producers, Designers and Installation Companies (Ogolnopolskie Stowarzyszenie Producentow, Projektantow I Instalatorow Systemow Alarmowych)
Mr. Bogdan Tatarowski, President
ul. Marszalkowska 60 m. 27
00-545 Warsaw
tel:(48-22)625-34-00, 625-32-96
fax:(48-22) 625-26-75

Polish Franchise Association (PFA)
Polskie Stowarzyszenie Franchisingu
Ms. Jolanta Kramarz, President
ul. Szpitalna 1, II floor, room 5
00-020 Warsaw
tel: (48-22) 826-80-30/-39, ext. 120, 123
tel/fax: (48-22) 625-69-56

Association of Leasing Companies in Poland
Konferencja Przedsiebiorstw Leasingowych
Mr. Andrzej Plochocki, Director
ul. Filtrowa 71a apt. 3
02-055 Warsaw
tel/fax: (48-22) 25-19-43

Association of Polish Druggists
Stowarzyszenie Drogistow Polskich
Mr. Przemyslaw Solecki, President
ul. Podwale 3
00-952 Warsaw
tel: (48-22) 635-60-96

Polish Cosmetics Association
Polskie Stowarzyszenie Kosmetyczne
Ms. Iwona Tomas, President
ul. Smocza 30, Apt. 32
01-048 Warsaw
tel/fax: (48-22) 38-61-59

Packaging Materials and Packaging Manufacturers Association
Stowarzyszenie Producentow I Uzytkownikow Materialow Opakowaniowych I Opakowan (PROPAK)
Mr. Tomasz Romanowski, President
ul. Czackiego 3/5
00-950 Warsaw
tel: (48-22) 826-74-61 through 69, ext 211
tel/fax: (48-22) 632-89-75, 622-64-26, 773-19-32

Pro-Marka Polish Association of Branded Goods Producers (PABGP)
E. Wedel S.A.
Mr. Zbigniew Wrobel, Chairman
ul. Zamoyskiego 28/30
03-801 Warsaw
tel: (48-22) 670-75-11, 670-70-70
fax: (48-22) 670-75-12

Stowarzyszenie Marketingu Bezposredniego (SMB)
Mr. Andrz
Direct Marketing Associationej Miekusz, President
ul. Sienkiewicza 3
00-015 Warsaw
tel: (48-22) 827-50-70 through 79
fax: (48-22) 627-31-75

Economic Chamber of Energy and Environmental Protection
Mr. Zbigniew Bicki, President
Mr. Slawomir Krystek, Director
ul. Krucza 6/14
00-950 Warsaw
tel/fax: (48-22) 621-65-72

Polish Power Plant Association
(Towarzystwo Gospodarcze Polskie Elektrownie)
Mr. Slawomir Krystek, Director
ul. Krucza 6/14
00-950 Warsaw
tel: (48-22) 629-04-09
fax: (48-22) 628-60-00

Polish CHP Association
(Polskie Towarzystwo Elektrocieplowni Zawodowych)
Mr. Ryk, Director
ul. Krucza 6/14
00-950 Warsaw
tel: (48-22) 693-23-68
fax: (48-22) 628-69-93

Polish Power Transmission and Distribution Association
Mr. Stanislaw Filipiak, President
ul. Nowowiejskiego 10
60-967 Poznan
tel: (48-61) 56-10-60
fax: (48-22) 56-10-67

Heat Energy Chamber of Commerce
(Izba Gospodarcza Energetyki Cieplnej)
ul. Korotynskiego 23
02-123 Warsaw
tel/fax: (48-22) 22-28-38

Polish Chamber of Tourism
(Polska Izba Turystyki)
Mr. Wlodzimierz Sukiennik, President
ul. Wierzbowa 11
00-094 Warsaw
tel: (48-22) 628-57-31
fax: (48-22) 29-37-57

LIST OF POLISH BANKS WITH CORRESPONDENT U.S. BANKING ARRANGEMENTS

Bank Przemyslowo Handlowy S.A. (BPH)
ul. Na Zjezdzie 11

30-527 Krakow, skr. Poczt.57
tel: (48-12) 22-72-24, 18-78-05
fax: (48-12) 21-69-14

Pomorski Bank Kredytowy S.A. (PBKS)
ul. Bogurodzicy 5, skr.poczt.105
70-105 Szczecin
tel: (48-91) 88-00-39
fax: (48-91) 33-59-69

Powszechny Bank Gospodarczy S.A.
Al. J. Pilsudskiego 12, skr. Poczt.12
90-950 Lodz
tel:(48-42) 361-470
fax:(48-42) 367-772

Bank Polska Kasa Opieki, S.A. (PBKO)
(Pekao, SA)
ul. Grzybowska 53/57
00-950 Warsaw
tel:(48-22)656-0780, 656-0781
fax:(48-22)656-0453

Bank Zachodni S.A. (BZ)
Rynek 9/11, skr. poczt. 1109
50-950 Wroclaw
tel: (48-71) 72-31-38
fax: (49-71) 72-37-63

Gornoslaski Bank Gospodarczy S.A. (BGBK)
Bank Slaski SA
ul. Warszawska 6, skr. poczt. 1138
40-006 Katowice
tel: (48-32)59-62-31
fax: (48-32) 58-64-97

Bank Inicjatyw Gospodarczych BIG S.A. (BIG)
ul. Kopernika 36/10, skr. poczt. 6
00-924 Warsaw
tel: (48-22) 657-50-50, 657-50-00
fax: (48-22) 626-71-80, 657-50-09

Bank Gdanski S.A. (BGSA)
ul. Targ Drzewny 1, skr. poczt. 436
80-958 Gdansk
tel: (48-58) 37-92-22
fax: (48-58) 31-73-61, 31-15-00

Bank Handlowy w Warszawie S.A. (BH)
(Commercial Bank SA)
ul. Koszykowa 54
00-950 Warsaw
tel:(48-22)630-8625
fax:(48-22)630-8609

Bank Rozwoju Eksportu, S.A. (BRE)
(Export Development Bank SA)
Plac Bankowy 2, skr. poczt. 728
00-950 Warsaw
tel:(48-22)637-2800
fax:(48-22)637-1879

Powszechna Kasa Oszczednosci, Bank Panstwowy (PKO BP)
ul. Nowy Swiat 6/12, skr. poczt. 639
00-950 Warsaw
tel:(48-22)637-1618
fax:(48-22)635-5855

Bank Gospodarki Zywnosciowej S.A. (BGZ)
(Bank for the Food Economy)
ul. Chelmska 19
00-916 Warsaw
tel/fax:(48-22) 416-131

Bank Depozytowo-Kredytowy S.A. (BDK)
ul. Chopina 6
20-954 Lublin
tel:(48-81)532-0171
fax:(48-81)532-3318

Bank Gospodarstwa Krajowego (BGK)
ul. Swietokrzyska 12, skr. poczt. 57
00-916 Warsaw
tel: (48-22) 826-23-51, 20-03-11
fax: (48-22) 20-07-30

Narodowy Bank Polski (NBP)
ul. Swietokrzyska 11/21, skr. poczt. 1011

00-919 Warsaw
tel: (48-22) 653-23-35, 653-25,71
fax: (48-22) 653-13-21

STRATEGIC STATISTICS

INVESTMENT STATISTICS

The investment climate in Poland has improved noticeably over the past year. Foreign companies chose Poland for a variety of reasons, including: its size, skilled work force, and low labor cost. As a result Poland is rapidly moving up the list of top countries for foreign investment.

Note: State Agency for Foreign Investment (PAIZ) tracks only foreign investment in Poland by "major" investments, or those made by "large" foreign investors, totaling USD 1 million or more. According to PAIZ, at the end of 1996 there were 492 companies representing 28 countries which invested more than USD 1 million.

FOREIGN DIRECT INVESTMENTS (BY COUNTRIES OF ORIGIN)

Country	Total Equity & Loans
U.S.A.	2965.6
Germany	1524.4
International	1493.0
Italy	1223.8
Holland	951.7
France	899.9
Great Britain	509.0
Sweden	361.3
Switzerland	357.7
Australia	328.1
Austria	315.3
Denmark	238.2
South Korea	184.5
Ireland	105.7
Spain	94.3
Canada	94.1
Finland	92.9

Norway	80.1
Belgium	46.5
Japan	32.5
South Africa	25.0
China	25.0
Turkey	23.0
Russia	20.0
Singapore	13.0
Liechtenstein	12.3
Slovenia	4.9
Greece	3.6
Luxembourg	2.3
GRAND TOTAL	12027.7

FOREIGN DIRECT INVESTMENTS (BY INDUSTRY SECTOR DESTINATION –

Sector	Equity & Loans	Commitments
Industry total	7482.9 -- *62.2%*	6816.9
of this:		
fuel-energetic	182.8	1491.1
metallurgical	108.3	183.7
electro-machinery	2039.6 -- *17.0%*	2538.7
chemical	642.4 -- *0.05%*	239.4
mineral	748.0 -- *0.06%*	796.2
wood and paper	608.4 -- *0.05%*	89.1
light	301.2	220.4
food	2535.3 -- *21.1%*	1224.9
others	316.9	33.4

Construction	607.2 -- *0.05%*	251.1
Agriculture	15.0	0.0
Transportation	48.0	4.5
Telecommunications	587.6 -- *0.05%*	380.7
Trade	709.6 -- *0.06%*	297.8
Municipal Economy	24.8	6.7
Finance	2522.9 -- *21.0%*	273.4
Insurance	29.7	2.2
TOTAL	12027.7	7933.3

THE TOP 20 U.S. INVESTORS IN POLAND

USD Millions	Company	Value of investments
	Polish American Enterprise Fund	464.0
	International Paper Corp.	370.0
	Pepsico	292.0
	Philip Morris	227.0
	Procter and Gamble	130.0
	Goodyear	112.0
	D.Chase Enterprises	100.0
	MARS Inc.	100.0
	Curtis	100.0
	Epstein	90.0
	R.J.Reynolds	70.0
	Schooner Capital Corp.	64.6

	Ford Motor Co.	54.0
	Cargill Inc.	53.0
	McDonald's	50.0
	Citibank	50.0
	Ameritech	45.0
	US West	45.0
	Wrigley's	40.0
	Air Touch International	36.5
Source: PAIZ		

THE TOP TWENTY FOREIGN INVESTORS IN POLAND (USD MILLIONS)

Investor	Equity & Loans	Origin	Branch
Fiat	888.1	Italy	car manufacture
EBRD	613.8	International	banking-capital participation in enterprises
Polish-American Enterprise Fund	464.0	USA	capital cooperation with private firms and participation in privatization
Int'l Paper Corp.	370.0	USA	paper industry
ING Group	350.0	Netherlands	banking
Pepsico	292.0	USA	sweets-soft drinks-chips

Coca-Cola Amatil	285.0	Australia	soft drinks production
International Finance Corporation	277.3	private sector	investment in International projects across all ind. sectors
Nestle	248.0	Switzerland	confectionery
Philip Morris	227.0	USA	tobacco industry
ABB	200.0	International	power supply systems
Thomson Consumer Electronics	185.0	France	TV tubes and sets
Pilkington	168.9	UK	glass plant
Saint Gobain	150.0	France	glass- insulating materials-production construction
SHV Macro	148.0	Netherlands	wholesale trade centers

Unilever	140.0	International	washing powder- food processing
Procter and Gamble products	130.0	USA	personal hygiene
Reemtsma	130.0	Germany	tobacco industry
Daewoo	129.5	Korea	electronics equip.-car production
Michelin	112.0	France	tire production
Source: PAIZ			

Domestic Economy	**1995**	**1996**	**2004(f)**
GDP Current (USD Billions)	113.9	129.9	140.1
GDP Growth Rate (real % change)	7%	6%	5.5%
GDP Per Capita (in current USD)	3086	3460	3700
(at purchasing power parity)	6350	7400	7900
Gov't Spending (% of GDP)	31.9%	30.0%	29.6%
Inflation (% change Dec-Dec)	21.6%	18.5%	13.0%
Unemployment (Percent)	14.9%	13.6%	12.9%
Foreign Exchange Reserves(mn USD)			
-gross	14830	17980	18000
-net	20400	21700	21000
Average Exchange Rate (**)	2.42	2.69	3.16
Foreign Hard Curr. Debt(mln USD)	41780	43750	39375

Foreign Debt Service (&)(mln USD) (as a % of exports)	9.0%	10.2%	N/a

Notes:
Polish Government Statistics, unless otherwise noted
f = Forecast, straight line projections
N/a = Data not available
**** = Polish Zloty per USD 1**

TRADE

The following figures are from Poland's Ministry of Foreign Economic Relations and are in USD millions, unless otherwise noted.

	1995	1996	2004*
Total Poland Exports	22900	24440	28811**
Total Poland Imports	24700	37137	38272**
U.S. Imports from Poland	664	627	627
U.S. Exports to Poland	776	968	1200
U.S. Share of Polish Imports	3.8%	4.4%	6.0%

Agricultural Data Total Polish Agricultural Imports (a): 3989
Agricultural Imports from the U.S.(b): 225
U.S. Percent of Import Market (a): 6.6%
Agricultural Trade Balance with U.S. (a): -204.6

a report on U.S. agriculture exports to Poland is available at http://ffas.usda.gov/cgi-bin/bico-get/1063

FIVE PRINCIPAL U.S. EXPORTS TO POLAND (HS)

1. **Machinery (157.760 mln)**
2. **Electrical (110.673 mln)**
3. **Cereals (104.539 mln)**
4. **Special Other (74,372 mln)**
5. **Vehicles, not Railway (67,052 mln)**

Five Principal U.S. Imports from Poland (HS)

1. **Machinery (129.008 mln)**
2. **Electrical (54,808 mln)**
3. **Woven Apparel (40,430 mln)**
4. **Glass (39,763 mln)**
5. **Iron and Steel (34.976 mln)**

GLOSSARY

Bolsheviks

Members of the radical political faction that, under the leadership of Vladimir I. Lenin, staged the Bolshevik Revolution and in 1918 formed the Russian Communist Party (Bolshevik), precursor of the Communist Party of the Soviet Union.

Byzantine

Medieval Christian civilization that combined European and Asian cultures on an ancient Greco-Roman foundation. Centered at Byzantium (known as Constantinople 330-1930, and later called Istanbul), the Byzantine Empire occupied western Turkey and the Balkans and, as the center of Orthodox Christianity, exerted strong influence on many of the Slavic peoples of Eastern Europe.

CoCom (Coordinating Committee for Multilateral Export Controls)

Loose arrangement of Western governments formed in 1949 to prevent the transfer of military-useful (dual-use) technology from the West to the Soviet Union and Eastern Europe; the group (whose membership was almost identical to that of the North Atlantic Treaty Organization, *q.v.*) operated on the basis of informal agreements covering items having military or nuclear applications.

Comecon (Council for Mutual Economic Assistance)

A multilateral economic alliance headquartered in Moscow; it existed from 1949-91. Members in 1990 included Bulgaria, Cuba, Czechoslovakia, the German Democratic Republic (East Germany), Hungary, Mongolia, Poland, Romania, the Soviet Union, and Vietnam. Also referred to as CMEA and CEMA.

Commonwealth of Independent States (CIS)

official designation of the former republics that remained loosely federated in economic and security matters of common concern, after the Soviet Union disbanded as a unified nation in 1991. Members in 1993 were Armenia, Azerbaijan, Belarus, Kazakhstan, Kyrgyzstan, Moldova, Russia, Tajikistan, Turkmenistan, Ukraine, and Uzbekistan.

Conference on Security and Cooperation in Europe (CSCE)

Originating at the meeting that produced the Helsinki Accords (*q.v.*) in 1975, a grouping of all European nations (the lone exception, Albania, joined in 1991) that subsequently sponsored joint sessions and consultations on political issues vital to European security.

Conventional Forces in Europe (CFE) Treaty

An agreement signed in 1990 by the members of the Warsaw Pact (*q.v.*) and the North Atlantic Treaty Organization (*q.v.*) to establish parity in conventional weapons between the two organizations from the Atlantic to the Urals. Included a strict system of inspections and information exchange.

Czech and Slovak Federative Republic (CSFR)

official name of the former Czechoslovakia, adopted in December 1990 to recognize the two ethnic components of that country. (Czechoslovakia was still used as the short form designation after that date.) In January 1993, divided into two independent states, the Czech Republic and Slovakia, which retained some economic and security ties.

Enlightenment

Philosophical and spiritual movement in Europe in the seventeenth and eighteenth centuries, concerned with the relationship of God, nature, reason, and man, often challenging the tenets of conventional Christianity.

European Bank for Reconstruction and Development (EBRD)

A bank founded under sponsorship of the European Community (*q.v.*) in 1990, to provide loans to East European countries (Bulgaria, the Czech and Slovak Federative Republic, Hungary, Poland, Romania, the Soviet Union, and Yugoslavia) to establish independent, market-driven economies and democratic political institutions. Some fifty-eight countries were shareholders in 1992.

European Community (EC)

A group of primarily economic communities of Western European countries, including the European Atomic Energy Community (Euratom or EAEC) and the European Coal and Steel Community (ECSC). Executive power rested with the European Commission, which implemented and defended the community treaties in the interests of the EC as a whole. Members in 1993 were Belgium, Britain, Denmark, France, Germany, Greece, Ireland, Italy, Luxembourg, the Netherlands, Portugal, and Spain. Name changed to European Union (EU), December 1993.

Gdansk Agreement

The first of several major concessions made by the Polish communist government in late 1980 to the rising Solidarity movement. The agreement granted public expression to many groups in Polish society hitherto restricted, promised new economic concessions, removed discredited communist officials, and recognized workers' right to establish free trade unions.

glasnost'

Russian term, literally meaning "openness," applied in the Soviet Union beginning in the mid-1980s to official permission for public discussion of issues and public access to information. Identified with the tenure of Mikhail S. Gorbachev as leader of the Soviet Union.

gross domestic product (GDP)

The total value of goods and services produced exclusively within a nation's domestic economy, in contrast to gross national product (*q.v.*), usually computed over one year.

gross national product (GNP)

The total value of goods and services produced within a country's borders and the income received from abroad by residents, minus payments remitted abroad by nonresidents. Normally computed over one year.

Habsburg Empire

Also known as the House of Austria, one of the principal European dynasties between the fifteenth and twentieth centuries. Controlled a variety of separate monarchies, reaching its most powerful stage in the sixteenth century under Emperor Charles V of the Holy Roman Empire (*q.v.*). After 1867 what remained of the empire was commonly known as Austria-Hungary.

Helsinki Accords

Signed in 1975 by all countries of Europe except Albania (which signed in 1991), plus Canada and the United States, at the initial Conference on Security and Cooperation in Europe (*q.v.*). The pact outlined general principles of international behavior and security and addressed some economic, environmental, and humanitarian issues.

Holy Roman Empire

Enduring from A.D. 800 to 1806, official successor under papal authority to the Roman Empire. The title *king of the Romans*, first given to Charlemagne, was borne by a long succession of German kings. Centered in Germany, the empire at its peak (thirteenth century to sixteenth century) extended from the Low Countries to Czechoslovakia and southward into Italy. Weakened by struggles with Roman Catholic Church and the Reformation, then scattered by the results of the Thirty Years' War (*q.v.*), 1648.

International Monetary Fund (IMF)

Established with the World Bank (*q.v*) in 1945, a specialized agency affiliated with the United Nations and responsible for stabilizing international exchange rates and payments. Its main business was providing loans to its members when they experienced balance of payments difficulties.

Jacobinism

Political philosophy of the leaders of the French revolutionary government. After reaching power in the revolutionary dictatorship of 1793, the Jacobins set about safeguarding the values of the revolution and public virtue by a Reign of Terror against opposing views.

London Club

A group of 500 major international commercial banks lending money under auspices of the International Monetary Fund (*q.v.*) to Poland for economic development, under conditions of continued economic reform.

net material product (NMP)

In countries having centrally planned economies, the official measure of the value of goods and services produced within the country. Roughly equivalent to the Western gross national product (*q.v.*), NMP was based on constant prices and did not account for depreciation.

North Atlantic Treaty Organization (NATO)

An alliance founded in 1949 by the United States, Canada, and their postwar European allies to oppose Soviet military presence in Europe. Until the dissolution of the Warsaw Pact (*q.v.*) in 1991, NATO was the primary collective defense agreement of the Western powers. Its military and administrative structure remained intact after the threat of Soviet expansionism had subsided.

Organisation for Economic Co- operation and Development (OECD)

Founded in 1961 to replace the all-European Organisation for European Economic Cooperation, assists member governments to form and coordinate economic and social aid policies in developing countries. In 1992, twenty-four nations had full membership, including Australia, Canada, New Zealand, and the United States.

Ottoman Empire

A Muslim empire that controlled southeastern Europe, the Middle East, and most of North Africa between the sixteenth and eighteenth centuries, and lesser territories from 1300 until 1913. Ottoman occupation was a major influence on all civilizations of southeastern Europe and caused ethnic animosities that remained after the disintegration of the empire.

Paris Club

A group of seventeen Western countries lending money under auspices of the International Monetary Fund (*q.v.*) to Poland for economic development, under conditions of continued economic reform.

perestroika

Russian word meaning "restructuring," applied in the late 1980s to an official Soviet program of revitalization of the communist party, economy, and society, by adjusting economic, social, and political mechanisms. Identified with the tenure of Mikhail S. Gorbachev as leader of the Soviet Union (1985-1991).

Prague Spring

Period of attempts to institute political and economic reforms in Czechoslovakia, led by communist party First Secretary Alexander Dubcek, in 1968. The Soviet Union and four Warsaw Pact (*q.v.*) allies responded by invading Czechoslovakia and forcing Dubcek out of power.

Reformation

Sixteenth-century movement against dogma of the Roman Catholic Church, in favor of grace through faith, the authority of the Scriptures, and the direct relationship of believers with God. Met with resounding force by the established church, the Reformation influenced Christian practice to varying degrees in all European countries, resulting in a schism between the Roman Catholic church and Protestant reformers.

Teutonic Knights

In full, Knights of the Teutonic Order, an organization of German crusaders founded in Palestine in 1190. From their base in Prussia, consolidated the Eastern Baltic into a powerful feudal state in the fourteenth century, nominally as agents of the Roman Catholic Church. Expansion aroused hostility and revolts, which with Polish and Lithuanian support defeated the knights decisively at Grunwald in 1410. After rapid decline of military power and influence in the fifteenth century, disbanded in 1525.

Thirty Years' War

Conventional name for a fifty-year struggle (1610-60) of various factions including Protestant nobles and French kings against the Holy Roman Empire (*q.v.*) and its ruling Habsburg Dynasty for control of parts of Europe, including the Baltic coast. The fiercest period of the war was 1618-48, hence the misnomer *Thirty Years' War*.

Treaty of Versailles

Signed at the Paris Peace Conference, June 1919, dictating peace terms ending World War I. Harsh terms imposed by the Allies on Germany were cited as a major factor in the rise of Adolf Hitler and genesis of World War II.

Warsaw Pact

Informal name for Warsaw Treaty Organization, a mutual defense organization founded in 1955, including the Soviet Union, Albania (which withdrew in 1961), Bulgaria, Czechoslovakia, the German Democratic Republic (East Germany), Hungary, Poland, and Romania. The Warsaw Pact enabled the Soviet Union to station troops in the countries to its west to oppose the forces of the North Atlantic Treaty Organization (*q.v.*). The pact was the basis of the invasions of Hungary (1956) and Czechoslovakia (1968). Disbanded in July 1991.

Western European Union (WEU)

Signed in 1948 by Western European states as a regional defense, cultural, and economic pact, became inactive in 1954 but was revived in 1984 to improve European military preparedness and activity in the North Atlantic Treaty Organization (*q.v.*). Subsequently issued statements on European security and other international issues. Members in 1993 were Belgium, Britain, France, Germany, Greece, Italy, Luxembourg, the Netherlands, Portugal, and Spain.

World Bank

Informal name for a group of four affiliated international institutions: the International Bank for Reconstruction and Development (IBRD), the International Development Association (IDA), the International Finance Corporation (IFC), and the Multilateral Investment Guarantee Agency (MIGA). The IBRD, established in 1945, had as its primary purpose making loans to developing countries for specific projects. The IDA, legally separate but administered by the IBRD, furnished credits to the poorest developing countries on terms easier than those of the IBRD. The IFC supplemented IBRD activity through loans to stimulate private enterprise in the less developed countries. The MIGA was founded in 1988 to insure private foreign investment in developing countries against noncommercial risks. The four institutions were owned by the governments of the countries that subscribed their capital. For a state to participate in the World Bank group, prior membership in the International Monetary Fund (IMF--*q.v.*) was required.

zloty

Polish national currency (Polish spelling zloty) nominally divided into 100 groszy. Became convertible with Western currencies January 1, 1990. In March 1990, US$1 equalled 9,824 zloty; in March 1991, the exchange rate was US$1=9,520 zloty; in March 1993, it was US$1=16,330 zloty.

X. OPERATING IN POLAND

Forms of Business Entities

Polish regulations allow the following legal forms of businesses:

- enterprises run by a natural person; these are small businesses run by private individuals,
- civil partnerships established under the regulations of the Polish Civil Code,
- commercial companies, established by natural or legal persons under the regulations of the Polish Code of Commercial Companies,
- co-operatives established by natural or legal persons,
- state-owned enterprises,
- societas europaea (SE) and European Economic Interest Grouping (EEIG) can be set up in Poland as of 19 May 2005 (in accordance with EU Council regulations).

The Code of Commercial Companies of 15 September 2000 regulates two groups of companies:

- partnerships (registered partnership, limited partnership, professional partnership and limited joint-stock partnership),
- corporations (joint-stock company and limited liability company).

Societies, foundations, and trade unions may also carry out economic activity.

Operations in some business areas require a license or a permit, on the grounds of the Law on Economic Freedom of 2 July 2004, or may be carried out following the company's entry in the register of regulated activities, regardless of whether the company is domestic or foreign. For some basic information on corporations, as well as licensing and permits, please refer to Legal Considerations in Chapter V.

On the basis of the Law on Economic Freedom of 2 July 2004, foreign persons (as defined by the aforementioned law) from EU and EFTA states – members of the European Economic Area – may operate in Poland in accordance with the principles applicable to domestic entrepreneurs.

Other foreign persons may conduct their operations solely (unless stated otherwise in international agreements) in the form of a limited partnership, limited joint-stock partnership, limited liability company, and joint-stock company. Moreover, foreign persons may open branch offices and representative offices in Poland. For more information on subsidiaries please refer to the next sub-chapter.

Establishing a Company

Joint-Stock Companies and Limited Liability Companies

Before the registration procedure for a company may be started, the company charter (joint-stock company) or the articles of association (limited liability company) must be prepared and duly signed and notarised. Prior to their finalisation in consultation with a notary, a draft should be prepared by the legal advisers of the company's founders.

In the case of a joint-stock company, the notarial deed should contain the following:

- business name and company seat,
- type of activity,
- duration of the company, if limited,
- amount of share capital, capital paid-in before registration, the nominal value of the shares and their number, the indication whether they are registered shares or bearer shares,
- number of each type of shares and rights associated with specific share types, if applicable,
- names and addresses of the founders,
- number of members of the governing and supervisory bodies, or at least a minimum or a maximum number and an entity authorised to appoint the members,
- at least an approximation of costs resulting from the company's formation,
- a newspaper / periodical for publishing announcements, if the company intends to publish announcements in other than the Court and Economic Monitor (*Monitor Sądowy i Gospodarczy*).

Apart from the above, the charter should include provisions concerning the number and type of instruments that entitle the holder to participate in the profits or in the division of company assets, along with the rights associated with these instruments, any additional obligations related to the purchase of the shares, the conditions and manner in which the shares may be re-deemed, any limitations concerning shares' transfer or sale and any extra rights granted to specific shareholders.

In the case of a limited liability company, the notarial deed should contain the following:

- business name and company seat,
- type of activity,
- duration of the company, if limited,
- amount of share capital,
- whether a shareholder is entitled to one or more shares,
- number and nominal value of shares held by individual shareholders.

Apart from the above, the deed should include provisions concerning in-kind contributions and stipulations concerning additional shareholder benefits and/or obligations, if applicable.

Other documents required at the notary office are:

- a list of names of shareholders and the value and number of shares held by the founders,
- a draft of the appointment of the Board of Management,
- a draft of the appointment of the Supervisory Board (obligatory for joint-stock companies) and Control Committee, if provided by law or the articles of association.

If the shareholder is a legal person, he is required to submit:

- a copy of the company's entry in the commercial register (valid for three months),
- a resolution of the appropriate body of the company agreeing to the company's participation in the new company to be formed,
- notarialy authorised proxies, if the persons authorised to sign on behalf of the shareholder are not appearing in person and are to be represented by a proxy.

Documents in a foreign language should be confirmed by the local Polish embassy or consulate as having been prepared in accordance with local law and must be accompanied by a certified translation.

It should be noted that for limited liability companies the founding capital must be fully paid up on incorporation, while for joint-stock companies at least 25 % of the founding capital must be paid up / contributed on incorporation and at least 25 % of the cash capital must be paid up.

The next step is to register the company in the National Court Register. This is performed by the Registry Court, which acts after receiving an application for registration submitted by the Board of Management and containing information on:

- business name and company seat, and scope of business,
- the value of the initial capital (and the number of shares and their nominal value for joint-stock companies),
- the names of Board of Management members and how the company is represented (and members' addresses for limited liability companies),
- the names of Supervisory Board members (obligatory for joint-stock companies) and Control Committee, if required by law, or the articles of association,
- the duration of the company, if limited,

- a newspaper / periodical for publishing announcements, if indicated in the charter / articles of association,
- a statement on in-kind contributions made by the partners,
- whether a shareholder is entitled to one or more shares (limited liability companies),
- number of privileged shares and type of privileges (joint-stock companies),
- final share capital amount, if provided by the charter (joint-stock companies),
- amount of capital paid-in before registration (joint-stock companies),
- any extra rights granted to specific shareholders, if provided by the charter.

Other documents required upon registration include:

- The company charter or articles of association;
- Documents appointing the company's governing bodies, with a specification of appointed members. In the case of a limited liability company only when these were not defined in the articles;
- A statement from all members of the Board of Management that the contributions towards initial capital have been made by all shareholders in full (limited liability companies), or that the share payments and contributions in kind envisaged by the charter have been effected lawfully (joint-stock companies);
- A list, signed by all members of the Board of Management, giving the names of the shareholders (individuals and companies) and the number and nominal value of shares held;
- Specimens of the signatures of the Board of Management members, certified by a notary or made in person in the presence of the Court;
- Personal details of the members of the Board of Management.

There are some further requirements concerning documents required upon registration of a joint-stock company, specified in the Code of Commercial Companies, article 320. There is a registration fee amounting to PLN 1,000.

The registration has to be officially announced, as required by the law, in the Court and Economic Monitor. The announcement fee is PLN 500.

After its registration in the Court, each company must obtain its statistical number (REGON) from the local statistical office (free of charge). To receive it the company is required to fill-in and submit a simple RG-1 form, accompanied by a copy of the articles or charter and a certified copy of the entry in the Commercial Register. Although statistical offices are obliged to issue the REGON within seven days, if you show up in person it can take as little as twenty or thirty minutes, depending on the length of the queue.

Finally, the company must be registered with the Social Security Institution (ZUS) and the local tax office (after opening a bank account).

Limited Partnership

A limited partnership is a partnership wherein at least one partner is fully liable against creditors (general partner) and the liability of at least one partner (the limited partner) is limited. The partnership agreement must be notarised and it should contain:

- business name and company seat,
- type of activity,
- duration of the company, if limited,
- contributions made by each partner and their value,
- liability of each limited partner against creditors (value),
- if a limited partner contributes in kind, the contribution must be specified, along with its value and the name of the contributing partner.

The next step is to register the company in the National Court Register. The same registration and announcement fees apply as in the case of other commercial companies. A limited partnership's registration application should contain:

- business name and company seat,
- type of activity,
- name(s) of general partners and, separately, names(s) of limited partners, as well as circumstances pertaining to limitations on partners' active capacity, if applicable,
- names of persons authorised to represent the company, and how the company is represented, and, should general partners entrust the running of the company to some of their number alone, this circumstance should be mentioned,
- amount up to which the limited partners are liable.

A limited partnership is established upon its registration. After this, just as for corporations, the company must obtain its statistical number, and register with the Social Security Institution (ZUS) and with the local tax office (after opening a bank account).

Limited Joint-Stock Partnership

A limited joint-stock partnership is a partnership wherein at least one partner is fully liable against creditors (the general partner) and at least one of the partners is the company's shareholder. The minimum share capital of a limited joint-stock partnership amounts to PLN 50,000. The partnership agreement must be notarised and it should contain:

- business name and company seat,
- type of activity,
- duration of the company, if limited,
- contributions made by each partner and their value,
- amount of share capital, how it was collected, the nominal value of the shares and their number, an indication whether they are registered shares or bearer shares,
- number of each type of shares and rights associated with specific share types, if applicable,
- name(s) of general partners, with their seats / addresses,
- structure of the General Meeting and of the Supervisory Board, if establishment of the Supervisory Board is required by law, or the partnership agreement.

The next step is to register the company in the National Court Register. The same registration and announcement fees apply as in the case of other commercial companies. A limited joint-stock partnership's registration application should contain:

- business name and company seat,
- type of activity,
- duration of the company, if limited,
- amount of share capital, the nominal value of the shares and their number,
- number of privileged shares and type of privileges, if envisaged in the partnership agreement,
- amount of capital paid-in before registration,
- name(s) of general partners, as well as circumstances pertaining to limitations on partners' active capacity, if applicable,
- names of persons authorised to represent the company, and how the company is represented, and, should general partners entrust the running of the company to some of their number alone, this circumstance should be mentioned,
- a statement on in-kind contributions of the shareholders, if applicable.

A limited joint-stock partnership is established upon its registration. After this, just as for corporations, the company must obtain its statistical number, and register with the Social Security Institution (ZUS) and with the local tax office (after opening a bank account).

Subsidiaries of Foreign Companies

Foreign companies may open branch offices and representative offices in Poland pursuant to the provisions contained in the Law on Economic Freedom of 2 July 2004.

Branch Office

Foreign companies may establish branch offices in Poland, on the basis of reciprocity, subject to the provisions of international agreements ratified by Poland, in order to conduct business activity in Poland within the scope of their business objectives, exclusively.

Foreign persons (as defined by the aforementioned law) from EU and EFTA states – members of the European Economic Area – may establish branch offices in Poland in accordance with the principles applicable to domestic entrepreneurs.

Branch offices are obliged to use the name of the mother company in the language of the country where it is registered, along with the name of its legal form translated into Polish and the words *oddział w Polsce* (branch in Poland) added.

A foreign entity setting up its branch office is obliged to appoint a person at the branch who is authorised to represent this entity. A branch may commence its operations only after it has been registered with the National Court Register.

Branch offices are to maintain separate accounting books in Polish, pursuant to Polish accounting regulations. Another requirement stipulates that branch offices are required to notify the Polish Minister of Economic Affairs of:

- the commencement of liquidation of the foreign entity that has opened the branch in Poland,
- the loss by that foreign entity of the right to conduct business activity.

Liquidation of branch offices is carried out following the liquidation procedure for limited liability companies contained in the Code of Commercial Companies of 15 September 2000.

Representative Office

Foreign companies may establish representative offices in Poland solely in order to promote and advertise the company establishing the office. Establishment of a representative office requires registration in the Register of Representative Offices of Foreign Business Entities kept by the Minister of Economic Affairs. Registration is effected based on an application from the foreign company concerned.

The application, in Polish, should contain the following:

- name, place of registration, and legal form of the foreign company opening its representative office,
- scope of the business activity of the foreign company opening its representative office,
- name and address in Poland of a person in the representative office authorised to represent the foreign company,
- representative office's address in Poland.

The above-mentioned application should be accompanied by the documents listed below:

- deed of formation (articles of association, charter) of the foreign company, if applicable,
- copy of its entry in the Commercial Register or its equivalent, if applicable,
- statement of the foreign company on establishing its representative office in Poland,
- document certifying the foreign company's rights to the real estate wherein its representative office will carry out the activities.

The enclosures in a foreign language contained in this list should be accompanied by a certified translation into Polish.

Representative offices are obliged to use the name of the mother company in the language of the country where it is registered, along with the name of its legal form translated into Polish and the words *przedstawicielstwo w Polsce* (representative office in Poland) added.

Just take branch offices, representative offices are required to maintain separate accounting books in Polish, pursuant to Polish accounting regulations. Furthermore, representative offices are obliged to notify the Polish Minister of Economic Affairs of:

- the commencement or end of liquidation of the foreign entity that has opened a representative office in Poland,
- the loss by that foreign entity of the right to conduct business activity,
- the loss by that foreign entity of the right to dispose of its assets, as well as
- any change pertaining to the information contained in the application for registering of the representative office.

Liquidation of representative offices is conducted in accordance with following the liquidation procedure for limited liability companies contained in the Code of Commercial Companies of 15 September 2000.

Competition and Consumer Protection

The Office for Competition and Consumer Protection (UOKIK) is the Polish competition authority guarding freedom of competition and consumer interests. Its major mission is to examine conformity with the Competition and Consumer Protection Law of 15 December 2000 (in force as of 1 April 2001), which forms the legal basis for competition and consumer protection in Poland.

The UOKIK's head-office is located in Warsaw and there are 9 branch-offices in major Polish cities. Its key activities include acting against monopolistic practices, merger control, consumer protection, and public aid monitoring. As of 1 May 2004 the UOKiK is a part of the European Competition Network, formed by the European Commission and competition protection authorities of the member countries. From a foreign investor's point of view probably the most interesting activities of the Office for Competition and Consumer Protection and its regional agencies are the ones pertaining to mergers.

A merger of companies is subject to the UOKiK is approval if the companies' combined turnover in the preceding year exceeded EUR 50 million. This obligation refers, in particular, to:

- the merger of two or more independent companies;
- the takeover, through acquisition or by entering into the possession of stocks, other securities, shares, of the entirety or a part of the property, or in any other way obtaining direct or indirect control over one or several companies;
- the creation of a joint venture;
- the takeover or acquisition of stocks or shares of another company resulting in gaining at least 25 % of the votes at the general assembly or assembly of partners;
- the same person assuming the function of a member of the managing or controlling body of competing companies.

There are, however some exclusions from the obligation of obtaining the UOKiK's approval, most notably these pertaining to taking over companies with an annual turnover below EUR 10 million (in the territory of Poland, during each of the two accounting years immediately preceding the merger), to companies of the same holding, and to acquiring only temporary control. A merger can take place if UOKiK grants a favourable decision.

In order to increase the efficiency of the UOKiK, in cases where a company's practice may be restricting competition, an explanatory investigation may be instituted instead of the more complex and costly anti-monopoly proceedings, and a decision may be made on the evidence gathered in the shorter proceedings.

Furthermore, the question arose as to the obligation of notification of trans-national mergers. It was decided that, on the basis of Article 1 of the Act on Competition and Consumer Protection, which provides that the act will apply to all anti-competitive practices "which cause or may cause effects within the territory of the Republic of Poland", the parties to trans-national mergers are obliged to notify the UOKiK of their intention to merge if:

- any of the enterprises has subsidiaries in Poland; or
- they have distribution networks in Poland; or
- they conduct permanent sales on the territory of Poland.

It should be noted that as of 1 May 2004, art. 13 clause 2 of the Competition and Consumer Protection Law, providing an exemption from the obligation to notify the UOKiK about mergers as a result of which the joint market share of the merging partners will not exceed 20 % is no longer in force. Therefore, all mergers that had not been effected by 1 May 2004 and that were excluded from the obligation to obtain the UOKiK approval on the grounds of the aforementioned clause, need to obtain such an approval regardless of the partners' market share.

The same law prohibits agreements that aim at, or result in, the elimination, restriction, or any other infringement of competition on the relevant market, and in particular, those agreements consisting in:

- fixing, directly or indirectly, prices and other conditions for the purchase or sale of products;
- limiting or controlling production or supply, or technical development or investments;
- sharing markets of supply or purchase;
- applying onerous, or different contract terms in like transactions with third parties, thus creating different conditions of competition for these parties;
- making the conclusion of an agreement subject to the acceptance or fulfilment by the other party of another performance, having neither substantial nor customary relation with the subject of the agreement;
- limiting access to the market or eliminating from the market entrepreneurs who are not party to the agreement;
- fixing the conditions of offers to be submitted by entrepreneurs participating in a tender, in particular in relation to the scope of works or price.

There are, however, some exclusions from the above, most notably pertaining to companies with a joint market share of below 5 %. Abusing a dominant market position, as defined in art. 8 of the law is, also prohibited.

In 2004, the UOKiK issued 152 decisions on the grounds of anti-monopoly regulations regarding practises limiting competition. Of this number, 16 cases involved horizontal agreements (in 8 cases practises limiting competition were discovered), 10 cases involved vertical agreements (in 6 cases practises limiting competition were discovered), and 126 cases involved abuse of a dominant position (in 45 cases practises limiting competition were discovered).

In the same year the UOKiK examined 256 cases pertaining to mergers and completed 218. In 175 instances, the decision was favourable to the merging companies; in one case the favourable decision was conditional; and in one case the intended merger was banned.

Accounting and Auditing

The accounting and auditing regulations are based on the Accounting Law of 29 September 1994, as amended. The law does not apply to the State Treasury and the National Bank of Poland.

All businesses having their registered seat, or the seat of management in Poland must adhere to Polish accounting and auditing regulations. However, as of 1 January 2005, entities keeping accounts in line with International Accounting Standards (IAS) and following International Financial Reporting Standards (IFRS) and the related interpretations announced as directives of the European Commission are required to apply the Accounting Law only to the matters not regulated therein.

Application of the law by the following business entities is voluntary, providing that their net sales do not exceed EUR 800,000:

- enterprises run by a natural person,
- civil partnerships established by natural persons,
- registered partnerships established by natural persons, and
- professional partnerships.

The required accounting procedures are based on a double-entry system. Each company must establish its own book of accounts. Except for state organisations, no uniform book of accounts is imposed. Nevertheless, a book of accounts must still meet certain requirements, such as the ability to show the company's assets, the cost of production, and the profitability of the company. The accounting records, the annual balance sheet, and the profit and loss account must be maintained in Polish currency and prepared in the Polish language.

The requirements regarding the correctness and clarity of accounting records and vouchers do not differ from those normally applied in other European countries. Accounting records, documentation, reports, etc., have to be kept for 5 years.

The accounting law provides for the (optional) application of Polish Accounting Standards (only a few exist, presently), and where there is no Polish standard, the appropriate International Accounting Standard (IAS) may be used. In practise, this means that many companies will not comply with IAS where the accounting law is silent on a particular issue.

In light of the commercial activity regulations, if a transaction is concluded between entrepreneurs, it is always to be done via a bank account. In the case of transactions between entrepreneurs and other parties, this obligation arises only if the amount of the transaction exceeds EUR 15,000, regardless of the number of payments.

The entrepreneur must notify the appropriate tax office of his intention to operate a bank account for business purposes. If he has opened more than one bank account, he is obliged to indicate one of them as basic and to inform both the bank and the relevant tax office which is his the principal bank account.

The law specifies information to be included in financial reports. There is also a provision allowing for simplified financial reports. Such reports can be used by companies meeting at least two of the following three criteria in the year to be reported and in the previous year:

- the average number of employees (in full-time terms) does not exceed 50,
- balance sheet assets do not exceed EUR 2 million,
- net income does not exceed EUR 4 million.

However, simplified reports are not allowed in the case of banks and insurance companies.

Holdings, joint-stock companies (excluding companies in the process of organisation), banks and insurers, and entities operating according to the provisions concerning the public turnover of securities, the organisation and operation of pension funds, and investment funds, are required to hold an annual audit. Other companies must be audited if two of the following three conditions are met in the preceding year:

- the number of employees exceeds 50,
- balance sheet assets exceed EUR 2.5 million,
- net income exceeds EUR 5 million.

The auditor's report must be submitted to the company's local tax office, as well as to the registration court. The report is available for public inspection. All auditors must be members of, and are governed by, the National Registered Auditors' Chamber and the list of auditors entitled to perform audits may be obtained there.

Public Procurement

The Polish public procurement system is governed by the Law on Public Procurement of 29 January 2004, as amended. It came into force on 2 March 2004, in order to harmonize the Polish law on public procurement with EU requirements. The law specifies the rules and procedures for awarding public contracts, law enforcement measures, monitoring of the award of public contracts and the competent authorities with respect to matters addressed therein. Public procurement activities are supervised by the Public Procurement Office (UZP).

Generally, the law applies to all public contracts with a value exceeding EUR 6,000, including for example, those awarded by state and local governments, co-operatives, public health care centres and all other entities which use public funds to finance at least 50 % percent of a given project. Entities from some sectors, such as water management, power, transport and telecommunications are subject to the law if they operate on the basis of special or exclusive rights, or if they are subordinated to dominant entities from the public finance sector. However, it should be noted that defence related purchases are excluded from public tender requirements. Moreover, there are other exclusions, including contracts related to the performance of an international obligation, and labour and real estate transactions.

Depending on the value and nature of the tender, one of seven tender procedures envisaged by the law is to be applied. The seven are:

- public tenders,
- limited tenders,
- published competitive negotiations,
- unpublished competitive negotiations,
- open orders,
- price inquiries, and finally,
- internet auctions.

Public tenders and limited tenders are the primary procedures. The others may be used only in cases specified in the aforementioned law.

Generally, public contracts involving the sale of goods and / or services up to EUR 60,000 may be carried out using simplified tender procedures, and thus avoid the need to follow all public tender requirements. If a value of tender for the sale of goods and / or services exceeds EUR 130,000 (EUR 5,000,000 in the case of construction services), public tender announcements are published in the Official Journal of the European Union. However, a public agency administering the tender is allowed a certain degree of discretion to utilize the limited tender procedure as opposed to the formal public tender, regardless of the value of the contract.

Specifying the subject of a contract by identifying trademarks, patents, or origin is not allowed. Still, if such a degree of specification necessarily arises out of the very nature of the contract, or the ordering party cannot describe the contract in any other manner, this ban can be avoided.

A bidder is entitled correct obvious mistakes in his tender, including mistakes in calculations. In such case the bidder is obliged to inform all the other bidders accordingly. Moreover, regardless of the value of the tender, an unsuccessful bidder has the right to appeal. Even if just one bid is received, the tender may continue without the need to cancel it, or call for a new one. Polish entities no longer receive preferential treatment as compared to their EU counterparts. On the other hand, non-EU based entities may find themselves at a competitive disadvantage.

Bankruptcy and Insolvency

Bankruptcy and insolvency are governed by the Law on Corporate Insolvency and Recovery of 28 February 2003. The Law applies to all types of economic entities, including state enterprises, companies, and natural persons conducting business activity.

The aim of the Law on Corporate Insolvency and Recovery is to create greater protection for creditors and also to encourage reorganisation schemes during the course of the insolvency process. The primary objective is to ensure that the entity can continue its economic activities, with the objective of maintaining employment and the integrity of the enterprise.

Moreover, the law aims at the corporate recovery of the enterprise, creditor satisfaction, the prevention of further insolvency, debt rescheduling, and the encouragement of responsible business practices amongst entrepreneurs. The legislation applies to entrepreneurs, limited liability companies, joint-stock companies, partners in partnerships, and branches of foreign banks operating in Poland.

Insolvency of any business may be declared when a business entity has ceased to pay its debts. However, if the situation is short-lived only, due to some temporary difficulties, it does not give grounds to declare bankruptcy.

In the case of state-owned enterprises, co-operatives, joint-stock companies, limited liability companies, other legal persons conducting economic activity, liquidated general partnerships, registered partnerships, professional partnerships, or limited joint-stock partnerships, bankruptcy is also declared if the assets of such subjects cannot satisfy existing debts. In all cases, the court always closely supervises proceedings.

An insolvent debtor is obliged to lodge a formal application within 14 days of the occurrence of conditions of insolvency. Failure to comply can lead to civil law consequences, prohibition from conducting economic activity by the individual and prohibition from acting as a director or supervisory board member of any entity. In addition, persons acting dishonestly or impeding the process of insolvency can be prosecuted under criminal law.

The legislation has a restrained scope of application to individuals, where its application is limited to personal insolvency caused by factors outside the control of the individual. This law does not apply to non-commercial entities.

The insolvency process is divided into two phases. The first concerns the declaration and publication of insolvency and the process of establishing whether there are grounds for declaring insolvency. The second phase regards the execution of the insolvency process, ending in the complete or partial satisfaction of creditors, or in some compromise scheme.

The choice of the method to satisfy creditors' claims is determined by the court.

A creditor of the company may also file a motion for bankruptcy, as well as any of his creditors. Further, in the case of general partnerships, registered partnerships, professional partnerships, or limited joint-stock partnerships, any partner or shareholder is entitled to file a motion for bankruptcy, while in the case of legal persons and other organisational units this right is granted to any person representing such an entity.

There are the following types of insolvency procedures:

- bankruptcy,
- arrangements within bankruptcy proceedings,
- voluntary agreements,
- banking arrangements.

The bankruptcy of a company results in the sale of all assets, the meeting of all commitments, and the collection of all debts. Where possible, companies with no financial liquidity should be sold as going concerns. The law aims to avoid the bankruptcy of economic entities that are facing short-term liquidity problems.

Under the legislation it is not possible to place the following into insolvency:

- The State Treasury,
- Local authorities and their entities,
- Public health service units,
- Institutions and legal entities set up by an act of Parliament, or those set up under delegated authority arising from legislation,

- Farmers,
- Education establishments.

Recovery of a business entity which, as a result of exceptional circumstances beyond its control, has ceased to pay its debts or foresees that its payments will cease, may demand the opening of proceedings for arrangements with creditors in order to make a voluntary arrangement.

Entrepreneurs should note, however, that bankruptcy proceedings are very slow and do not give creditors protection at a level foreign investors may be used to.

The law introduced the concept of securing the assets of an insolvent entity. The aim is to ensure that the insolvent entity does not dispose of its assets in the period between the declaration of insolvency and the moment of appointment of a liquidator / administrator or the appointment of a court official.

The law provides for the possibility to conduct a process of corporate restructuring. The process is designed to ensure speed of action and in practise is carried out by the insolvent enterprise itself. It is designed to be applied to enterprises which are still capable of meeting some of their liabilities, but which are in danger of becoming insolvent. Conducting this process is subject to presenting a restructuring plan. Restructuring, however, can only be conducted by enterprises entered in the National Court Register.

The law also extends the application of cross-border insolvency and restructuring. When a foreign entity is put into liquidation, its Polish registered branches and representative offices become subject to the insolvency law. The Polish law imposes the model legal solutions of the 1997 UNCITRAL rules. However, as at the date of Poland's accession to the European Union, intra-EU insolvency became subject to the EU law. The main consequence of the above is that the insolvency process of a branch or a representative office is conducted on the grounds of the law of the country of registration of the parent entity.

Employees

All major employment issues are regulated by the Labour Code of 26 June 1974, as amended. These include employer-employee relations, working conditions, salaries and wages, holidays, etc. Another important act concerning employment, and employment of foreigners in particular, is the Law on the Promotion of Employment and Labour Market Institutions of 20 April 2004.

An employer must conclude a written employment contract with an employee. The contract should describe the type of work to be carried out, the commencement date, place of work, working hours, and the salary. The employment contract may be for an unlimited or limited period of time or can be limited to the carrying out of a specific task. There are several types of employment contracts:

- unlimited duration contract, which is a permanent employment contract,
- limited duration contract, concluded for a probationary period. The term of this contract can not exceed three months. Often it leads to the conclusion of an unlimited duration contract, for which the contractual conditions may be renegotiated. If the parties do not reach an agreement concerning future contract terms, the contract expires at the end of the probationary period,
- personal service contract *(umowa zlecenie)* is a fixed term contract concluded for the performance of a specified activity,
- specific task contract *(umowa o dzieło)* is a fixed term contract concluded for the performance of a commissioned activity, which is to bring specified results. This type of contract is regulated by the provisions of the Civil Code.

Employers are allowed to forbid employees from co-operating with rival companies. Non-competition clauses in the contract may take the form of an absolute ban on co-operation with companies with a similar business profile or a ban on working in a rival company after the employee leaves the job. If an employee violates such a clause, he or she is financially liable.

The employee is bound to work with due care, to comply with the hours of work laid down within the company and to use such time effectively, always to have in mind the benefit of the company, and to obey those instructions of his superiors that relate to his work. The employment contract can be cancelled without previous notice if the employee commits a serious breach of contract, commits a crime, or, through his own fault, loses any licence required for the carrying out of his or her work.

Generally, employees must be at least 18 years old. There are, however, specific rules for employing minors. Employees who have less than 4 years to work before attaining pensionable age and pension rights (65 years for men and 60 years for women) may only be dismissed in the event of the bankruptcy or liquidation of the company. This is also true for employees during periods of vacation, illness, maternity leave, or leave of absence requested in advance by the employee.

Upon termination of the employment contract the company must complete a reference with respect to the employee. The reference should include information necessary for a new employer to determine the type of work carried out, the employment period, the position given to the employee, and the type of termination or reasons for ending the employment contract. The employee is entitled to request a reference. If the employee is not satisfied with the reference he or she can request a correction: if necessary, by applying to the labour courts.

Wages and salaries are paid in Polish currency at least once a month. There is a minimum salary requirement, obligatory for all business entities in Poland. In 2005, the minimum gross salary for any full-time employee amounts to PLN 849, approximately USD 250. However, the minimum gross salary in the first year of work is set at 80 % of the above mentioned amount, and at 90 % in the second year.

Working hours are to amount to an average of 8 hours a day and 40 hours a week. There are twelve public holidays: New Year (January 1), Easter Sunday and Easter Monday, May 1 and 3, Whitsunday, Corpus Christi, August 15, All Saints Day (November 1), Independence Day (November 11), and Christmas (December 25 and 26).

In specific cases, working 12 hours a day is permitted. The overtime work relates to duties performed during the time beyond the limit set by the Labour Code's regulations. The circumstances under which such work may be done are thoroughly specified, and include, in particular:

- an emergency action to protect human life, or health, or property, or the natural environment, or to eliminate breakdowns, failures, etc.
- a case of the specific needs of the employer.

The number of overtime hours worked in the second above-mentioned circumstance can not exceed 150 hours per person in the calendar year.

For working overtime an employee, beside his or her usual wages, is entitled to a bonus in the amount of:

- 50 % of remuneration for each hour of overtime work on working days and on holidays which are working days;
- 100 % of remuneration for each hour of overtime work on holidays which are non-working days, and at night.

Employees have a right to annual leave, paid in accordance with their remuneration. The employee starting a job acquires a right to annual leave in the same calendar year after each month of work in the amount of 1/12 of the annual leave. The right to the next annual leave is acquired in each following calendar year. The length of annual leave depends on the length of employment. It amounts to 20 days (up to 10 years of employment), or to 26 days (10 years or over of employment).

Women are entitled to paid maternity leave of 16 weeks after the first birth and 18 weeks after the second or any subsequent birth and 26 weeks for giving birth to more than one child at a time. Employees, who have been employed for at least six months are also entitled to a 3 year leave (paid by the Social Security Institution – ZUS) to raise their children of up to 4 years of age. This leave may be taken in up to 4 separate periods. In addition, 2 extra work-free days are permitted to take care of children up to 14 years old.

In 2005, the total social security charges amount to 48 % of the salary. This amount is split as follows: the social insurance contribution, constituting the major charge and accounting for 36.90 % (encompassing pension insurance – 19.52 %, disability pension insurance – 13 %, insurance against sickness – 2.45 % and accident insurance – average 1.93 %), health insurance, accounting for 8.50 %, the Labour Fund contribution, accounting for 2.45 % and the FGŚP fund (*Fundusz Gwarantowanych Świadczeń Pracowniczych*) contribution of 0.15 %. The Social Security Institution (ZUS) transfers 7.3 % out of the 19.52 % of the pension insurance collected to the open pension funds for all employees that are pension fund members.

Please note that the accident insurance contribution rate ranges between 0.97 and 3.86 %, depending on the company's size and activities. Moreover, the health insurance contribution rate is to increase by 0.25 % a year, to reach 9 % in 2007.

Some of these contributions are paid by the employer, some by the employee, and some are divided between them. Employers are obliged to pay for accident insurance, as well as the Labour Fund contribution and the FGŚP fund contribution. The employee pays for insurance against sickness, and for health insurance, while pension insurance and disability pension insurance charges are split between them equally. Therefore, the social security contribution paid by the employer amounts to 20.79 % of the salary. The maximum base for calculating most elements of the social security contribution is limited to 30 times the average monthly wages envisaged for a given year by the budgetary law. In 2005, the maximum base is equal to PLN 72,690.

It is important to note that a company must register with the ZUS department responsible for the region in which the company is located within 7 days after the first employee has started work.

Employment of Foreigners

Foreigners from Cyprus, the Czech Republic, Estonia, Hungary, Ireland, Latvia, Lithuania, Malta, Slovakia, Slovenia, Sweden and United Kingdom are allowed to work in Poland without any permits.

Moreover, foreigners who meet any of the following criteria do not need a permit to work in Poland:

- a permit for settlement in Poland was received, or
- a consent for tolerated stay was obtained, or
- a refugee status granted in the Republic of Poland was obtained, or
- a temporary protection within the territory of Poland is enjoyed.

Other foreign employees require a work permit issued by the district authorities, however foreigners from other EU countries than those already mentioned have easier access to work permits in comparison to non-EU citizens.

Still, there are numerous instances where the work permit is not required. These include, but are not limited to:

- foreigners resident abroad and delegated by their foreign employer to Poland for up to 3 months for:
    - the assembly, maintenance and repair of machinery, equipment, constructions, etc., produced by their employer,
    - the acceptance of machinery, equipment, etc., ordered from a Polish producer,
    - the training of staff of the Polish employer accepting machinery, equipment, constructions, etc., produced by their employer in servicing and operations thereof,
    - the assembly and disassembly of fair stalls, if their foreign employer is the exhibitor.
- foreign language teachers and teachers teaching in a foreign language, working within the framework of international agreements executed by the Minister of Education and Science,
- foreigners – spouses of Polish citizens, resident in Poland on the grounds of a residence permit for a specified time, granted because of marriage,
- NATO military and civil staff,
- actors, singers, conductors, etc., performing in Poland for up to 30 days a year,
- students attending regular courses in Poland, for up to 3 months during holidays.

No permit is needed from the Polish authorities for employees who work outside Poland for the Polish employer. Furthermore, subject to meeting certain conditions, employees from EU and EFTA countries – members of the EEA – delegated to work in Poland do not require a work permit on the grounds of Directive 96/71/EC of the European Parliament and of the Council concerning the posting of workers in the framework of the providing services. Foreign companies can also accept unpaid assistance from persons delegated by a foreign business partner. Such persons would be neither employed nor paid by the foreign company.

Living in Poland

Standards of living in Poland have improved vastly since the political and economic transformations started in 1989. Accommodation of various types is readily available. Most native city dwellers live in blocks of relatively small apartments; however, the newly constructed flats are usually quite spacious. Houses tend to be considerably more expensive, but there are a lot to choose from on the real estate market. The options range from relatively small semi-detached buildings to grand estates with swimming pools and tennis courts. There are many real estate agencies all over Poland, offering a wide range of properties. In Warsaw alone there are well over a hundred licensed real estate agencies in operation. For more information on the real estate market, please refer to Chapter VIII.

For tourists and visitors, Poland offers a whole range of accommodation, from modern hotels to bed-and-breakfast in private houses. The best hotels offer excellent rooms, restaurants, and room service, but just as everywhere they tend to be expensive. Reservations can be made through travel agencies or directly with a chosen hotel. For more information on tourist accommodation in Poland, please refer to Chapter XI. There are hundreds of travel agencies that provide accommodation, transport, and other logistical services.

Most worldwide best-selling foreign newspapers are on sale in Poland, as well as Polish periodicals published in foreign languages, such as the weekly *The Warsaw Voice*, and *Warsaw Business Journal*. In the largest cities there are bookshops with books in foreign languages, though the languages are often limited to English.

In some larger cities there are schools for foreign children, where lessons are taught in a language other than Polish. In Warsaw, for example, there are American, English, French, and German schools, as well as some others.

Most cities offer a well-developed bus and tram system. Tickets must be bought beforehand and punched or stamped in the bus/tram (or the underground) to validate them. However, in some cities, in Warsaw for example, those who are forgetful can buy a ticket directly from the driver. Crowded in peak hours, buses and trams tend to run quite frequently until ten or eleven in the evening. Bus and tram routes are shown on most city maps. In many cases it is also possible to find them, as well as the schedules, on the net. The number of cars in Warsaw, as well as in other major cities, has been rapidly increasing over the past few years and traffic jams are everyday reality now. Inter-city train connections are good and reliable.

The private medical sector is booming with many small and medium-size private clinics opening throughout the country at a rapid rate. Some of them provide fully comprehensive services supported by English speaking staff. Home visits are among the variety of health care services designed to give foreign guests reassurance while staying in Poland. It is advisable to carefully examine insurance policies to find out exactly what risks are involved and to find a provider whose services cover prevention and cure.

Poland has regular direct air connections with most major European countries, as well as some intercontinental connections provided by the national airline LOT and foreign carriers. Charter flights to popular holiday destinations are available. There are also domestic flights between the major cities in Poland. Competition in the Polish sky is rapidly increasing, and with several low-cost carriers on the market the prices are falling fast, to the passengers benefit.

Visitors travelling by car can enter Poland through many border crossings. Please refer to the next Chapter XI, sub-chapter "Visiting Poland" for visa / currency requirements. Rent-a-car services are at hand; cars can be rented in major cities or at the airports. Generally, to rent a car one has to be 21, and have a driving licence, a passport, and a credit card.

A foreigner must register within 2 days of crossing into Poland. However, individuals staying in hotels, motels, camping grounds, etc., are relieved from this responsibility, as it is done for them by the facility. The procedure is simple and requires only a few minutes of time. The registered person receives an official document of registration, which is required upon leaving Poland at the border. In the case of longer trips, exceeding two months, the red tape is slightly more complex and requires some more time, as well as the assistance of the person having legal title to the accommodation where the foreigner is staying. The registration takes place in the Office of the Commune (*Urząd Gminy*) in which the foreigner is staying, in the Division of Citizens' Affairs.

Opening hours vary, but generally shops are open from 10 a.m. to 7 p.m. Groceries usually start much earlier and some are open round the clock. Shopping is easy. Everything is now more or less available, just as in any other European country. In small shops payment is usually possible in cash only, especially in the country. Larger shops and restaurants, especially these in cities and tourist resorts, increasingly accept cheques and internationally recognised credit cards, such as Visa, American Express, MasterCard, etc. Their opening hours are usually longer, too. There are also many large supermarket chains in Poland, including Auchan, Carrefour, Castorama, E.Leclerc, Geant, Real, Tesco, etc.

All in all, there are approximately 120,000 places accepting credit card payments, as the use of credit cards is becoming increasingly popular in Poland (see Chapter II, the end of the section on banking). In the country, it is considerably more difficult to do without cash, but the prices are substantially lower.

As far as prices are concerned, Warsaw is certainly cheaper for foreigners than New York, Moscow, or St. Petersburg, but probably more expensive than Prague or Budapest. Everything depends on what one wants to do, and how.

After a hard day at the office, a little relaxation is very welcome. Restaurants offering various cuisine, charm, and quality abound. One can find many restaurants offering foreign cuisine, often run by expats. On the other hand, Polish traditional food is also delicious and tasting traditional Polish food, such as *bigos* and various types of *pierogi*, is a must. The number of pubs is growing rapidly, although they tend to be rather expensive. There are also many clubs with various types of music, so it is not difficult to find something for one's taste, especially in larger cities.

Cinemas have a good and up-to-date repertoire, and they are all non-smoking. Films are usually shown in their original version, with Polish subtitles. There are also many theatres worth visiting. The Teatr Wielki (Grand Theatre) in Warsaw has an impressive ballet and opera programme, and there are often very good concerts at the Warsaw Philharmonic, and, in the summer time, outdoors at the Chopin monument in the beautiful Royal Łazienki Park. Warsaw and Cracow are also famous for their art galleries, with frequently changing exhibitions ranging from the old masters to contemporary experimental artists.

However, despite very good macro-economic results and many advantages, Poland and its capital, Warsaw, face a number of problems. The number of underground parking lots, and the supply of financial, recreational, and exhibition centres are still insufficient. The road network is quite extensive, but the very few highways and the large amount of roads in need of major repairs slow down car travel considerably. Companies, both Polish and foreign alike, often complain of the ever-changing legal environment and less than clear executive provisions and administrative procedures. The European Union membership acquired in 2004 should assist substantially in dealing with the shortcomings mentioned, especially in the area of infrastructure and the legal environment.

Living in Poland presents its own difficulties, as in all different cultures. There are many contradictions in Polish society, but with persistence it is easy to be accepted and make many lasting friendships. Everything considered, Poland is a very nice place to live.

XI. TOURISM IN POLAND

- **Border requirements; EU and EEA citizens are required just to present a valid travel document or another document attesting to their identity and citizenship**
- **Residence permits are valid for five years with the possibility of extension for further five-year periods**
- **12 Polish sites on the UNESCO World Heritage List**
- **62 million foreign arrivals**
- **Total foreign currency receipts from tourists and same-day visitors of USD 5.8 billion**
- **Over 7 thousand tourist accommodation facilities offering 600,000 beds**

XIII. SOURCES OF BUSINESS INFORMATION IN POLAND

Considering information distribution methods and accessibility, one can basically group sources of business information into three categories:

- institutions,
- newspapers, magazines, and other printed publications,
- internet pages.

Usually an institutional source of information provides access to its information in many ways: direct consultation, publications, and information on its website.

For English speaking foreigners, accessing business and financial news in Poland is quite easy. Nowadays state and research institutions employ highly-qualified staff and finding somebody who speaks English there is not a problem. Whether this particular person will be an expert in the issues you would like to discuss is another matter.

English-language publications pertaining to the Polish economy cover the whole spectrum of information, from daily stock market news and reports, to the legal aspects of setting up a business in Poland, and market analysis. Finally, one can always order a specific report to be prepared in a language of choice from Poland's many consulting and corporate intelligence companies. Last but not least the easiest and cheapest way of accessing a wealth of information is surfing the web. There are many exclusively business and finance oriented websites and if one is patient enough one will find most of the information required right there.

Institutions

State and research institutions are among the most reliable sources of information. Appendix 18 provides a list of central institutions and ministries with contact information (including websites). Nearly all of them issue various publications (some in English) and maintain websites, usually with an English language version.

Of course, a foreigner's obvious first choice is his / her embassy in Poland, or a Polish embassy abroad. A list of embassies in Poland is contained in Appendix 30 and a list of the economic and commercial sections of Polish embassies and consulates abroad is presented in Appendix 31. Next, there are various bilateral chambers of commerce, some of which are listed in Appendix 29.

Obviously, which institution to contact depends on the nature of one's business in Poland, therefore it is not possible to indicate the single best contact that would suit everyone's needs. However, if one considers direct investment, PAIiIZ (the Polish Information and Foreign Investment Agency) is a prime choice. PAIiIZ produces a series of high quality English-language titles under different headings, covering areas ranging from the construction sector to banking, and offers a whole range of free of charge services to foreign investors. For more information on PAIiIZ see the Institutional Structure for Foreign Direct Investments in Chapter V. The Warsaw UNIDO Office, publisher of this guide, is also helpful.

For a company wanting to participate in the privatisation processes in Poland, the Ministry of the Treasury (described in Chapter IV) is the institution to turn to, while the Ministry of Economic Affairs deals with state economic policy, foreign trade regulations, investment incentives, state aid, etc., and will provide useful general and specific information. It is also worth to note that the Ministry of Finance supervises the customs system. Some information in English, regarding customs regulations one may find via their website (Customs Service). An outline of basic functions of some major government institutions is provided in Chapter I.

The Central Statistical Office (GUS) disseminates a wide range of detailed data covering all aspects of the economy. Some of it is readily available in English in their bilingual publications, such as the Statistical Bulletin, published monthly. Accessing the information is very simple. The best way is to visit the Inquiry Office, which has a small reading room and a very helpful staff, ready to help you find the required publications, or to assist you in searching their databanks. A fair range of information is also available through the website.

The National Bank of Poland (NBP) is an invaluable source of reliable information concerning the Polish financial system, system of payments, and, obviously, the banking sector. Up to date information includes the balance of payments, foreign reserves, and foreign debt, not to mention monetary policy and exchange rates.

The Office for Competition and Consumer Protection (UOKiK) protects freedom of competition and consumer interests. It counteracts monopolistic practices, controls mergers, and monitors public aid. The register of dangerous products can also be found on their website, as well as reports concerning the above mentioned activities. For more information on UOKIK please refer to Chapter X.

The Insurance and Pension Funds Supervisory Commission (KNUiFE) provides detailed information regarding the insurance sector and pension funds. This includes insurance agents, pension societies, individual pension accounts, employee pension plans, etc. Information on the Polish insurance sector is contained in Chapter II.

In the case of the tourism industry, the Institute of Tourism is highly recommended. It provides a lot of current information regarding the tourism sector in Poland free of charge, and in-depth analyses of particular aspects of the market are available through their publications. Moreover, it also offers consulting services, such as compiling specific reports upon request, at very reasonable prices.

Trade and co-operation offers are collected and distributed by, among other bodies, the Polish Chamber of Commerce, which also offers corporate due diligence services. This organisation produces regular bulletin-type publications on business trends and financial news in Poland.

The Polish Press Agency (PAP) offers an informative and comprehensive, if somewhat expensive, guide to Polish politics and business, as well as general issues. It provides Warsaw Stock Exchange and currency rate listings. The English is not free of lapses, although it serves its purpose.

International news agencies, like Reuters, Bloomberg, and the German Press Agency (dpa) are all accessible for in-depth daily and weekly financial news, although for the uninformed they pose the problem of little or no contextual analysis, and for the average news seeker they pose questions of price.

There are also many international organisations and institutions present in Poland, usually based in Warsaw, which are willing and able to provide various facts and figures. Some of them are listed in Appendix 20.

Finally, business reports from corporate intelligence companies are becoming increasingly popular in Poland. The companies undertaking to draw up such reports will take an in-depth look at a given company on your behalf and offer confidential, if often costly, advice on the company's financial credibility, in Polish or in a foreign language. For the potential business partner in search of company details, such information may prove to be well worth its price.

Newspapers, Magazines and Other Publications

English-language newsprint publications in Poland cover a broad selection of areas for the English-speaking foreigner, from the general interest weekly, *The Warsaw Voice*, the oldest and highest circulation newspaper, to the purely entertainment-based Warsaw Insider (*http://www.warsawinsider.pl*). The *Voice* also produces a *Business and Economy Yearbook*, which is available on request from the *Warsaw Voice* office.

The Warsaw Business Journal provides perhaps the most comprehensive coverage of financial and business news, although the *Voice* has decent weekly reports on the stock market and currency, and often in-depth studies of key markets and industries. The *Warsaw Business Journal* publishes its well-known *Book of Lists*, which is a useful database for companies. *Book of Lists* is also available on-line as a paid service. The *WBJ* web page, *http://www.wbj.pl*, contains some articles from the *Warsaw Insider*, as well as from *Poland A.M.*, a morning news digest published by the same house. There is also *Polen am Morgen*, a German version of *Poland A.M.*

The Warsaw Voice's internet site, *http://www.warsawvoice.pl* is well presented, easy to access, and offers comprehensive coverage of financial and business stories. Its weekly updates on the currency market, Warsaw Stock Exchange, and the odd feature or news article on sectors of industry in the news, are found on these pages, free of charge. There is also an extensive archive available, with a search option.

The Polish Market, a business focused monthly, presents a valuable compendium of data and information about the government's economic policy. It covers investment, commodity and service markets' issues, and provides information on leading Polish companies and high quality prize-winning products. It promotes various Polish regions, presenting their development strategies and investment offers. One may also notice alticles on Polish business leaders and the biggest Polish and foreign investors. Many interesting articles from current and past issues are available at their website *http://www.polishmarket.com.pl.* Accessing most of the materials requires a free registration.

Another major information supplier is BOSS Information and Publishing Agency, which has been on the market as an independent specialist information provider for the past twelve years. It offers analyses and reports on various aspects of the economy, as well as three publications. The latter include *Business News Poland* – an English language weekly offering in-depth business, economic, and legal information aimed at foreign investors. Regular features include sector analyses, statistics, forecasts, trends, commentaries, tax and legal regulations, company news, and business/economic news round-ups. Their website is available at *http://www.boss.com.pl.*

Several other sources of business and financial news are published outside Poland and can be found in Poland at any of the major hotels, English-language book shops, and, if one is lucky, at kiosks.

For the upper end of the business information market, one may look towards The Economist Intelligence Unit's *Quarterly Business Report on Poland*, updated monthly. Other sources include the reports of international organisations such as the IMF, World Bank, OECD, and the European Commission, which are usually published at least once a year and are available through their respective websites.

Internet

A real flurry of internet pages has appeared (and sometimes, vanished) in recent years on Polish business and finance, each new one stepping on the toes of the last, while offering something slightly different, in format as well as content. The following are outlines of the main sources of internet business and finance news. For those in search of current data and hard economic news, as well as commercial and business offers and practical guidance concerning legal, tax, or, for example, insurance matters, the internet is an ideal source of information, especially for the English-speaking persons, and persons not based in Poland, who don't have access to other sources.

From the point of view of reliability of information, and of its being up to date, it is certainly best to hear it 'straight from the horse's mouth'. Speaking in terms of the internet, this translates into seeking information on the pages of the information providers. Anyone seeking reliable business information on Poland is best advised to turn to the official pages of various Polish ministries and other government and quasi-government institutions. Most of their websites have an English language version covering if not all, then at least the major topics available on the Polish site. However, quite often the information in English is not quite up to date, so it is highly advisable to verify whether the information presented reflects the current state of affairs. Frequently this can be done by a simple phone call to the institution involved, or by checking the part of the website in Polish.

As far as business information is concerned, the sites especially recommended include the ones administered by the Ministry of Economic Affairs, the Ministry of the Treasury, the Ministry of Finance, PAIiIZ, and the Central Statistical Office. Furthermore, one may find specific business information on the pages of the Warsaw Stock Exchange, the National Bank of Poland, and other financial institutions. Please refer to Appendix 18 for the web pages of various state institutions.

Below, there is a short description of a few general sites on Poland and on doing business in Poland. However, please remember that the internet is a very dynamic medium and by the time this information reaches the reader, there may be many other, equally good, websites.

Poland Home Page

http://www.poland.pl

This page is the official web-site of Poland. It offers some general information on Poland, as well as the latest news. Moreover, it provides access to a wide range of information through redirecting to various specialised sites. The major topics include the economy, science and education, the natural environment, tourism and recreation, culture and art. The site provides access to business, financial and economic news, although not all the pages to which one is redirected have their English versions. It is highly recommended as a good starting point for anyone, who wants to learn about Poland, regardless whether from business, leisure, or any other point of view.

There is also *http://www.poland.gov.pl*, another high quality and easy to navigate official website of Poland, managed by the Ministry of Foreign Affairs. Its considerable advantage is that apart from Polish and English, it is also available in French, German, Russian and Spanish. The information is divided into three sections: for travellers, for businessmen, and for info-seekers. The content covers both current news, and general information concerning the economy, tourism, culture, and the history of Poland. It is particularly focused on tourism and culture and provides a lot of interesting material, such as information on the most famous Poles, Polish traditions and customs, interesting castles and landscapes, etc.

Polish Export Promotion Portal

http://www.polishproducts.gov.pl, *http://www.exporter.gov.pl*

This useful service is provided by the Ministry of Economic Affairs. It contains some general economic reports, as well as brief and up to date information on the Polish economy, including facts and figures pertaining to industry, agriculture, foreign trade, prices, salaries and wages, etc. Furthermore, the portal contains a database of Polish exporters, with an option to search for particular products, and an option to submit a query.

BMB Promotions

http://www.export-import.pl

This internet service is a window onto the world of Polish exports. The service enables users to access thousands of offers of Polish firms looking for export and import opportunities. It is available in seven language versions, including English, French, and German. The service is run by BMB Promotions, which also offers a printed version of the catalogue in several languages, as well as a CD-ROM version. Furthermore, BMB

Promotions has prepared a general access database containing information about the economic potential and investment environment of all local self-government units. It contains thousands of investment projects in Polish districts, towns, communes, etc. This service is available at *www.gminy.pl.* The site contains a very useful feature which ranks communes based on a selected set of criteria. This service is also available in several languages, in print, and on CD-ROM.

In addition, there are some very good pages created by the economic and commercial divisions of various Polish embassies and consulates. The ones well-worth visiting certainly include *www.handelsratpolen.at* (Austria), *www.poland-canada.org* (Canada), *www.wirtschaft-polen.de* (Germany), *www.polishemb-trade.co.uk* (United Kingdom), *www.brhusa.com* and *www.polandembassy.org* (both USA). Of course the others are also quite useful. For a complete list of the economic and commercial sections of Polish embassies and consulates please refer to Appendix 31. An updated list is also available at the Polish Export Promotion Portal, *www.exporter.gov.pl.*

Finally, anyone interested in commercial relations will be glad to take a look at *Targi i Wystawy w Polsce* (*www.targi.com*) which lists all the major trade fairs in Poland. This site is simple to navigate, is updated on a regular basis, and provides information on some 400 trade fairs organised in Poland each year. There are also information and/or links to some 100 fair organisers. The information is available in Polish and in English. Alternatively, one can use the Polish Trade Fair Corporation (*www.polfair.com.pl*), which offers a similar service, available in the same languages. It also offers some basic statistics on trade fairs in Poland, albeit only in Polish.

APPENDIX 1

MAIN ECONOMIC INDICATORS IN 2004

Gross Domestic Product growth	5.4 %
Gross fixed capital formation	5.3 %
Industrial output growth	11.6 %
Productivity growth	13 %
Construction growth	-1 %
Unemployment rate	19.1 %
Inflation rate	3.5 %
Rediscount rate (December)	7.00 %
Budget deficit	4.7 % of GDP
Foreign debt	52.3 % of GDP
Public debt	48.8 % of GDP
Foreign trade, SAD and INTRASTAT statistics: Export revenue Import expenditures Trade deficit	 USD 73.8 bn USD 88.2 bn USD 14.4 bn
Liquidity – import coverage	5 months
Foreign debt/export ratio	1.7
Foreign reserves (December)	USD 36.8 bn
Foreign direct investments	USD 7.86 bn
Cumulative foreign direct investments	USD 84.5 bn
Average exchange rate	3.6540 PLN/USD 4.5340 PLN/EUR
Wages (average gross monthly)	PLN 2,289.57
Minimum gross salary (as of 1 Jan. 2005)	PLN 849

SELECTED ECONOMIC INDICATORS IN 2005 AVAILABLE AT THE TIME OF PRINT

Gross Domestic Product growth (second quarter)	2.8 %
Industrial output growth (January-September)	2.5 %
Unemployment rate (end of September)	17.6 %
Inflation rate (January-September)	2.5 %
Rediscount rate (October)	4.75 %
Foreign trade, SAD and INTRASTAT statistics (January-August): Export revenue Import expenditures Trade deficit	 USD 57.15 bn USD 64.71 bn USD 7.56 bn
Foreign reserves (October)	USD 41.7 bn
Average exchange rate (October)	3.2600 PLN/USD 3.9261 PLN/EUR

APPENDIX 2

ESTABLISHMENT OF A LIMITED LIABILITY COMPANY - CONSECUTIVE STEPS

Stage of Company Formation	Institution	Comments	Cost
1. Signing of Articles of Association / Deed of Formation	Notarial Office	According to the provisions of the Code of Commercial Companies, Articles of Association or Deed of Formation of a limited liability company must be executed as a notarial deed.	1. Notarial fee. 2. Tax on civil and legal proceedings. The amount of both charges depends on the amount of the company's initial capital.
2. Company registration	National Court Register	The registration takes place at the Economic Court having jurisdiction in the principal place of business of the company being formed. Upon being entered into the register the company acquires a legal personality.	Fixed charge of PLN 1,000.
3. Announcement of the company's registration in "Monitor Sądowy i Gospodarczy"	Office for the publishing of "Monitor Sądowy i Gospodarczy", Ministry of Justice - through the secretariat of the competent economic court		The charge is paid in advance to the Office account in an amount not lower than PLN 500.
4. Assigning the company's statistical number	Provincial Statistical Office (Wojewódzki Urząd Statystyczny)	Applications for the company's registration in the REGON system are to be submitted at the Provincial Statistical Office that has jurisdiction in the company's principal place of business.	No charge.
5. Company's registration with the Social Security Institution (ZUS)	Social Security Institution (Zakład Ubezpieczeń Społecznych)	Within seven days of employing the first employee the company should register in the district office of the Social Security Institution (ZUS).	No charge.
6. Obtaining a licence or permit, if required	Competent licensing body	A list of business activities requiring licences or permits is available at PAIiIZ.	Stamp duty in an amount depending on the type of licence or permit.
7. Opening the company's bank account	Bank	A company is obliged to open a bank account in Polish złotys and may also hold foreign currency accounts with a bank authorised to deal in foreign currency.	According to the bank's regulations.

Stage of Company Formation	Institution	Comments	Cost
8. Registration of the company with the Tax Office in respect of income tax and VAT	Local Tax Office	Upon commencing business activity, that is issuing the first invoice, the company is obliged to register with the competent tax office.	Tax Identification Number (NIP) - no charge. VAT registration - stamp duty - PLN 152.

Source: Various acts

Notarial Fees – maximum rates determined by the Minister of Justice

Company's Initial Capital	Fees
To PLN 3,000	PLN 100
Over PLN 3,000 to PLN 10,000	PLN 100 + 3 % of an amount in excess of PLN 3,000
Over PLN 10,000 to PLN 30,000	PLN 310 + 2 % of an amount in excess of PLN 10,000
Over PLN 30,000 to PLN 60,000	PLN 710 + 1 % of an amount in excess of PLN 30,000
Over PLN 60,000 to PLN 1,000,000	PLN 1,010 + 0.5 % of an amount in excess of PLN 60,000
Over PLN 1,000,000	PLN 5,710 + 0.25 % of an amount in excess of PLN 1,000,000

Please note:

- the maximum notarial fee for an individual service is PLN 13,200.
- the above fees are subject to 22 % VAT.

Tax on Civil and Legal Proceedings – the Company's Deed of Formation

Tax on civil and legal proceedings with respect to a company's deed of formation amounts to 0.5 % of the company's initial capital.

APPENDIX 3

ESTABLISHMENT OF A JOINT-STOCK COMPANY - CONSECUTIVE STEPS

Stage of Company Formation	Institution	Comments	Cost
1. Signing the Deed of Formation and Charter	Notarial Office	According to the provisions of the Code of Commercial Companies, the Deed of Formation and Charter of a joint-stock company must be executed as a notarial deed.	1. Notarial fee. 2. Tax on civil and legal proceedings. The amount of both charges depends on the amount of the company's share capital.
2. Accumulation of the company's share capital	The Securities Commission (in certain cases)	- Immediate formation (through subscription for shares by the founders and third parties). - Consecutive formation (through public subscription of shares; in which case a permit from the Securities Commission is required).	
3. Company registration	National Court Register	The registration takes place at the Economic Court having jurisdiction in the principal place of business of the company being formed. Upon being entered into the register the company acquires legal personality.	Fixed charge of PLN 1,000.
4. Announcement of the company's registration in "Monitor Sądowy i Gospodarczy"	Office for the publishing of "Monitor Sądowy i Gospodarczy", Ministry of Justice - through the Secretariat of the competent economic court		The charge is paid in advance to the Office account in an amount not lower than PLN 500.
5. Assigning the company's statistical number	Provincial Statistical Office (Wojewódzki Urząd Statystyczny)	Applications for the company's registration in the REGON system are to be submitted at the Provincial Statistical Office that has jurisdiction in the company's principal place of business.	No charge.
6. Company's registration with Social Security Institution (ZUS)	Social Security Institution (Zakład Ubezpieczeń Społecznych)	Within seven days of employing the first employee the company should register with the district office of the Social Security Institution (ZUS).	No charge.
7. Obtaining a licence or permit, if required	Competent licensing body	A list of business activities requiring licences or permits is available at PAIiIZ.	Stamp duty in an amount depending on the type of licence or permit.

Stage of Company Formation	Institution	Comments	Cost
8. Opening the company's bank account	Bank	A company is obliged to open a bank account in Polish złotys and may also hold foreign currency accounts with a bank authorised to deal in foreign currency.	According to the bank's regulations.
9. Registration of the company with the Tax Office in respect of income tax and VAT	Local Tax Office	Upon commencing business activity, that is issuing the first invoice, the company is obliged to register with the competent tax office.	Tax Identification Number (NIP) - no charge. VAT registration - stamp duty - PLN 152.

Source: Various acts

For notarial fees and taxes on civil and legal proceedings please refer to Appendix 2.

APPENDIX 4

FUNDAMENTAL BUSINESS REGULATIONS

REGULATION	Published in Journal of Laws (Dz. U.)
Accounting Law of 29 September 1994	Dz. U. No. 76, item 694 of 2002 – uniform text
Acquisition of Real Estate by Foreigners Law of 24 March 1920	Dz. U. No. 167, item 1758 of 2004 – uniform text
Administration of Foreign Trade in Goods Law of 16 April 2004	Dz. U. No. 97, item 963 of 2004
Banking Law of 29 August 1997	Dz. U. No. 72, item 665 of 2002 – uniform text
Civil Code of 23 April 1964	Dz. U. No. 16, item 93 of 1964
Code of Commercial Companies of 15 September 2000	Dz. U. No. 94, item 1037 of 2000
Commercialisation and Privatisation of State Enterprises Law of 30 August 1996	Dz. U. No. 171, item 1397 of 2002 – uniform text
Competition and Consumer Protection Law of 15 December 2000	Dz. U. No. 122, item 1319 of 2000
Construction Law of 7 July 1994	Dz. U. No. 89, item 414 of 1994
Copyright and Related Rights Law of 4 February 1994	Dz. U. No. 24, item 83 of 1994
Corporate Insolvency and Recovery Law of 28 February 2003	Dz. U. No. 60, item 535 of 2003
Customs Law of 19 March 2004	Dz. U. No. 68, item 622 of 2004
Economic Freedom Law of 2 July 2004	Dz. U. No. 173, item 1807 of 2004
Financial Assistance for Investments Law of 20 March 2002	Dz. U. No. 41, item 363 of 2002
Financial Restructuring of Banks and Enterprises Law of 3 February 1993	Dz. U. No. 18, item 82 of 1993
Foreign Exchange Law of 27 July 2002	Dz. U. No. 141, item 1178 of 2002
Formation of the Agricultural System Law of 11 April 2003	Dz. U. No. 64, item 592 of 2003
Industrial Property Law of 30 June 2000	Dz. U. No. 49, item 508 of 2001

REGULATION	Published in Journal of Laws (Dz. U.)
Insurance Law of 22 May 2003	Dz. U. No. 124, item 1151 of 2003
Labour Code of 26 June 1974	Dz. U. No. 21, item 94 of 1998 – uniform text
National Investment Funds and their Privatisation Law of 30 April 1993	Dz. U. No. 44, item 202 of 1993
Promotion of Employment and Labour Market Institutions Law of 20 April 2004	Dz. U. No. 99, item 1001 of 2004
Public Aid Procedure Law of 30 April 2004	Dz. U. No. 123, item 1291 of 2004
Public Procurement Law of 29 January 2004	Dz. U. No. 19, item 177 of 2004
Refinancing the Interest on Fixed Interest Rate Export Credits Law of 8 June 2001	Dz. U. No. 73, item 762 of 2001
Spatial Zoning Law of 27 March 2003	Dz. U. No. 80, item 717 of 2003
Special Economic Zones Law of 20 October 1994	Dz. U. No. 123, item 600 of 1994
State Enterprises Law of 25 September 1981	Dz. U. No. 112, item 981 of 2002 – uniform text
Suppressing Unfair Competition Law of 16 April 1993	Dz. U. No. 47, item 211 of 1993
Tax Laws	See Appendix 5

APPENDIX 5

BASIC TAX LIABILITIES

Tax	Rate	Remitters	Notes	Legal Base
Corporate income tax	19 %	Legal persons	Revenue earned abroad is also subject to this tax	Act on Income Tax on Legal Persons (Dz.U. of 2000 No. 54, item 654, as amended)
VAT	22 % 7 % 3 % 0 %	Legal and natural persons	Indirect tax 22 % - basic rate 7 % - preferential rate 3 % - unprocessed products 0 % - export rate some goods & services are exempted	Act on Value Added Tax (Dz.U. of 2004 No. 54 item 535)
Excise duty	Various	Legal and natural persons	Indirect tax limited to some 60 commodity groups	Act on Excise Duty (Dz.U. of 2004 No. 29 item 257, as amended)
Tax on dividends	19 %	Shareholders in companies, legal and natural persons	Holdings are effectively exempted. Rate may be reduced by Agreements on Avoiding Double Taxation. Tax residence certificate for shareholder required if lower rate to be applied	Act on Income Tax on Legal Persons (Dz.U. of 2000 No. 54, item 654, as amended)
Personal income tax	19 % 30 % 40 %	Natural persons	Foreigners staying temporarily in Poland pay tax only on the income earned in Poland and from work carried out in Poland (limited tax liability)	Act on Income Tax on Natural Persons (Dz.U. of 2000 No. 14 item 176, as amended) Act on Lump-sum Income Tax on Some Income Derived by Natural Persons (Dz.U. of 1998 No. 144 item 930, as amended)
Agricultural tax		Legal and natural persons	Calculated on the area of land on which agricultural activity is carried out. The rates vary according to the category of land.	Act on Agricultural Tax (Dz.U. of 1993 No. 94 item 431, as amended)
			LOCAL TAXES	
Real estate tax	Various	Real estate owners, legal and natural persons	Rates determined by local authorities, per m^2	Act on Local Taxes and Charges (Dz.U. of 1991 No. 9 item 31, as amended)

Source: Various acts

APPENDIX 6

AGREEMENTS ON AVOIDING DOUBLE TAXATION

No.	Country	Agreement			
		Signed on	Entry into Force	Applied from	Published in *Dziennik Ustaw*
1.	Albania	05.03.1993	27.06.1994	01.01.1995	1994/No 101, item 492
2.	Algeria	31.01.2000			
3.	Armenia	14.07.1999	27.02.2005	01.01.2006	2005/No 66, item 576
4.	Australia	07.05.1991	04.03.1992	01.01.1993	1992/No 41, item 177
5.	Austria*	02.10.1974 13.01.2004	21.09.1975	01.01.1974	1975/No 24, item 129
6.	Azerbaijan	26.08.1997			
7.	Bangladesh	08.07.1997	28.01.1999	01.01.2000	2000/No 106, item 1121
8.	Belgium	14.09.1976 20.08.2001	21.09.1978 29.04.2004	01.01.1979 01.01.2005	1978/No 24, item 109 2004/No 211, item 2139
9.	Belarus	18.11.1992	30.07.1993	01.01.1994	1993/No 120,item 534
10.	Bulgaria	11.04.1994	10.05.1995	01.01.1996	1995/No 137, item 679
11.	Canada	04.05.1987	30.11.1989	01.01.1989	1990/No 38, item 216
12.	Chile	10.03.2000	30.12.2003	01.01.2004	2004/No 193, item 1976
13.	China	07.06.1988	07.01.1989	01.01.1990	1989/No 13, item 65
14.	Croatia	19.10.1994	11.02.1996	01.01.1997	1996/No 78, item 370
15.	Cyprus	04.06.1992	07.07.1993	01.01.1994	1993/No 117, item 523
16.	Czech Republic	24.06.1993	20.12.1993	01.01.1994	1994/No 47, item 189
17.	Denmark	06.12.2001	13.12.2002	01.01.2003	2003/No 43, item 368
18.	Egypt	24.06.1996	16.07.2001	01.01.2002	2003/No 78, item 690
19.	Estonia	09.05.1994	09.12.1994	01.01.1995	1995/No 77, item 388
20.	Finland Protocol	26.10.1977 28.04.1994	30.03.1979 25.01.1995	01.01.1980 01.01.1996	1979/No 12, item 84 1995/No 106, item 517
21.	France	20.06.1975	12.09.1976	01.01.1974	1977/No 1, item 5
22.	Georgia	05.11.1999			
23.	Germany Protocol	18.12.1972 24.10.1979 14.05.2003	14.09.1975 19.12.2004	01.01.1972 01.01.2005	1975/No 31, item 163 1982/No 1, item 1 2005/No 12, item 90
24.	Greece	20.11.1987	28.09.1991	01.01.1992	1991/No 120, item 524
25.	Hungary Protocol	23.09.1992 27.06.2000	10.09.1995 01.05.2002	01.01.1996 01.08.2002	1995/No 125, item 602 2002/No 108, item 946
26.	Iceland	19.06.1998	20.06.1999	01.01.2000	1999/No 79, item 890
27.	India	21.06.1989	26.10.1989	01.01.1990	1990/ No 8, item 46
28.	Indonesia	06.10.1992	25.08.1993	01.01.1994	1994/No 46, item 187
29.	Iran	02.10 1998			
30.	Ireland	13.11.1995	22.12.1995	01.01.1996	1996/No 29, item 129
31.	Israel	22.05.1991	30.12.1991	01.01.1992	1992/No 28, item 124
32.	Italy	21.06.1985	26.09.1989	01.01.1984	1989/No 62, item 374
33.	Japan	20.02.1980	23.12.1982	01.01.1983	1983/No 12, item 60
34.	Jordan	04.10.1997	22.04.1999	01.01.2000	1999/No 61, item 654
35.	Kazakhstan	21.09.1994	13.05.1995	01.01.1996	1995/No 121, item 586
36.	Kyrgyzstan	19.11.1998	22.06.2004	01.09.2004** 01.01.2005***	2004/No 228, item 2304
37.	Kuwait	16.11.1996	25.04.2000	01.01.1996	2000/No 69, item 811

* Agreement re-negotiated (signed)

** Income tax collected at source

*** Other taxes

No.	Country	Agreement			
		Signed on	Entry into Force	Applied from	Published in *Dziennik Ustaw*
38.	Latvia	17.11.1993	30.11.1994	01.01.1995	1995/No 53, item 285
39.	Lebanon	26.07.1999	07.11.2003	01.01.2004	2004/No 244, item 2445
40.	Lithuania	20.01.1994	19.07.1994	01.01.1995	1995/No 51, item 277
41.	Luxembourg	14.06.1995	11.07.1996	01.01.1997	1996/No 110, item 527
42.	Macedonia FYR	28.11.1996	17.12.1999	01.01.2000	2002/No 206, item 1744
43.	Malaysia	16.09.1977	05.12.1978	01.01.1977	1979/No 10, item 62
44.	Malta	07.01.1994	24.11.1994	01.01.1995	1995/No 49, item 256
45.	Mexico	30.11.1998	06.09.2002	01.01.2003	2003/No 13, item 131
46.	Moldova	16.11.1994	27.10.1995	01.01.1996	1996/No 38, item 166
47.	Mongolia	18.04.1997	21.07.2001	01.01.2002	2002/No 206, item 1746
48.	Morocco	24.10.1994	29.03.1995	01.01.1996	1996/No 110, item 529
49.	Netherlands	13.02.2002	18.03.2003	01.01.2004	2003/No 216, item 2120
50.	Nigeria	12.02.1999			
51.	Norway	24.05.1977	30.10.1979	01.01.1976	1979/No 27, item 157
52.	Pakistan	25.10.1974	24.11.1975	01.01.1973	1976/No 9, item 47
53.	Philippines	09.09.1992	07.04.1997	01.01.1998	1997/No 127, item 817
54.	Portugal	09.05.1995	04.02.1998	01.01.1999	1998/No 48, item 304
55.	Romania	23.06.1994	15.09.1995	01.01.1996	1995/No 109, item 530
56.	Russia	22.05.1992	22.02.1993	01.01.1994	1993/No 125, item 569
57.	Singapore	23.04.1993	25.12.1993	01.01.1994	1994/No 38, item 139
58.	Slovakia	18.08.1994	21.12.1995	01.01.1996	1996/No 30, item 131
59.	Slovenia	28.06.1996	10.03.1998	01.01.1999	1998/No 35, item 198
60.	South Africa	10.11.1993	05.12.1995	01.01.1996	1996/No 28, item 124
61.	South Korea	21.06.1991	21.02.1992	01.01.1991	1992/No 28, item 126
62.	Spain	15.11.1979	06.05.1982	01.01.1983	1982/No 17, item 127
63.	Sri Lanka	25.04.1980	21.10.1983	01.01.1983	1988/No 5, item 38
64.	Sweden*	05.06.1975 19.11.2004	18.02.1977	01.01.1978	1977/No 13, item 51
65.	Switzerland	02.09.1991	25.09.1992	01.01.1992	1993/No 22, item 92
66.	Syria	15.08.2001	23.12.2003	01.01.2004	2004/No 193, item 1972
67.	Tajikistan	27.05.2003	24.06.2004	01.09.2004 01.01.2005	2005/No 12, item 92
68.	Thailand	08.12.1978	13.05.1983	01.01.1983	1983/No 37, item 170
69.	Tunisia	29.03.1993	15.11.1993	01.01.1994	1994/No 78, item 357
70.	Turkey	03.11.1993	01.10.1996	01.01.1998	1997/No 11, item 58
71.	Ukraine	12.01.1993	11.03.1994	01.01.1995	1994/No 63, item 269
72.	United Arab Emirates	31.01.1993	21.04.1994	01.01.1995	1994/No 81, item 373
73.	United Kingdom	16.12.1976	25.02.1978	01.04.1975	1978/No 7, item 20
74.	Uruguay	02.08.1991			
75.	USA	08.10.1974	23.07.1976	01.01.1974	1976/No 31, item 178
76.	Uzbekistan	11.01.1995	29.04.1995	01.01.1996	1995/No 116, item 560
77.	Vietnam	31.08.1994	20.01.1995	01.01.1996	1995/No 49, item 258
78.	Yugoslavia	12.06.1997	17.06.1998	01.01.1999	2001/No 101, item 1137
79.	Zambia	19.05.1995			
80.	Zimbabwe	09.07.1993	28.11.1994	01.01.1995	1995/No 62, item 318

Source: Ministry of Finance, 2005

* Agreement re-negotiated (signed)

APPENDIX 7

AGREEMENTS ON THE RECIPROCAL PROMOTION AND PROTECTION OF INVESTMENTS

No.	Country	Signed on	Entry into Force	Published in *Dziennik Ustaw*
1.	Albania	05.03.1993	09.08.1993	1993/No 122, item 547
2.	Argentina	31.07.1991	01.09.1992	1993/No 124, item 567
3.	Australia	07.05.1991	27.03.1992	1992/No 39, item 166
4.	Austria	24.11.1988	01.11.1989	1989/No 54, item 321
5.	Azerbaijan	26.08.1997	10.02.1999	1999/No 61, item 656
6.	Bangladesh	08.07.1997	19.11.1999	2000/No 43, item 492
7.	Belarus	24.04.1992	18.01.1993	1993/No 122, item 545
8.	Belgium-Luxembourg	19.05.1987	02.08.1991	2001/No 15, item 153
9.	Bulgaria	11.04.1994	09.03.1995	1995/No 62, item 322
10.	Canada	06.04.1990	22.11.1990	1991/No 27, item 114
11.	Chile	05.07.1995	17.01.2000	2000/No 21, item 266
12.	China	07.06.1988	07.01.1989	1989/No 13, item 67
13.	Croatia	21.02.1995	04.10.1995	1995/No 26, item 126
14.	Cyprus	04.06.1992	06.07.1993	1993/No 117, item 521
15.	Czech Republic	16.07.1993	29.06.1994	1994/No 97, item 469
16.	Denmark	01.05.1990	13.10.1990	1992/No 28, item 122
17.	Egypt	01.07.1995	17.01.1998	1998/No 48, item 302
18.	Estonia	06.05.1993	06.08.1993	1995/No 39, item 196
19.	Finland	25.11.1996	13.03.1998	1998/No 54, item 342
20.	France	14.02.1989	10.02.1990	1990/No 38, item 220
21.	Germany	10.11.1989	17.04.1990	1991/No 27, item 116
22.	Greece	14.10.1992	20.02.1995	1995/No 51, item 275
23.	Hungary	23.09.1992	16.06.1995	1995/No 113, item 512
24.	India	07.10.1996	31.12.1997	1998/No 34, item 186
25.	Indonesia	06.10.1992	01.07.1993	1994/No 46, item 185
26.	Iran	17.04 1997	30.10.2001	2002/No 22, item 217
27.	Israel	22.05.1991	06.05.1992	1993/No 124, item 562
28.	Italy	10.05.1989	09.01.1993	1994/No 42, item 157
29.	Jordan	04.11.1997	14.08.1999	2001/No 143, item 1603
30.	Kazakhstan	21.09.1994	25.05.1995	1995/No 121, item 584
31.	Kuwait	05.03.1990	18.12.1993	1994/No 50, item 199
32.	Latvia	26.04.1993	19.07.1993	1993/No 122, item 549
33.	Lithuania	28.09.1992	06.08.1993	1993/No 122, item 543
34.	Macedonia	28.11.1996	22.04.1997	1997/Nr 63, item 393
35.	Malaysia	21.04.1993	23.03.1994	1994/No 78, item 359
36.	Moldova	16.11.1994	27.07.1995	1995/No 118, item 568
37.	Mongolia	08.11.1995		
38.	Morocco	24.10.1994	29.05.1995	1999/No 76, item 858
39.	Netherlands	07.09.1992	01.02.1994	1994/No 57, item 235
40.	Norway	06.05.1990	24.10.1990	1990/No 84, item 488
41.	Portugal	11.03.1993	09.10.1993	1995/No 19, item 90
42.	Romania	23.06.1994	30.12.1995	1995/No 77, item 386

No.	Country	Signed on	Entry into Force	Published in *Dziennik Ustaw*
43.	Russia	02.10.1992		
44.	Singapore	03.06.1993	29.12.1993	1994/No 57, item 237
45.	Slovakia	18.08.1996	14.03.1996	1996/No 55, item 246
46.	Slovenia	28.06.1996	31.03.2001	2001/No 106, item 1119
47.	South Korea	01.11.1989	02.02.1990	1990/No 8, item 48
48.	Spain	30.07.1992	01.05.1993	1993/No 124, item 563
49.	Sweden	13.10.1989	04.01.1990	1990/No 38, item 218
50.	Switzerland	08.11.1989	18.04.1990	1990/No 63, item 366
51.	Thailand	18.12.1992	10.08.1983	1994/No 8, item 26
52.	Tunisia	29.03.1993	22.09.1993	1994/No 8, item 28
53.	Turkey	11.08.1991	19.08.1994	1994/No 112, item 539
54.	Ukraine	12.01.1993	14.09.1993	1993/No 125, item 575
55.	United Arab Emirates	31.01.1993	09.04.1994	1994/No 81, item 371
56.	United Kingdom	08.12.1987	14.04.1988	1988/No 12, item 93
57.	Uruguay	02.08.1991	21.10.1994	1995/No 55, item 291
58.	USA	21.03.1990	06.08.1994	1994/No 97, item 366
59.	Uzbekistan	01.11.1995	29.04.1995	1995/No 116, item 561
60.	Vietnam	31.08.1994	24.11.1994	1995/No 41, item 209
61.	Yugoslavia	03.09.1996	23.01.1997	1997/No 39, item 236

Source: Ministry of Economic Affairs and Labour, 2005

APPENDIX 8

LIST OF COUNTRIES WHOSE CITIZENS DO NOT REQUIRE A POLISH VISA WHEN ENTERING POLAND FOR LESS THAN 90 DAYS

Countries A - F	Countries G - M	Countries N - Z
Andorra	Guatemala	Norway
Argentina	Honduras	Panama
Australia	Hong Kong	Paraguay
Austria	Hungary	Portugal
Belgium	Iceland	Romania
Bolivia	Ireland	Salvador
Brazil	Israel	San Marino
Brunei	Italy	Singapore
Bulgaria	Japan	Slovakia
Canada	Latvia	Slovenia
Chile	Liechtenstein	South Korea
Costa Rica	Lithuania	Spain
Croatia	Luxembourg	Sweden
Cyprus	Macao	Switzerland
Czech Republic	Malaysia	United Kingdom
Denmark	Malta	United States of America
Estonia	Mexico	Uruguay
Finland	Monaco	Vatican
France	Netherlands	Venezuela
Germany	Nicaragua	
Greece	New Zealand	

Source: Ministry of Foreign Affairs, 2005

Citizens from other countries, not listed above, need to have a Polish visa when visiting Poland. For further information, also concerning studies, work and stay of over 3 months, please contact your nearest Embassy or Consulate of Poland.

APPENDIX 9

TOP 50 COMPANIES BY SALES REVENUE IN 2004 (in thousand PLN)

	Name of Company	Net Sales Revenue	Total Revenue	Pre-tax Profit	Net Profit
1.	Polski Koncern Naftowy ORLEN SA, Płock	40 810 810	41 137 175	3 114 903	2 569 712
2.	Telekomunikacja Polska SA GK, Warszawa	18 563 556	19 270 772	3 204 805	2 324 455
3.	PZU SA GK, Warszawa	16 016 080	n.a.	2 705 742	2 188 099
4.	Polskie Sieci Elektroenergetyczne SA, Warszawa	15 784 171	16 050 883	736 505	482 718
5.	Metro AG Polska, Warszawa	12 400 000	n.a.	n.a.	n.a.
6.	Grupa Lotos S.A., Gdańsk	10 333 161	10 357 119	673 927	538 153
7.	Fiat Auto Poland S.A., Bielsko-Biała	10 077 251	n.a.	n.a.	104 563
8.	Mittal Steel Poland S.A. GK, Katowice	9 650 000	n.a.	n.a.	n.a.
9.	Kompania Węglowa, Katowice	9 111 421	10 296 949	499 613	429 947
10.	PGNiG SA, Warszawa	8 502 510	9 817 395	1 252 003	861 866
11.	PKO BP S.A. GK, Warszawa	7 565 259	7 880 774	1 872 007	1 514 381
12.	Volkswagen Poznań Sp. z o.o., Poznań	7 557 345	n.a.	320 156	244 958
13.	PZU Życie S.A., Warszawa	7 313 927	n.a.	934 169	759 500
14.	KGHM Polska Miedź S.A. GK, Lubin	7 149 416	7 247 393	1 516 566	1 392 864
15.	BOT Górnictwo i Energetyka S.A. GK Łódź	6 818 328	n.a.	n.a.	n.a.
16.	Polska Telefonia Cyfrowa Sp. z o.o. GK, Warszawa	6 419 571	6 500 364	1 198 047	937 902
17.	Poczta Polska PPUP, Warszawa	6 408 730	6 443 580	170 403	101 448
18.	PKP Cargo S.A., Warszawa	5 975 207	6 031 384	243 787	212 379
19.	Bank Pekao SA,GK Warszawa	5 782 247	5 945 342	1 512 431	1 343 001
20.	Polkomtel S.A. Warszawa	5 743 871	n.a.	1 186 300	923 603
21.	PTK Centertel Sp. z o.o. Warszawa	5 635 498	5 869 701	820 871	652 857
22.	Polski Koks S.A. Katowice	5 627 603	5 628 924	-6 887	- 6 907
23.	Węglokoks S.A., Katowice	4 993 217	5 104 937	52 706	25 435
24.	Energia Koncern Energetyczny S.A., Gdańsk	4 934 436	5 007 719	148 578	104 335
25.	Jastrzębska Spółka Węglowa S.A. Jastrzębie Zdrój	4 823 073	5 051 190	2 153 276	1 547 569

	Name of Company	Net Sales Revenue	Total Revenue	Pre-tax Profit	Net Profit
26.	Jeronimo Martins Dystrybucja Sp. z o.o., Poznań	4 730 000	4 760 000	n.a.	n.a.
27.	Lasy Państwowe PP, Warszawa	4 666 638	4 758 355	74 177	73474
28.	BP Polska Sp. z o.o. Kraków	4 620 000	n.a.	180 000	5 000
29.	Tesco GK, Kraków	4 616 000	n.a.	n.a.	n.a.
30.	Bank BPH S.A. GK, Kraków	4 375 748	4 536 450	1 020 857	788 301
31.	Volkswagen Motor Polska sp. z o.o., Polkowice	4 367 939	4 378 397	195 274	194 588
32.	Grupa Energetyczna Enea S.A., Poznań	4 265 556	4 312 426	70 679	36 608
33.	Isuzu Motors Polska Sp. z o.o. Tychy	3 855 678	n.a.	n.a.	n.a.
34.	Ruch SA, Warszawa	3 850 515	3 871 018	39 858	24 796
35.	Grupa Shell Polska, Warszawa	3 824 621	n.a.	n.a.	n.a.
36.	Carrefour Polska, Warszawa	3 800 000	n.a.	n.a.	n.a.
37.	Auchan Polska, Warszawa	3 680 000	n.a.	n.a.	n.a.
38.	Geant Polska Sp. z o.o., Warszawa	3 678 469	n.a.	n.a.	n.a.
39.	Grupa Vattenfall Poland, Warszawa	3 678 120	n.a.	408 737	322 437
40.	Polska Grupa Farmaceutyczna S.A. GK, Łódź	3 655 320	3 680 089	57 845	41 362
41.	Grupa Żywiec SA GK, Żywiec	3 629 089	3 698 556	329 373	276 854
42.	Południowy Koncern Energetyczny SA, Katowice	3 552 678	3 593 152	357 784	294 821
43.	Imperial Tobacco Polska S.A., Tarnowo Podgórne	3 456 616	3 532 983	162 563	128 516
44.	J&S Energy S.A. Warszawa	3 411 326	3 412 798	42 976	34 014
45.	Fiat-GM Powertrain Polska Sp. z o.o. Bielsko-Biała	3 359 463	3 369 182	154 484	154 484
46.	Thomson Multimedia Polska Sp. z o.o., Piaseczno	3 309 717	3 344 462	9 640	-55 584
47.	Ahold Polska sp. z o.o. Kraków	3 120 000	n.a.	n.a.	n.a.
48.	EnergiaPro Koncern Energetyczny S.A., Wrocław	3 119 298	n.a.	n.a.	n.a.
49.	Katowicki Holding Węglowy SA, Katowice	3 105 864	3 210 380	207 131	138 727
50.	PKP Polskie Linie Kolejowe SA, Warszawa	2 993 902	3 495 441	- 167 754	-167 754

Source: Rzeczpospolita, 20 April 2005

APPENDIX 10

OUTPUT OF MAJOR GOODS AND RAW MATERIALS IN 2004*

Product	Units	Output
Hard coal	million tons	101.0
Brown coal	million tons	61.1
Coke	million tons	10.2
Fuel oils	million tons	4.6
Petrol (incl. aviation)	million tons	4.6
Diesel oil	million tons	5.3
Cement	million tons	12.3
Crude steel	million tons	10.6
Copper ore	million tons	31.9
Pure sulphur	th. tons	953
Sugar	th. tons	1,974
Paper and cardboard	th. tons	2,533
Passenger cars	ths.	522
Farm tractors	ths.	8.0
TV sets (incl. monitors other than for computers)	ths.	6,997
Sea-going vessels	th. DWT	582
Sawn timber	cubic decametres	2,111
Natural gas	cubic hectometres	5,608
Electricity	TWh	150.8

* *Data for companies employing over 49 persons*

Source: Central Statistical Office, 2005

APPENDIX 11

AVERAGE RETAIL PRICES OF SELECTED FOOD PRODUCTS AND OTHER ARTICLES (as of April 2005)

Product	Quantity	Price (PLN)
Milk, fat content 2 - 2.5%	1 litre	1.45
Wheat-rye bread	0.5 kg	1.35
Wheat flour	1 kg	1.57
Fresh butter, fat content 82.5%	0.2 kg	3.16
Beef, boneless (gammon)	1 kg	20.79
Pork ham, boiled	1 kg	20.00
White sugar, crystallised, in sacks	1 kg	3.14
Men's suit, polyester staple fibres and wool	set	448.23
Men's shirt, long-sleeve, polyester staple fibres and cotton	piece	79.07
Women's suits, wool	set	358.99
Fridge-freezer 320 l	unit	1479
Washer-dryer machine	unit	2020
TV-set, 21 inch	unit	821.17
Washing powder for washing machines	0.6 kg	4.50
Toilet soap 100 g.	one	1.95
Shampoo 200 ml.	one	5.41
Toothpaste 125 ml	one	8.27
Electricity, for households	kWh	0.42
Natural gas for households	1 m^3	1.44
Hot water supply	1 m^3	13.87
Central heating, for dwellings	1 m^2 of usable floor area	3.09
Petrol, Euro-Super	1 litre	3.96
Regular fast train ticket, 2nd class, 181-200 km	one	34.03
Regular long-distance bus ticket, 41-50 km	one	8.12
Taxi, daily fare, 5km	trip	12.85
Regular ticket, urban bus	one	1.91
Regular cinema ticket	one	12.62

Source: Central Statistical Office, 2005

APPENDIX 12

FOREIGN DIRECT INVESTMENTS IN POLAND BY COUNTRY OF REGISTRATION (as of 31 December 2004)

No.	Country	Investments USD million	Number of Companies
1.	France	16,026.1	101
2.	The Netherlands	11,154.2	126
3.	USA	10,163.7	118
4.	Germany	10,149.5	258
5.	International	4,648.7	14
6.	United Kingdom	4,337.2	56
7.	Italy	4,089.3	67
8.	Sweden	3,715.2	60
9.	Belgium	2,902.6	27
10.	Denmark	2,096.2	50
11.	Switzerland	1,617.5	28
12.	Austria	1,223.7	40
13.	South Korea	1,167.9	6
14.	Cyprus	1,110.5	4
15.	Ireland	1,026.2	6
16.	Portugal	678.4	4
17.	Luxembourg	673.0	19
18.	Finland	578.5	20
19.	Greece	561.6	4
20.	Spain	486.3	11
21.	Russia	409.1	3
22.	Japan	362.3	18
23.	Norway	345.2	14
24.	Croatia	219.0	2
25.	Canada	210.9	13
26.	Australia	159.5	3
27.	Turkey	100.1	4
28.	Czech Republic	75.0	5
29.	Israel	70.4	4
30.	Slovenia	70.3	2
31.	South Africa	57.2	1
32.	Hungary	55.8	4
33.	China	45.0	2
34.	Philippines	40.0	1
35.	Liechtenstein	16.9	5
36.	Monaco	6.8	1
Total value of FDI of USD 1 million and over		**80,649.8**	**1101**
Estimated value of FDI below USD 1 million		**3,827.8**	
T O T A L FDI in Poland		**84,477.6**	

Source: PAIiIZ, 2005

APPENDIX 13

FOREIGN DIRECT INVESTMENTS IN POLAND BY FIELD OF ACTIVITY (as of 31 December 2004)

Branch of Activity according to the European Activity Classification	Investments USD million	Share (%)
Manufacturing	**32,199.9**	**39.9**
Transport equipment	6,663.6	8.3
Food processing	6,624.8	8.2
Other non-metal goods	4,205.5	5.2
Electrical machinery and apparatus	3,250.0	4.0
Chemicals and chemical products	3,245.2	4.0
Pulp and paper	2,086.0	2.6
Wood and wooden products	1,692.1	2.1
Rubber and plastics	1,459.0	1.8
Metals and metal products	1,278.3	1.6
Machinery and equipment	1,023.7	1.3
Furniture production	349.7	0.4
Fabrics and textiles	290.5	0.4
Leather and leather products	31.4	0.0
Financial mediation	**18,875.5**	**23.4**
Trade and repairs	**9,517.4**	**11.8**
Transport, storage and communication	**7,861.4**	**9.7**
Power, gas and water supply	**3,207.6**	**4.0**
Real estate and business activities	**2,952.7**	**3.7**
Community, social and personal services	**2,732.2**	**3.4**
Construction	**2,110.1**	**2.6**
Hotels and restaurants	**885.3**	**1.1**
Mining and quarrying	**228.6**	**0.3**
Agriculture	**76.3**	**0.1**
Value of FDI of USD 1 million and over	**80,649.8**	**100.0 %**
Estimated value of FDI below USD 1 million	**3,827.8**	
T O T A L FDI in Poland	**84,477.6**	

Source: PAIiIZ, 2005

APPENDIX 14

FOREIGN DIRECT INVESTMENTS IN POLAND BY PROVINCE (as of 31 December 2004)

Province	Number of locations	%
Mazowieckie	834	26.7
Śląskie	392	12.5
Dolnośląskie	317	10.1
Wielkopolskie	257	8.2
Łódzkie	245	7.8
Pomorskie	185	5.9
Małopolskie	185	5.9
Kujawsko-Pomorskie	144	4.6
Lubuskie	103	3.3
Zachodniopomorskie	101	3.2
Podkarpackie	81	2.6
Opolskie	62	2.0
Warmińsko-Mazurskie	62	2.0
Lubelskie	59	1.9
Świętokrzyskie	52	1.7
Podlaskie	49	1.6
TOTAL	**3128**	**100.0 %**

Source: PAIiIZ, 2005

APPENDIX 15

LIST OF 20 MAJOR FOREIGN INVESTORS IN POLAND (as of 31 December 2004)

No.	Investor	Investments USD million	Country of registration	Sector
1.	**France Telecom**	4,470.4	France	Transport, storage and communication
2.	**European Bank for Reconstruction and Development (EBRD)**	4,000.0	International	Financial intermediation
3.	**Fiat**	1,800.6	Italy	Manufacture of transport equipment; financial intermediation
4.	**KBC Bank N.V.**	1,743.4	Belgium	Financial intermediation
5.	**Metro Group AG**	1,508.0	Germany	Wholesale and retail trade
6.	**HVB Group**	1,336.0	Germany	Financial intermediation
7.	**Citigroup**	1,300.0	USA	Financial intermediation
8.	**Tesco Plc**	1,300.0	United Kingdom	Wholesale and retail trade
9.	**Apollo-Rida Poland Llc**	1,300.0		Construction, real estate and business activities
10.	**Vivendi Universal**	1,243.4	France	Transport, storage and communication; real estate, renting and business activities; wholesale and retail trade
11.	**United Pan-Europe Communications N.V.**	1,200.0	Netherlands	Other community, social and personal service activities
12.	**UniCredito Italiano SpA**	1,200.0	Italy	Financial intermediation
13.	**Kronospan Holdings Ltd.**	1,061.8	Cyprus	Manufacture of wood and wood products
14.	**Vattenfall AB**	1,029.2	Sweden	Electricity, gas and water supply
15.	**General Motors Corporation**	1,010.0	USA	Manufacture of transport equipment
16.	**ING Group NV**	990.0	Netherlands	Financial intermediation, real estate
17.	**Carrefour**	980.0	France	Retail trade
18.	**Daewoo**	936.4	South Korea	Manufacture of electrical machinery and apparatus, financial intermediation
19.	**Enterprise Investors**	914.5	USA	Financial intermediation
20.	**Volkswagen AG**	873.1	Germany	Manufacture of transport equipment, financial intermediation

Source: PAIiIZ, 2005

APPENDIX 16

WSE – EQUITY

KEY FIGURES	2004	2003	2002	2001	2000
INDICES & INDICATORS					
WIG (end of period)	26,636.19	20,820.07	14,366.65	13,922.16	17,847.55
WIG20 (end of period)	1,960.57	1,574.04	1,175.64	1,208.34	1,816.19
MIDWIG (end of period)	1,730.10	1,269.34	950.24	1,020.49	1,004.68
PLN return on the WIG index (%)	27.94	44.9	3.2	-22	-1.3
PLN return on the WIG20 index (%)	24.56	33.9	-2.7	-33.5	3.4
PLN return on the MIDWIG index (%)	26.30	33.6	-6.9	1.6	-8.6
COMPANIES					
Number of listed companies (end of period)	230	203	216	230	225
Capitalisation at year-end (PLN million)	291,697	167,717	110,565	103,370	130,085
Total turnover value (PLN million)	**118,518**	**79,774**	**63,662**	**80,443**	**169,096**
Number of sessions	255	251	249	250	250
Number of investment accounts at end of period (thousand)	851	947	1,016	1,085	1,236
CONTINUOUS TRADING					
Number of listed companies (end of period)	206	159	152	141	102
Number of transactions per session	15,270	12,085	11,190	12,097	6,157
Total turnover value (PLN million)	109,531	66,281	47,599	60,032	58,329
SINGLE-PRICE AUCTION					
Number of listed companies (end of period)	24	44	64	89	123
Number of transactions per session	195	140	165	409	8,777
Total turnover value (PLN million)	244	162	130	516	45,329
BLOCK TRADES (TOTAL)					
Number of transactions (single-counted)	778	703	688	1,159	2,681
Average value of transaction (PLN million)	5.62	9.48	11.6	8.6	12.20
Total turnover value (PLN million)	8,743	13,331	15,933	19,895	65,438

Source: WSE, 2005

APPENDIX 17

WSE – BONDS

	2004	2003	2002	2001	2000
Order book transactions					
Number of bonds at the year-end	81	70	61	53	48
Turnover value (PLN mill)	7,820	7,840	3,986	5,093	4,381
Average turnover per session (PLN mill)	31	31	16	20	18
Number of transactions per session	411	410	331	525	534
Average transaction value (PLN)	37,287	38,130	24,222	19,386	16,408
Negotiated deals					
Number of transactions	113	1,278	45	13	45
Average transaction value (PLN mill)	2.36	1.89	1.61	1.55	2.32
Turnover value (PLN mill)	533	4,834	145	40	209

Source: WSE, 2005

APPENDIX 18

CENTRAL INSTITUTIONS AND MINISTRIES

Chancellery of the President of the Republic of Poland
Kancelaria Prezydenta RP
ul. Wiejska 10; 00-902 Warszawa
tel.: (+48-22) 6952900; fax: 6951109
www.prezydent.pl

Sejm Chancellery
Kancelaria Sejmu RP
ul. Wiejska 4/6/8; 00-902 Warszawa
tel.: (+48-22) 6942500; fax: 6942252
www.sejm.gov.pl

Senate Chancellery
Kancelaria Senatu RP
ul. Wiejska 6; 00-902 Warszawa
tel.: (+48-22) 6942500; fax: 6942224
www.senat.gov.pl

Chancellery of the Prime Minister
Kancelaria Premiera
Al. Ujazdowskie 1/3; 00-583 Warszawa
tel.: (+48-22) 6946000; fax: 6218827
www.kprm.gov.pl

Constitutional Tribunal
Trybunał Konstytucyjny
Al. Szucha 12a; 00-918 Warszawa
tel.: (+48-22) 6574531; fax: 6574532
www.trybunal.gov.pl

Supreme Court
Sąd Najwyższy
Pl. Krasińskich 2/4/6; 00-951 Warszawa
tel.: (+48-22) 5308000; fax: 6201354
www.sn.pl

Supreme Administrative Court
Naczelny Sąd Administracyjny
ul. Jasna 6; 00-013 Warszawa
tel.: (+48-22) 8276031; fax: 8276687
www.nsa.gov.pl

Supreme Chamber of Control
Najwyższa Izba Kontroli
ul. Filtrowa 57; 00-950 Warszawa
tel.: (+48-22)8254481; fax: 8257376
www.nik.gov.pl

National Bank of Poland
Narodowy Bank Polski
ul. Świętokrzyska 11/21; 00-919 Warszawa
tel.: (+48-22) 6531000; fax: 8264123
www.nbp.pl

Ministry of Agriculture and Rural Development
Ministerstwo Rolnictwa i Rozwoju Wsi
ul. Wspólna 30; 00-930 Warszawa
tel.: (+48-22) 6231000; fax: 6232750
www.minrol.gov.pl

Ministry of Culture and National Heritage
Ministerstwo Kultury i Dziedzictwa Narodowego
Krakowskie Przedmieście 15/17
00-071 Warszawa
tel.: (+48-22) 4210100
www.mkidn.gov.pl

Ministry of Defence
Ministerstwo Obrony Narodowej
ul. Klonowa 1; 00-909 Warszawa
tel.: (+48-22) 6280031 ... 34; fax: 8455378
www.wp.mil.pl

Ministry of Economic Affairs
Ministerstwo Gospodarki
Plac Trzech Krzyży 3/5; 00-507 Warszawa
tel.: (+48-22) 6935000; fax: 6934048
www.mg.gov.pl

Ministry of Education and Science
Ministerstwo Edukacji i Nauki
Al. Szucha 25; 00-918 Warszawa
tel.: (+48-22) 6280461; fax: 6297241
www.men.gov.pl

Ministry of the Environment
Ministerstwo Środowiska
ul. Wawelska 52/54; 00-922 Warszawa
tel.: (+48-22) 5792900
www.mos.gov.pl

Ministry of Finance
Ministerstwo Finansów
ul. Świętokrzyska 12; 00-916 Warszawa
tel.: (+48-22) 6945555; fax: 8266352
www.mofnet.gov.pl

Ministry of Foreign Affairs
Ministerstwo Spraw Zagranicznych
Al. Szucha 23; 00-580 Warszawa
tel.: (+48-22) 5239000; fax: 6298635
www.msz.gov.pl

Ministry of Health
Ministerstwo Zdrowia
ul. Miodowa 15; 00-952 Warszawa
tel.: (+48-22) 6349600; fax: 6359245
www.mz.gov.pl

Ministry of Internal Affairs and Administration
Ministerstwo Spraw Wewnętrznych i Administracji
ul. Batorego 5; 02-591 Warszawa
tel.: (+48-22) 6212020, 6289979; fax: 497494
www.mswia.gov.pl

Ministry of Justice
Ministerstwo Sprawiedliwości
Al. Ujazdowskie 11; 00-950 Warszawa
tel.: (+48-22) 5212888; fax: 6282575
www.ms.gov.pl

Ministry of Labour and Social Policy
Ministerstwo Pracy i Polityki Społecznej
ul. Nowogrodzka 1/3/5; 00-513 Warszawa
tel.: (+48-22) 6610100; fax: 6611124
www.mps.gov.pl

Ministry of Regional Development
Ministerstwo Rozwoju Regionalnego
Plac Trzech Krzyży 3/5; 00-507 Warszawa

Ministry of Sport
Ministerstwo Sportu
Al. Róż 2, 00-559 Warszawa
tel.: (+48-22) 5223399; fax: 8262172
www.msport.gov.pl

Ministry of Transport and Construction
Ministerstwo Transportu i Budownictwa
ul. Chałubińskiego 4/6; 00-928 Warszawa
tel.: (+48-22) 6301000; fax: 6301116
www.mi.gov.pl

Ministry of the Treasury
Ministerstwo Skarbu Państwa
ul. Krucza 36; 00-522 Warszawa
tel.: (+48-22) 6958000; fax: 6280872
www.mst.gov.pl

Agricultural Market Agency
Agencja Rynku Rolnego
ul. Nowy Świat 6/12; 00-400 Warszawa
tel.: (+48-22) 6617203; fax: 6289353
www.arr.gov.pl

Agricultural Property Agency
Agencja Nieruchomości Rolnych
ul. Dolańskiego 2; 00-215 Warszawa
tel.: (+48-22) 6358009; fax: 6350060
www.anr.gov.pl

Office of Technical Inspection
Urząd Dozoru Technicznego
ul. Szczęśliwicka 34; 02-353 Warszawa
tel.: (+48-22) 572 21 00; fax: 8227209
www.udt.gov.pl

Central Office of Measures
Główny Urząd Miar
ul. Elektoralna 2; 00-139 Warszawa
tel.: (+48-22) 6200241; fax: 6208378
www.gum.gov.pl

Central Statistical Office
Główny Urząd Statystyczny
Al. Niepodległości 208; 00-925 Warszawa
tel.: (+48-22) 6083000; fax: 6083863
www.stat.gov.pl

Office for Competition and Consumer Protection
Urząd Ochrony Konkurencji i Konsumenta
Pl. Powstańców Warszawy 1; 00-950 Warszawa
tel.: (+48-22) 5560800; fax: 8265076
www.uokik.gov.pl

General Administration of Domestic Roads and Highways
Generalna Dyrekcja Dróg Krajowych i Autostrad
ul. Żelazna 59; 00-848 Warszawa
tel.: (+48-22) 3758888; fax: 558600
www.gddkia.gov.pl

Government Centre for Strategic Studies
Rządowe Centrum Studiów Strategicznych
ul. Wspólna 4; 00-926 Warszawa
tel.: (+48-22) 6618600; fax: 6212550
www.rcss.gov.pl

State Mining Authority
Wyższy Urząd Górniczy
ul.Poniatowskiego 31; 40-956 Katowicze
tel.: (+48-32) 2511471; fax: 2514884
www.wug.gov.pl

Industrial Development Agency
Agencja Rozwoju Przemysłu S.A.
ul. Domaniewska 41; 02-672 Warszawa
tel.: (+48-22) 4603799; fax: 4603701

Institute of National Remembrance
Instytut Pamięci Narodowej
ul. Towarowa 28; 00-839 Warszawa
tel.: (+48-22) 5308690
www.ipn.gov.pl

National Broadcasting Council
Krajowa Rada Radiofonii i Telewizji
Skwer Kard. Stefana Wyszyńskiego 9
01-015 Warszawa
tel.: (+48-22) 5973000; fax: 5973180
www.krrit.gov.pl

National Police Headquarters
Komenda Główna Policji
ul. Puławska 148/150; 02-514 Warszawa
tel.: (+48-22) 6210251; fax: 8488494
www.kgp.gov.pl

Office of the Committee for European Integration
Urząd Komitetu Integracji Europejskiej
Al. Ujazdowskie 9; 00-918 Warszawa
tel.: (+48-22) 4555500; fax: 4555348
www.ukie.gov.pl

Office for Veterans and Repressed Persons
Urząd ds. Kombatantów i Osób Represjonowanych
ul. Wspólna 2/4; 00-926 Warszawa
tel.: (+48-22) 6618129; fax: 6618740
www.udskior.gov.pl

Polish Academy of Sciences
Polska Akademia Nauk
Plac Defilad 1; 00-901 Warszawa; PO Box 24
tel.: (+48-22) 6204970; fax: 6204910
www.pan.waw.pl

Polish Information and Foreign Investment Agency
Polska Agencja Informacji i Inwestycji Zagranicznych
ul. Bagatela 12; 00-585 Warszawa
tel.: (+48-22) 3349800; fax: 3349999
www.paiz.gov.pl

Polish Agency For Enterprise Development
Polska Agencja Rozwoju Przedsiębiorczości
ul. Pańska 81/83; 00834 Warszawa
tel.: (+48-22) 4328080; fax: 4328620
www.parp.gov.pl

Polish Chamber of Commerce
Krajowa Izba Gospodarcza
ul. Trębacka 4; 00-074 Warszawa
tel.: (+48-22) 6309600; fax: 8274673
www.kig.pl

Polish Committee for Standardisation
Polski Komitet Normalizacyjny
ul. Świętokrzyska 14; 00-050 Warszawa
tel.: (+48-22) 5567755; fax: 5567416
www.pkn.pl

Polish Centre for Testing and Certification
Polskie Centrum Badań i Certyfikacji
ul. Kłobucka 23a; 02-699 Warszawa
tel.: (+48-22) 4645200; fax: 6471222
www.pcbc.gov.pl

Polish Patent Office
Urząd Patentowy RP
Al. Niepodległości 188/192
00-950 Warszawa
tel.: (+48-22) 8258001; fax: 8750680
www.uprp.pl

Public Procurement Office
Urząd Zamówień Publicznych
Al. Szucha 2/4; 00-582 Warszawa
tel.: (+48-22) 4587777; fax: 4587700
www.uzp.gov.pl

State Atomic Agency
Państwowa Agencja Atomistyki
ul. Krucza 36; 00-522 Warszawa
tel.: (+48-22) 6959800; fax: 6290164
www.paa.gov.pl

State Committee for Scientific Research
Komitet Badań Naukowych
ul. Wspólna 1/3; 00-529 Warszawa
tel.: (+48-22) 5292718; fax: 6280922
www.kbn.gov.pl

State Hygiene Department
Institute of Scientific Research
Państwowy Zakład Higieny
Instytut Naukowo-Badawczy
ul. Chocimska 24; 00-791 Warszawa
tel.: (+48-22) 5421400; fax: 8497484
www.pzh.gov.pl

State Environmental Protection Inspectorate
Główny Inspektorat Ochrony Środowiska
ul. Wawelska 52/54; 00-922 Warszawa
tel.: (+48-22) 5792900; fax: 8250465
www.gios.gov.pl

State Inspection of Labour
Chief Labour Inspectorate
Państwowa Inspekcja Pracy
Główny Inspektorat Pracy
ul. Krucza 38/42; 00-926 Warszawa
tel.: (+48-22) 6618111; fax: 6254770
www.pip.gov.pl

Stock Exchange Commission
Komisja Papierów Wartościowych i Giełd
Pl. Powstańców Warszawy 1
00-950 Warszawa
tel.: (+48-22) 3326600; fax: 3326793
www.kpwig.gov.pl

Insurance and Pension Funds Supervisory Office
Komisja Nadzoru Ubezpieczeń i Funduszy Emerytalnych
ul. Niedźwiedzia 6E; 02-737 Warszawa
tel. (+48-22) 5487240; fax: 5487245
www.knuife.gov.pl

Export Credit Insurance Corporation
Korporacja Ubezpieczeń Kredytów Eksportowych
KUKE S.A.
ul. Sienna 39; 00-121 Warszawa
tel. (+48-22) 3568300; 3130110; fax: 3130119
www.kuke.com.pl

Foreign Investors' Chamber of Industry and Commerce in Poland
Izba Przemysłowo-Handlowa Inwestorów Zagranicznych w Polsce
ul. Pańska 73, 00-834 Warszawa
tel.: (+48-22) 3147575; fax: 3147576
www.iphiz.com.pl

Institute of Tourism
Instytut Turystyki
ul. Merliniego 9a; 02-511 Warszawa
tel. (+48-22) 8446347; fax: 8441263
www.intur.com.pl

Polish Chamber of Patent Attorneys
Polska Izba Rzeczników Patentowych
ul. Madalińskiego 20 lok. 2.; 02-513 Warszawa
tel/fax: (+48-22) 6464143; tel./fax: 6464012
www.rzecznikpatentowy.org.pl

Polish Federation of Valuers' Associations
Polska Federacja Stowarzyszeń Rzeczoznawców Majątkowych
ul. Złota 79, 00-819 Warszawa
tel.: (+48-22) 6202321; fax: 6202594
www.pfva.com.pl

Polish Real Estate Federation
Polska Federacja Rynku Nieruchomości
ul. Śliska 52, 00-826 Warszawa
tel.: (+48-22) 6545869; fax: 8253495
www.pfrn.pl

Polish Tourism Organisation
Polska Organizcja Turystyczna
ul. Chałubińskiego 4/6; 00-928 Warszawa
tel.: (+48-22) 6301736; fax: 6301742
www.pot.gov.pl

Warsaw Stock Exchange
Giełda Papierów Wartościowych
ul.Książęca 4; 00-498 Warszawa
tel.: (+48-22) 6283232; fax: 6281754
www.gpw.com.pl

APPENDIX 19

REGIONAL OFFICES OF THE MINISTRY OF THE TREASURY

REGIONAL OFFICE	PROVINCES COVERED	ADDRESS	TELEPHONE FAX NUMBER E-MAIL
Białystok	podlaskie	15-085 Białystok ul. Branickiego 17a	Tel.: (+48-85) 7322387, 7327981, 7328053 Fax: 7322387 e-mail: delegatura.bialystok@msp.gov.pl
Ciechanów	mazowieckie	06-400 Ciechanów ul. 17 Stycznia 7	Tel.: (+48-23) 6722393 Fax: 6722393 e-mail: delegatura.ciechanow@msp.gov.pl
Gdańsk	pomorskie, warmińsko-mazurskie	80-852 Gdańsk ul. Dyrekcyjna 6	Tel.: (+48-58) 3013306, 3012972, 3016035 Fax: 3012972 e-mail: delegatura.gdansk@msp.gov.pl
Katowice	śląskie	40-038 Katowice ul. Powstańców 34	Tel.: (+48-32) 2552601, 2552617, 2553065 ext. 324 Fax: 2552585 e-mail: delegatura.katowice@msp.gov.pl
Kielce	świętokrzyskie	25-955 Kielce ul. IX Wieków Kielc 3	Tel.: (+48-41) 3445287, 3421295, 3421763 3421371, 3421484 Fax: 3444008
Kraków	małopolskie	31-503 Kraków ul. Lubicz 25	Tel.: (+48-12) 4120726, 4210433 ext. 1132, 1139, 1147, 1149 Fax: 4210015 e-mail: delegatura.krakow@msp.gov.pl
Lublin	lubelskie	20-072 Lublin ul. Lubomelska 1-3	Tel.: (+48-81) 5323424, 7424521, 7404527, 7402272 Fax: 5323424 e-mail: delegatura.lublin@msp.gov.pl
Łódź	łódzkie	90-051 Łódź ul Piłsudskiego 8	Tel.: (+48-42) 6363409, 6362277 Fax: 6363809, 6370237 e-mail: delegatura.lodz.@msp.gov.pl
Poznań	wielkopolskie, lubuskie	60-734 Poznań ul. Głogowska 26	Tel.: (+48-61) 8654023, 8654441, 8654442 Fax: 8654443 e-mail:delegatura.poznan@msp.gov.pl
Rzeszów	podkarpackie	35-959 Rzeszów ul. Grunwaldzka 15	Tel.: (+48-17) 8627384 Fax: 8627199 e-mail:delegatura.rzeszow@msp.gov.pl
Szczecin	zachodnio-pomorskie	70-603 Szczecin ul. Bytomska 9	Tel.: (+48-91) 4623923, 4623924, 4623925 Fax: 4623924 e-mal:delegaura.szczecin@msp.gov.pl
Toruń	kujawsko-pomorskie	87-100 Toruń ul. Szosa Chełmińska 30/32	Tel.: (+48-56) 6224786, 6221352 Fax: 6222936 e-mail: delegatura.torun@msp.gov.pl
Wrocław	dolnośląskie, opolskie	53-333 Wrocław ul. Powstańców Śląskich 28/30	Tel.: (+48-71) 3350311 Fax: 3350313 e-mail: delegatura.wroclaw@msp.gov.pl

Source: Ministry of the Treasury, 2005

APPENDIX 20

INTERNATIONAL ORGANISATIONS AND UN AGENCIES IN POLAND

The World Bank
ul. Emilii Plater 53; 00-113 Warsaw
tel.: (+48-22) 5208000; fax: 5208001
www.worldbank.org.pl

International Monetary Fund
ul. Emilii Plater 53; 00-113 Warsaw
tel.: (+48-22) 5207100; fax: 5207101
www.imf.org

European Bank for Reconstruction and Development
ul. Emilii Plater 53; 00-113 Warsaw
(Warsaw Financial Centre, 13th floor)
tel.: (+48-22) 5205700; fax: 5205800
www.ebrd.org

International Finance Corporation
ul. Emilii Plater 53; 00-113 Warsaw
(Warsaw Financial Centre, 9th floor)
tel.: (+48-22) 5206100; fax: 5206101
www.ifc.org

Delegation of the European Commission
ul. Emilii Plater53; 00-113 Warsaw
tel.: (+48-22) 5208200; fax: 5208282
www.europa.delpopl.pl

International Labour Office
National Correspondent in Poland
ul. Nowogrodzka 1/3; Office no 617
00-513 Warsaw
tel.: (+48-22) 6214019, fax: 6610650

United Nations Development Programme
Al. Niepodległości 186; 00-608 Warsaw
tel.: (+48-22) 8259245; fax: 8254958
e-mail: registry.pl@undp.org
www.undp.org.pl

United Nations Industrial Development Organization
Al. Niepodległości 186; 00-608 Warsaw
tel.: (+48-22) 8259186; fax: 8258970
e-mail: ips-waw@unido.pl
www.unido.pl

United Nations International Drug Control Programme
United Nations House
Al. Niepodległości 186, 1st Floor, 00-608 Warsaw
tel.: (+48-22) 8259245, fax: 8254958

United Nationas Economic Commission for Europe
Trans-European North-South Motorway Central Office
ul. Golędzinowska 10; 03-302 Warsaw
tel.: (+48-22) 6145397; fax: 6145401
e-mail: untem@ibdim.edu.pl

Environmental Information Centre
United Nations Environment Programme
GRID Warsaw
ul. Sobieszyńska 8; 00-764 Warsaw
tel.: (+48-22) 8406664; fax: 8516201
e-mail: grid@gridw.pl
www.gridw.pl

United Nations Population Fund
United Nations House
Al. Niepodległości 186, 00-608 Warsaw
tel.: (+48-22) 8259245; fax: 8254958

United Nations High Commissioner for Refugees
Branch Office in Poland
Al. Róż 2; 00-556 Warsaw
tel.: (+48-22) 6286930; fax: 6256124
e-mail: polwa@unhcr.ch
www.unhcr.pl

United Nations Information Centre in Warsaw
United Nations House
Al. Niepodległości 186, 00-608 Warsaw
tel.: (+48-22) 8252557, 8259245; fax: 8254958
www.unic.un.org.pl

World Food Programme
United Nations House
Al. Niepodległości 186, 1st Floor, 00-608 Warsaw
tel.: (+48-22) 8259245; fax: 8254958

World Health Organization
Liaison Office in Poland
ul. Długa 38/4; 00-238 Warsaw
tel.: (+48-22) 6359496; fax: 8310892
e-mail: wholo@who.un.org.pl
www.who.int

Polish FAO National Committee
Ministry of Agriculture and Rural Development
Department for Foreign Relations
ul. Wspólna 30; 00-930 Warsaw
tel.: (+48-22) 6231303; fax: 6212326

Polish Committee for UNICEF
Pl. Defilad 1; 00-901 Warsaw
tel.: (+48-22) 6566610; fax: 6566613
e-mail: unicef@unicef.pl
www.unicef.org.pl

The Polish National Commission for UNESCO and the Permanent Secretariat of the Commission
Pałac Kultury i Nauki; 7th Floor; 00-901 Warsaw
tel./fax: (+48-22) 6203355, 6203362
e-mail: komitet@unesco.pl
www.unesco.pl

APPENDIX 21

LOCAL AUTHORITIES – PROVINCIAL GOVERNMENTS

Dolnośląskie
Dolnośląski Urząd Wojewódzki
Pl. Powstańców Warszawy 1, 50-951 Wrocław
tel.: (+48-71) 3406100; fax: 7907119
www.uwoj.wroc.pl

Kujawsko-Pomorskie
Kujawsko-Pomorski Urząd Wojewódzki
ul. Jagiellońska 3, 85-950 Bydgoszcz
tel.: (+48-52) 3497913; fax: 3497460
www.uwoj.bydgoszcz.pl

Lubelskie
Lubelski Urząd Wojewódzki
ul. Spokojna 4, 20-914 Lublin
tel.: (+48-81) 5324543; fax: 7424319
www.lublin.uw.gov.pl

Lubuskie
Lubuski Urząd Wojewódzki
ul. Jagiellończyka 8, 66-400 Gorzów Wlkp.
tel.: (+48-95) 7215600; fax: 7223680
www.wojewodalubuski.pl

Łódzkie
Łódzki Urząd Wojewódzki
ul. Piotrkowska 104, 90-926 Łódź
tel.: (+48-42) 6641000; fax: 6641040
www.lodz.uw.gov.pl

Małopolskie
Małopolski Urząd Wojewódzki
ul. Basztowa 22, 31-156 Kraków
tel.: (+48-12) 6160200; fax: 4227208
www.uwoj.krakow.pl

Mazowieckie
Mazowiecki Urząd Wojewódzki
Pl. Bankowy 3/5, 00-950 Warszawa
tel.: (+48-22) 6956997; fax: 6203704
www.mazowsze.uw.gov.pl

Opolskie
Opolski Urząd Wojewódzki
ul. Piastowska 14, 45-082 Opole
tel.: (+48-77) 4524100; fax: 4544575
www.opole.uw.gov.pl

Podkarpackie
Podkarpacki Urząd Wojewódzki
ul. Grunwaldzka 15, 35-959 Rzeszów
tel.: (+48-17) 8671000; fax: 8671950
www.uw.rzeszow.pl

Podlaskie
Podlaski Urząd Wojewódzki
ul. Mickiewicza 3, 15-213 Białystok
tel.: (+48-85)7439201; fax: 7429231
www.bialystok.uw.gov.pl

Pomorskie
Pomorski Urząd Wojewódzki
ul. Okopowa 21/27, 80-810 Gdańsk
tel.: (+48-58) 3077695; fax: 3011417
www.uw.gda.pl

Śląskie
Śląski Urząd Wojewódzki
ul. Jagiellońska 25, 40-032 Katowice
tel.: (+48-32) 2077777; fax: 2654245
www.katowice.uw.gov.pl

Świętokrzyskie
Świętokrzyski Urząd Wojewódzki
Al. IX Wieków Kielc 3, 25-516 Kielce
tel.: (+48-41) 3421222; fax: 3444832
www.kielce.uw.gov.pl

Warmińsko-Mazurskie
Warmińsko-Mazurski Urząd Wojewódzki
Al. Piłsudskiego 7/9, 10-575 Olsztyn
tel.: (+48-89) 5232200; fax: 5237754
www.uw.olsztyn.pl

Wielkopolskie
Wielkopolski Urząd Wojewódzki
Al. Niepodległości 16/18, 61-713 Poznań
tel.: (+48-61) 8541071; fax: 8527327
www.poznan.uw.gov.pl

Zachodniopomorskie
Zachodniopomorski Urząd Wojewódzki
ul. Wały Chrobrego 4, 70-502 Szczecin
tel.: (+48-91) 4303011; fax: 4330250
www.zuw.szczecin.uw.gov.pl

APPENDIX 22

ECONOMIC DIVISIONS OF DISTRICT COURTS (REGISTERING COMPANIES)

XII Wydział Gospodarczy
15-017 **Białystok** ul. Łąkowa 3
tel.: (0-85) 7408980

VIII Wydział Gospodarczy
43-300 **Bielsko-Biała** ul. Bogusławskiego 24
tel.: (0-33) 4997910, 4997900

XIII Wydział Gospodarczy
85-023 **Bydgoszcz** ul. Toruńska 64A
tel.: (0-52) 3262736

XVII Wydział Gospodarczy KRS
42-200 **Częstochowa** ul. Rejtana 6
tel.: (0-34) 3779921

XII / XVI Wydział Gospodarczy
80-169 **Gdańsk** ul. Piekarnicza 10
tel.: (0-58) 3213785, 3213835

X Wydział Gospodarczy
44-100 **Gliwice** ul. Kościuszki 15
tel.: (0-32) 3380212

VIII Wydział Gospodarczy
40-040 **Katowice** ul. Lompy 14
tel.: (0-32) 7313469

X Wydział Gospodarczy
25-312 **Kielce** ul. Warszawska 44
tel. (0-41) 3441056-58 ext. 116

IX Wydział Gospodarczy Rejestrowy
75-626 **Koszalin** ul. Wł. Andersa 34
tel.: (0-94) 3428260

XI / XII Wydział Gospodarczy
31-547 **Kraków** ul. Przy Rondzie 7
tel.: (0-12) 6195172; 6195178

XI Wydział Gospodarczy
20-340 **Lublin** ul. Garbarska 20
tel.: (0-81) 7454711

XX Wydział Gospodarczy Rejestrowy
90-928 **Łódź** ul. Pomorska 37
tel.: (0-42) 6305200 ext. 207

VIII Wydział Gospodarczy
10-523 **Olsztyn** ul. Partyzantów 70
tel. (0-89) 5354099

VIII Wydział Gospodarczy
45-057 **Opole** ul. Ozimska 19
tel. (0-77) 4543834

XXI / XXII Wydział Gospodarczy
61-752 **Poznań** ul. Grochowe Łąki 6
tel. (0-61) 8566481; 8566466

XII Wydział Gospodarczy
35-324 **Rzeszów** ul. Trembeckiego 11a
tel. (0-17) 8628933

XVII Wydział Gospodarczy
70-485 **Szczecin** ul. Królowej Korony Polskiej 31
tel.: (0-91) 4225347

VII Wydział Gospodarczy Rejestrowy
87-100 **Toruń** ul. Młodzieżowa 31
tel.: (0-56) 6105864

XIX / XX / XXI Wydział Gospodarczy
02-315 **Warszawa** ul. Barska 28/30
tel. (0-22) 5705112; 5705118; 5705116

VI / IX Wydział Gospodarczy
53-234 **Wrocław** ul. Grabiszyńska 269
tel. (0-71) 3348210; 3348200

VIII Wydział Gospodarczy
65-364 **Zielona Góra** ul. Kożuchowska 8
tel.: (0-68) 3220263

APPENDIX 23

REGIONAL BRANCHES AND SUBSIDIARY OFFICES OF AGRICULTURAL PROPERTY AGENCY

		Address	Phone / E-mail	Fax
Head Office		00-215 Warszawa ul. Dolańskiego 2	(0-22) 6358009	6350060
1.	Warsaw	00-095 Warszawa Plac Bankowy 2	(0-22) 6351000	6354000
	Subsidiary office	91-420 Łódź ul. Północna 27/29	(0-42) 6362972, 6365326 lodz@anr.gov.pl	6329133
2.	Bydgoszcz	85-039 Bydgoszcz ul. Hetmańska 38	(0-52) 3493773 bydgoszcz@anr.gov.pl	3493797
3.	Gdańsk	83-000 Pruszcz Gdański ul. Powstańcow Warszawy 28	(0-58) 3004841, 3023817 gdansk@anr.gov.pl	3004843
4.	Gorzów Wlkp.	66-400 Gorzów Wlkp. ul. Jagiellończyka 8	(0-95) 7215340	7215433
	Subsidiary office	65-001 Zielona Góra ul. Lwowska 25	(0-68) 3254641, 3272389 gryszczuk@anr.gov.pl	3272006
5.	Lublin	20-027 Lublin ul. Karłowicza 4	(0-81) 5325967, 5322112	5320211
6.	Olsztyn	10-448 Olsztyn ul. Głowackiego 6	(0-89) 5235029	5235685
	Subsidiary office	16-400 Suwałki ul. Sportowa 22	(0-87) 5651847, 5663591	5665861
7.	Opole	45-068 Opole ul. 1 Maja 6	(0-77) 4000900	4000929
8.	Poznań	61-701 Poznań ul. Fredry 12	(0-61) 8560601 poznan@anr.gov.pl	8515092
	Subsidiary office	64-920 Piła ul. Motylewska 7	(0-67) 2123001 pila@anr.gov.pl	2123527
9.	Rzeszów	35-959 Rzeszów ul. 8 Marca 13	(0-17) 8537800 rzeszow@anr.gov.pl	8537816
10.	Szczecin	70-500 Szczecin ul. Wały Chrobrego 4	(0-91) 8144200 szczecin@anr.gov.pl	8144222
	Subsidiary office	75-411 Koszalin ul. Partyzantów 15a	(0-94) 3433930 koszalin@anr.gov.pl	3433695
11.	Wrocław	54-610 Wrocław ul. Mińska 60	(0-71) 3563900	3579097

APPENDIX 24
POLISH TECHNOLOGIES AND TECHNOLOGY PROVIDERS

Industrial Research Institute for Automation and Measurements, Warsaw
The SMR - 100 Expert Anti-Terrorist Neutralisation and Assistance Robot
Inventors: A group of project engineers under the direction of Piotr Szynkarczyk made up of Adam Andrzejuk, Mariusz Kozak, Tomasz Krakówka, Sebastian Pawłowski, Ignacy Bojanek, Michał Kulawiec, Sławomir Kapelko, Stanisław Nycz, Rafał Czupryniak, Wiesław Zalewski, and Przemysław Wieczorek, with the participation of Prof. Andrzej Masłowski.

The SMR-100 Expert Anti-Terrorist Neutralisation and Assistance Robot has been designed within the framework of the Polish National Science Foundation program. During the project engineers consulted with various specialists from the Police, the Government Protection Office, the Security Department of Warsaw Airport, and the National Border Guard. The principal purpose of the robot is the identification and neutralisation of hazardous explosive devices (IED) in tight indoor environments and in mass transit vehicles such as aircrafts, buses, and railroad cars. With the use of the robot it is possible to carry out a remote inspection of a threatened area, the recognition of IEDs, the removal or destruction of IED, and negotiations with terrorists. The robot can be send to area threatened by an explosion (or subject to other dangers, such as chemical contamination) instead of a person.

The SMR-100 Expert is made up of a crawler mounted mobile platform, with a manipulator with gripping device mounted on top, and an operator's station. The collapsible operator's station is designed in the form of a suitcase resistant to mechanical damage. The mobile base moves on caterpillar tracks. The additional front mini-track angle position can be remotely altered. The robot is stabilised by two movable lateral stabilisers. The manipulator, with six degrees of freedom, is fitted with a gripping device. It can be easily equipped with a variety of accessories. The robot is remotely controlled by radio or cable. It is equipped with a set of colour cameras and lighting devices.

The miniaturisation of electronic devices designed in SMT technology, a distributed multiprocessor controller architecture, unconventional stabilisation of the mobile base (providing for a wide manipulator reach) contribute to the robot's efficiency. To the best of the robot's designers knowledge, the SMR-100 Expert is the only robot in the world capable of carrying out comprehensive assignments inside aircrafts.

This technology is the winner of the 2003 edition of the Polish Product of the Future competition in the Product of the Future category.

P.P.U.H MARBET-WIL Sp. z o.o., Bielsko-Biała
MARWIL®-REFBET® - Technology of Applying Protective Layers on Concrete and Reinforced Concrete Surfaces
Inventor: Włodzimierz Mysłowski

The MARWIL®- REFBET® technology created to apply protective layers on concrete and reinforced concrete surfaces, uses SULCEM®, a sulphur polymer. The SULCEM® sulphur polymer production technology was developed by the MARBET®-WIL company (the first industrial application in Europe). The technology is based on the modification of waste sulphur generated in the process of removing sulphur from natural gas and oil in Claus-type installations.

The development of the MARWIL®- REFBET® technology, required the construction of the SULSPRAY® system, a device unique in the world that is used to spray SULCEM® sulphur

polymer on concrete surfaces. SULCEM® sulphur polymers and the SULSPRAY® device facilitated the development of the MARWIL®- REFBET® technology, which protects road curbs and other concrete road elements against the destructive action of salt and frost.
Through the addition of reflective particles and luminescent material, the MARWIL®- REFBET® system enhances road aesthetics and traffic safety by improving visibility both day and night. The system seals and reinforces the structure of concrete through surface and deep sealing injection, making it water-repellent and smooth.
The SULSPRAY® device is designed for the application of a sulphur polymer layer on concrete and reinforced concrete structures to impregnate and seal them as well as to protect the surface against corrosion. The SULSPRAY® device can also be used as a sulphur polymer batcher when reeling the aggregate in mixing devices.
The MARWIL®-REFBET® system ensures high resistance to aggressive media, high sealing properties, good adherence to concrete surfaces, a water and oil repellent surface, an increased resistance to frost and abrasive agents. It also hampers the growth of bacteria, mould, lichen, and fungi on the coating. The SULCEM® system is available in a wide range of colours.
Innovativeness of the technology consists in a novel use of sulphur polymers that is less expensive than the agents commonly used so far, and in that thermoplastic properties ensures better concrete impregnation. So far, sulphur polymer has not been applied as a protective coating for concrete and reinforced concrete elements, nor as a surface sealing, impregnation, and corrosion-proofing agent.
This technology is the winner of the 2003 edition of the Polish Product of the Future competition in the Technology of the Future category.

Plastic Waste Processing System
Inventors: Stanisław Lewandowski and Izabella Bogacka, with the cooperation of Piotr Banaszuk from the Białystok Institute of Technology.

Today's waste disposal sites contain plastics mixed with other types of waste. This system, designed to process such waste into liquid fuels, is small and efficient. It can be used to produce most types of benzines and oils, as well as larger quantities of paraffins and heavy hydrocarbons. The system is made up of three elements: a loading device, a depolymeriser, and a vapour condenser.
The loading device feeds plastics into the system on a continual or intermittent basis. The depolymeriser, heart of the system, is a diaphragm-heated reservoir. Unsegregated plastics are transformed here. This process generates depolymerisate vapour. The nature of this solution allows for effective and quick transmission of the burning fuel energy without a loss. The combustion method and its duration results in unusually pure combustion gases. Moreover, the leftover combustion energy is used to dry, heat and de-oxidise the charge. The vapour condenser allows for the zonal out-dropping of the depolymerisate, which enables good isolation of products in the form of a broad fraction of oil-like hydrocarbons, or its division into relevant fractions. Incondensable high-energy gases can be used for the generation of any type of energy for the needs of the system (thermal, rotational, or electric energy). This makes the system usable anywhere, without the need to connect it to electricity and water.
This system's innovativeness consists in a highly-efficient and fast transmission and distribution of burned fuel energy, thanks to which the heating elements are not subject to coking. It makes it possible to set-up and operate a very efficient installation operating continuously, with no need to

shutdown for cleaning. Impurities loaded along with the plastics can be evacuated without interrupting the system's operation.
This technology won a distinction in the 2003 edition of the Polish Product of the Future competition in the Technology of the Future category.

Hydromega Sp. z o.o., Gdynia
Pulsation Method for Swilling Oil Pipelines
Inventors: Zbigniew Zienowicz and a group of consultants from the Gdańsk Polytechnic directed by Prof. Andrzej Osiecki

The pulsation method for the swilling of oil pipes technology combines two flows of hydraulic oil. The final effect is achieved by combining the pulsation flow with the constant capacity flow of specific technical parameters. This method allows to define the distribution of pollutants along and across the pipeline, which in turn was vital for setting of parameters of the swilling processes and for the construction of a new swilling device. On the basis of results obtained in laboratory, a new swilling device was designed, the HM/MR-500, followed by another one, the HM/MR-50, for swilling pipelines of a diameter from 8 to 168 mm. Both devices are designed to monitor changes in oil purity. This method allows for the reduction of swilling time to a minimum, and it was shown that it ensures real pipeline cleanliness.
The technology has been tested in the field. The failures of pressurised hydraulic systems caused by assembly-related contamination were eliminated. Moreover, the life of all the hydraulic elements was prolonged. Considering that heavy industry widely employs hydraulic power and control units, pulsation swilling of oil pipes has considerable market potential. Its innovativeness consists in a combination of two swilling methods, constant capacity and pulsation methods, which ensures the removal of contaminants left over from the assembly process. It considerably reduces swilling time, even to a few hours, thus eliminating the need to shut down assembly lines on account of post-assembly contamination.
This technology won a distinction in the 2003 edition of the Polish Product of the Future competition in the Technology of the Future category.

Road and Bridge Research Institute, Warsaw
GUFI Modified Bituminous Mix for Laying of Crack-Resistant and Sound-Absorbing Pavements
Inventors: Dariusz Sybilski, Andrzej Wróbel, Janusz Kopaniewski, Renata Horodecka, Wojciech Bańkowski, and Krzysztof Mirski

The GUFI bituminous mix, in addition to standard components such as mineral aggregate and bituminous binder, contains granulated rubber and polymer fibres, giving the mix many unique and useful properties, which make it very different from ordinary bituminous mixes. Specifically, it consists of plain bitumen or polymer modified bitumen, mineral aggregate with coarse and fine particles (sand), granulated rubber and polymer fibres (preferably polyester) with melting temperature of no less than 200°C.
The mix's production process consists of adding – either continuously or in portions – granulated rubber and polymer fibres to the heated mineral aggregate and, after mixing, binder is added after which the mixture is mixed to consistency. Additives, such as rubber and fibres, in combination with the modified-polymer binder, make for specific properties of pavements made of the GUFI

mixture, such as resistance to cracking. The mixture can be used as an anti-crack membrane on the road pavement. It presents very good adherence properties with regards to all kinds of base surfaces, including concrete, stone slabs and blocks, paving stones, etc. It also leads to a reduction in tire-pavement contact noise. The result of applying the GUFI mix to pavements is twofold: Technical – longer pavement durability, and environmental – lower traffic noise (silent pavement) and the use of industrial waste material (granulated used tire rubber). Traffic noise reduction is of the order of 3 to 5 dB (A), which is equivalent a reduction of road traffic intensity by half. Furthermore, this mixture is suitable for bicycle paths, sports fields, and playgrounds, as the granulated rubber in the mix decreases the hardness of the pavement, making it safer in case of a fall.
This technology won a distinction in the 2003 edition of the Polish Product of the Future contest in the Product of the Future category.

Industrial Chemistry Research Institute
Reactive Extrusion Technology for the Production of PET Bottle Based Structural Elements
Inventors: Regina Jeziórska, Jacek Dzierżawski, Teresa Jaczewska, Agnieszka Szadkowska, Piotr Chrzanowski, Grażyna Chrzanowska, Marek Borensztejn, Stanisław Kalinowski, Piotr Krzyżanowski, Zbigniew Wielgosz, Witold Zieliński, and Maria Zielonka

As a result of chemical reactions taking place during the reactive extrusion process between functional PET groups and the modifier's functional group, stable chemical bonds are created. The polymer thus obtained has structural properties. Structural plastics sold under the trademark of Reylan® and produced by King-Plast Ltd. on the basis of waste can be applied in a variety of leading branches of industry, such as mechanical and electrical engineering, the automotive and electronic industries, etc.
The environmental impact of this technology is also very important. A single production line uses 1,200 tons of plastic waste annually, that's approximately 240 million PET bottles. This project takes advantage of the newest achievements in the field of chemical modification of thermoplastic polymers and results in the production of structural plastics with unique, high quality parameters with a wide range of uses. This technology is patented (PL 183 370).
This technology won a distinction in the 2003 edition of the Polish Product of the Future competition in the Technology of the Future category.

VIGO System S.A., Warszawa
The V-20 Thermographic Camera
Inventors: Prof. Józef Piotrowski, Mirosław Brudnowski, Maciej Rzeczkowski, and Robert Słomka

The V-20 thermographic camera serves for remote temperature measurement and visualisation of its distribution without physical contact. The camera records infrared radiation that is emitted by all bodies with a temperature of above 0 K. The device operates within a 3-5μm range and uses a high-sensitivity detector (NEDT @20°C:0.05°C) made by VIGO Systems SA.
The camera is controlled by two microprocessors, using 16-bit analog-to-digital conversion. The measurement data collected in the camera's memory is sent to a computer, typically through a USB 2.0 port. A user can connect any type of computer to the camera. If the camera is used for laboratory measurements on measuring stands, a traditional PC or laptop is used. In other cases, where measurements are taken in the field and when the camera is carried from one measuring point to another, it is recommended to use a palmtop. It acts as a display device, playing a role similar to that of a large video-camera viewfinder.

In the camera, measuring ranges were defined in the 10 to 1,500°C range. The user can assign colours from the colour palette corresponding to selected temperatures. Measurement results in a set of data presented in a form of a colour map, the thermogram. The thermogram consists of 57,600 measuring points (240 points on 240 lines). The user can select a point and read out its coordinates and temperature. The built-in laser indicator makes framing easier, indicating precisely the point that lies in the camera's optical axis (the point of coordinates x=120, y=120) and peripheral points in the field of vision.
The V-20 camera finds an application in various fields, such as preventive inspections of power grid equipment, diagnostics of machines in industrial plants, and searching for sources of heat loss from buildings. Thanks to its high sensitivity, it can also be used in medical and veterinary diagnostics and various types of research into slow-change thermal processes.
The heart of the camera is a relatively cheap, ultra-fast, un-cooled and high-sensitivity detector, also designed by VIGO System S.A. on the basis of its own infrared detector manufacturing technology that makes it possible to obtain high parameters without the necessity of using expensive liquid nitrogen cooling systems. A single element detector is used in combination with a mechanical scanning system. An advantage of this design is that the temperature of each elementary field of vision area of the camera is measured by means of the same detector, thus increasing the measurement's accuracy. In the case of matrix cameras, which make it possible to obtain real-time images, there are sensitivity differences between the matrix pixels that lead to errors in measurements. Presently, the V-20 Camera is the cheapest device for temperature distribution measurement without physical contact offered on the market.
This technology won a distinction in the 2003 edition of the Polish Product of the Future contest in the Product of the Future category.

Transition Technologies S.A., Warsaw
Digital Platform for the Optimisation of Electric Energy Generation
Inventors: Paweł D. Domański, Konrad Świrski, Jarosław Arabas

Modern control systems allow for the gathering of huge amounts of information concerning the control process and they are becoming progressively more elaborate for bigger control systems. However, processes are often so complex and unstable that traditional methods fail to produce an optimal solution. The aim of this system is to address this problem.
The software system includes highly specialised optimisation and control modelling procedures which take into account the economy of production and environmental protection at the level of the entire power station. It combines the latest scientific achievements (neural networks, optimisers) of Polish research centres. The most recent regulation techniques are used in this solution, i.e. predictive models with neural networks, fuzzy logic controllers, fuzzy neural networks, genetic optimisation, advanced validation algorithms – wavelet conversions, Kohonen neural networks and other methods. Many of the unique technical solutions applied in this tool are protected by patents. Currently all versions of the software are undergoing significant modernisation and are fully web-enabled. Its innovativeness consists in:

- modern, open-scaled information structure,
- the use of innovative calculation algorithms,
- the integration of information technologies and algorithm solutions into an industrial platform for control and optimisation.

This technology was the winner of the 2002 edition of the Polish Product of the Future competition in the Technology of the Future category.

Med & Life Polska Sp. z o.o., Komorów
Viofor JPS System Clinic - Equipment for Therapy with Magnetic Field and Light Energy
Inventors: Prof. Feliks Jaroszyk, Prof. Janusz Paluszak, Prof. Aleksander Sieroń, Prof. Wiesław Stręk, the design team directed by Waldemar Deka, the team from Institute of Optoelectronics (Military University of Technology) directed by Prof. Zygmunt Mierczyk

This equipment has been designed for physiotherapy using a magnetic field and the energy of light. Viofor JPS System Clinic combines the functions of a magneto stimulation device, a simplified version of a magneto therapy device, as well as applicators for the associated action of a magnetic field and monochromatic light. Associated action applicators are produced in three versions: red light, infrared light and mixed - red with infrared. A unique JPS magneto stimulation system elaborated by prominent Polish scientists is used in this equipment.
The system consists of a microprocessor controller with an LCD graphic display and applicators for magneto stimulation: homogeneous and heterogeneous magnetic fields, for magneto therapy heterogeneous field applicator as well as applicators for associated impact of magneto stimulation and monochromatic light, with a similar effect and power as those of bio stimulating medical lasers, but safer for the users. Communication with the user takes place by way of the menu system from the equipment's keyboard or the infrared remote control.
The device is destined for use in hospital therapy conditions, in physiotherapy and in medical offices. It is effective in the treatment, assisted treatment and recovery following many sicknesses, e.g., illnesses and contusions of the locomotive system, neurological diseases and injuries. It has analgestic, antiphlogistic and anti-inflammatory properties. In many cases, the use of this method results in a reduction of medication consumed and in a shorter recovery period. So far, no side-effects have been observed. Combining three methods of physical therapy in one device leads to cost reduction, economy of space and increases the effectiveness of therapy by enabling the use of different methods simultaneously or consecutively. Therapy parameters may be programmed by the user.
This technology is the winner of the 2002 edition of the Polish Product of the Future competition in the Product of the Future category.

Pharmaceutical Research Institute, Warsaw
Manufacturing of Tacalcitol, an Active Ingredient of Antipsoriasic Drug
Inventors: Andrzej Kutner, Michał Chodyński, Wanda Wojciechowska, Hanna Fitak, Małgorzata Krupa

Tacalcitol is an analogue of vitamin D_3. It is an active substance of a drug used in dermatology. The main clinical use of tacalcitol is local treatment of light and mild forms of ordinary and plaque psoriasis. Among similar drugs, tacalcitol stands out due to its high efficiency and low level of side effects (skin irritation). Therefore, it seems that tacalcitol will soon account for a substantial share of the dermatological market.
The absence of tacalcitol on the pharmaceutical market presents an opportunity to manufacture a pharmaceutical compound (ointment or cream) containing tacalcitol as an active substance, in keeping with the latest GMP European requirements for domestic and foreign markets. Its high price and short supply on the pharmaceutical market is an indication of the difficulties in its manufacturing. Among the group of active analogues and metabolites of vitamin D used as drugs, tacalcitol is the most difficult one to synthesise.
The synthesis of tacalcitol was elaborated in the Vitamin Laboratory of the Chemistry Department of the Pharmaceutical Institute. The method is based on the coupling of the s.c. C-22 vitamin

synthon, which includes the main part of a molecule, with a separately obtained side chain. The substrates in the elaborated method are commercially available (norcholenic acid acetate and L-valine). As usual in the case of vitamin D metabolites, the most difficult part of the process was to obtain a final compound with a high degree of chemical and pharmaceutical purity, providing for an adequate stability of the substance in the finished pharmaceutical form.
The innovativeness of the project consists in the elaboration of a completely new process for the production of tacalcitol. The multistage synthesis yields a pharmaceutically pure product that complies with relevant quality requirements.
This technology won a distinction in the 2002 edition of the Polish Product of the Future competition in the Technology of the Future category.

Foundry Research Institute, Cracow
Aluminium Composite Brake Disks And Drums
Inventors: Prof. Jerzy Sobczak, Andrzej Wojciechowski, Adam Nowak, Natalia Sobczak

This technology consists in the introduction of hard particles of silicon carbide to a relatively soft aluminium alloy matrix in an amount of approximately 20 % in terms of volume and/or some selected fractions of fly-ash (micro granules or micro spheres) in an amount of approximately 10 % in terms of volume. This type of metal-ceramic composite material, through the combination of the advantages of both materials, achieves performance characteristics exceeding even the best quality grades of cast iron. The proposed solution represents a new approach in the field of materials and the design of braking system elements. Besides a significant reduction in weight, the use of this new material reduces the maximum operating temperature several times. It also introduces a new definition of operating time, since the expected life of new brake disks may reach even hundreds of thousands of kilometres of failure-free performance.
The new material proposed, as well as the brake disk and drum manufacturing technology, can be used effectively in the car industry, in vehicles designed for large-scale production, as well as in racing cars, special-purpose and luxury vehicles, and in railway transport.
This technology won a distinction in the 2002 edition of the Polish Product of the Future competition in the Technology of the Future category.

Institute of Plastic Processing METALCHEM, Toruń
Technological Line for Single-Stage Polyolefin Pipes Extrusion, Particularly PP Pipes, Highly Filled with Mineral Components in the Double-Screw Concurrent Plastifying Process
Inventors: Joachim Stasiek, Grzegorz Kubiak, Józef Mazur, Jerzy Przytuła, Edmund Kopaczewski, Stanisław Skotarczak, Janisław Baraniak, and Roman Cybulski

This is a direct pipe extrusion technology for the extrusion of filled plastic pipes, without the need for an intermediate pre-compounding stage. The proper amount of plastic and additional components are measured by gravimetric feeder and are batched to specific positions in the extruder's barrel (of a segmental modular structure), in which a composite is intermixed and homogenised, and then placed in the gear pump. The gear pump forces the malleable plastic composite into the die of the extruder, which forms the pipe. The main advantages of direct extrusion include:

- a reduction of manufacturing costs – mineral fillers cost several times less than plastic,
- a shorter manufacturing time – decrease in energy consumption,
- higher pipe quality – as a result of plastic heat load reduction.

The direct extrusion method for highly filled PP pipes is used for pipe manufacturing, especially non-pressurised ones, i.e., for ventilation and sewage pipes used in sewage disposal. The technology allows for the manufacturing of pipes containing chalk up to 50 % of mass. This is an environment-friendly technology, due to the presence of an ecological mineral component in the pipe, which considerably simplifies the recycling process.
This technology won a distinction in the 2002 edition of the Polish Product of the Future contest in the Technology of the Future category.

Institute of Natural Fibres, Poznań
Technology of Hemp and Flax Fibres and Oil Flax Manufacturing, Serving as an Alternative Raw Material for the Ecological Manufacture of Chemical Paper Pulp and Composite Materials
Inventors: Prof. Ryszard Kozłowski, Jerzy Mańkowski, and Andrzej Kubacki
Presently, the production of chemical pulp and paper is based mainly on logged spruce-pine wood pulp. Considering the growing ecological consciousness of society, this technology presents an alternative to the use of wood. This alternative is to use fibre crops, especially hemp, which yields 10 tonnes of straw and ca 2.5 tonnes of fibre per ha. Conducted analyses have confirmed the high usefulness of flax and hemp fibres in the process of thermoplastic strengthening. These natural fibres are characterised by high endurance, elasticity, and lower specific gravity. Therefore, they are perfectly able to replace synthetic fibres (carbon fibres, glass fibres, etc.) currently used in such applications.
This innovative technology consists in processing fibre crop straw and in fibre production with non-standard devices used in the retting industry. It provides considerable simplification of the processing method used so far as well as cost reduction through a lower consumption of energy and labour in the fibre extraction process. In contrast to traditional production methods, the suggested raw material processing eliminates the labour-consuming and expensive straw retting and drying processes. The resulting fibre, due to an application of some new devices, has a form which makes it suitable, after an appropriate thorough cleaning, for technical purposes.
New technological solutions largely simplify the manufacturing processes and reduce production costs. In practice, one extracting device equipped with thorough cleaning devices, make it possible to obtain fibre with the parameters required by pulp mills, and which are still considerably cheaper in comparison to the traditional raw material. The equipment for the extraction of fibres from fibre crops applied in this technology is 2-3 times cheaper than that used by competitors.
This technology won a distinction in the 2002 edition of the Polish Product of the Future competition in the Technology of the Future category.

KOMAG Mining Mechanisation Centre, Gliwice
Universal KSW-750E High-Power Longwall Shearer
Inventors: Andrzej Meder, Ryszard Diederichs, Ryszard Bednarz, Jan Dziura, Piotr Drabik, Tadeusz Mazurkiewicz, Artur Tarkowski

The KSW-750E shearer has been designed in order to increase the efficiency of the coal extraction process in hard coal mines. Operational tests of the shearer have demonstrated that the applied innovative solutions result in the tripling of output in comparison to the present average production rates as well as in an increase of safety and reliability.
The KSW-750E shearer makes it possible to reduce the large number of longwall faces of limited efficiency, and its auxiliary infrastructure in order to introduce a model of 2-3-face mine of a several times higher degree of efficiency. The expected economic effect can be obtained only by

a high-power shearer installed and equipped with an automatic haulage system allowing for the continuous and optimal use of this power. Another challenge consists in ensuring a high degree of availability which can only be achieved through the use of technically advanced equipment of the highest life and reliability parameters. The electric KSW-750E longwall shearer fully meets the requirements of the modern mining industry.
The unique set of features of the KSW-750E longwall shearer sets it apart from other equipment currently being produced. Eight innovative solutions embodied in this product immensely increase its operational parameters, as well as improve its life and reliability, and are under patent protection of the Polish Patent Office.
This technology won a distinction in the 2002 edition of the Polish Product of the Future contest in the Product of the Future category.

Institute of Communication, Warsaw
Portable Device for Programmed and Controlled Discharging and Charging of Accumulator Batteries 48/50V – Converter TBA2-IŁ
Inventors: Tadeusz Kunert, Paweł Godlewski, Kazimierz Niechoda, Krzysztof Olechowski, Zbigniew Mąkosza. Consultations and research: Jan Komorowski

The TBA2-IŁ converter is the only such device (at least in Europe), which allows the process of discharging and charging batteries for accumulators of the 48/50V VRLA type in telecommunication structures to be wholly automated. The accumulators in these structures, in order to increase their operational life, must be temporarily discharged and recharged (in large devices with a current of up to 200 A), which normally requires the use of "discharging resistance" and constant process supervision, lasting up to 48 hours. This can all change with the use of the TBA2-IŁ converter.
The TBA2-IŁ converter, after connecting to the accumulator batteries and programming, can do its job without supervision and, after completing an assigned programme (e.g., a cycle: equalising charging – discharging – recovery charging), it turns itself off and transmits, via computer or telephone network, information to the user about the termination of the process and the recorded characteristics of the battery. The charging and discharging parameters are automatically corrected according to the ambient temperature of the battery and its characteristics. While discharging a battery, the device converts its energy into alternating sinusoidal current energy and transmits it to an 230V/50Hz electrical network. Therefore, even during long-lasting operations the room doesn't heat up, contrary to the "discharging resistance" method, where excess heat must be evacuated via an air-conditioning system. In order to increase the current efficiency while operating at the largest structures, a few devices may be connected in parallel and the computer appropriately adjusted so that one of them records overall results.
The TBA2-IŁ converter embodies high-current technology, precise measurement techniques, microprocessor technology to control and program work, and remote-control communication through various media. Due to the modern solutions used, the converter is of very small dimensions and weight, and has a very user-friendly software interface.
This technology won a distinction in the 2002 edition of the Polish Product of the Future competition in the Product of the Future category.

Foundry Research Institute
ul. Zakopiańska 73; 30-418 Kraków
tel.: (+48-12) 2618111
fax: (+48-12) 2660870
e-mail: iod@iod.krakow.pl
www.iod.krakow.pl

HYDROMEGA Spółka z o.o.
ul. Wrocławska 93; 81-553 Gdynia
tel.: (+48-71) 6647704
fax: (+48-71) 6647292
e-mail: hydromega@hydromega.com.pl
www.hydromega.com.pl

Industrial Chemistry Research Institute
ul. Rydygiera 8; 01-793 Warszawa
tel.: (+48-22) 6338298
fax: (+48-22) 6338295
e-mail: zbigdo@ichp.waw.pl

Institute of Communication
ul. Szachowa 1; 04-894 Warszawa
tel.: (+48-22) 5128169
fax: (+48-22) 5128185
e-mail: info@itl.waw.pl
www.itl.waw.pl

Institute of Heavy Organic Synthesis BLACHOWNIA
ul. Energetyków 9, 47-225 Kędzierzyn-Koźle
tel.: (+48 77) 4873199, fax: (+48 77) 4873060
e-mail: info@icso.com.pl
www.icso.com.pl

Institute of Industrial Organic Chemistry
ul. Annopol 6, 03-236 Warszawa
tel.: (+48 22) 8111231
fax: (+48 22) 8110799
e-mail: ipo@ipo.waw.pl
www.ipo.waw.pl

Institute of Microbiology, Warsaw University
Department of Bacterial Genetics
ul. Miecznikowa 1, 02-096 Warszawa
tel.: (+48 22) 5541403, 5541216
e-mail: kjkryn@biol.uw.edu.pl
www.biol.uw.edu.pl

Institute of Natural Fibres
ul. Wojska Polskiego 71 B; 60-630 Poznań
tel.: (+48-61) 8480061
fax: (+48-61) 8417830
e-mail: sekretar@inf.poznan.pl
www.iwn.inf.poznan.pl

Institute of Plastics Processing „METALCHEM"
ul. M. Skłodowskiej-Curie 55; 87-100 Toruń
tel.: (+48-56) 6500044
fax: (+48-56) 6500333
e-mail: sekretariat@ipts-metalchem.torun.pl
www.ipts-metalchem.torun.pl

KOMAG Mining Mechanization Centre
ul. Pszczyńska 37; 44-101 Gliwice
tel.: (+48-22) 2374100
fax: (+48-22) 2310843
e-mail: info@komag.gliwice.pl
www.komag.gliwice.pl

Med & Life Polska Sp. z o.o.
ul. Marii Dąbrowskiej 45; 05-806 Komorów
tel.: (+48-22) 7591515
fax: (+48-22) 7591519
e-mail: info@medandlife.com
www.medandlife.com

Pharmaceutical Research Institute
ul. Rydygiera 8; 01-793 Warszawa
tel.: (+48-22) 6338555
fax: (+48-22) 6338296
e-mail: ichp@ichp.pl
www.ichp.waw.pl

Road and Bridge Research Institute
ul. Jagiellońska 80; 03-301 Warszawa
tel.: (+48-22) 8113231
fax: (+48-22) 8111792
e-mail: ibidim@ibidim.edu.pl

Rokita-Agro S.A.
ul. Sienkiewicza 4, 56-120 Brzeg Dolny
tel.: (+48 71) 7942040
fax: (+48 71) 7942150
e-mail: agro@rokita-agro.com.pl
www.rokita-agro.com.pl

Transition Technologies S.A.
ul. Pawia 55; 01-130 Warszawa
tel.: (+48-22) 3318020
fax: (+48-22) 3318030
e-mail: tt@tt.com.pl www.tt.com.pl

VIGO System S.A.
ul. Świetlików 3; 01-389 Warszawa
tel.: (+48-22) 6660145
fax: (+48-22) 6660159
e-mail: info@vigo.com.pl
www.vigo.com.pl

X-Serwis Sp. z o.o.
ul. Piłsudskiego 200; 05-260 Marki
tel.:(+48-22) 7619168
fax: (+48-22) 7619168
www.x-serwis.casper.pl

Association of Polish Inventors
Stowarzyszenie Polskich Wynalazców
i Racjonalizatorów
ul. Rydygiera 8; 01-793 Warszawa
tel./fax: (+48-22) 6338482, 6339511 ext.2105
e-mail: spwir@spwir.org.pl
www.spwir.org.pl

European Institute of Technology
Europejski Instytut Technologiczny
ul. Spółdzielcza 10, 87-800 Włocławek
tel./fax: (+48-54) 4119020
e-mail: eit@w3wl.pl, rcie@w3wl.pl

APPENDIX 25

SPECIAL ECONOMIC ZONES

Special Economic Zone in Kamienna Góra
Kamiennogórska Specjalna Strefa Ekonomiczna
Małej Przedsiębiorczości S.A.
ul. Jana Pawła II 11a; 58-400 Kamienna Góra
tel.: (+48-75) 6451503 do 06; fax: 7442017
e-mail: strefa@ssemp.pl www.ssemp.pl

Special Economic Zone in Katowice
Katowicka Specjalna Strefa Ekonomiczna S.A.
ul. Sienkiewicza 28; 40-032 Katowice
tel.: (+48-32) 2510736; fax: 2513766
e-mail: ksse@ksse.com.pl www.ksse.com.pl

Special Economic Zone in Kostrzyn-Słubice
Kostrzyńsko-Słubicka Specjalna Strefa Ekonomiczna
ul. Orła Białego 22; 66-470 Kostrzyn n. Odrą
tel.: (+48-95) 7219800; fax: 7524167
e-mail: info@kssse.pl www.kssse.pl

Special Economic Zone in Kraków
Specjalna Strefa Ekonomiczna
Krakowski Park Technologiczny
Centrum Zaawansowanych Technologii-Kraków
ul. Jana Pawła II 37; 31-864 Kraków
tel.: (+48-12) 6401940; fax: 6401945
e-mail: biuro@sse.krakow.pl www.sse.krakow.pl

Special Economic Zone in Legnica
Legnicka Specjalna Strefa Ekonomiczna S.A.
ul. Kardynała B. Kominka 9; 59-220 Legnica
tel.: (+48-76) 8522446/7; fax: 8522443
e-mail: strefaleg@cuprum.com.pl
www.cuprum.com.pl/strefa

Special Economic Zone in Łódź
Łódzka Specjalna Strefa Ekonomiczna
ul. Ks. Tymienieckiego 22/24; 90-349 Łódź
tel./fax: (+48-42) 6762753; fax: 6762755
e-mail: info@sse.lodz.pl www.sse.lodz.pl

Special Economic Zone in Mielec
Agencja Rozwoju Przemysłu Oddział w Mielcu
EURO-PARK Mielec
ul. Partyzantów 25; 39-300 Mielec
tel.: (+48-17) 7887236; fax: 7887769
e-mail: europark@europark.com.pl
www.europark.com.pl

Special Economic Zone in Olsztyn
Warmińsko-Mazurska
Specjalna Strefa Ekonomiczna S.A.
ul. Mickiewicza 21/23; 10-508 Olsztyn
tel.fax: (+48-89) 5350241
e-mail: wmsse@wmsse.com.pl www.wmsse.com.pl

Special Economic Zone in Słupsk
Słupska Specjalna Strefa Ekonomiczna
Pomorska Agencja Rozwoju Regionalnego S.A.
ul. Poznańska 1a; 76-200 Słupsk
tel./fax: (+48-59) 8425116, 8413261
e-mail: office@parr.slupsk.pl www.sse.slupsk.pl

Special Economic Zone in Starachowice
Specjalna Strefa Ekonomiczna Starachowice S.A.
ul. Radomska 29; 27-200 Starachowice
tel.: (+48-41) 2754101; fax: 2754102
e-mail: sekretariat@sse.com.pl www.sse.com.pl

Special Economic Zone in Suwałki
Suwalska Specjalna Strefa Ekonomiczna S.A.
ul. Noniewicza 49; 16-400 Suwałki
tel/fax: (+48-87) 5652217
e-mail: ssse@ssse.com.pl www.ssse.com.pl

Special Economic Zone in Tarnobrzeg
Agencja Rozwoju Przemysłu S.A.
Tarnobrzeska Specjalna Strefa Ekonomiczna
EURO-PARK Wisłostan
ul. Zakładowa 48; 39-405 Tarnobrzeg-Machów
tel.: (+48-15) 8229999 tel/fax: 8236888
e-mail: biuro@tsse.pl www.tsse.pl

Special Economic Zone in Wałbrzych
Wałbrzyska Specjalna Strefa Ekonomiczna
Invest-Park Sp. z o.o.
ul. Uczniowska 21; 58-306 Wałbrzych
tel.: (+48-74) 6649164; fax: 8410177
e-mail: invest@invest-park.com.pl
www.invest-park.com.pl

Special Economic Zone in Gdańsk
Pomorska Specjalna Strefa Ekonomiczna
ul. Władysława IV 9; 80-703 Sopot
tel.: (+48-58) 5559700; fax: 5559711
e-mail: marketing@strefa.gda.pl www.strefa.gda.pl

APPENDIX 26

BANKS OPERATING IN POLAND
(Head Offices – Excluding Co-operative Banks)

Name of Bank	Address	Telephone Fax
Narodowy Bank Polski	00-919 Warszawa ul. Świętokrzyska 11/21	0-22 6531000 8264123
ABN AMRO Bank (Polska) SA	02-134 Warszawa ul. 1 Sierpnia 8A	0-22 5730500 5730501
AIG Bank Polska SA	00-450 Warszawa ul. Przemysłowa 26A	0-22 5235300 5235350
Bank BPH SA	31-548 Kraków ul. Pokoju 1	0-12 6187411 6187593
Bank Gospodarki Żywnościowej SA	01-211 Warszawa ul. Kasprzaka 10/16	0-22 8604000 8605000
Bank Gospodarstwa Krajowego	00-955 Warszawa Al. Jerozolimskie 7	0-22 5229112 6270378
Bank Handlowy w Warszawie SA	00-923 Warszawa ul. Senatorska 16	0-22 6577200 6577580
Bank Inicjatyw Społeczno-Ekonomicznych SA	00-184 Warszawa ul. Dubois 5A	0-22 8601100 8601103
Bank Millenium SA	02-017 Warszawa Al. Jerozolimskie 123A	0-22 6575718 6575059
Bank Ochrony Środowiska SA	00-950 Warszawa Al. Jana Pawła II 12	0-22 8508735 8508891
Bank of Tokyo-Mitsubishi (Polska) SA	00-113 Warszawa ul. Emilii Plater 53	0-22 5208165 5205236
Bank Pocztowy SA	85-959 Bydgoszcz ul. Jagiellońska 17	0-52 3499100 3270407
Bank Polska Kasa Opieki SA Grupa Pekao SA	00-950 Warszawa ul. Grzybowska 53/57	0-22 6560000 6560203
Bank Przemysłowo-Handlowy PBK SA	31-548 Kraków Al. Pokoju 1	0-12 4223333 4216914
Bank Przemysłowy SA	90-365 Łódź ul. Tymienieckiego 5	0-42 6402790 6845513
Bank Rozwoju Budownictwa Mieszkaniowego SA	00-099 Warszawa ul. Senatorska 29/31	0-22 3329010 8275470
Bank Rozwoju Cukrownictwa SA	60-959 Poznań ul. Mickiewicza 33	0-61 8532201 8532385
Bank Svenska Handelsbanken (Polska) SA	02-135 Warszawa ul. Iłżecka 26	0-22 8787387 8787388
Bank Współpracy Europejskiej SA	00-082 Warszawa ul. Senatorska 14	0-22 3386800 8260261
Bank Zachodni WBK SA	50-950 Wrocław Rynek 9/11	0-71 3701000 3702787
Banque PSA Finance S.A. Oddział w Polsce	00-095 Warszawa pl. Bankowy 2	0-22 5311811 5311817

Name of Bank	Address	Telephone Fax
BNP - Paribas Bank Polska SA	00-108 Warszawa ul. Zielna 41/43	0-22 6546263 6972329
BPH Bank Hipoteczny SA	00-805 Warszawa ul. Chmielna 132/134	0-22 6562169 6562188
BRE Bank Hipoteczny SA	00-609 Warszawa Al. Armii ludowej 26	0-22 5797500 5797589
BRE Bank SA	00-950 Warszawa ul. Senatorska 18	0-22 8290000 8290033
CC - Bank SA	60-324 Poznań ul. Marcelińska 90	0-61 8609400 8609402
Calyon Bank Polska SA	00-950 Warszawa Al. Jerozolimskie 65/79	0-22 6306888 6354500
Cetelem Bank SA	03-738 Warszawa ul. Kijowska 1	0-22 5118888 5118800
DaimlerChrysler Services Bank Polska SA	02-460 Warszawa ul. Gottlieba Daimlera 1	0-22 3127800 3126710
Danske Bank Polska SA	00-688 Warszawa ul. Emilii Plater 28	0-22 3377100 3377101
Deutsche Bank PBC SA	31-047 Kraków ul. J. Sarego 2 i 4	0-12 6182388 4219652
Deutsche Bank Polska SA	00-609 Warszawa al. Armii Ludowej 26	0-22 5799000 5799001
DOMINET BANK SA	59-300 Lubin ul. Tysiąclecia 2	0-76 8404100 8404103
Dresdner Bank Polska SA	02-017 Warszawa al. Jerozolimskie 123	0-22 5253112 5253159
DZ Bank Polska SA	Pl. Piłsudskiego 3 00-078 Warszawa	0-22 5057000 5057442
Euro Bank SA	50-126 Wrocław ul. Świętego Mikołaja 72	0-71 7955500 7955501
FCE Bank Polska SA	02-222 Warszawa Al. Jerozolimskie 181	0-22 6086900 6086901
Fiat Bank Polska SA	02-678 Warszawa ul. Szturmowa 2	0-22 6074801 6074849
Fortis Bank Polska SA	02-676 Warszawa ul. Postępu 15	0-22 5669000 5669010
GE Bank Mieszkaniowy SA	02-822 Warszawa ul. Poleczki 21	0-22 5450500 5450501
GE Capital Bank SA	80-853 Gdańsk ul. Wały Jagiellońskie 36	0-58 3040634 3007952
GE Money Bank SA	80-894 Gdańsk ul. Elżbietańska 2	0-58 3007001 3040701
Getin Bank SA	40-479 Katowice ul. Pszczyńska 10	0-32 2008823 2008685
GMAC Bank Polska SA	02-515 Warszawa ul. Puławska 15	0-22 5215400 5215401
Gospodarczy Bank Wielkopolski SA	61-725 Poznań ul. Mielżyńskiego 22	0-61 8562400 8522730

Name of Bank	Address	Telephone Fax
Górnośląski Bank Gospodarczy SA	40-006 Katowice ul. Warszawska 6	0-32 2008500 2008685
HSBC Bank Polska SA	00-073 Warszawa ul. Piłsudskiego 2	0-22 3540500 3540510
ING Bank Śląski SA	40-086 Katowice ul. Sokolska 34	0-32 3577000 7353740
INVEST - BANK SA	04-175 Warszawa ul. Ostrobramska 77	0-22 5145100 5145106
Jyskie Bank A/S S.A. Oddział w Polsce	00-103 Warszawa ul. Królewska 16	0-22 5386996 5386997
Kredyt Bank SA	01-211 Warszawa ul. Kasprzaka 2/8	0-22 6345400 6345335
LUKAS Bank SA	53-605 Wrocław ul. Orląt Lwowskich 1	0-71 3559511 3553005
Mazowiecki Bank Regionalny SA	01-747 Warszawa ul. Elbląska 15/17	0-22 5600400 5600409
NORD.LB Bank Polska Norddeutsche Landesbank SA	00-380 Warszawa ul. Kruczkowskiego 8	0-22 5250700 5254110
Nordea Bank Polska SA	81-303 Gdynia ul. Kielecka 2	0-58 6691111 6691110
Nykredit Bank Hipoteczny SA	00-103 Warszawa ul. Królewska 16	0-22 5386000 5386001
Powszechna Kasa Oszczędności - Bank Polski SA	00-975 Warszawa ul. Puławska 15	0-22 5356565
PTF Bank SA	50-062 Wrocław Plac Solny 16	0-71 3748666 3748500
Rabobank Polska SA	00-958 Warszawa al. Jana Pawła II 27	0-22 6535000 6535004
Raiffeisen Bank Polska SA	00-549 Warszawa ul. Piękna 20	0-22 5852000 5852585
Societe Generale SA - Succursale de Varsovie	00-102 Warszawa ul. Marszałkowska 111	0-22 5284000 5284444
Svenska Handelsbanken AB SA Oddział w Polsce	02-135 Warszawa ul. Iłżecka 26	0-22 8787387 8787388
Sygma Banque Societe Anonyme (SA) Oddział w Polsce	00-807 Warszawa Al. Jerozolimskie 92	0-22 4564704 4564701
Śląski Bank Hipoteczny SA	02-587 Warszawa ul. Wiktorska 63	0-22 5401700 5401701
Toyota Bank Polska SA	02-672 Warszawa ul. Domaniewska 41	0-22 8744755 8744754
Volkswagen Bank Polska SA	00-828 Warszawa Al. Jana Pawła II 15	0-22 5387000 5387888
WesLB Bank Polska SA	02-781 Warszawa ul. Rtm. Witolda Pileckiego 65	0-22 6530500 6530501
Wschodni Bank Cukrownictwa SA	20-022 Lublin ul. Okopowa 1	0-81 5322220 5329005

Source: National Bank of Poland, 2005

APPENDIX 27

REPRESENTATIVE OFFICES OF FOREIGN BANKS IN POLAND

Name of the Bank	Address	Telephone Fax
American Express Bank Ltd., New York	00-121 Warszawa ul. Sienna 39	0-22 5815268 5815269
BELARUSBANK, Minsk	02-511 Warszawa ul. Bielawska 6 m.57	0-22 6460595 8444480
BELPROMSTROJBANK, Minsk	00-950 Warszawa ul. Krucza 6/14 apt. 206,207	0-22 6218979 6210693
BELINVESTBANK, Minsk	02-611 Warszawa ul. Krasickiego 12A m.1	0-22 8443301 8443301
BELVNESHECONOMBANK, Minsk	02-703 Warszawa ul. Bukowińska 24A apt.118	0-22 8530127 8475180
BANCA-INTESA S.p.A., Milan	00-175 Warszawa al. Jana Pawła II 80 lok. 58	0-22 4354710 4354712
Banca Nazionale del Lavoro S.p.A., Rome	00-697 Warszawa Al. Jerozolimskie 65/79 p.1824	0-22 6306780 6306781
Bank of America, National Association, Charlotte	02-135 Warszawa ul. Iłżecka 26	0-22 5757200 5757406
Crédit Industriel et Commercial, Paris	00-193 Warszawa ul. Stawki 2	0-22 8606503 8606504
EUROHYPO Aktiengesellschaft Europaeische Hypothekenbank der Deutschen Bank	00-609 Warszawa ul. Armii Ludowej 26	0-22 5797780 5797780
HSH Nordbank AG, Hamburg	00-113 Warszawa ul. Emilii Plater 53	0-22 4561060 4561069
Investkredit Bank AG, Wien	00-121 Warszawa ul. Sienna 39	0-22 8503300 8503301
Istituto Bancario San Paolo di Torino - Istituto Mobiliare Italiano S.p.A., Turin	00-193 Warszawa ul. Stawki 2	0-22 8606200 8606205
JPMorgan Chase Bank, New York	00-113 Warszawa ul. Emilii Plater 53	0-22 5205100 5205120
Landesbank Baden - Wuerttemberg, Stuttgart	00-845 Warszawa ul. Łucka 20 apt. 15	0-22 6541689 6541687
The Export-Import Bank, Taiwan, Taipei	02-672 Warszawa ul. Domaniewska 41	0-22 8743582 8743583
UBS AG, Zurych & Basel	00-536 Warszawa Al. Ujazdowskie 51	0-22 5258400 5258433

Source: National Bank of Poland, 2005

APPENDIX 28

NATIONAL INVESTMENT FUNDS

I National Investment Fund
FUND 1. SA
Ballinger Capital Sp. z o.o.
ul. Dworkowa 3; 00-784 Warszawa
tel.: (+48-22) 6468546; fax: 6468536
www.ballinger.com.pl

II National Investment Fund SA
NIF Management Sp. z o.o.
ul.Emilii Plater 53, 00-113 Warszawa
tel: (+48-22) 520 93 50, fax: 520 93 51
e-mail: management@ca-ib.com.pl
www.ca-ib.com.pl

IV National Investment Fund
PROGRESS SA
NIF Management Sp. z o.o.
ul.Emilii Plater 53, 00-113 Warszawa
tel: (+48-22) 5209350, fax: 5209351
e-mail: management@ca-ib.com.pl
www.ca-ib.com.pl

V National Investment Fund
VICTORIA SA
Ballinger Capital Sp. z o.o.
ul. Dworkowa 3; 00-784 Warszawa
tel.: (+48-22) 6468546; fax: 6468536
www.ballinger.com.pl

VI National Investment Fund
MAGNA POLONIA SA
AIB WBK Fund Management Sp. z o.o.
Al. Jana Pawła II 25; 00-854 Warszawa
tel.: (+48-22) 6534700; fax: 6534707
e-mail: aibfund@aib.pl
www.magnapolonia.com.pl

VII National Investment Fund
KAZIMIERZ WIELKI SA
ul. Zwycięzców 28/51; 03-938 Warszawa
tel.: (+48-22) 7406740; fax: 6725115
e-mail: biuro@7nfi.pl

VIII National Investment Fund
OCTAVA SA
ul. Królewska 16, 00-103 Warszawa
tel.: (+48-22) 3306333, fax:3306300
www.octava.com.pl

IX National Investment Fund
E. KWIATKOWSKI SA
NIF Management Sp. z o.o.
ul. Emilii Plater 53, 00-113 Warszawa
tel: (+48-22) 5209333, fax: 5209351
e-mail: management@ca-ib.com.pl
www.ca-ib.com.pl

X National Investment Fund
FOKSAL SA
ul. Zwycięzców 28/18A; 03-938 Warszawa
tel.: (+48-22) 7406770...74; fax: 6728051
e-mail: office@foksalnfi.com.pl
www.foksalnfi.com.pl

III and XI National Investment Fund
JUPITER SA
Trinity Management Sp. z o.o.
ul. Nowogrodzka 47a; 00-695 Warszawa
tel.: (+48-22) 5259900; fax: 5259988
e-mail: jupiter@jupiter-nfi.pl
www.jupiter-nfi.pl

XII National Investment Fund
PIAST SA
ul. Królewska 16, 00-103 Warszawa
tel.: (+48-22) 3306333, fax: 3306300
www.piast.com.pl

XIII National Investment Fund
FORTUNA SA
Ballinger Capital Sp. z o.o.
ul. Dworkowa 3; 00-784 Warszawa
tel.: (+48-22) 6468546; fax: 6468536
www@ballinger.com.pl

XIV National Investment Fund
ZACHODNI SA
ul. Żurawia 22, 00-515 Warszawa
tel.: (+48-22) 4389220; fax:4389221
e-mail: info@zachodninfi.pl

XV National Investment Fund
NFI Empik Media & Fashion S.A.
ul. Żurawia 8, 00-508 Warszawa
tel.: (+48-22) 5833771; fax: 6234057
e-mail: info@emf.pl
www.emf.pl

APPENDIX 29

SELECTED BILATERAL CHAMBERS OF TRADE AND INDUSTRY

Association of Cooperation between Poland and the East
ul. Marszałkowska 115; 00-102 Warszawa
tel.(+48-22) 6200301; fax: 8269601
e-mail: zkswpw@wp.pl

American Chamber of Commerce in Poland
Amerykańska Izba Gospodarcza w Polsce
ul. Emilii Plater 53; 00-113 Warszawa
tel.: (+48-22) 5205999; fax: 5205998
www.amcham.com.pl

Polish-Azerbaijan Chamber of Commerce
Polsko-Azerbejdżańska Izba Gospodarcza
ul. Kawia 13/15; 42-200 Częstochowa
tel.: (+48-34) 3612550; fax: 3613126 ext.18
e-mail: paig@bigduo.pl

British Chamber of Commerce in Poland
Brytyjska Izba Handlowa w Polsce
ul. Fabryczna 16/22, 00-446 Warszawa
tel.: (+48-22) 6545971; fax: 6211937
www.bpcc.org.pl

French Chamber of Trade & Industry in Poland
Francuska Izba Handlowo-Przemysłowa w Polsce
ul. Mokotowska 19, 00-560 Warszawa
tel.: (+48-22) 6967580; fax: 6967590
www.ccifp.pl

Italian Foreign Trade Institute
Włoski Instytut Handlu Zagranicznego
ul. Marszałkowska 72, 00-545 Warszawa
tel.: (+48-22) 6280243; fax: 6280600
www.italtrade.com/polska

Poland-Israel Chamber of Commerce
Izba Gospodarcza Polska-Izrael
ul. Trębacka 4; 00-074 Warszawa
tel.: (+48-22) 6309798; fax: 8274673

Polish-Belarussian Chamber of Trade & Industry
Polsko-Białoruska Izba Handlowo-Przemysłowa
ul. Trębacka 4, 00-074 Warszawa
tel: (+48-22) 6309844; fax: 6309946
e-mail: pbihp@chamber.pl
www.chamber.pl

Polish-Belgian-Luxembourgian Chamber of Commerce
Polsko-Belgijsko-Luksemburska Izba Handlowa
ul. Trębacka 4; 00-074 Warszawa
tel.: (+48-22) 6309773; fax: 6309974
www.polbelux.pl

Polish-German Chamber of Commerce
Polsko-Niemiecka Izba Przemysłowo-Handlowa
ul. Miodowa 14; 00-952 Warszawa
tel.: (+48-22) 5310500; fax: 5310600
e-mail: info@ihk.pl
www.ihk.pl

Polish-Kazakhstan Chamber of Commerce
Polsko-Kazachstańska Izba Gospodarcza
ul. Nowowiejska 10; 00-643 Warszawa
tel./fax: (+48-22) 8758567

Union of Chambers of Commerce and Industry of Kazakhstan - Representative Office in Poland
Przedstawicielstwo Związku Izb Handlowo-Przemysłowych Republiki Kazachstan w Polsce
ul. Nowowiejska 10; 00-643 Warszawa
tel.: (+48-22) 8758567

Polish-Latvian Chamber of Commerce
Polsko-Łotewska Izba Gospodarcza
ul. Trębacka 4; 00-074 Warszawa
tel.: (+48-22) 6309823; fax: 8274673

Polish-Lithuanian Chamber of Commerce
Polsko-Litewska Izba Gospodarcza Rynków Wschodnich
ul. Kościuszki 76, 16-400 Suwałki
tel. (+48-87) 5632600 fax: 5632602
www.plig.org.pl

Polish-Russian Chamber of Trade & Industry
Polsko-Rosyjska Izba Handlowo-Przemysłowa
ul. Zimna 16, 00-138 Warszawa
tel.: (+48-22) 6547373, 6547399; fax: 6547388

Polish-Swiss Chamber of Industry & Trade
Polsko-Szwajcarska Izba Przemysłu i Handlu
ul. Szpitalna 6/11; 00-031 Warszawa
tel.: (+48-22) 8277621; fax: 8277623
e-mail: psiph@psiph.pl
www.psiph.pl

Polish-Ukrainian Chamber of Commerce
Polsko-Ukrainska Izba Gospodarcza
ul. Trębacka 4, 00-074 Warszawa
tel: (+48-22) 6309929; fax: 6309793
e-mail: puig@chamber.pl
www.chamber.pl

Scandinavian-Polish Chamber of Commerce
Skandynawsko-Polska Izba Gospodarcza
Wiśniowa 40b apt.3, 02-520 Warszawa
tel.: (+48-22) 8497414; fax: 6464930
www.spcc.pl

APPENDIX 30

EMBASSIES AND COMMERCIAL COUNSELLORS' OFFICES IN POLAND

Embassy of Afghanistan
ul. Goplańska 1, 02-954 Warsaw
tel.: (+48-22) 8855410, fax: 8856500
www.afghanembassy.com.pl

Embassy of the Republic of Albania
ul. Altowa 1, 02-386 Warsaw
tel.: 8241427; fax: 8241426
e-mail: alb@atos.warman.com.pl

Embassy of the People's Democratic Republic of Algeria
ul. Dąbrowiecka 21, 03-932 Warsaw
tel.: (+48-22) 6175855; fax: 6160081
e-mail: ambalgva@zigzag.pl

Embassy of the Republic of Angola
ul. Balonowa 20, 02-635 Warsaw
tel.: (+48-22) 6463529
e-mail: embaixada@emb-angola.pl

Embassy of the Argentine Republic
ul. Brukselska 9, 03-973 Warsaw
tel.: (+48-22) 6176028; fax: 6177162
Economic Section:
e-mail: epolo@home.pl

Embassy of the Republic of Armenia
ul. A. Waszkowskiego 11, 02-913 Warsaw
tel.: (+48-22) 8408620; fax: 6420643
e-mail: main@embarmenia.it.pl

Australian Embassy
ul. Nowogrodzka 11, 3rd floor, 00-513 Warsaw
tel.: (+48-22) 5213444; fax: 6273500
e-mail: ambasada@australia.pl
www.australia.pl

Embassy of the Republic of Austria
ul. Gagarina 34, 00-748 Warsaw
tel.: (+48-22) 8410081…84; fax: 8410085
e-mail: warschau-ob@bmaa.gv.at
Commercial Section:
ul. Idzikowskiego 7/9, 02-704 Warsaw
tel.: (+48-22) 8437909, 8439932; fax: 8439505
e-mail: warschau@austriantrade.org

Embassy of the Republic of Azerbaijan
ul. Zwycięzców 12, 03-941 Warsaw
tel.: (+48-22) 6162188, fax: 6161949
e-mail: info@azer-embassy.pl

Embassy of the Republic of Belarus
ul. Wiertnicza 58, 02-952 Warsaw
tel.: (+48-22) 7420990, 8425202; fax: 7420980
www.belembassy.org/poland

Embassy of the Kingdom of Belgium
ul. Senatorska 34, 00-095 Warsaw
tel.: (+48-22) 5512800; fax: 5512888
e-mail: ambabel.warsaw@pol.pl
Economic and Commercial Office for the Flemish Region:
ul. Senatorska 34; 00-095 Warsaw
tel.: (+48-22) 8280878, 8263897; fax: 8278136
e-mail: vlev.warschau@pol.pl
Economic and Commercial Office for the Walloon Region (AWEX):
ul. Skorupki 5, 00-546 Warsaw
tel.: (+48-22) 5837011; fax: 5837019
e-mail: awex.varsovie@pol.pl
Economic and Commercial Office for the Brussels Capital Region:
pl. Bankowy 2, 00-095 Warsaw
tel.: (+48-22) 5311824, 5311825; fax: 5311826
e-mail: brussels-polska@pol.pl

Embassy of the Federative Republic of Brazil
ul. Poselska 11, 03-931 Warsaw
tel.: (+48-22) 6174800; fax: 6178689
e-mail: brasil@brasil.org.pl
www.brasil.org.pl

British Embassy
Al. Róż 1, 00-556 Warsaw
tel.: (+48-22) 3110000; fax: 3110311
e-mail: info@britishembassy.pl
Commercial Section:
ul. Emilii Plater 28, 2nd floor, 00-688 Warsaw
tel.: (+48-22) 3110000; fax: 3110250

Embassy of the Republic of Bulgaria
Al. Ujazdowskie 33/35, 00-540 Warsaw
tel.: (+48-22) 6294071...75; fax: 6282271
e-mail: office@bgemb.com.pl
Commercial Section:
tel.: (+48-22) 6294111, 6212535; fax: 6255989
e-mail: n.kostov@mi.government.bg

Canadian Embassy
ul. Matejki 1/5, 00-481 Warsaw
tel.: (+48-22) 5843100, fax: 5843182
e-mail: wsaw@international.gc.ca
www.canada.pl

Embassy of Chile
ul. Okrężna 62, 02-925 Warsaw
tel.: (+48-22) 8582330…33; fax: 8582329
www.embachile.pl
Commercial Section e-mail: prochile@onet.pl

Embassy of the People's Republic of China
ul. Bonifraterska 1, 00-203 Warsaw
tel.: (+48-22) 8313836; fax: 6354211
www.chinaembassy.org.pl
Commercial Counsellor
ul. Bonifraterska 1, tel.: (+48-22) 8313861

Embassy of the Republic of Colombia
ul. Zwycięzców 29, 03-936 Warsaw
tel.: (+48-22) 6170973; fax: 6176684
e-mail: embcol@medianet.pl

Embassy of the Democratic Republic of Congo
ul. Miączyńska 50, 02-637 Warsaw
tel.: (+48-22) 8496999, fax: 8485215
e-mail: ambardcvarsovia@yahoo.fr

Embassy of the Republic of Costa Rica
ul. Kubickiego 9 m. 5, 02-954 Warsaw
tel.: (+48-22) 8589112; fax: 6427832
e-mail: emcoripol@neostrada.pl

Embassy of the Republic of Croatia
ul. Ignacego Krasickiego 10, 02-628 Warsaw
tel.: (+48-22) 8442393; fax: 8444808
e-mail: croemb@croatia.pol.pl

Embassy of the Republic of Cuba
ul. Rejtana 15 m. 8, 02-516 Warsaw
tel.: (+48-22) 8481715; fax: 8482231
e-mail: embacuba@medianet.pl

Embassy of the Republic of Cyprus
ul. Pilicka 4, 02-629 Warsaw
tel.: (+48-22) 8444577; fax: 8442558
e-mail: embassyofcyprus@neostrada.pl

Embassy of the Czech Republic
ul. Koszykowa 18, 00-555 Warsaw
tel.: (+48-22) 6287221...25; fax: 6298045
e-mail: warsaw@embassy.mzv.cz
www.mfa.cz/warsaw
Economic and Commercial Section
tel.: (+48-22) 6281957; fax: 6219880

Royal Danish Embassy
ul. Rakowiecka 19, 02-517 Warsaw
tel.: (+48-22) 5652900; fax: 5652970
e-mail: wawamb@um.dk
www.danishembassy.pl
Commercial and Economic Section
tel.: (+48-22) 5652917; fax: 5652973

Embassy of the Republic of Ecuador
ul. Rejtana 15 m. 15, 02-516 Warsaw
tel.: (+48-22) 8487230; fax: 8488196
e-mail: mecuapol@it.com.pl
www.mmrree.gov.ec

Embassy of the Arab Republic of Egypt
ul. Alzacka 18, 03-972 Warsaw
tel.: (+48-22) 6176973; fax: 617 90 58
e-mail: embassyofegypt@neostrada.pl
Commercial Section:
ul. Alzacka 3 C, 03-972 Warsaw
tel.: (+48-22) 6161368; fax: 6161370
e-mail: office@egyptcomoff.org.pl

Embassy of the Republic of Estonia
ul. Karwińska 1, 02-639 Warsaw
tel.: (+48-22) 8811810; fax: 8811812
e-mail: embassy.varssavi@mfa.ee
www.estemb.pl

Embassy of Finland
ul. Chopina 4/8, 00-559 Warsaw
tel.: (+48-22) 6294091; fax: 6213442
e-mail: sanomat.var@formin.fi
Commercial Section: fax: 6216394
e-mail: info@ftc.com.pl

Embassy of France
ul. Piekna 1, 00-477 Warsaw
tel.: (+48-22) 5293000; fax: 5293001
e-mail: presse@ambafrance-pl.org
www.ambafrance-pl.org
Commercial Service:
tel.: (+48-22) 5293100; fax: 5293101
e-mail: varsovie@missioneco.org
http://www.missioneco.org/pologne/

Embassy of Georgia
ul. Wąchocka 1 S, 03-934 Warsaw
tel./fax: (+48-22) 3531650, fax: 4997752
e-mail: geoemb@mfa.go.ge

Embassy of the Federal Republic of Germany
ul. Dąbrowiecka 30, 03-932 Warsaw
tel.: (+48-22) 5841700; fax: 5841729
e-mail: zreg@wars.auswaertiges-amt.de
www.ambasadaniemiec.pl
Commercial and Economic Section:
ul. Jazdów 12 B, 00-467 Warsaw
tel.: (+48-22) 5841900; fax: 5841919

Embassy of Hellenic Republic
ul. Górnośląska 35, 00-432 Warsaw
tel.: (+48-22) 6229460; fax: 6229464
e-mail: embassy@greece.pl
www.greece.pl

Economic and Commercial Office:
Krakowskie Przedmieście 47/51, 00-071 Warsaw
tel.: (+48-22) 8264828; fax: 8264008
e-mail: ecotrade@greece.pl

Embassy of the Republic of Hungary
ul. Chopina 2, 00-559 Warsaw
tel.: (+48-22) 6284451...55; fax: 6218561
e-mail: varsnk@2a.pl
Commercial Section:
ul. Szwoleżerów 10, 00-464 Warsaw
tel.: (+48-22) 8413551; fax: 8413863
e-mail: itdwarszawa@business2hungary.pl

Embassy of India
ul. Rejtana 15 apt. 2-7, 02-516 Warsaw
tel.: (+48-22) 8495800; fax: 8496705
e-mail: goi@indem.it.pl
www.indianembassy.pl

Embassy of the Republic of Indonesia
ul. Estońska 3/5, 03-903 Warsaw
tel.: (+48-22) 6175179; fax: 6174455
e-mail: info@indonesianembassy.pl
www.indonesianembassy.pl

Embassy of the Islamic Republic of Iran
ul. Królowej Aldony 22, 03-928 Warsaw
tel.: (+48-22) 6171585; fax: 6178452
e-mail: iranemb@iranemb.warsaw.pl
www.iranemb.warsaw.pl

Liaison Office of the Republic of Iraq
ul. Dąbrowiecka 9 A, 03-932 Warsaw
tel.: (+48-22) 6175773, 6174911; fax: 6177065
e-mail: ambasada.iraku@neostrada.pl

Embassy of Ireland
ul. Mysia 5, 00-498 Warsaw
tel.: (+48-22) 8496633, 8496655; fax: 8498431
e-mail: ambasada@irlandia.pl
www.irlandia.pl
Commercial Section:
tel.: (+48-22) 6469797; fax: 6465015

Embassy of Israel
ul. Krzywickiego 24, 02-078 Warsaw
tel.: (+48-22) 8250028, 8250923; fax: 8251607
e-mail: publicaffairs@warsaw.mfa.gov.il
www.israel.pl

Embassy of Italy
pl. Dąbrowskiego 6, 00-055 Warsaw
tel.: (+48-22) 8263471; fax: 8278507
e-mail: ambasciata@italianembassy.pl
www.italianembassy.pl

Embassy of Japan
ul. Szwoleżerów 8, 00-464 Warsaw
tel.: (+48-22) 6965000; fax: 6965001
e-mail: kazdipmis@hot.pl
www.emb-japan.pl

Embassy of the Republic of Kazakhstan
ul. Królowej Marysieńki 14, 02-954 Warsaw
tel.: (+48-22) 6425388; fax: 6423427
www.kazakhstan.pl

Embassy of the Democratic People's Republic of Korea
ul. Bobrowiecka 1 A, 00-728 Warsaw
tel.: (+48-22) 8405813; fax: 8405710
e-mail: dprkemb_pl@hotmail.com

Embassy of the Republic of Korea
ul. Szwoleżerów 6, 00-464 Warsaw
tel.: (+48-22) 5592900; fax: 5592905
e-mail: koremb_waw@mofat.go.kr

Embassy of the State of Kuwait
ul. Franciszka Nullo 13, 00-486 Warsaw
tel.: (+48-22) 6222860; fax: 6274314
e-mail: embassy@kue.com.pl

Embassy of the Lao People's Democratic Republic
ul. Rejtana 15 m. 26, 02-516 Warsaw
tel.: (+48-22) 8484786; fax: 8497122
e-mail: embassylaos@yahoo.com

Embassy of the Republic of Latvia
ul. Królowej Aldony 19, 03-928 Warsaw
tel.: (+48-22) 6174389; fax: 6174289
e-mail: embassy.poland@mfa.gov.lv

Embassy of Lebanon
ul. Starościńska 1 B m. 10-11, 02-516 Warsaw
tel.: (+48-22) 8445065; fax: 6460030
e-mail: embleban@pol.pl

People's Bureau of the Great Socialist People's Libyan Arab Jamahiriya
ul. Kryniczna 2, 03-934 Warsaw
tel.: (+48-22) 6174822; fax: 6175091
e-mail: alfath2@ikp.atm.com.pl

Embassy of the Republic of Lithuania
al. Jana Chrystiana Szucha 5, 00-580 Warsaw
tel.: (+48-22) 6253368, 6290596; fax: 6253440
e-mail: ambasada@lietuva.pl
Commercial Section:
Al. Ujazdowskie 51, 00-536 Warsaw
tel.: (+48-22) 5847050; fax: 5847053
e-mail: com.attache_lit@post.pl

Embassy of the Republic of Macedonia FYR
ul. Królowej Marysieńki 40, 02-954 Warsaw
tel.: (+48-22) 6517291; tel./fax: 6517292
e-mail: ambrmwar@zigzag.pl
www.ambasadarm.zigzag.pl

Embassy of Malaysia
ul. Gruzińska 3, 03-902 Warsaw
tel.: (+48-22) 6173144; fax: 6176256
e-mail: mwwarsaw@it.com.pl

Embassy of Mexico
ul. Starościńska 1 B m. 4-5, 02-516 Warsaw
tel.: (+48-22) 6468800; fax: 6464222
e-mail: embamex@ikp.pl

Embassy of the Republic of Moldova
ul. Miłobędzka 12, 02-634 Warsaw
tel./fax: (+48-22) 6462099
e-mail: embassy@moldova.pl
www.moldova.pl

Embassy of Mongolia
ul. Rejtana 15 m. 16, 02-516 Warsaw
tel.: (+48-22) 8499391; fax: 8482063
e-mail: mongamb@ikp.atm.com.pl
www.ambmong.net7.pl

Embassy of the Kingdom of Morocco
ul. Starościńska 1 m. 11-12, 02-516 Warsaw
tel.: (+48-22) 8496341; fax: 8481840
e-mail: info@moroccoembassy.org.pl
www.moroccoembassy.org.pl

Royal Netherlands Embassy
ul. Kawalerii 10, 00-468 Warsaw
tel.: (+48-22) 5591200; fax: 8402638
e-mail: war@minbuza.nl
www.nlembassy.pl
Commercial Section:
tel.: (+48-22) 5591239
e-mail: war-ea@minbuza.nl

Embassy of the Federal Republic of Nigeria
ul. Wiertnicza 94, 02-952 Warsaw
tel.: (+48-22) 8486944; fax: 8485379
e-mail: info@nigeriaembassy.pl
www.nigeriaembassy.pl

Royal Norwegian Embassy
ul. Chopina 2 A, 00-559 Warsaw
tel.: (+48-22) 6964030; fax: 6280938
e-mail: emb.warsaw@mfa.no
www.amb-norwegia.pl
Commercial Section:
ul. Chmielna 85/87, 00-805 Warsaw
tel.: (+48-22) 5810581; fax: 5810981
e-mail: warsaw@invanor.no

Embassy of the Islamic Republic of Pakistan
ul. Starościńska 1 m. 1-2, 02-516 Warsaw
tel.: (+48-22) 8494808; fax: 8491160
e-mail: parepwarsaw@wp.pl
www.pakembwaw.com.pl

Embassy of Palestine
ul. Starościńska 1 m. 7, 02-516 Warsaw
tel.: (+48-22) 8497772; fax: 8567376
e-mail: info@palestyna.pl

Embassy of the Republic of Peru
ul. Starościńska 1 m. 3-4, 02-516 Warsaw
tel.: (+48-22) 6468806; fax: 6468617
e-mail: embperpl@atomnet.pl
www.perupol.pl

Embassy of Portugal
ul. Francuska 37, 03-905 Warsaw
tel.: (+48-22) 5111010; fax: 5111013
E-mial: embaixada@embport.internetdsl.pl
Commercial and Tourism Office:
ul. Francuska 37, 03-905 Warsaw
tel.: (+48-22) 6176460; fax: 6174477
e-mail: icepvars@icep.pl

Embassy of Romania
ul. Chopina 10, 00-559 Warsaw
tel.: (+48-22) 6283156; fax: 6285264
e-mail: embassy@roembassy.com.pl
Economic Section - tel.: (+48-22) 6283300

Embassy of the Russian Federation
ul. Belwederska 49, 00-761 Warsaw
tel.: (+48-22) 6213453, 6215575; fax: 6253016
e-mail: embassy@russia.internetdsl.pl
www.poland.mid.ru

Royal Embassy of Saudi Arabia
ul. Stępińska 55, 00-739 Warsaw
tel.: (+48-22) 8400000; fax: 8405636
e-mail: info@saudiembassy.pl
www.saudiembassy.pl

Embassy of Serbia and Montenegro
Al. Ujazdowskie 23/25, 00-540 Warsaw
tel.: (+48-22) 6285161; fax: 6297173
e-maill: yuabapl@zigzag.pl

Embassy of the Slovak Republic
ul. Litewska 6, 00-581 Warsaw
tel.: (+48-22) 5258110; fax: 5258122
e-mail: slovakia@ambasada-slowacji.pl
www.ambasada-slowacji.pl
Commercial Section:
tel.: (+48-22) 5258110; fax: 6252452
e-mail: obeo@varsava.mfa.sk

Embassy of the Republic of Slovenia
ul. Starościńska 1 m. 23-24, 02-516 Warsaw
tel.: (+48-22) 8498282; fax: 8484090
e-mail: vvr@mzz-dkp.gov.si

Embassy of the Republic of South Africa
ul. Koszykowa 54, 6th floor, 00-675 Warsaw
tel.: (+48-22) 6256228; fax: 6256270
e-mail: saembassy@supermedia.pl

Embassy of the Kingdom of Spain
ul. Myśliwiecka 4, 00-459 Warsaw
tel.: (+48-22) 6224250; fax: 6225408
e-mail: embesppl@mail.mae.es
Commercial Office:
ul. Genewska 16, 03-963 Warsaw
tel.: (+48-22) 6179408, 6176368; fax: 6172911
e-mail: varsovia@mcx.es

Embassy of the Democratic Socialist Republic of Sri Lanka
Al. Wilanowska 313 A, 02-665 Warsaw
tel.: (+48-22) 8538896; fax: 8435348
e-mail: lankaemb@medianet.pl
www.srilanka.pl

Embassy of Sweden
ul. Bagatela 3, 00-585 Warsaw
tel.: (+48-22) 6408900; fax: 6408983
e-mail: ambassaden.warszawa@foreign.ministry.se
www.swedishembassy.pl
Commercial Section:
ul. Wołodyjowskiego 74, 02-724 Warsaw
tel.: (+48-22) 8532030; fax: 8532021
e-mail: johan.holmberg@swedishtrade.se
www.swedishtrade.se

Embassy of Switzerland
Al. Ujazdowskie 27, 00-540 Warsaw
tel.: (+48-22) 6280481...82; fax: 6210548
e-mail: vertretung@var.rep.admin.ch

Embassy of the Syrian Arab Republic
ul. Narbutta 19 A, 02-536 Warsaw
tel.: (+48-22) 8484809, 8491456; fax: 8491847
www.syrian-embassy.com

Royal Thai Embassy
ul. Willowa 7, 00-790 Warsaw
tel.: (+48-22) 8492655; fax: 8492630
e-mail: thaiemb@ids.pl
Office of Commercial Affairs:
ul. Migdałowa 4/27, 02-796 Warsaw
tel.: (+48-22) 6451210; fax: 6451250
e-mail: info@ttcwarsaw.neostrada.pl

Embassy of the Republic of Tunisia
ul. Myśliwiecka 14, 00-459 Warsaw
tel.: (+48-22) 6286330; fax: 6216295
e-mail: at.varsovie@it.com.pl

Embassy of Turkey
ul. Malczewskiego 32, 02-622 Warsaw
tel.: (+48-22) 6464321…22; fax: 6463757
e-mail: turkemb@zigzag.pl
Commercial Counsellor's Office:
tel.: (+48-22) 6461408; tel./fax: 6463447
e-mail: trcomm@poczta.neostrada.pl

Embassy of Ukraine
al. Jana Chrystiana Szucha 7, 00-580 Warsaw
tel.: (+48-22) 6293446, 6224797; fax: 6298103
e-mail: emb_pl@mfa.gov.ua
www.ukraine-emb.pl
Trade and Economic Office:
tel./fax: (+48-22) 6224743

Embassy of the United States of America
Al. Ujazdowskie 29/31, 00-540 Warsaw
tel.: (+48-22) 5042000; fax: 5042688
http://poland.usembassy.gov/
Foreign Commercial Service:
ul. Poznańska 2/4, 00-680 Warsaw
tel.: (+48-22) 6254374
e-mail: warsaw.office.box@mail.doc.gov

Embassy of the Eastern Republic of Uruguay
ul. Rejtana 15 m. 12, 02-516 Warsaw
tel.: (+48-22) 8495040; fax: 6466887
e-mail: urupol@ikp.atm.com.pl

Embassy of Uzbekistan
ul. Wernyhory 21, 02-727 Warsaw
tel.: (+48-22) 847 52 53, fax: 853 22 88
www.uzbekistan.pl

Embassy of the Bolivarian Republic of Venezuela
ul. Rejtana 15 m. 10, 02-516 Warsaw
tel.: (+48-22) 6461846; fax: 6468761
e-mail: embavenez.pl@qdnet.pl

Embassy of the Socialist Republic of Vietnam
ul. Resorowa 36, 02-956 Warszawa
tel.: (+48-22) 6516098; fax. 6516095
e-mail: office@ambasadawietnamu.org
www.ambasadawietnamu.org
Commercial Section:
ul. Polna 48 m. 17, 00-644 Warsaw
tel.: (+48-22) 8258163; fax: 8258106
e-mail: pl@mot.gov.vn

Embassy of the Republic of Yemen
ul. Zwycięzców 18, 03-941 Warsaw
tel.: (+48-22) 6176025...26; fax: 6176022
e-mail: warsaw@yemen-embassy.pl
www.yemen-embassy.pl

APPENDIX 31

ECONOMIC AND COMMERCIAL SECTIONS OF POLISH EMBASSIES AND CONSULATES

Albania
Embassy of the Republic of Poland
Rruga e Durresit 123, Tirana
tel.: (+355-4) 234-190
fax: (+355-4) 233-364
e-mail: polemb@albaniaonline.net

Algeria
Ambassade de la République de Pologne
Service Economique et Commercial
4 bis, rue Rabah Bourbia
16606 El-Biar, Alger BP 148
tel.: (+213-21) 921706, 921828; fax: 921622
e-mail: brhalger@wissal.dz

Ambassade de la République de Pologne
37 Av. Mustapha Ali Khodja
16030 El-Biar, Alger BP 60
tel.: (+213-21) 923474, 922533; fax: 921435
e-mail: marekmal@wissal.dz

Angola
Embaixada da Republica da Polonia
Rua Comandante N´zaji 21/23, Alvalade
Luanda; CP 1340
tel.: (+244) 222 323 088; tel./fax: 222 323 086
e-mail: embpol@netangola.com
www.embpolonia-ang.info

Argentina
Embajada de la Republica de Polonia
Departamento Economico y Comercial
Virrey del Pino 3147
1426 Buenos Aires
tel.: (+54-11) 45515397; fax: 45515097
e-mail: brhbaires@house.com.ar
www.polonia-wehbaires.com.ar

Embajada de la Republica de Polonia
Calle Alejandro Maria de Aguado 2870
1425 Buenos Aires
tel.: (+54-11) 4802 9681/82; fax: 4802 9683
e-mail: polemb@datamarkets.com.ar

Armenia
Embassy of the Republic of Poland
44A Hanrapetutyan Str., Erewan
tel. (+374-1) 542493
fax.(+374-1) 542498
e-mail: polemb@arminco.com

Azerbaijan
Embassy of the Republic of Poland
2 Kichik Gala street, Icheri Sheher, AZ-1000 Baku
tel.: (99-412) 4920114, fax: 4920214
e-mail: embpol@azeurotel.com
www.embpol.azeurotel.com

Australia
Embassy of the Republic of Poland
Economic and Commercial Section
10 Trelawney Str., Woollahra
NSW 2025, Sydney
tel.: (+61-2) 9363 9821; fax: 9327 8568
e-mail: brhsydney@bigpond.com.au
www.poland.org.au/trade

Embassy of the Republic of Poland
7 Turrana Str., Yarralumla, ACT 2600 Canberra
tel.: (+61-2) 6272 1000, 6273 1208; fax: 6273 3184
e-mail: polamb@tpg.com.au
www.poland.org.au

Austria
Botschaft der Republik Polen
Wirtschafts-und Handelsbeteilung;
Titlgasse 15; 1130 Wien
tel.: (+43-1) 877 8341; fax: 877 3597
e-mail: info@handelsratpolen.at
www.handelsratpolen.at

Botschaft der Republic Polen
Hietzinger Hauptstraβe 42c
A-1130 Wien; PO Box 17
tel.: (+43-1) 87015-0 ...46; fax: 87015-222
e-mail: sekretariat@botschaftrp.at
www.botschaftrp.at

Belgium
Ambassade de la République de Pologne
Service Economique et Commercial
18, Avenue de l'Horizon; 1150 Bruxelles
tel.: (+32-2) 771 6815; fax: 771 1839
e-mail: info@poleconomie.be
www.poleconomie.be

Ambassade de la République de Pologne
Avenue des Gaulois 29, 1040 Bruxelles
tel.: (+32-2) 739 0101; fax: 736 1881
e-mail: info@polembassy.be
www.polembassy.be

Belarus
Ambassade de la République de Pologne
Service Economique et Commercial
ul. Wołodarskiego 6; 220030 Minsk
tel.: (+375-17) 222 4819; fax: 220 4974
e-mail: weh@nsys.by

Ambassade de la République de Pologne
P. Rumiancewa 6, 220034 Minsk
tel.: (+375-17) 288 2313; fax: 236 4992
e-mail:ambminsk@nsys.by
www.embassypoland.nsys.by

Brazil
Embaixada da Republica da Polonia
Escritorio do Conselheiro Comercial
Avenida das Naçoes, Quadra 809, Lote 33
Brasilia D.F. CEP 70423-900
tel.: (+55-61) 242 8698; fax: 242 8738
e-mail: brh-b@conectanet.com.br
www.polonia.org.br

Departamento Econômico e Comercial
da Embaixada em São Paulo
Rua Zequinha de Abreu, 240, Pacaembu
CEP: 01250-050 São Paulo, SP
tel.: (+55-11) 3673-2776, fax: 3673-0354
e-mail: wehsp@poloniatrade.org.br

Bosnia and Herzegovina
Embassy of the Republic of Poland
ul. Dola 13, 71000 Sarajevo
tel.: (+387-33) 201142; 215862; fax: 233796
e-mail: amsar@bih.net.ba

Bulgaria
Ambassade de la République de Pologne
Service Economique et Commercial
ul. Ewłogi Georgiew 125; 1504 Sofia
tel.: (+359-2) 943 4245; fax: 943 4814
e-mail: brh_pl_sofia@bsbg.net
www.brhplsofia.bsbg.net

Ambassade de la République de Pologne
Chan Krum 46, 1000 Sofia
tel.: (+359-2) 987 2610, 987 2660; fax. 987 2939
e-mail: polamba@internet-bg.net

Cambodia
Ambassade de la République de Pologne
767 Monivong Boulevard,
Phnom Pehn Cambodge, P.O. Box 58
tel. (+855-23) 217782/3; fax: 217781
e-mail: emb.pol.pp@online.com.kh
www.polishembassy-cambodia.org

Canada
Embassy of the Republic of Poland
443 Daly Avenue, Ottawa 2, Ontario K1N 6H3
tel.: (+1-613) 7890-468, 7893-376; fax: 7891-218
e-mail: ottawa@polishembassy.ca
www.polishembassy.ca

Economic and Commercial Division of the Embassy
3501 Ave du Musee, Montreal, Quebec H3G 2C8
tel.: (+1-514) 282-1732, 282-1734, fax: 282-1784
e-mail: weh.kanada@poland-canada.org
www.poland-canada.org

Polish Trade Comission - Toronto Branch
3300 Bloor Street West, Suite 2860 - Centre Tower
Toronto, Ontario M8V 2X3
tel.:(+1-416) 233-6571, fax: 233-9578
e-mail: tradeoffice.toronto@poland-canada.org
www.poland-canada.org

People's Republic of China
Embassy of the Republic of Poland
Economic and Commercial Section
1, Ri Tan Lu, Beijing, 100600 Beijing
tel.: (+86-10) 6532-1888; fax: 6532-1235
e-mail: polcom@public3.bta.net.cn
www.polecom.com.cn

Consulate General of the Republic of Poland
Economic and Commercial Section
1375 Huai Hai Zhong Rd., Shanghai, 200031
tel.: (+86-21) 6433-4735; fax: 6433-0161
e-mail: commoff@uninet.com.cn
www.polandshanghai.com

Consulate General of the Republic of Poland
Economic and Commercial Section
Shamian Dajie 63, Guangzhou, 510130
tel.: (+86-20) 8121-8991; fax: 8121-8992
e-mail: info@ polandguangzhou.com
www.polandguangzhou.com

Consulate General of the Republic of Poland
Economic and Commercial Section
Suite 2009, Two Pacific Place
88 Queensway, Central Hong Kong
tel.: (+852) 2840-0814; fax: 2918-9109
e-mail: kgcommhk@netvigator.com
www.polandtrade.com.hk

Chile
Embajada de la República de Polonia
Mar del Plata 2055, Providencia, Santiago de Chile
tel.: (+562) 2041213, 2690212; fax: 2049332
e-mail: embchile@entelchile.net
www.embpolonia.cl

Colombia
Embajada de la República de Polonia
Apartado Aereo 101363 Unicentro
Calle 104a, No 23-48, Bogota
tel.:(+57-1) 2140400, 2142931; fax: 2140854
e-mail: polemb@cable.net.co
www.embajadadepolonia.com

The Democratic Republic of the Congo
Embassy of the Republic of Poland
63, Avenue de la Justice, Kinshasa Gombe
tel./fax: (+243-81) 7006327, 7006326
e-mail: kinpolamb@yahoo.com

Costa Rica
Embajada de la República de Polonia
Avenida 9, Calle 33 No 3307, Barrio Escalante
San Jose, 664-2010 Correos Zapote
tel.: (+506) 2347411, 2346024; fax: 2347900
e-mail: embajpolonia1@racsa.co.cr
www.polonia-emb-cr.com

Croatia
Ambassade de la République de Pologne
Service Economique et Commercial
ul. Rokefellerova 49; 10000 Zagreb
tel.: (+385-1) 468-4202; tel/fax: 468-3128
e-mail: weh.zagreb@zg.htnet.hr
www.wehzagreb.com.hr

Ambassade de la République de Pologne
Krlezin Gvozd 3, 10000 Zagreb
tel.: (+385-1) 4899-444; fax: 4834-577
e-mail: ambasada-polska@zg.htnet.hr
www.ambasadapoljska.hr

Cuba
Embajada de la República de Polonia
Calle G No.452, esq.19, Vedado, La Habana
tel.: (+53-7) 8332439; fax: 8332442
e-mail: havpolemb@ct.futuro.pl
www.embajadapolonia.cu

Cyprus
Embassy of the Republic of Poland
Economic and Commercial Section
11 Acharnon str., 2027 Stravolos, Nicosia
tel.: (+357-2) 242-7007; fax: 251-0611
e-mail: wans@cytanet.com.cy
www.wehcypr.org.cy

Embassy of the Republic of Poland
12-14 Kennedy Ave. flat 302, 1087 Nicosia
tel.: (+357-2) 275-3517; fax: 275-1981
e-mail: polamb@cytanet.com.cy

Czech Republic
Ambassade de la République de Pologne
Service Economique et Commercial
ul. Hradešinska 1931/58; 10100 Praha 10
tel.: (+420-2) 71732342; fax: 72735442
e-mail: weh@weh.cz
www.weh.cz

Ambassade de République de Pologne
Valdštejnská 8, 11801 Praha 1
tel.: (+4202) 57099500; fax: 57530399
e-mail: ambrpczechy@mbox.vol.cz
www.ambpol.cz

Consulat Général de la République de Pologne
Service Economique et Commercial
Blahoslavova 4, 70100 Ostrava
tel.: (+420-596) 120460
e-mail: weh.ostrawa@volny.cz
www.wehostrawa.cz

Denmark
Embassy of the Republic of Poland
Economic and Commercial Section
Ryvangs Alle 46,
Copenhagen - 2900 Hellerup
tel.: (+45) 3962-2633; fax: 3962-2554
e-mail: mail@brh-dania.dk
www.brh-dania.dk

Embassy of the Republic of Poland
Richelieus Allé 12,
Copenhagen - 2900 Hellerup
tel.: (+45) 3946-7700; fax: 3946-7766
e-mail: mail@ambpol.dk
www.ambpol.dk

Egypt
Embassy of the Republic of Poland
Economic and Commercial Section
8, Ahmed Nessim St.304, Giza-Cairo
tel.: (+202) 337-9683; fax: 760-9353
e-mail: info@wehkair.com

Embassy of the Republic of Poland
5 El Aziz Osman Str., Zamalek, Cairo
tel.: (+202) 736-7456, fax: 735-5427
e-mail: sahafa@bolanda.org
www.bolanda.org

Estonia
Ambassade de la République de Pologne
Service Economique et Commercial
Narva mnt. 9A, 10503 Tallinn, BP 240
tel.: (+372) 6604-378; fax: 6604-380
e-mail: poola@poola.ee
www.poola.ee

Ambassade de la République de Pologne
Pärnu Mnt. 8, 10503 Tallinn, BP 247
tel.: (+372) 6278-206; fax: 6445-221
e-mail: info@poola.info
www.poola.info

Ethiopia
Embassy of the Republic of Poland
PO Box 27207/1000 Addis Abeba
Bole Sub-city, Kebele 03, House No 2111
tel.: (+251-1) 185401; 637635; fax: 610000
e-mail: polemb@telecom.net.et

European Communities
Mission de la République de Pologne
Auprès des Communautés Européennes
282-284 Av. de Tervuren; 1150 Bruxelles, Belgique
tel.: (+32-2) 7777-200; fax: 7777-297
e-mail: mail@pol-mission-eu.be
www.polrepeu.be

Finland
Embassy of the Republic of Poland
Economic and Commercial Section
Risto Rytin tie 7; 700-570 Helsinki
tel.: (+358-9) 684-9188; fax: 684-8907
e-mail: weh.helsinki@kolumbus.fi
www.embassyofpoland.fi/weh

Embassy of the Republic of Poland
Armas Lindgrenin tie 21, F-00570 Helsinki
tel.: (+358-9) 684-8077; fax: 684-7477
e-mail: amb.poland@helsinki.inet.fi
www.embassyofpoland.fi

France
Ambassade de la République de Pologne
Service Economique et Commercial
86, rue de la Faisanderie; 75116 Paris
tel.: (+33-1) 4504-1020; fax: 4504-6317
e-mail: info@eco.amb-pologne.fr
www.eco.amb-pologne.fr

Ambassade de la République de Pologne
1 rue de Talleyrand, 75343 Paris
tel.: (+33-1) 4317-3405; fax: 4317-3507
e-mail: info@ambassade.pologne.net
www.ambassade.pologne.net

Consulat Général de la République de Pologne
Service Economique et Commercial
79, rue Crillon, 69006 Lyon
tel.: (+33-4) 3751-1233; fax: 3751-1238
e-mail: pol-eco-lyon@tiscali.fr
www.lyon.consulat.pologne.net

Georgia
Embassy of the Republic of Poland
ul. Zubałaszwili 19, 0108 Tbilisi
tel. (+995-32) 920398
fax. (+995-32) 920397
e-mail: ambpolgruzja@access.sanet.ge

Germany
Botschaft der Republik Polen
Lassenstr. 19-21, 14193 Berlin
tel.: (+49-30) 223-130; fax: 2231-3155
e-mail: info@botschaft-polen.de
www.botschaft-polen.de

Botschaft der Republik Polen
Wirtschafts-und Handelsabteilung
Glinkastrasse 5-7, 10117 Berlin
tel.: (+49-30) 220-2551; fax: 229-2451
e-mail: info@wirtschaft-polen.de
www.wirtschaft-polen.de

Generalkonsulat der Republik Polen
Wirtschafts- und Handelsabteilung
An der Alteburger Mühle 6,
50968 Köln 51, Marienburg
tel.: (+49-221) 34990, 349913; fax: 349910
e-mail: info.koeln@wirtschaft-polen.de
www.wirtschaft-polen.de

Generalkonsulat der Republik Polen
Wirtschafts- und Handelsabteilung
Röntgenstraße 5, 81679 München
tel.: (+49-89) 4702-7747, 4186-0842; fax: 4707-223
e-mail: info.muenchen@wirtschaft-polen.de
www.wirtschaft-polen.de

Generalkonsulat der Republik Polen
Wirtschafts-und Handelsabteilung
Grundgenstr. 20; 22309 Hamburg
tel.: (+49-40) 611870; fax: 6325030
e-mail: info.hamburg@wirtschaft-polen.de
www.wirtschaft-polen.de

Generalkonsulat der Republik Polen
Wirtschafts-und Handelsabteilung
Gorber str.14/411-412, 04105 Leipzig
tel.: (+49-341) 980-0281; fax: 980-2043
e-mail: info.leipzig@wirtschaft-polen.de
www.wirtschaft-polen.de

Greece
Embassy of the Republic of Poland
Economic and Commercial Section
1, Kondoleondos st., 154-52 Paleo Psychico, Athens
tel.: (+30-210) 672 6176; fax: 672 1952
e-mail: wehateny@ath.forthnet.gr
www.wehateny.gr

Embassy of the Republic of Poland
22 Chrysanthemon st.
154-52 Paleo Psychico, Athenes
tel.: (+30-210) 679 7700; fax: 679 7711
e-mail: info@poland-embassy.gr
www.poland-embassy.gr

The Holy See
Ambassade de la République de Pologne
Via dei Delfini 16 int.3, 00186 Roma
tel.: (+39-06) 6990958; fax: 6990978
e-mail: polamb.wat@agora.it

Hungary
Embassy of the Republic of Poland
Economic and Commercial Section
Stefania ut 65, H-1143 Budapest XIV
tel.: (+36-1) 251-4677; fax: 252-9289
e-mail: ambpl-weh@axelero.hu
www.ambpl-weh.hu

Embassy of the Republic of Poland
Városligeti fasor 16, 1068 Budapest
tel.: (+36-1) 413-8200; fax: 351-1722
e-mail: info@polishemb.hu
www.lengyelorszag.hu

India
Embassy of the Republic of Poland
Economic and Commercial Section
50-M, Shantipath, Chanakyapuri; New Delhi 110021
tel.: (+91-11) 5149-6922, fax: 2687-2033
e-mail: morhan2@vsnl.net.in
www.poltradeindia.org

Consulate of the Republic of Poland
Economic and Commercial Section
Manavi Apartments, 36, B.G. Kher Marg,
Malabar Hill, Mumbai 400 006
tel.: (+91-22) 363-3863/4; fax: 363-3376
e-mail: poland@vsnl.com
www.polishconsulate.com

Indonesia
Embassy of the Republic of Poland
Economic and Commercial Section
JL.H.R.Rasuna Said, Kav.X Blok IV/3
Jakarta 12950
tel.: (+62-21) 2525-947; fax: 2525-960
e-mail: radca@polandembjak.org
www.polandembjak.org

Iran
Embassy of the Republic of Poland
Africa Expressway, Pirouz Str. 1/3
P.O.Box 11365-3489, 19-174 Tehran
tel.: (+9821) 8787-262/4, fax: 8788-774
e-mail: info@embpoltehran.com
www.embpoltehran.com

Iraq
Embassy of the Republic of Poland
Baghdad, Hay Al-Wahda, Mahalla 904,
Zukak 60, House 20/24
tel.: +964 7901 909506; fax: (sat) +873-762 05 3415
e-mail: poltrade@tlen.pl; ambaspol@tlen.pl

Ireland
Embassy of Republic of Poland
Economic and Commercial Section
4 The Vicarage St John`s Road; Dublin 4
tel.: (+353-1) 269-1370; fax: 269-7662
e-mail: radca@dublin.polishembassy.ie
www.dublin.polishembassy.ie

Embassy of the Republic of Poland
5, Ailesbury Road, Ballsbridge, Dublin 4
tel.: (+3531) 283-0855; fax: 269-8309
e-mail: polembas@iol.ie
www.polishembassy.ie

Israel
Embassy of the Republic of Poland
Economic and Commercial Section
79, Yehuda Hamaccabi St.; 62-300 Tel-Aviv
tel.: (+972-3) 5446-246; fax: 5446-247
e-mail: brhtlv@inter.net.il
www.polemb.org/economic.htm

Embassy of the Republic of Poland
16, Soutine St., Tel-Aviv 64-484
tel.: (+972-3) 5240-186, fax: 5237-806
e-mail: embpol@netvision.net.il
www.polemb.org

Italy
Ambassade de la République de Pologne
Service Economique et Commercial
Via Olona 2; 00198 Roma
tel.: (+39-6) 854-1128; fax: 855-3391
e-mail: info@infopolonia.it
www.infopolonia.it

Embassy of the Republic of Poland
Via P.P. Rubens 20, 00197 Roma
tel.: (+39-6) 362 04 200; fax: 321 7895
e-mail: ufficio.stampa@ambasciatapolonia.it
www.ambasciatapolonia.it

Consulat Général de la République de Pologne
Service Economique et Commercial
Via Capecelatro 53/4, 20148 Milano
tel.: (+39-2) 487 131 64; fax: 405 303
e-mail: economia@infopolonia.it

Japan
Embassy of the Republic of Poland
Economic and Commercial Section
2-13-5 Mita, Meguro-ku, Tokyo 153-0062
tel.: (+81-3) 5794 7050; fax: 5794 7053
e-mail: brhtokio@twics.com
www.poland.or.jp

Jordan
Embassy of the Republic of Poland
No 3 Mahmoud Seif Al-Din Al-Irani St.
PO Box 942050, Amman 11194
tel. (+9626) 5512593, 5512594; fax: 5512595
e-mail: polemb@nol.com.jo

Kazakhstan
Embassy of the Republic of Poland
Economic and Commercial Section
ul. Baturina 4, Almaty 480051
tel./fax: (+7-3272) 647911, 534427
e-mail: brhala@nursat.kz

Embassy of the Republic of Poland
Dżarkentskaja 9 / Iskanderowa 11/13,
480099 Almaty, P.O.Box 228
tel.: (+7-3272) 581 551, fax: 581 550
e-mail: ambpol@maiz.kz

Kenya
Embassy of the Republic of Poland
Kabarnet Road, Nairobi, PO Box 30086
tel.: (+254-20) 3872 811, 3872 812; fax: 3872 814
e-mail: ambnairo@kenyaweb.com

Democratic People's Republic of Korea
Ambassade de la République de Pologne
Tedonggang - Munsudong, Pyongyang, D.P.R.K.
tel. (+8502) 3817325, 3817328; fax: 3817634
www.msz.gov.pl/amb/phenian

Republic of Korea
Embassy of the Republic of Poland
Economic and Commercial Section
4F, Dongkyung B/D, 604 Hannam-dong,
Yongsan-Ku, Seoul 140-210
tel.: (+82-2) 3785 2471 fax: 797 0853
e-mail: marekm@kornet.net
www.buypoland.or.kr

Embassy of the Republic of Poland
70, Sagan-dong, Jongno-gu, Seoul
tel.: (+82-2) 723 9681; fax: 723 9680
e-mail : embassy@polandseoul.org
www.polandseoul.org

Kuwait
Embassy of the Republic of Poland
P.O. Box 5066, Safat, 13501 Kuwait
tel.: (+965) 5311 571/2, fax: 5311 576
e-mail: polamba@qualitynet.net
www.polambakuw.gov.kw

Lao People's Democratic Republic
Ambassade de la République de Pologne
263 Thadeua Rd., km. 3
P.O. Box 1106 Vientiane
tel.: (+856 21) 312-940; fax: 312-085
e-mail: polvte7@laotel.com

Latvia
Embassy of the Republic of Poland
Economic and Commercial Section
11 Elizabetes str., 1010 Riga
tel.: (+371) 735-8251; fax: 735-8250
e-mail: weh@poltrade.lv
www.poltrade.lv

Embassy of the Republic of Poland
Miednieku iela 6B, 1010 Riga
tel.: (+371) 703-1500; fax: 705-1549
e-mail: ambpol@apollo.lv

Lebanon
Ambassade de la République de Pologne
Av. President Suleiman Frangieh 52
Raymong Khalife Bldg
Baabda - PO Box 40-215
tel. 05-924-881, 05-468-951; fax: 05-924-882
e-mail: polamb@cyberia.net.lb

Libya
Ambassade de la République de Pologne
61 Sharia Ben Ashour Str.
Garden City Tripoli, PO Box 519
tel.(+218 21) 3608569, 3615972; fax: 3615199
e-mail: ambrp.trypolis@interia.pl
http://ambrp.trypolis.w.interia.pl

Lithuania
Ambassade de la République de Pologne
Service Economique et Commercial
Vasario 16-osios g.14/2, 01107 Vilnius-1
tel.: (+370-5) 261-7960; fax: 261-0686
e-mail: info@weh-wilno.lt
www.weh-wilno.lt

Embassy of the Republic of Poland
Smelio g. 20A. 10323 Vilnius
tel.: (+370-5) 270-9001; fax: 270-9007
www.polandembassy.lt

Macedonia FYR
Ambassade de la République de Pologne
ul. Djuro Djaković 50, 1000 Skopje
tel.: (+389 2) 3119744, 3112647
e-mail: ambpol@unet.com.mk

Malaysia
Embassy of the Republic of Poland
Economic and Commercial Section
Suite 6, level 7, Mesiara Dato'Onn,
P.O.Box 47 & 48, Putra World Trade Centre,
45 Jalan Tun Ismail, 50480 Kuala Lumpur
tel.: (+60-3) 4043 0940; fax: 4043 0216
e-mail: brh_msia@tm.net.my
www.wehkl.com

Embassy of the Republic of Poland
No 495, 4 ½ Miles Jalan Ampang,
68000 Ampang, Selangor 50704 Kuala Lumpur
tel.: (+60-3) 4257-6733; fax: 4257-0123
e-mail: polamba@tm.net.my

Mexico
Embajada de la República de Polonia
Calle Cracovia 40, Colonia San Angel,
01000 México D.F.
Apartado Postal 20383
tel.: (+52 55) 5550-4700, fax: 5616-0822
e-mail: embajadadepolonia@prodigy.net.mx
www.polonia.org.mx

Moldova
Embassy of the Republic of Poland
Economic and Commercial Section
MD-2009 Chisinau, str. Plamadeala 3
tel: (+373-22) 238956; fax: 238957
e-mail: weh@polonia.md
www.polonia.md

Embassy of the Republic of Poland
MD-2009 Chisinau, str. Plamadeala 3
tel: (+373-22) 238551; fax: 238553
e-mail: ambpolsk@ch.moldpac.md

Mongolia
Ambassade de la République de Pologne
Diplomat 95 Ajlyn Oron Suuc VI ORC
PO Box 1049, Ulaanbaatar-13
tel.: (+976-11) 320641, fax: 321926;
e-mail: polkonsulat@magicnet.mn

Morocco
Ambassade de la République de Pologne
Service Economique et Commercial
22, rue Khouribga, BP 384, 10000 Rabat
tel.: (+212-37) 768368; fax: 769068
e-mail: commerpl@menara.ma
www.wehrabat.ma
Ambassade de la République de Pologne
23, Rue Oqbah, Rabat, BP 425
tel.: (212-37) 771173; fax: 775320
e-mail: apologne@iam.net.ma
www.ambpologne.ma

Consulat Général de la République de Pologne
Service Economique et Commercial
9 rue d'Alger-Villa Beausoleil, 20000 Casablanca
tel.: (+212-22) 279138; fax: 279139
e-mail: conspl@iam.net.ma
www.consulatpl.net

Netherlands
Embassy of the Republic of Poland
Economic and Commercial Section
Van Lennepweg 51; 2597 LG Den Haag
tel.: (+31-70) 306-9944; fax: 354-3966
e-mail: weh@wehhaga.nl
www.wehhaga.nl

Embassy of the Republic of Poland
Alexanderstraat 25, 2514 JM Den Haag
tel.: (+31-70) 7990-100; fax: 360-2810
e-mail: ambhaga@polamb.nl
www.polamb.nl

New Zeland
Embassy of the Republic of Poland
17 Upland Road, Kelburn
Wellington 6005, P.O. Box 10211
tel.: (+644) 4759453, fax: 4759458
e-mail: polishembassy@xtra.co.nz
www.poland.org.nz

Nigeria
Embassy of the Republic of Poland
Economic and Commercial Section
1 Amado Tijani Street, Victoria Island, Lagos
tel.: (+234-1) 262-0660; fax: 262-0649
e-mail: brh.nig@hyperia.com

Embassy of the Republic of Poland
16, Ona Crescent, Maitama, Abuja
tel.: (+234-9) 41382-80…83; fax: 41382-81
e-mail: poembabu@linkserve.com

Norway
Embassy of the Republic of Poland
Economic and Commercial Section
Uranienborg terrasse 11; 0351-Oslo
tel.: (+47-22) 602448; fax: 565381
e-mail: tradepol@broadpark.no
www.wehoslo.com

Embassy of the Republic of Poland
Olav Kyrres plass 1, 0244 Oslo
tel.: (+47-24) 110850; fax: (+47-24) 444839
e-mail: ambpol@online.no
www.poland-embassy-no.com

Pakistan
Embassy of the Republic of Poland
Diplomatic Enclave II, Street 24, G-5/4,
Islamabad P.O. Box 1032
tel. (+92-51) 2279491, 2279493; fax: 2279498
e-mail: polemb@isb.comsats.net.pk

Panama
Embajada de la República de Polonia
Bella Vista, Calle 47,
Edificio "Vista Marina", piso 2.
Zona 5, Apartado Postal 8782, Panama
tel.: (+507) 2636254, 2635097; fax: 2233717
e-mail: polamb@cwpanama.net
www.embajadadepolonia.net

Peru
Embajada de la República de Polonia
Casilla de coreo 180174,
Miraflores, Lima 18
tel.: (+511) 4713-920, fax: 4713-925
e-mail: consrplima@amauta.rcp.net.pe
www.polonia.org.pe

Portugal
Embaixada da Republica da Polonia
Departamento Econômico e Comercial
Avenida da Pepublica, 9-7; 1050-185 Lisboa
tel.: (+351-21) 352-6170; fax: 352-6174
e-mail: brh.lizbona@mail.telepac.pt
www.negociosnapolonia.com

Embaixada da Republica da Polonia
Avenida das Descobertas 2, 1400-092 Lisboa
tel.: (+ 351-21) 301-2350; fax: 301-0202
e-mail: embpol@mail.telepac.pl
www.emb-polonia.pt

Republic of South Africa
Embassy of the Republic of Poland
Economic and Commercial Section
PO Box 1547, Houghton 2041, Johannesburg, RSA
tel.: (+27-11) 788-6597; fax: 442-5375
e-mail: brhpljhb@iafrica.com
www.brhjhb.org.za

Embassy of the Republic of Poland
14 Amos Street, Colbyn 0083, Pretoria
PO Box 12277, Queenswood 0121
tel.: (+27-12) 430-2621; fax: 430-2608
e-mail: amb.pol@pixie.co.za

Romania
Ambassade de la République de Pologne
Service Economique et Commercial
Bd Aviatorilor 24; 011862 Bucuresti
tel.: (+40-21) 230-7714; fax: 230-7732
e-mail: brh.buk@dnt.ro
www.polonia.ro

Ambassade de la République de Pologne
Al. Alexandru 23, 011821 Bucuresti
tel.: (+40-21) 308-2200; fax: 230-7832
e-mail: ambasada@bukareszt.ro
www.bukareszt.ro

Russia
Ambassade de la République de Pologne
Service Economique et Commercial
123557 Moscou, rue Klimashkina 4
tel.: (+7-095) 231-1611; fax: 231-1615
e-mail: poland@polweh.ru
www.polweh.ru

Consulat Général de la République de Pologne
Service Economique et Commercial
Rue 5-ya Sovietskaya 12; 193130 Sankt Petersburg
tel.: (+7-812) 274-4328; fax: 274-4318
e-mail: weh@sp.ru
www.weh.spb.ru

Consulat Général de la République de Pologne
Service Economique et Commercial
Prospekt Mira 81/2; 236000 Kaliningrad
tel.: (+7-0112) 218-741; fax: 216-287
e-mail: postmaster@tpol.koenig.ru
www.weh-kaliningrad.ru

Saudi Arabia
Embassy of the Republic of Poland
Abdullah Bin Dżafar Street, House No.20
Al-Woorood District Riyadh (Rijad)
P.O.Box 94016, Riyadh 11693
tel.: (+966-1) 4549274, 4508889; fax: 4549210
e-mail: rijadamb@shabakah.net.sa
www.polandembassy.org.sa

Senegal
Ambassade de la République de Pologne
Avenue des Ambassadeurs, Fann Residence
Dakar BP 343
tel.: (+221) 8252403, 8242354; fax: 8249526
e-mail: ambassade.pl@sentoo.sn
www.ambassade-pologne.sn

Serbia and Montenegro
Ambassade de la République de Pologne
Service Economique et Commercial
Il.Vladimira Popovica 6 ap 401, 11070 Beograd
tel.: (+381-11) 311-2340; fax: 311-2307
e-mail: wehfrj@eunet.yu

Ambassade de la République de Pologne
Kneza Milośa 38, 11000 Beograd
tel.: (+381-11) 206-5301; fax: 361-6939
e-mail: ambrpfrj@eunet.yu

Singapore
Embassy of the Republic of Poland
Economic and Commercial Section
435 Orchard Road, 10-01/02 Wisma Atria
Singapore 238877
tel.: (+65) 6734-0466; fax: 6734-6129
e-mail: polish_embassy@pacific.net.sg

Slovakia
Ambassade de la République de Pologne
Service Economique et Commercial
Zelena 6; 81101 Bratyslava
tel.: (+421-2) 5443-2744; fax: 5443-2007
e-mail: weh@polamb.sk
www.weh.polamb.sk

Ambassade de la République de Pologne
Hummelova 4, 81491 Bratyslava
tel.: (+421-2) 5441-3175, fax: 5441-3184
e-mail: bratampl@nextra.sk
www.polskevelvyslanectvo.sk

Slovenia
Embassy of the Republic of Poland
Economic and Commercial Section
Cesta 27 aprila 37, 1000 Lublana
tel./fax: (+386-1) 426-1448, 426-0505
e-mail: pl-brh@pl-brh.si
www.pl-brh.si

Embassy of the Republic of Poland
Bezigrad 10, 1000 Lublana
tel.: (+386-1) 436-4712; fax: 436-2521
e-mail: ambpol.si@siol.net
www.poland-embassy.si

Spain
Embajada de la República de Polonia
Sección de Economía y Comercio
Avenida del Dr. Arce, 25; 28002 Madrid
tel.: (+34-91) 590-1280; fax: 561-5108
e-mail: comercial@polonia.es

Embajada de la República de Polonia
Calle Guisando 23 bis, 28035 Madrid
tel.: (+34-91) 373-6605; fax: 373-6624
e-mail: embajada@polonia.es
www.polonia.es

Sweden
Embassy of the Republic of Poland
Economic and Commercial Section
Friggagatan 4, 11427 Stockholm
tel.: (+46-8) 453-8420; fax: 216-188
e-mail: info@polcommerce.com
www.polcommerce.com

Embassy of the Republic of Poland
Karlavägen 35, 11432 Stockholm
tel.: (+46-8) 5057-5000; fax: 5057-5086
e-mail: info.polen@tele2.se
www.polemb.se

Switzerland
Botschaft der Republik Polen
Wirtschafts- und Handelsabteilung
Elfenstrasse 9; CH-3000 Bern 6
tel.: (+41-31) 350-8282; fax: 351-3457
e-mail: postmaster@weh-pl-bern.ch
www.weh-pl-bern.ch

Botschaft der Republik Polen
Elfenstrasse 20a, CH-3000 Bern 6
tel.: (+41-31) 358-0202, fax: 358-0216
e-mail: polishemb@dial.eunet.ch
www.pol-amb.ch

Syria
Ambassade de la République de Pologne
Rue Georges Haddad, Damascus P.O. 501
tel.: (+963-11) 3333010, fax: 3315318
e-mail: damapol@scs-net.org
www.msz.gov.pl/amb/damaszek

Tanzania
Embassy of the Republic of Poland
63 Aly Khan Road, Upanga, Dar es Salaam
P. O. Box 2188
tel.: (+255-22) 2115271, tel./fax : 2115812
e-mail: polamb@wingrouptz.com

Thailand
Embassy of the Republic of Poland
Economic and Commercial Section
11th Fl., Two Pacific Place
142 Sukhumvit Road, Bangkok 10110
tel.: (+66-2) 653-2014; fax: 653-2013
e-mail: poltrade@loxinfo.co.th
www.polbizbkk.com

Embassy of the Republic of Poland
8A, Sriyukhon Bldg, Sukhumvit Soi 5
PO Box 1167, Bangkok 10110
tel.: (+66-2) 251-8891/2; fax: 251-8895
e-mail: info@polemb.or.th
www.polemb.or.th

Tunisia
Ambassade de la République de Pologne
Service Economique et Commercial
5, Rue Ibn Assaker, El Menzah I, 1004 Tunis
tel.: (+21671) 751 907; fax: 238 812
e-mail: ambweh.tunis@planet.tn
www.pologne.intl.tn

Ambassade de la République de Pologne
5, Impasse No 1, Rue de Cordoue,
2092 El Manar I, Tunis
tel.: (+21 6) 71 873 837; fax: 71 872 987
e-mail: amb-pologne@email.ati.tn

Turkey
Embassy of the Republic of Poland
Economic and Commercial Section
And Sokak No 8/17; 06680 Cankaya - Ankara
tel.: (+90-312) 468-0990; fax: 428-1234
e-mail: weh.ankara@superonline.com
www.polonya.org.tr/weh

Embassy of the Republic of Poland
Atatürk Bulvari 241, Kavaklidere PK 20
06650 Ankara
tel.: (+90-312) 467-5619; fax: 467-8963
e-mail: polamb@superonline.com
www.polonya.org.tr

Consulate General of the Republic of Poland
Economic and Commercial Section
Toprakkale Sok. No 6, Burak Apt. D-3
Etiler - 80630, Istanbul
tel.: (+90-212) 265-8609; fax: 265-0722
e-mail: commdivisionist@hotmail.com

Ukraine
Ambassade de la République de Pologne
Service Economique et Commercial
Volodymyrska 45, 01034 Kiev
tel.: (+380-44) 279-4537; fax: 278-1140
e-mail: wehamb@ukrnet.net
http://users.adamant.net/~wehamb/

Ambassade de la République de Pologne
Jaroslawiw Wal 12, 01034 Kiev
tel.: (+ 380-44) 230-0700, fax: 270-6336
e-mail: ambasada@polska.com.ua
www.polska.com.ua

Consulat Général de la République de Pologne
Economic and Commercial Section
Sarachowa 78a III, 79026 Lviv
tel/fax: (+380-322) 976-677, 971-353
e-mail: khpol@utel.net.ua
www.wehkg-Lv.txnet.com

Consulat Général de la République de Pologne
Service Economique et Commercial
Artioma 16 - 401, 61002 Charkiv
tel.: (+380-572) 585-424; fax: 585-425
e-mail: weh_khr@lin.com.ua

United Arab Emirates
Embassy of the Republic of Poland
Abu Dhabi, Delma Street,
Corner with Karama Street,
P.O. Box 2334, Abu Dhabi
tel.: (+971-2) 4465-200; fax 4462-967
e-mail: polemb@emirates.net.ae
www.plembassy.gov.ae

United Kingdom
Embassy of the Republic of Poland
Economic and Commercial Section
15, Devonshire Street; London W1G 7AP
tel.: (+44) 20 75 8054 81; fax: 20 73 23 01 95
e-mail: weh@polishemb-trade.co.uk
www.polishemb-trade.co.uk

Embassy of the Republic of Poland
47 Portland Place, London W1B 1JH
tel.: (+44) 87 07 74 27 00
fax: (+44) 20 72 91 35 75
e-mail: polishembassy@polishembassy.org.uk
www.polishembassy.org.uk

Urugway
Embajada de la República de Polonia
Jorge Canning 2389, C.P. 11600 Montevideo
tel.: (+59 82) 4801151, 4801313; fax: 4873389
e-mail: ambmonte@netgate.com.uy
www.embajadapoloniauruguay.com

USA
Embassy of the Republic of Poland
Economic and Commercial Section
675, 3rd Ave. (19th floor)
New York, NY 10017
tel.: (+1-212) 370-5300; fax: 818-9623
e-mail: brhusa@brhusa.com
www.brhusa.com

Embassy of the Republic of Poland
2640, 16th Street, N.W.,
Washington DC 20009
tel.: (+1-202) 234-3800; fax: 328-6271
e-mail: polemb.info@earthlink.net
www.polandembassy.org

Embassy of the Republic of Poland
Economic and Commercial Section
1503, 21st Street N.W.
Washington DC 20036
tel.: (+1-202) 467-6690; fax: 833-8343
e-mail: econcompl@wehwas.us
www.polandembassy.org

Consulate General of the Republic of Poland
Economic and Commercial Section
333 East Ontario Street, Suite 3906
Chicago, Illinois 60611
tel.: (+1-312) 642-4102; fax: 642-8829
e-mail: info@wehchicago.com
www.wehchicago.com

Consulate General of the Republic of Poland
Economic and Commercial Section
12400 Wilshire Blvd., Suite 555
Los Angeles, CA 90025
tel.: (+1-310) 442-8500 ext.113; fax: 442-8526
e-mail: wehla@consulplla.org
www.pan.net/tradeconsul

Uzbekistan
Embassy of the Republic of Poland
Economic and Commercial Section
Mahatma Gandi 1, tupik 4
700000 Tashkent
tel.: (+998-71) 133-9650; fax: 133-9750
e-mail: weh-amb@bcc.com.uz
http://weh-amb.ziyo.uz

Embassy of the Republic of Poland
Fridavsiy 66, Yunasabadskiy Rayon
700084 Tashkent
tel.: (+998-71) 120-8650; fax: 120-8651
email: embassy@poland.uz
www.poland.uz

Venezuela
Embajada de la República de Polonia
Av. Nicolas Copernico, Qta. "Ambar"
Valle Arriba, Sector Los Naranjos
Apartado 62293, Chacao, Caracas 1060-A
fel.: (+58-212) 991-6167; fax: 992-2164
e-mail: ambcarac@ambasada.org.ve
www.ambasada.org.ve

Vietnam
Ambassade de la République de Pologne
Service Economique et Commercial
5, Ba Huyen Thanh Quan
PO Box 21, Hanoi
tel.: (+84-4) 845-2836; fax: 843-0517
e-mail: brh.hanoi@fpt.vn

Ambassade de la République de Pologne
3 Chua Mot Cot, Hanoi
tel.: (+84-4) 845-2027, 845-3728; fax: 823-6914
e-mail: polamb@hn.vnn.vn

Yemen
Embassy of the Republic of Poland
Fajj Attan Area, Sana'a, Yemen
P.O. Box 16168
tel.: (+9671) 413523, 413524; fax: 413647
e-mail: polemb@y.net.ye
www.y.net.ye/polemb

Zimbabwe
Embassy of the Republic of Poland
16 Cork Rd, Belgravia
Harare, PO Box 3932
tel.: (+263-4) 253442; fax: 253710
e-mail: polamb@africaonline.co.zw

APPENDIX 32

UNIDO ESTABLISHED NETWORKS

INVESTMENT AND TECHNOLOGY PROMOTION OFFICES

UNIDO Investment and Technology Promotion Office in Bahrain
Mr. Hashim Hussein, Head
Bahrain Development Bank House
P.O. Box 10523, Bldg. No. 170.Road 1703, Manama 317, Bahrain
Telephone: +973 536881; Fax: +973 536883
e-mail: itpo.bahrain@unido.org

UNIDO Investment and Technology Promotion Office in Belgium
Ministère de la Region Wallonne
Agence Wallonne à l'Exportation
Place Sainctelette, 2; B-1080 Brussels, Belgium
Telephone: +32 2 4218211; Fax: +32 2 4218787
e-mail: itpo.walloon-region@unido.org http://www.awex.be

UNIDO Investment and Technology Promotion Office in Brazil
Mr. Valerio Veloso, Head
Rua do Apolo, 181
Bairro do Recife - PE; State of Pernambuco, Brasil – CEP: 50030-220
Telephone: +55-81 3419 8002/8004; Fax: +55-81 3419 8001
e-mail: valerio@portodigital.org

UNIDO Investment and Technology Promotion Office in China
Mr. Tao Dong, Head
UNIDO Shanghai Investment Promotion Center
16F New Town Center, 83, Loushanguan Road, Shanghai, 200336, China
Telephone: +8621 62368800; Fax: +8621 62368024
e-mail: itpo.shanghai@unido.org

Mr. Yuandong HU, Head
No. 17, Xi WU Jei, San Li tun, Chaoyang District, Beijing 100600, China
Telephone: +8610 65326140, 65326141; Fax: +8610 65326145
e-mail: itpo.beijing@unido.org http://www.unidoitpo.org.cn

UNIDO Investment Promotion Unit in Egypt
Mr. Enrico Sasdelli, Head
Sherif Street 30, Cairo, Egypt
Telephone: +202 392 5277, 393 7447; Fax: +202 3957631
e-mail: itpo.cairo@unido.org

UNIDO Investment and Technology Promotion Office in France
Mr. Gérard Gaveau, Head
9, rue Notre Dame des Victoires, F-75002 Paris, France
Telephone: +331 44550505; Fax: +331 49269726
e-mail: itpo.paris@unido.org

Mr. Jean Claude Plana, Head
271, corniche Président J.F. Kennedy, F-13007 Marseille, France
Telephone: +33-4-91525619, Fax: +33-4-91571728
e-mail: itpo.marseille@unido.org

UNIDO Investment and Technology Promotion Office in Greece
Mr. Ioannis Karmokolias, Head
7, Stadiou Street, 7th Floor, Syntagma Sqr, 10562 Athenes, Greece
Telephone: +302 10 3248319, 3248367; Fax: + 302 10 3248778
e-mail: itpo.athens@unido.org

UNIDO Investment and Technology Promotion Office in Italy
Ms. Diana Battaggia, Head
Via della Beverara, 123, I-40131 Bologna, Italy
Telephone: +39051 634 3031; Fax: +39051 634 1186
e-mail: itpo.bologna@unido.org

Ms.Diana Battaggia, Head
Via Panisperna 28, 00 184 Rome, Italy
Phone: +39 06 6962 153, 6962 129; Fax: +39 06 6962 122
e-mail: itpo.rome@unido.org

UNIDO Investment and Technology Promotion Office in Japan
Mr. Seiji Oshima, Head
Shin-Aoyama Building, W-16F, 1-1-1 Minami-Ayoama, Minato-Ku, Tokyo 107, Japan
Telephone: +81 3 340 29341; Fax: +81 3 340 29384
e-mail: itpotokyo@unido.or.jp

UNIDO Investment Promotion Unit in Jordan
Ms. Monica Carcó, Head
c/o Jordan Investment Board
P.O. Box 893; Amman 11821, Jordan
Telephone: +962 6 5608400; Fax: +962 65517626
e-mail: unido@jib.com.jo

UNIDO Investment and Technology Promotion Office in Republic of Korea
Mr. Wan-Gil Kang, Head
c/o Korea International Cooperation Agency (KOICA)
128, Yunkun-dong, Chongro-gru, Seoul 110-460, Republic of Korea
Telephone: +82 2 747 8191, 747 8192; Fax: +82 2 747 8193
e-mail: itpo.seoul@unido.org

UNIDO Investment and Promotion Unit in Morocco
Mr. Luca Ranieri, Officer-in-Charge
c/o Unité de Promotion des Investissements
Office pour le Développement Industriel
10 Rue Ghandi; BP 211 – Rabat, Morocco
Telephone: +212 37 737 979, 737 889; Fax: +212 37 738 070
e-mail: itpo.rabat@unido.org

UNIDO Investment and Technology Promotion Office in Poland
Mr. Krzysztof Loth, Head
Aleja Niepodległości 186, 00-608, Warsaw, P.O. Box 10, Warsaw 12, Poland
Telephone: +48 22 8259186 Fax: +48 22 8258970
e-mail: ips-waw@unido.pl

UNIDO Investment and Technology Promotion Office in Russian Federation
Mr. Mikhail V. Rytchev, Director
UNIDO Center for International Industrial Coop.
Ulitsa Kuusinena 21B, 125252 Moscow, Russian Federation
Telephone: +7 095 9430021, 1989809; Fax: +7 095 9430018
e-mail: itpo.moscow@unido.org http://www.unido.ru

UNIDO Investment Promotion Unit in Tunisia
Mr. Claudio Scaratti, Head
ONUDI Tunis
63, Rue de Syrie 6th floor, Tunis-Belvedere, Tunisia
Telephone: +216 71 283 923 / 216 98 652 979 [mobile]; Fax: +216 71 283 724
e-mail: office.tunisia@unido.org

UNIDO Center for Regional Cooperation in Turkey
Mr. Celal Armangil
Birlik Mahallesi, 2. Cadde, No:11, 06610, Çankaya, Ankara, Turkey
Tel: (+90 312) 4541078, 4541079; Fax: (+90 312) 496 14 75
e-mail: celal.armangil@un.org.tr http://www.un.org.tr/unido

UNIDO Investment and Technology Promotion Office in United Kingdom
Mr. John McFadzean, Head
Renaissance House
P.O. Box 37, Centre Park
Warrington Cheshire WA1 1XB, United Kingdom
Telephone: +44 1925 400224; Fax: +44 1925 400405
e-mail: info@nwda-unido.org.uk http://www.nwda-unido.org.uk

UNIDO Investment Promotion Unit in Uganda
Mr. Andrea Negri, OIC
c/o Uganda Investment Authority
The Investment Centre
Plot 28, Kampala Road
P.O. Box 7418, Kampala
Telephone: +256 41 251561/-5; 244733; Fax: +256 41 342903
e-mail: itpo.kampala@unido.org

INTERNATIONAL/NATIONAL TECHNOLOGY CENTRES COOPERATING WITH UNIDO

InterTec Ltd. Austria
Brahmsplatz 8/3
A-1040 Vienna, Austria
Telephone: +431 5044091; Fax: +431 5044094
General Information: info@intertec.co.at

The International Centre for Genetic Engineering and Biotechnology in Italy
Dott. Decio Ripandelli, ICGEB – Area di Ricerca, Padriciano 99
34012 Trieste – Italia
Telephone: +39 040 3757345; Fax: +39 040 3757363
e-mail: decio@icgeb.org

National Technology Transfer Centre – Kyiv (TTC) in Ukraina
Kyiv 03150, а/я 52, Ukraine
Telephone/fax: +044 – 2276502
e-mail: contact@uatechnology.org

National Technology Transfer Centre (NCTT) in Republic of Belarus
k.106, Академическая 1,
220072 Minsk, Republic of Belarus
Telephone/fax: +375 17 2841499
e-mail: ictt@pochtamt.ru

INTERNATIONAL TECHNOLOGY CENTRES AND COOPERATING NETWORKS

The International Centre for Application of Solar Energy (CASE) in Australia
Mr. Gordon Thompson, Managing Director
220 St. Georges Terrace
Perth, Western Australia 6000
Telephone: +618 93217600; Fax: +618 93217497
e-mail: case@case.gov.au

The International Materials Assessment and Application Centre (IMAAC) in Austria
Mr. Vladimir Kozharnovich, Programme Manager
Quality, Technology and Investment Branch
Investment Promotion & Institutional Capacity-Building Division
UNIDO
Vienna International Centre
P.O.Box 300, A-1400 Vienna, Austria
Telephone: +431 26026 3720/3702; Fax: +431 26026 6809
e-mail: vkozharnovich@unido.org

The International Centre for Advancement of Manufacturing Technology in India
Mr. Vinod Kumar Yadav, Project Director
Core 5A, Ist Floor, BMTPC Office
India Habitat Centre. Lodi Road
New Delhi – 110003 India
Telephone: +91 80 24647083; Fax: +91 80 24647082
e-mail: v.yadav@unido.org , vkuadav@icamt.org

The International Centre for Science and High Technology in Italy
Mr. Francesco Pizzio, Managing Director
AREA Science Park, Padriciano 99
34012 Trieste, Italy
Telephone: +39 040 9228101; Fax: +39 040 9228101
e-mail: info@ics.trieste.it

The International Centre for Small Hydro Power (ICSHP) in China
Prof. Tong Jiandong, Director
P.O.Box 202, 136 Nanshan Road
Hangzhou 310002, People's Republic of China
Telephone: +86 571 87023380; Fax: +86 571 87023353
e-mail: hic@mail.hz.zj.cn

The International Centre for Materials Technology Promotion (ICM) in China
Prof. Yan Yao (Ms)
President China Building Materials Academy
Guanzhuang, Chaoyang District
Beijing 100024, People's Republic of China
Telephone: +86 10 65750105, 65761325
Fax: +86 10 65762976
e-mail: yaoyan@public2.bta.net.cn

The International Centre of Medicine Biotechnology (ICMB) in Russian Federation
Mr. Nikolay Durmanov, International Coordinator
Ulitsa Kuusinena 21B
125252 Moscow, Russian Federation
Telephone: +7 095 2010051; Fax: +7 095 7254636
e-mail: durmanov@postman.ru

2007
WORLD INTERNATIONAL ORGANIZATIONS BUSINESS AND DEVELOPMENT LIBRARY

PRICE - $99.95 EACH

1. Abu Dhabi Fund for Development Handbook
2. African Development Bank Group(AfDB) Handbook
3. African Development Fund (AfDF) Handbook
4. Nigeria Trust Fund (NTF) Handbook
5. African Export-Import Bank (AFREXIMBANK) Handbook
6. Andean Community General Secretariat Handbook
7. Andean Development Corporation (CAF) Handbook
8. Arab Authority for Agricultural Investment and Development (AAAID) Handbook
9. Arab Bank for Economic Development in Africa (BADEA) Handbook
10. Arab Fund for Economic and Social Development (AFESD) Handbook
11. Arab Gulf Programme for United Nations Development Organizations (AGFUND) Handbook
12. Arab Maghreb Union (AMU) Handbook
13. Arab Monetary Fund (AMF) Handbook
14. Arab Organization for Agricultural Development (AOAD) Handbook
15. Arab Planning Institute - Kuwait Handbook
16. Arab Trade Financing Program (ATFP) Handbook
17. Asia-Pacific Economic Cooperation (APEC) Handbook
18. Asian and Pacific Coconut Community (APCC) Handbook
19. Asian Clearing Union (ACU) Handbook
20. Asian Development Bank (AsDB) Handbook
21. Association of Natural Rubber Producing Countries (ANRPC) Handbook
22. Association of South East Asian Nations (ASEAN) Handbook
23. Baltic Council of Ministers Handbook
24. Bank for International Settlements (BIS) Handbook
25. Bank of Central African States (BEAC) Handbook
26. Black Sea Trade and Development Bank (BSTDB) Handbook
27. Caribbean Centre for Monetary Studies (CCMS) Handbook
28. Caribbean Community (CARICOM) Handbook
29. Caribbean Development Bank (CDB) Handbook
30. Caribbean Regional Technical Assistance Centre (CARTAC) Handbook
31. Center for Latin American Monetary Studies (CEMLA) Handbook
32. Center for Marketing Information and Advisory Services for Fishery Products in Latin America and the Caribbean (INFOPESCA) Handbook
33. Central American Bank for Economic Integration (CABEI) Handbook
34. Central American Monetary Council (CAMC) Handbook
35. Central Bank of West African States (BCEAO) Handbook
36. Colombo Plan for Co-operative Economic and Social Development in Asia and the Pacific Handbook
37. Colombo Plan Staff College for Technician Education Handbook

38. Common Fund for Commodities Handbook
39. Common Market for Eastern and Southern Africa (COMESA) Handbook
40. Cooperation Council for the Arab States of the Gulf (GCC) Handbook
41. Council of the Baltic Sea States (CBSS) Handbook
42. Council of Europe Development Bank (CEB) Handbook
43. East African Development Bank (EADB) Handbook
44. Eastern Caribbean Central Bank (ECCB) Handbook
45. Economic Community of West African States (ECOWAS) Handbook
46. Economic Cooperation Organization (ECO) Handbook
47. European Bank for Reconstruction and Development (EBRD) Handbook
48. European Central Bank (ECB) Handbook
49. European Free Trade Association (EFTA) Handbook
50. European Investment Bank (EIB) Handbook
51. European Investment Fund (EIF) Handbook
52. European Union, The (EC) Handbook
53. Financial Fund for the Development of the River Plate Basin (FONPLATA) Handbook
54. Food and Agriculture Organization of the United Nations (FAO) Handbook
55. Fund for Co-operation, Compensation and Development (ECOWAS Fund) Handbook
56. Inter-American Development Bank (IDB) Handbook
57. Inter-American Institute for Cooperation on Agriculture (IICA) Handbook
58. Inter-Arab Investment Guarantee Corporation (IAIGC) Handbook
59. International Atomic Energy Agency (IAEA) Handbook
60. International Civil Aviation Organization (ICAO) Handbook
61. International Cocoa Organization (ICCO) Handbook
62. International Coffee Organization (ICO) Handbook
63. International Confederation of Free Trade Unions (ICFTU) Handbook
64. International Cotton Advisory Committee (ICAC) Handbook
65. International Fund for Agricultural Development (IFAD) Handbook
66. International Grains Council Handbook
67. International Labour Organization (ILO) Handbook
68. International Lead and Zinc Study Group Handbook
69. International Monetary Fund (IMF) Handbook
70. International Olive Oil Council (IOOC) Handbook
71. International Rubber Study Group Handbook
72. International Sugar Organization (ISO) Handbook
73. International Telecommunications Union (ITU) Handbook
74. International Tropical Timber Organization (ITTO) Handbook
75. Islamic Development Bank Group (IsDB) Handbook
76. Islamic Research and Training Institute (IRTI) Handbook
77. Joint Vienna Institute (JVI) Handbook
78. Kuwait Fund for Arab Economic Development Handbook
79. Lake Chad Basin Commission (LCBC) Handbook
80. Latin American Association of Development Financing Institutions (ALIDE) Handbook
81. Latin American Economic System (SELA) Handbook
82. Latin American Energy Organization (OLADE) Handbook
83. Latin American Export Bank (BLADEX) Handbook
84. Latin American Integration Association (ALADI) Handbook
85. Latin American Reserve Fund (LARF) Handbook
86. League of Arab States Handbook
87. Mekong River Commission (MRC) Handbook
88. Nordic Development Fund (NDF) Handbook

---

89. Nordic Investment Bank (NIB) Handbook
90. OPEC Fund for International Development Handbook
91. Organisation for Economic Co-operation and Development (OECD) Handbook
92. Organisation of Eastern Caribbean States (OECS) Handbook
93. Organization of American States (OAS) Handbook
94. Organization of Arab Petroleum Exporting Countries (OAPEC) Handbook
95. Organization of the Petroleum Exporting Countries (OPEC) Handbook
96. Pacific Financial Technical Assistance Centre Handbook
97. Pacific Islands Forum Secretariat Handbook
98. Pan American Health Organization (PAHO) Handbook
99. Regional Association of Oil and Natural Gas Companies in Latin America and the Caribbean (ARPEL) Handbook
100. Regional Electrical Integration Commission (CIER) Handbook
101. Saudi Fund for Development (SFD) Handbook
102. Secretariat for Central American Economic Integration (SIECA) Handbook
103. Secretariat of the Pacific Community Handbook
104. Sectorial Commission for the Common Market of the South (MERCOSUR) - Uruguay Handbook
105. South Asian Association for Regional Cooperation (SAARC) Handbook
106. South-East Asian Central Banks (SEACEN) Research and Training Centre Handbook
107. Training Centre for Regional Integration (CEFIR) Handbook
108. United Nations African Institute for Economic Development and Planning (IDEP) Handbook
109. United Nations Conference on Trade and Development (UNCTAD) Handbook
110. United Nations Development Program (UNDP) Handbook
111. United Nations Economic and Social Commission for Asia and the Pacific (ESCAP) Handbook
112. Asian and Pacific Centre for Transfer of Technology (APCTT) Handbook
113. Regional Coordination Centre for Research and Development of Coarse Grains, Pulses, Roots and Tuber Crops in the Humid Tropics of Asia and the Pacific (ESCAP CGPRT Centre) Handbook
114. Statistical Institute for Asia and the Pacific (SIAP) Handbook
115. United Nations Economic and Social Commission for Western Asia (ESCWA) Handbook
116. United Nations Economic Commission for Africa (UNECA) Handbook
117. United Nations Economic Commission for Europe (UN/ECE) Handbook
118. United Nations Economic Commission for Latin America and the Caribbean (ECLAC) Handbook
119. United Nations Educational, Scientific and Cultural Organization (UNESCO) Handbook
120. United Nations Industrial Development Organization (UNIDO) Handbook
121. United Nations Latin American and Caribbean Institute for Economic and Social Planning (ILPES) Handbook
122. Universal Postal Union (UPU) Handbook
123. West African Development Bank (BOAD) Handbook
124. West Africa Economic and Monetary Union Handbook
125. World Bank Group Handbook
126. World Food Program (WFP) Handbook
127. World Health Organization (WHO) Handbook
128. World Trade Organization (WTO) Handbook

INTERNATIONAL BUSINESS PUBLICATIONS USA

P.O.BOX 15343
WASHINGTON, DC 20003, USA
Ph. 202-546-2103, Fax. 202-456-3275
Email: ibpusa@comcast.net
rusric@erols.com
WWW.IBPUS.COM

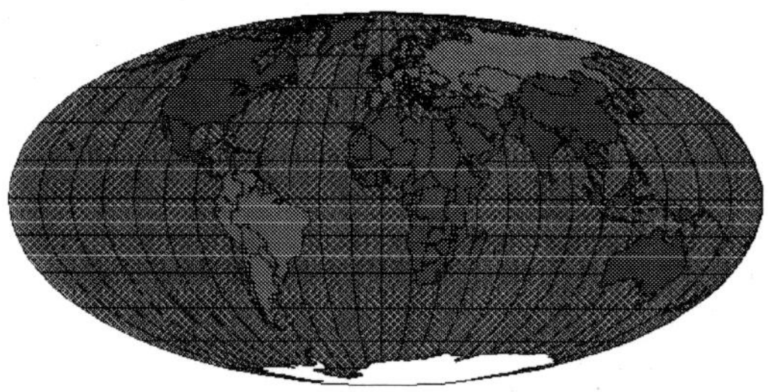

Poland Business and Investment Opportunities Yearbook
ISBN 0-7397-7717-3

ISBN 0-7397-7717-3
59995
9 780739 777176

WORLD BUSINESS INFORMATION CATALOG